GRAND CANYON HANDBOOK

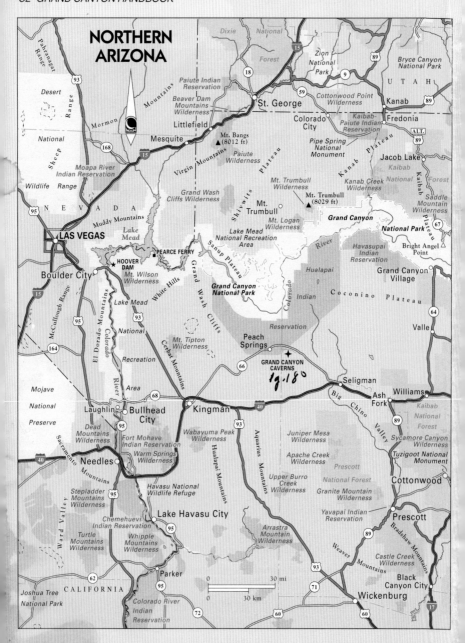

NORTHERN ARIZONA

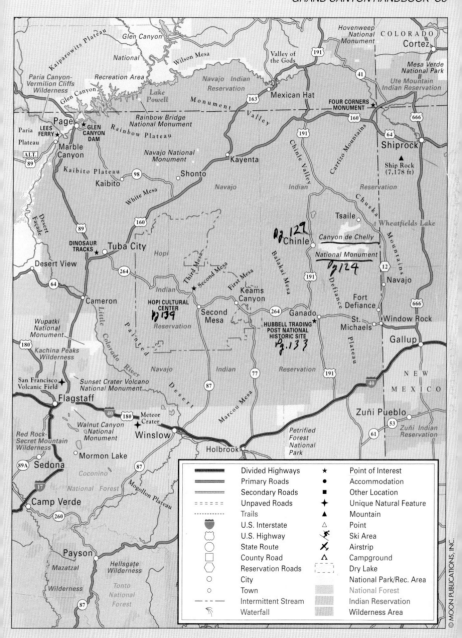

Map labels (selection):

Hovenweep National Monument · COLORADO · Cortez
Glen Canyon · Wilson Mesa · Valley of the Gods · 191
Kaiparowits Plateau · National · Navajo Indian Reservation · Mesa Verde National Park · 41
Paria Canyon-Vermilion Cliffs Wilderness · Recreation Area · Lake Powell · Mexican Hat · 163 · Ute Mountain Indian Reservation
Glen Canyon · Monument · Valley · 191 · 666
Page · LEES FERRY ★ · GLEN CANYON DAM · Rainbow Bridge National Monument · FOUR CORNERS MONUMENT · 160 · 64 · Shiprock
Paria Plateau · Marble Canyon · Rainbow Plateau · Chinle Valley · Carrizo Mountains · Ship Rock (7,178 ft)
ALT 89 · Navajo National Monument · Kayenta · Reservation · Chuska
Kaibito Plateau · 98 · Shonto · Navajo · Indian · Wheatfields Lake
Desert · 89 · White Mesa · Tsaile · Mountains
DINOSAUR TRACKS · 160 · Tuba City · Pg.127 · Chinle · Canyon de Chelly
Desert View · Hopi · Third Mesa · Balakai Mesa · National Monument · Pg.124 · 12
64 · 264 · Second Mesa · First Mesa · 191 · Navajo
Cameron · Indian · Keams Canyon · Defiance · Fort Defiance
Wupatki National Monument · HOPI CULTURAL CENTER · Pg.139 · Second Mesa · 264 · Ganado · St. Michaels · 666 · Window Rock
180 · Kachina Peaks Wilderness · Reservation · HUBBELL TRADING POST NATIONAL HISTORIC SITE · Pg.133 · Plateau · Gallup
San Francisco Volcanic Field · Sunset Crater Volcano National Monument · Navajo · Indian · Reservation · 191 · NEW
Flagstaff · 40 · 180 · Meteor Crater · 77 · 87 · MEXICO
Red Rock-Secret Mountain Wilderness · Walnut Canyon National Monument · Winslow · Marcou Mesa · Zuñi Pueblo · 53
Sedona · 89A · Mormon Lake · Holbrook · Petrified Forest National Park · 61 · Zuñi Indian Reservation
17 · Camp Verde · Coconino · 87 · Mogollon Plateau
260 · Payson · National Forest · Mazatzal Wilderness · Hellsgate Wilderness · Tonto National Forest · 87

Legend:

Divided Highways	★ Point of Interest
Primary Roads	● Accommodation
Secondary Roads	■ Other Location
Unpaved Roads	✛ Unique Natural Feature
Trails	▲ Mountain
U.S. Interstate	△ Point
U.S. Highway	Ski Area
State Route	Airstrip
County Road	Campground
Reservation Roads	Dry Lake
○ City	National Park/Rec. Area
○ Town	National Forest
Intermittent Stream	Indian Reservation
Waterfall	Wilderness Area

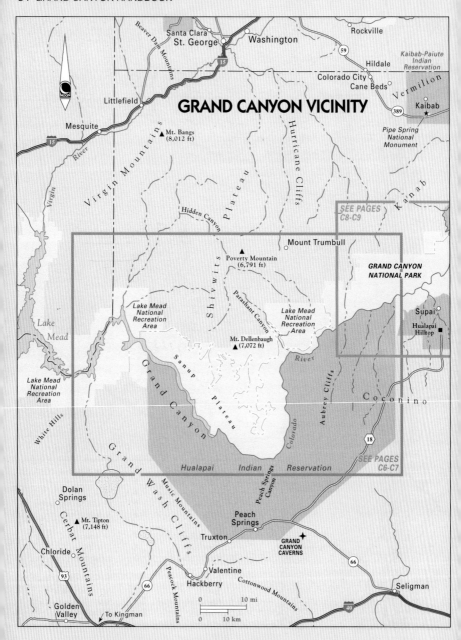

GRAND CANYON VICINITY

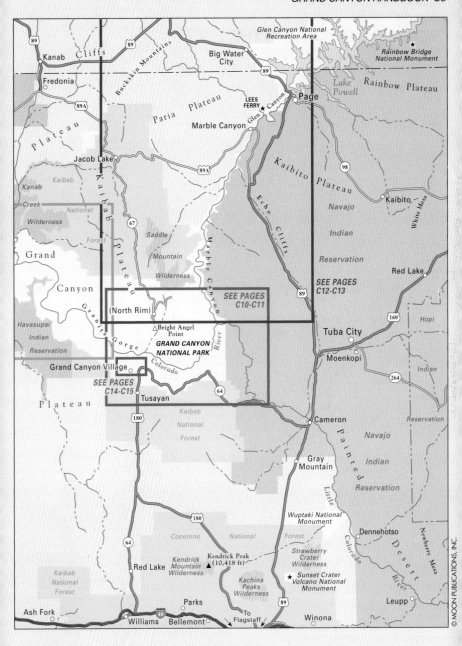

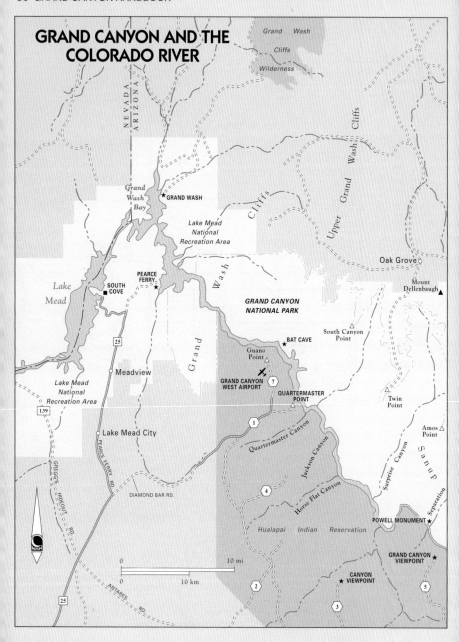

GRAND CANYON AND THE COLORADO RIVER

Grand Wash Cliffs Wilderness

NEVADA
ARIZONA

Grand Wash Bay

★ GRAND WASH

Lake Mead National Recreation Area

Cliffs

Upper Grand Wash Cliffs

Oak Grove

PEARCE FERRY

SOUTH COVE

Lake Mead

25

Grand Wash

GRAND CANYON NATIONAL PARK

Mount Dellenbaugh ▲

South Canyon Point △

★ BAT CAVE

Guano Point △

Meadview

Lake Mead National Recreation Area

139

Lake Mead City

GRAND CANYON WEST AIRPORT 7

QUARTERMASTER POINT △

Twin Point △

Amos Point △

1

Quartermaster Canyon

Jackson Canyon

Sanup

Surprise Canyon

Separation

GREGG'S HIDEOUT RD.

PEARCE FERRY RD.

DIAMOND BAR RD.

4

Horse Flat Canyon

POWELL MONUMENT ★

Hualapai Indian Reservation

GRAND CANYON VIEWPOINT ★

25

ANTARES RD.

0   10 mi

0   10 km

2

CANYON VIEWPOINT ★

3

5

MOON

Mount Trumbull

Mount Trumbull Wilderness

Shivwits Plateau

Mount Logan Wilderness

GRAND CANYON NATIONAL PARK

Whitmore Wash

Tuckup Canyon

TUWEEP (HISTORIC SITE)

TUWEEP LANDING STRIP

Fern Glen Canyon

The Dome ▲

TUWEEP RANGER STATION

Toroweap Point ▲

Big Point △

BAR TEN RANCH ■

Andrus Canyon

Whitmore Canyon

Whitmore Point

Vulcan's Throne ▲

Overlook ★

Vulcan's Anvil ★

Lava Falls Rapid (10)

WHITMORE WASH

Parashant Canyon

WHITMORE WASH HELIPAD ■

Prospect Point

Mohawk Canyon

National Canyon

Lake Mead National Recreation Area

Mollie's Nipple △

Prospect Canyon

Hualapai   Indian   Reservation

⬡ 11

⬡ 12

⬡ 10

205 Mile Rapid (7-8)

Price Point △

⬡ 11

GRANITE PARK ★

⬡ 15

⬡ 18

209 Mile Canyon

Granite Park Canyon

⬡ 13

⬡ 29

⬡ 10

⬡ 12

GRAND CANYON NATIONAL PARK

217 Mile Rapid (6-7)

⬡ 11

⬡ 18

Kelly Point △

217 Mile Canyon

THORNTON LOOKOUT ★

⬡ 17

Canyon

⬡ 10

⬡ 14

⬡ 14

Plateau

Gneiss Canyon Rapid (3-6)

Bridge Canyon Rapid (3-6)

Diamond Creek Rapid (4)

Diamond Creek

⬡ 46

Lower Granite Gorge

Travertine Falls ★

DIAMOND CREEK (RIVER ACCESS) ■

⬡ 21

⬡ 13

Travertine Canyon

Peach Springs Canyon

⬡ 6

Thumb △

Tower of Babylon △

⬡ 18

⬡ 20

Navajo Nation Land Big Boquillas Ranch

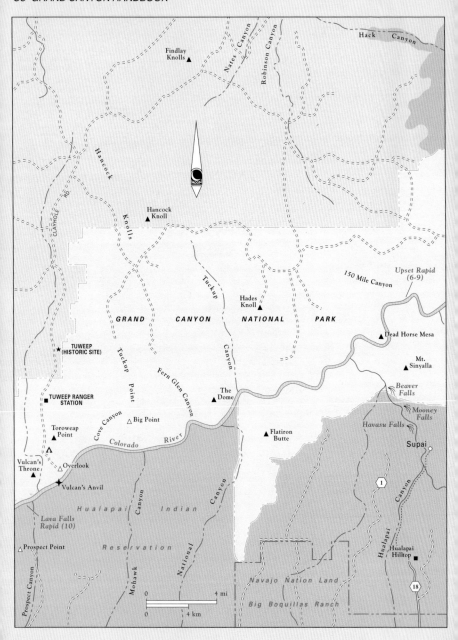

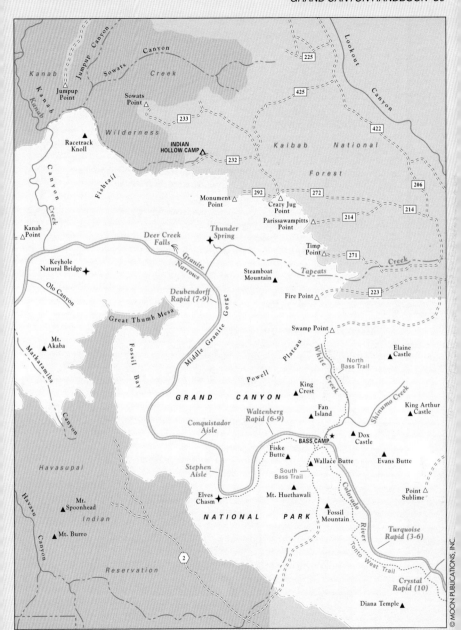

© MOON PUBLICATIONS, INC.

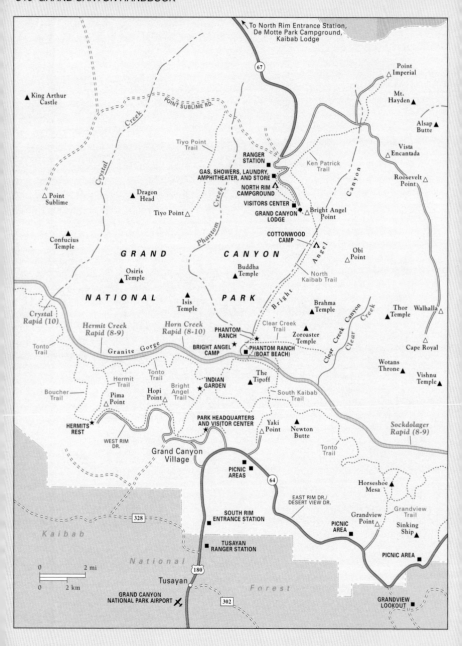

To North Rim Entrance Station,
De Motte Park Campground,
Kaibab Lodge

Point
△ Imperial

Mt.
Hayden ▲

67

▲ King Arthur
   Castle

POINT SUBLIME RD.

Crystal
Creek

Tiyo Point
Trail

Alsap ▲
Butte

Vista
Encantata

RANGER
STATION

GAS, SHOWERS, LAUNDRY,
AMPHITHEATER, AND STORE

Ken Patrick
Trail

Roosevelt △
Point

△ Point
  Sublime

▲ Dragon
   Head

NORTH RIM
CAMPGROUND

Phantom Creek

VISITORS CENTER

Tiyo Point △

GRAND CANYON
LODGE

△ Bright Angel
  Point

▲ Confucius
   Temple

COTTONWOOD
CAMP

Bright Angel Creek

Obi
△ Point

G R A N D   C A N Y O N

▲ Osiris
   Temple

Buddha
▲ Temple

North
Kaibab Trail

N A T I O N A L   P A R K

Crystal
Rapid (10)

Hermit Creek
Rapid (8-9)

Horn Creek
Rapid (8-10)

▲ Isis
   Temple

Brahma
▲ Temple

Thor ▲
Temple

Walhalla △

Tonto
Trail

Granite Gorge

PHANTOM
RANCH

Clear Creek
Trail

Zoroaster
△ Temple

Clear Creek Canyon

Clear Creek

Cape Royal

Boucher
Trail

Hermit Creek
Rapid (8-9)

Hermit
Trail

Tonto
Trail

BRIGHT ANGEL
CAMP

PHANTOM RANCH
(BOAT BEACH)

Wotans
△ Throne

Pima
△ Point

Hopi
Point △

Bright
Angel
Trail

INDIAN
★ GARDEN

The
▲ Tipoff

South Kaibab
Trail

Vishnu ▲
Temple

HERMITS
★ REST

WEST RIM
DR.

PARK HEADQUARTERS
AND VISITOR CENTER

Yaki
△ Point

Newton
△ Butte

Sockdolager
Rapid (8-9)

Grand Canyon
Village

Tonto
Trail

PICNIC
AREAS

64

Kaibab

328

SOUTH RIM
ENTRANCE STATION

EAST RIM DR./
DESERT VIEW DR.

Horseshoe
▲ Mesa

Grandview
Trail

National

TUSAYAN
RANGER STATION

Grandview
Point △

PICNIC
AREA

Sinking
Ship △

0   2 mi

0   2 km

180

Tusayan

Forest

PICNIC AREA

GRAND CANYON
NATIONAL PARK AIRPORT ✈

302

GRANDVIEW
LOOKOUT

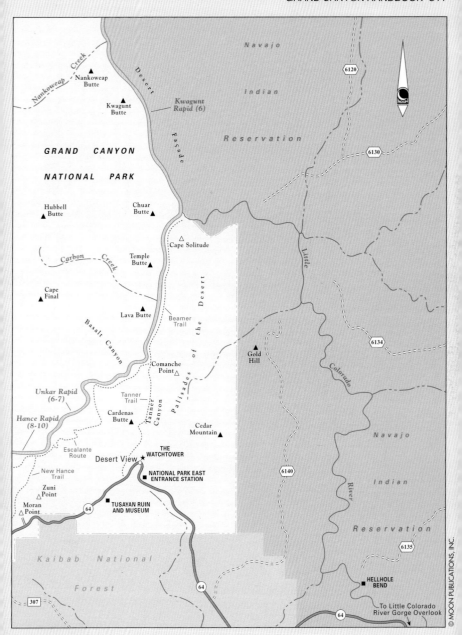

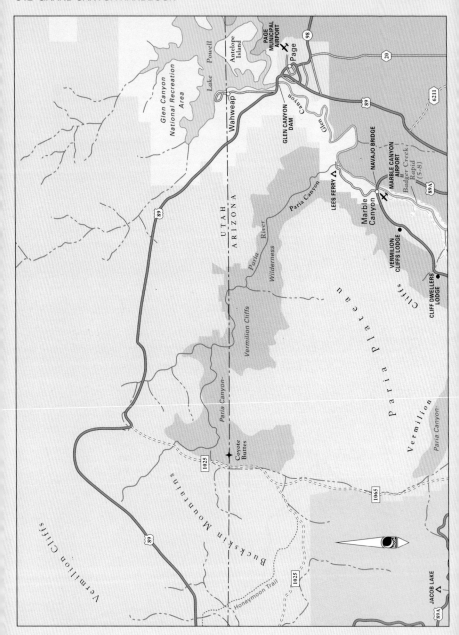

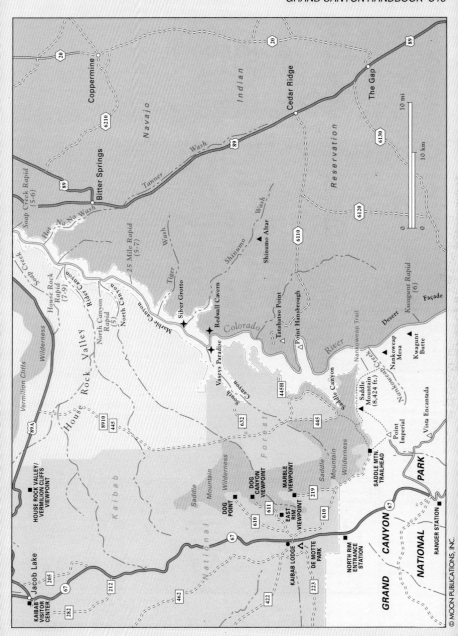

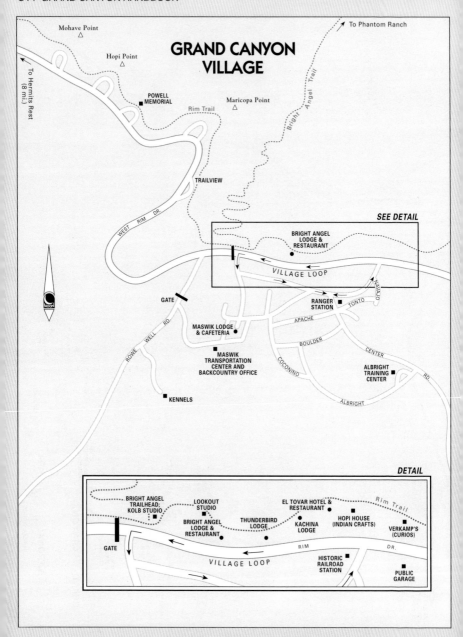

GRAND CANYON VILLAGE

Mohave Point △

Hopi Point △

To Phantom Ranch

POWELL MEMORIAL ■

Maricopa Point △

Rim Trail

To Hermits Rest (8 mi.)

TRAILVIEW

WEST RIM DR.

SEE DETAIL

Bright Angel Trail

BRIGHT ANGEL LODGE & RESTAURANT ■

VILLAGE LOOP

GATE

NAVAJO

RANGER STATION ■

TONTO

APACHE

MASWIK LODGE & CAFETERIA ■

ROWE WELL RD.

BOULDER

CENTER

MASWIK TRANSPORTATION CENTER AND BACKCOUNTRY OFFICE ■

COCONINO

ALBRIGHT TRAINING CENTER ■

RD.

KENNELS ■

ALBRIGHT

DETAIL

BRIGHT ANGEL TRAILHEAD; KOLB STUDIO ■

LOOKOUT STUDIO ■

EL TOVAR HOTEL & RESTAURANT ■

Rim Trail

BRIGHT ANGEL LODGE & RESTAURANT ■

THUNDERBIRD LODGE ■

KACHINA LODGE ■

HOPI HOUSE (INDIAN CRAFTS) ■

VERKAMP'S (CURIOS) ■

GATE

VILLAGE LOOP

RIM

DR.

HISTORIC RAILROAD STATION ■

PUBLIC GARAGE ■

MOON

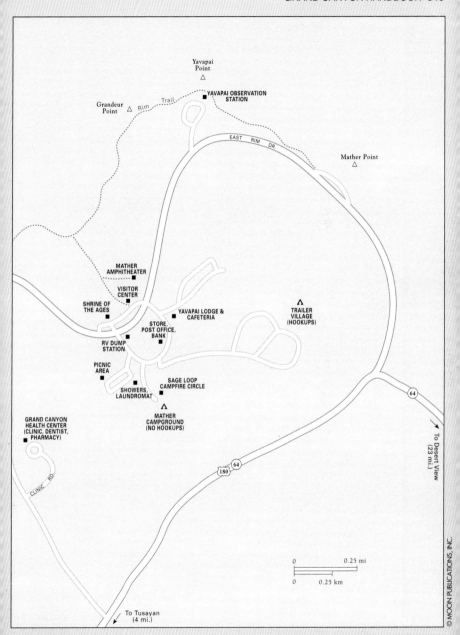

Yavapai
Point

YAVAPAI OBSERVATION
STATION

Grandeur
Point Rim Trail

EAST RIM DR.

Mather Point

MATHER
AMPHITHEATER

VISITOR
CENTER

SHRINE OF
THE AGES

YAVAPAI LODGE &
CAFETERIA

TRAILER
VILLAGE
(HOOKUPS)

STORE,
POST OFFICE,
BANK

RV DUMP
STATION

PICNIC
AREA

SAGE LOOP
CAMPFIRE CIRCLE

SHOWERS,
LAUNDROMAT

64

GRAND CANYON
HEALTH CENTER
(CLINIC, DENTIST,
PHARMACY)

MATHER
CAMPGROUND
(NO HOOKUPS)

To Desert View
(23 mi.)

CLINIC RD.

180 64

0   0.25 mi

0   0.25 km

To Tusayan
(4 mi.)

GRAND CANYON HANDBOOK

INCLUDING ARIZONA'S INDIAN COUNTRY
FIRST EDITION

BILL WEIR

MOON
TRAVEL
HANDBOOKS

GRAND CANYON HANDBOOK
FIRST EDITION

Published by
Moon Publications, Inc.
P.O. Box 3040
Chico, California 95927-3040, USA

Printed by
Colorcraft Ltd.

© Text and photographs copyright Bill Weir, 1999.
All rights reserved.

© Illustrations and maps copyright Moon Publications, Inc., 1999.
All rights reserved.

Some photos and illustrations are used by permission
and are the property of the original copyright owners.

ISBN: 1-56691-152-4
ISSN: 1522-3485

Editor: Karen Gaynor Bleske
Map Editor: Gina Wilson Birtcil
Copy Editor: Valerie Sellers Blanton
Production & Design: Carey Wilson
Cartography: Chris Folks, Allen Leech, and Mike Morgenfeld
Index: Sondra Nation

Front cover photo: South Rim of the Grand Canyon by John Henley; courtesy of Picturesque Stock Photo

All photos by Bill Weir unless otherwise noted.
All illustrations by Bob Race unless otherwise noted.

Distributed in the United States and Canada by Publishers Group West

Printed in China

Please send all comments,
corrections, additions,
amendments, and critiques to:

GRAND CANYON HANDBOOK
MOON TRAVEL HANDBOOKS
P.O. BOX 3040
CHICO, CA 95927-3040, USA
e-mail: travel@moon.com
www.moon.com

Printing History
1st edition—June 1999
5 4 3 2 1 0

CONTENTS

Cross-references in **bold type** within the text of the book refer to citations in the general index.

ABOUT THE BANNERS

The historic images that illustrate the beginning of each
chapter in this book come from the collection of Aislinn
Race and from J.W. Powell's *The Exploration of the Colorado
River and Its Canyons.*

Introduction: *The Grand Canyon* 1

Grand Canyon National Park:
   "A Section of the Colorado River in the Cañon" 12

Western Grand Canyon and the Arizona Strip:
   "Mount Trumbull, from Mount Logan" 72

Indian Country of Northeastern Arizona:
   A Passageway in Mishongnovi 110

Flagstaff and Vicinity:
   "The San Francisco Volcanoes". 142

Canyon Country Basics: *Railroad Car at Flagstaff* . . . 181

MAPS

*For detailed coverage within and around Grand Canyon National Park,
please refer to the color section.*

MAP SYMBOLS

═══ Superhighway	☐ County or Forest Road	⚡ Ski Resort
══ Primary Road	★ Point of Interest	✗ Airfield/Airstrip
── Secondary Road	• Accommodation	⚑ State Park
------- Trail	▼ Restaurant/Bar	Λ Campground
—+—+— Railroad	▪ Other Location	⋔ Waterfall
⬭ U.S. Interstate	+ Unique Natural Feature	▲ Mountain
⬡ U.S. Highway	⊛ State Capitol	△ Point
◯ State Highway	○ City	⌓ Golf Course
⬡ Indian Route	○ Town	

ABBREVIATIONS

a/c—air conditioning
ATV—all-terrain vehicle
B&B—bed and breakfast
BLM—Bureau of Land
 Management
ca.—circa

CCC—Civilian Conservation
 Corps
d—double
elev.—elevation
F—Fahrenheit
FR—Forest Road
hp—horsepower

4WD-four-wheel drive
RV—recreational vehicle
s—single
tel.—telephone
U.S.G.S.—United States
 Geological Survey

ACKNOWLEDGMENTS

Many thanks go to the hundreds of people who assisted in making the *Grand Canyon Handbook* as complete and accurate as it is! I am especially indebted to my mother, Doris Weir, for editing the entire book—diligently rearranging words and commas to make the text easier and clearer to read. I've been fortunate also to have a top-notch editor at Moon Travel Handbooks, Karen Bleske, who helped polish and fit all the sentences into this book. The rest of the Moon Crew—see title page for credits—drew the maps, laid out the pages, and helped the book on its way into your hands.

Staff of the National Park Service at the Grand Canyon took time out from their busy schedules to assist in many ways. Just a few of those who aided the author in the park are Lon Ayer (Grand Canyon Interpretation), who read the entire section on the park, then made many detailed suggestions; Clair Roberts (Tuweep Ranger), who offered ideas and updates for the Toroweap area; and Colleen Hyde (photo archives), who led the author into the park's huge collection of historic photos. Many other National Park Service people helped with research and fact checking at the region's national monuments and at Glen Canyon National Recreation Area. Foresters with the U.S. Forest Service provided many helpful ideas for their forests on both sides of the Grand Canyon. Staff at offices of the Bureau of Land Management gave me valuable advice on exploring the remote and beautiful Arizona Strip. Chambers of commerce supplied valuable ideas, travel tips, and maps. Barton Wright's excellent drawing of the Hopi Reservation, which he kindly gave permission to use in the *Grand Canyon Handbook,* appears in the Hopi Country section.

The friendly crews of Grand Canyon Dories and Canyon Explorations introduced the author to the Grand Canyon from river level with skill and style. Also for this edition, the author enjoyed a Colorado River trip through Glen Canyon with Wilderness River Adventures. Back in the saddle after many years, the author rode to the South Rim of the Grand Canyon with the entertaining wranglers of Apache Stables. From the skies, Grand Canyon Airlines and Airstar Helicopters provided the author new perspectives over the Grand Canyon.

HELP MAKE THIS A BETTER BOOK

Nothing stays the same, it seems. Although this book has been carefully researched, the Grand Canyon and its surrounding areas will continue to grow and change. New sights and services will open while others change hands or close. Your comments and ideas on making Grand Canyon Handbook more useful to other readers will be highly valued. If you find something new, discontinued, or changed, please let me know so that the information can be included in the next printing or edition. Please send e-mails with your thoughts and experiences to travel@moon.com.

Perhaps a map or worthwhile place to visit has been overlooked; please bring it to my attention. All contributions (letters, maps, and photos) will be carefully saved, checked, and acknowledged. Businesses, too, are most welcome to send an e-mail, postcard, or letter with updates. If you have a question about an order or other business transaction, please contact Moon Travel Handbooks directly—as I may be off at some remote monastery or mountain!

If Moon Travel Handbooks uses your photos or artwork, you will be mentioned in the credits and receive a free copy of the book. Be aware, however, that the author and publisher are not responsible for unsolicited manuscripts, photos, or artwork and, in most cases, cannot undertake to return them unless you include a self-addressed, stamped envelope. Address your letters to:

> *Grand Canyon Handbook*
> c/o Moon Travel Handbooks
> P.O. Box 3040
> Chico, CA 95927 USA
> e-mail: travel@moon.com

ACCOMMODATIONS RATINGS

Accommodations in this book are rated by price category, based on double-occupancy, high-season rates.

> Budget: under $35
> Inexpensive: $35-60
> Moderate: $60-85
> Expensive: $85-110
> Premium: $110-150
> Luxury: $150 and up

PREFACE

As one of the Seven Natural Wonders of the World, the Grand Canyon certainly lives up to its billing! The many rim viewpoints help you get the big picture. You'll also find that the Grand Canyon contains countless canyons within canyons, each a little world of its own with distinct geology, plants, and animals. Trails and routes inside will lead to discovery of some of these canyon worlds. A river trip down the Colorado rates as one of the world's greatest adventures, opening up even more areas to appreciation and exploration.

Fascinating areas surround the Grand Canyon. Travels on the lands of the Havasupai, Hualapai, Navajo, and Hopi provide cultural insights and spectacular scenery. Arizona's highest summit, Humphrey's Peak, soars from the San Francisco Volcanic Field south of the Grand Canyon. The high Kaibab Plateau north of the Grand Canyon offers not only beautiful forests of spruce, fir, ponderosa pine, and aspen, but some of the best Canyon viewpoints. If you're looking for grand scenery and solitude, then you've got it on the remote Arizona Strip between the Grand Canyon and the Utah border. Very few visitors travel the wilderness trails and jeep roads here.

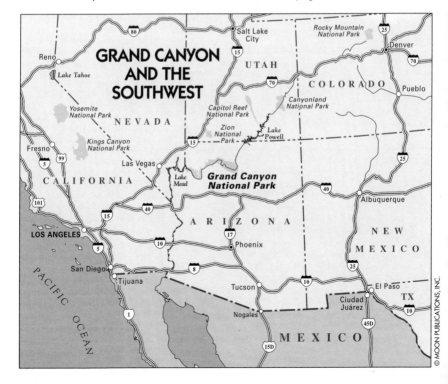

COURTESY: AISLINN RACE

INTRODUCTION

A collision of the earth's forces—uplifting of the massive Colorado Plateau and vigorous down-cutting by the Colorado River—created the awe-inspiring Grand Canyon and its many tributaries. Neither pictures nor words can fully describe the sight. You have to experience the Canyon by traveling along the rim, descending into the depths, riding the waves of the Colorado River, and watching the continuous show of colors and patterns as the sun moves across the sky.

The Canyon's grandeur stretches 277 miles across northern Arizona, measuring as much as 18 miles wide—10 miles on average—and one mile deep. Roads provide access to developed areas and viewpoints on both rims. Trails lead hikers and mule riders down the precipitous cliffs to the Colorado River, yet most of the park remains as remote as ever, rarely visited by humans.

THE LAND

This is a land of time. Massive cliffs reveal limestone composed of animals that lived in long-departed seas, sandstone formed of ancient desert sand dunes, and shale made of silt from now-vanished rivers and shores. Volcanic eruptions deposited layers of ash, cinders, and lava. Deeper into the Canyon lie the roots of mountain ranges, whose peaks towered over a primitive land two billion years ago. Time continues to flow in the Canyon with the cycles of the plants and animals that live here, and with the erosive forces of water ever widening and deepening the chasm.

GEOGRAPHY

Colorado Plateau
This giant uplifted landmass in northern Arizona also extends across much of adjacent Utah,

Colorado, and New Mexico. Rivers have cut deeply into the plateau, creating the Grand Canyon of the Colorado and other vast gorges. Volcanoes breaking through the surface have left hundreds of cinder cones, such as multicolored Sunset Crater, and larger volcanic complexes, such as the San Francisco Peaks. The most recent burst of volcanic activity in Arizona took place near Sunset Crater about 700 years ago. Most elevations on the plateau range from 5,000 to 8,000 feet. Sheer cliffs of the Mogollon (MUGGY-own) Rim drop to the desert, marking the plateau's south boundary. To the west, the plateau ends at Grand Wash Cliffs.

Forming of the Grand Canyon

Geologists have a difficult time pinpointing the age of the Grand Canyon itself, though it is far younger than even the most recent rock layers—those on the rim, which are about 250 million years old. These lay at sea level 65 million years ago, when the earth's crust began a slow uplift. Somewhere between five and 20 million years ago, the ancestral Colorado River settled on its present course and began to carve the Canyon. Gradual uplift continued, giving the waters a steeper gradient and thus greater power. Today, the South Rim reaches elevations of 7,000 to 7,500 feet, while the North Rim towers about 1,500 feet higher. The Colorado River drops through the Canyon at an average gradient of 7.8 feet per mile, 25 times that of the lower Mississippi.

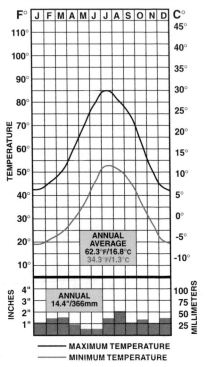

GRAND CANYON SOUTH RIM AREA CLIMATE

ANNUAL AVERAGE
62.3°F/16.8°C
34.3°F/1.3°C

ANNUAL
14.4"/366mm

——— MAXIMUM TEMPERATURE
------- MINIMUM TEMPERATURE

Angels Window at Cape Royal on the North Rim

PHANTOM RANCH CLIMATE

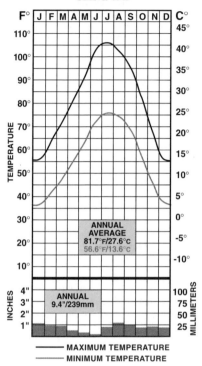

ANNUAL AVERAGE
81.7°F/27.6°C
56.6°F/13.6°C

ANNUAL
9.4"/239mm

MAXIMUM TEMPERATURE
MINIMUM TEMPERATURE

NORTH RIM CLIMATE (BRIGHT ANGEL POINT)

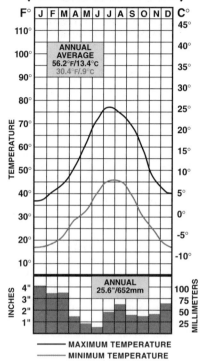

ANNUAL AVERAGE
56.2°F/13.4°C
30.4°F/.9°C

ANNUAL
25.6"/652mm

MAXIMUM TEMPERATURE
MINIMUM TEMPERATURE

CLIMATE

The Grand Canyon has been compared with an inverted mountain. Temperatures change with elevation as on a mountainside, but with added canyon peculiarities. In winter, the sun's low angle allows only a few hours of sunlight a day to reach the Inner Gorge, creating a cooling effect. The situation reverses during the summer, when the sun's high angle turns the Canyon into an oven. At night, temperatures often drop lower than you'd expect, when cold, dense air on the rims pours over the edge into the depths.

The Seasons

In one day, a hiker can travel from the cold fir and aspen forests of the North Rim to the hot cactus country of the Canyon bottom—a climate change equal to that between Canada and Mexico. In the Inner Gorge (elev. 2,480 feet at Phantom Ranch), summer temperatures soar, with average highs over 100° F; the thermometer commonly tops 115° in early July. Spring and autumn offer pleasantly warm weather and are the best times to visit. Winter down by the river can be fine too; even in January, days warm up to the 50s or low 60s and it rarely freezes. Only 9.4 inches of precipitation makes it to the bottom in an average year; snow and rain often evaporate completely while falling through the mile of warm Canyon air.

The South Rim enjoys pleasant weather most of the year. Summer highs reach the mid-80s, cooling during winter to highs in the upper 30s and lower 40s. Winter campers need warm sleeping bags to combat frosty nights when temperatures plunge into the teens. Yearly precipitation at the South Rim's Grand Canyon Village (elev. 6,950 feet) is 14.4 inches, with snow accumulations seldom exceeding two feet.

Although averaging only 1,500 feet higher, the North Rim really gets socked in by winter storms. Snow piles up to depths of 6-10 feet in an average season, and the National Park Service doesn't even try to keep the roads open there from early November to mid-May. Summers can be a joy in the cool, fresh air; highs then run in the 60s and 70s. Bright Angel Ranger Station (elev. 8,400 feet) on the North Rim receives 25.6 inches of annual precipitation.

Most moisture falls during the winter and late summer (mid-July to mid-September). Summer rains often arrive in spectacular afternoon thunderstorms, soaking one spot in the Canyon and leaving another bone dry even though it's only a short distance away. The storms put on a great show from the rim viewpoints, but you should take cover if lightning gets close (less than seven seconds between the flash and the thunder) and especially if the hair on your head stands on end or if you smell ozone. As in mountain areas, the Grand Canyon's weather can change rapidly. Always carry water and raingear when heading down a trail.

Storm Hazards

Rainwater runs quickly off the rocky desert surfaces and into gullies and canyons. Flash floods can form and sweep away anything in their paths, including boulders, cars, and campsites. Take care not to camp or park in potential flash-flood areas. If you come to a section of flooded roadway, a common occurrence on desert roads after storms, just wait until the water goes down—usually only an hour or so. Summer lightning causes forest and brush fires and poses a danger to hikers foolish enough to be exposed when storms threaten.

FLORA AND FAUNA

The seemingly endless variations of elevation, exposure, and moisture allow for an astonishing range of plant and animal communities. The Canyon also acts as a barrier to many nonflying creatures who live on just one side of the Colorado River or only in the Inner Gorge. Some mammals, such as the Abert's (South Rim) and Kaibab (North Rim) squirrels, spotted skunk, cliff chipmunk, and common pocket gopher, evolved into separate subspecies on each rim.

VEGETATION ZONES AND WILDLIFE

Spruce-Fir Forest

You'll find dense forests of spruce and fir and groves of quaking aspen on the Kaibab Plateau of the North Rim, mostly above 8,200 feet. Common trees include spruce (Engelmann and blue), fir (Douglas, white, and subalpine), aspen, and mountain ash. Lush meadows, dotted with wildflowers in summer, spread out in shallow valleys at the higher elevations.

Animals of the spruce-fir forest include the mule deer, mountain lion, porcupine,

red and Kaibab squirrel, Uinta chipmunk, longtailed vole, and northern pocket gopher. The shy Kaibab squirrel, easily identified by an all-white tail and tufted ears, lives only on the North Rim. The Kaibab probably evolved from Abert's squirrels that crossed the Colorado River long ago, perhaps during the Pleistocene epoch. Birds you might see include the turkey, great horned owl, saw-whet owl, broad-tailed hummingbird,

common raven
(Corvus corax)

hairy woodpecker, hermit thrush, Clark's nut-cracker, Steller's jay, and mountain bluebird.

Ponderosa Pine Forest

Stands of tall ponderosas grow between elevations of 7,000 and 8,000 feet on both rims. Mature forests tend to be open, allowing in sunlight for Gambel oak, New Mexican locust, mountain mahogany, greenleaf manzanita, cliffrose, wildflowers, and grasses.

Animals and birds found here include most of those resident in the spruce-fir forests. The Abert's squirrel, though common in the Southwest, lives within the park only on the South Rim. This squirrel has tufted ears and a body and tail that are mostly gray with white undersides.

Pinyon Pine-Juniper Woodland

These smaller trees abound in drier and more exposed places between elevations of 4,000 and 8,000 feet. Their neighbors commonly include broadleaf yucca, cliffrose, rabbit brush, Mormon tea, sagebrush, fernbrush, serviceberry, and Apache plume.

Mule deer, mountain lions, coyotes, gray foxes, desert cottontails, Stephen's woodrats, pinyon mice, rock squirrels, cliff chipmunks, lizards, and snakes (including rattlesnakes) make their homes here. Birds include the mourning dove, plain titmouse, Bewick's wren, black-throated gray warbler, and pinyon and scrub jays.

Desert Scrub

Except near permanent water, the low-desert country below 4,500 feet cannot support trees. Instead, you'll find such hardy plants as blackbrush, Utah agave, narrowleaf yucca, various cacti, desert thorn, Mormon tea, four-wing saltbush, and snakeweed.

Animals include the bighorn sheep, black-tailed jackrabbit, spotted skunk, desert woodrat, antelope ground squirrel, and canyon mouse. Most reptiles hole up during the day, though lizards seem to tolerate higher temperatures than snakes. Chuckwallas, spiny and collared lizards, common king snakes, whipsnakes, and Grand Canyon rattlesnakes live in this part of the Canyon. The shy

OLD-GROWTH FORESTS

Only five percent of Arizona's original forest remains. The surviving systems endure in remote canyons and on a few mountains, some of which receive federal protection. Scientists find them an amazingly complex interaction of life and decay. Hundreds of species of fungi, insects, birds, animals, and plants all feed and protect each other in ways still being discovered. We've also learned about forest management from the old systems. Checks and balances in these forests limit damage of insect and mistletoe infestations, an advantage that managed forests of single-aged trees don't share. Fires in the old growths burn cool and close to the ground and do little harm because the shade from mature trees prevents excessive growth of brush and thickets of small trees; also, the branches of mature trees lie above the reach of most fires. Natural fires move through every five to seven years, clearing the underbrush and fertilizing the soil with ash. Even in death, a large tree can stand 50 years, providing generations of birds and insects with a home. Foresters once removed these old snags as fire hazards, but now we know that many birds depend on them.

Grand Canyon or pink rattlesnake, a subspecies of the western rattlesnake, lives nowhere else. Birds of the desert scrub have to either look elsewhere for nesting trees or choose a spot in cliffs or on the ground. Species you might see include the common raven, turkey vulture, golden eagle, red-tailed hawk, rock and canyon wrens, and black-throated sparrow. You'll probably hear the song of the water-loving canyon wren without ever seeing him; he sings in an unforgettable descending scale.

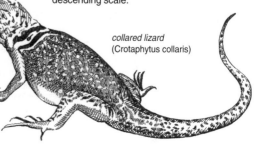

collared lizard
(Crotaphytus collaris)

Riparian Woodlands
Until 1963, seasonal flooding of the Colorado River washed away most vegetation below the high-water mark. Then, when the Glen Canyon Dam was completed upstream, tamarisk (an exotic species originally from the Arabian deserts) accelerated its takeover of formerly barren beaches. Native cattail, coyote willow, and arrowweed now thrive too. Seeps and springs support luxuriant plant growth and supply water for wildlife.

Beavers, river otters, ringtail cats, raccoons, white-footed deermice, spotted sandpipers, blue grosbeaks, Lucy's warblers, Woodhouse's toads, and tree lizards make their homes near the streams. Fremont cottonwood trees in the tributaries provide welcome shade for overheated hikers. The cold, clear waters that flow from Glen Canyon Dam have upset breeding patterns of the seven native fish species; they now spawn in warmer waters at the mouths of the Little Colorado River and Havasu Creek. Rainbow trout and 10 other species have been introduced.

HISTORY

PREHISTORY

The First Peoples
Indians knew of this land and its canyons centuries before white people arrived. At least 4,000 years ago, a hunting and gathering society stalked the plateaus and canyons of northern Arizona, leaving behind stone spear points and some small split-twig figures resembling deer or sheep. Preserved in caves in the Grand Canyon, these figurines date from approximately 2000 B.C. This culture departed about 1000 B.C., leaving the Canyon apparently unoccupied for the next 1,500 years.

The Ancestral Pueblo People Arrive
Prehistoric ancestral pueblo people came to the Grand Canyon area about A.D. 500. Like their predecessors, they hunted deer, bighorn sheep, jackrabbits, and other animals, while gathering such wild plant foods as pinyon nuts and agave. The ancestral pueblo people also crafted fine baskets and sandals. At their peak, between 1050 and 1150, they grew crops, crafted pottery, and lived in above-ground masonry villages. Toward the end of this period, drought hit the region. By 1150 nearly all the ancestral pueblo people had departed from the Grand Canyon, leaving more than 2,000 sites behind. Most likely they migrated east to the Hopi mesas.

Archaeologists have used the term Anasazi for this culture, but the Navajo word means "ancient enemies"—not a phrase that modern-day pueblo people care to use in reference to their ancestors! So this book uses the more respectful phrase "ancestral pueblo people."

Other Indians Come to the Canyon
While the ancestral pueblo people kept mostly to the east half of the Grand Canyon (east of today's Grand Canyon Village), another group of hunter-gatherers and farmers, the Cohonina, lived downstream between A.D. 600 and 1150. They adopted many of the agricultural and building techniques and crafts of their neighbors to the east. In 1300 the Cerbat, probable ancestors of the modern Havasupai and Hualapai, migrated

DIANA LASICH HARPER

onto the Grand Canyon's South Rim from the west. They lived in caves or brush shelters and ranged as far upstream as the Little Colorado River in search of game and wild plant foods. The Cerbat also planted crops in areas of fertile soil or permanent springs. It's possible that the Cerbat had cultural ties with the earlier Cohonina.

Paiute Indians living north of the Grand Canyon made seasonal trips to the North Rim, occasionally clashing with the Cerbat. The Paiute lived in brush shelters and relied almost entirely on hunting and gathering. They spent their summers on the Kaibab Plateau and in other high country, then moved to lower elevations for the winter. Hopi Indians knew of the Grand Canyon too; they came for religious pilgrimages and to collect salt.

EXPLORATION

Spanish and American Explorers

In 1540, when Francisco Vásquez de Coronado led an expedition in search of the Seven Cities of Cíbola, Hopi Indians told a detachment of soldiers about a great canyon to the west. Hopi guides later took a party of Coronado's men, led by García López de Cárdenas, to the South Rim but kept secret the routes into the depths. The Spaniards failed to find a way to the river and left discouraged. Franciscan priest Francisco Tomás Garcés, looking for souls to save, visited the Havasupai and Hualapai in 1776 and was well received. Historians credit Garcés with naming the Río Colorado ("Red River").

Mountain Men

James Ohio Pattie and other American fur trappers probably came across the Grand Canyon in the late 1820s, but they provided only sketchy accounts of their visits. Lieutenant Joseph Ives led the first real exploration of the Colorado River. He chugged 350 miles by steamboat upstream from the river's mouth in 1857-58 before crashing into a rock in Black Canyon. The party then continued overland to the Diamond Creek area in the western Grand Canyon.

The First Grand Canyon Expeditions

Most of the Canyon remained a dark and forbidding unknown until Major John Wesley Powell

Major John Wesley Powell

bravely led a boat expedition through the chasm in 1869. On this trip and on a second journey in 1871-72, he and his men made detailed drawings and took notes on geology, flora and fauna, and Indian ruins. Powell recorded his experiences in *Canyons of the Colorado,* now published as *The Exploration of the Colorado River and Its Canyons.*

SETTLING IN

Ranching on the Arizona Strip

Not many pioneers took an interest in the prairie here—the ground proved nearly impossible to plow and lacked water for irrigation. Determined Mormons began ranching in the 1860s despite the isolation and occasional Navajo raids. They built Winsor Castle, a fortified ranch, in 1870 as a base for a large church-owned cattle herd. Mormons also founded the towns of Fredonia, Short Creek (now Colorado City), and Littlefield.

Some of these settlers had fled Utah to escape federal laws prohibiting polygamy. About 3,000 members of a polygamous, excommunicated Mormon sect still live in Colorado City and neighboring

Hilldale, Utah. Federal and state officials raided Colorado City several times, most recently in 1953, when 27 arrests were made—those charged received one year of probation. Now government policy seems to be "live and let live."

Miners and Tourists

After about 1880, prospectors entered the Grand Canyon to search for copper, asbestos, silver, and lead deposits. Their trails, many following old Indian routes, are still used by modern hikers.

In 1883, stagecoaches began bringing tourists to the Canyon at Diamond Creek, where J.H. Farlee opened a four-room hotel the following year. Prospectors Peter Berry and Ralph and Niles Cameron built the Grandview Hotel in 1895 at Grandview Point and led tourists down a trail to Horseshoe Mesa. Other prospectors, such as John Hance and William Bass, also found

guiding visitors more profitable than mining. Tourism began on a large scale soon after the railroad reached the South Rim in 1901. The Fred Harvey Company bought Bright Angel Lodge, built the deluxe El Tovar Hotel, and took over the smaller operators.

The Park Is Born

As the Canyon became better known, President Theodore Roosevelt and others pushed for greater federal protection. First a forest reserve in 1893, the Grand Canyon became a national monument in 1908, and finally a national park in 1919. The park's size doubled in 1975 when legislation extended the boundaries west to Grand Wash and northeast to Lees Ferry. Grand Canyon National Park now includes 1,892 square miles and receives about five million visitors annually.

THE PEOPLE

INDIANS OF THE GRAND CANYON AREA

Havasupai

Long before the first white people arrived, this tribe farmed the fertile Havasu Canyon floor in the Grand Canyon during the summer, moving to the plateau after harvest to gather abundant wild foods and firewood during winter. Spanish missionary Francisco Garcés visited the Havasupai in 1776, finding them a happy and industrious people.

Though a peaceful tribe, the Havasupai suffered the usual fate of American Indians—confinement to a tiny reservation while white people grabbed their lands. The Havasupai protested, but it wasn't until 1975 that the tribe's winter homelands were returned. The Havasupai Reservation now spans 188,077 acres; most of the 500-600 tribal members on the reservation live in Supai village.

Supai lies 35 air miles northwest of Grand Canyon Village in Havasu Canyon, a major Grand Canyon tributary. The waterfalls, travertine pools, and greenery of the remote canyon have earned it fame as a Shangri-La.

Hualapai

The "Pine Tree People" once occupied a large area of northwestern Arizona. In language and culture, they're closely tied to the Havasupai and Yavapai tribes. Early white visitors enjoyed friendly relations with the Hualapai, but land seizures and murders by the newcomers led to warfare. Army troops defeated the Hualapai and herded them south onto the Colorado River Reservation, where many died. Survivors fled back to their traditional lands, part of which later became the Hualapai Indian Reservation. About half of the 1,500 tribal members live on the 993,000-acre reservation, which includes much of the lower Grand Canyon's South Rim. Highlights for visitors include the drive into the Grand Canyon to Diamond Creek, one- and two-day Colorado River trips, and spectacular viewpoints from the rim of the lowermost Grand Canyon.

Peach Springs, a small town 54 miles northeast of Kingman on AZ 66, is the only town on the reservation. A road from here descends to the Colorado River in the Grand Canyon.

Paiute

A small band of Paiute Indians lives on the Kaibab-Paiute Reservation, west of Fredonia in far northern Arizona. In earlier times they used this area as a winter home and spent summers in the forests of the Kaibab Plateau to the east. About 250 Paiute, who speak a Uto-Aztecan language, live on the reservation. The tribe arrived sometime after 1300, though members believe themselves related to the ancestral pueblo people who had once lived on this land. The adjacent Pipe Spring National Monument preserves pioneer traditions.

The Navajo

The semi-nomadic Navajo, relatives of the Athabaskans of western Canada, wandered into the area east of the Grand Canyon between A.D. 1300 and 1600. This adaptable tribe learned agriculture, weaving, pottery, and other skills from its Pueblo neighbors and became skilled horsemen and sheepherders with livestock obtained from the Spanish.

The Navajo habit of raiding neighboring tribes—this time, white people—almost caused the tribe's downfall. In 1863-64 the U.S. Army rounded up all the Navajo it could find, forcing the survivors to make "The Long Walk" from Fort Defiance in eastern Arizona to a bleak camp at Fort Sumner in eastern New Mexico. This attempt at forced domestication failed dismally, and the Navajo were released four years later to return to their homeland. The colorful velveteen blouses and long, flowing skirts worn by some Navajo women date back in style to this period; it was what U.S. Army wives were then wearing!

The Hopi

Legends and long-abandoned pueblos indicate that the tribe has lived here for more than a thousand years. Old Oraibi, a Hopi village dating from at least A.D. 1150, is thought to be the oldest continuously inhabited settlement in the United States, and some Hopi identify even older village sites as the homes of their ancestors, whom they call *Hisatsinom.*

Spanish explorers entered the region in the 1500s, looking for gold and treasure, but they left empty-handed. Desiring to save Hopi souls, Spanish friars arrived about 1630 and had some success until traditional Hopi leaders, fearing the loss of their own culture, joined with the New Mexico Pueblo Indians in a revolt against the Spanish in 1680. Hopi killed any foreigner unable to escape, massacred many of their own people who were Christians, and tore down the mission buildings. During the 1800s, American frontierspeople arrived seeking mineral wealth and fertile lands, but they too usually met with disappointment. So the Hopi continued to farm in relative peace, raising crops of corn, squash, and beans.

Curious tourists overwhelm the tribe at times, but the Hopi welcome visitors who respect local culture and regulations. Highlights of reservation visit include: a trip to Walpi, a traditional stone village that seemingly grows out of its spectacular ridge-top setting on First Mesa; the museum at the Cultural Center on Second Mesa; and the kachina and other dances performed on many weekends (not all are open to the public).

THE EXPLORATION OF THE COLORADO RIVER AND ITS CANYONS

Navajo with silver ornaments, late 19th century

Visiting the Indian Reservations

Privacy of the tribal residents needs to be respected; permits are required for sightseeing or other activities off the main highways. Indians prefer *not* to be treated as anthropological subjects, so it's important to ask permission before taking photos. The Hopi generally forbid photography, so don't even think of pulling a camera out on the reservation!

You'll find at least one motel and campground on all of the reservations noted above except for the Kaibab-Paiute, which has only a campground. The Navajo and Hopi Reservations have good tribal museums.

Two other museums of Indian culture, the Heard in Phoenix and the Museum of Northern Arizona in Flagstaff, provide especially good introductions to the tribes and their crafts.

REGIONAL BESTS~ OUTDOOR RECREATION

Hiking

Entering the Grand Canyon under your own power gives you the best feel for its size, grandeur, and details. Easy paths follow sections of the rims, a few wide and well-graded trails enter the depths, narrower and more difficult trails extend farther out into the backcountry, and some very difficult routes go to places rarely seen by humans. Because of the Grand Canyon's immensity and potential hazards, hikers need to give some thought to what they wish to do, then carry sufficient water, food, maps, and supplies for the trip.

The region also has fine hiking in tributaries of the Colorado River, such as Paria Canyon north of Lees Ferry and Havasu Canyon farther downstream. The hike to Rainbow Bridge on the Navajo Indian Reservation offers many awe-inspiring views. You can squeeze into the cave-like passages of Antelope/Corkscrew Canyon, also on Navajo lands. Mountains of the Arizona Strip north of the Grand Canyon have some great little climbs, as do the many peaks of the San Francisco Volcanic Field to the south.

Whitewater

The Colorado River through the Grand Canyon has it all—big-water rapids, contemplative smooth water, gorgeous canyons, and an amazing tour of the Earth's geology. The 280 river miles from Lees Ferry to the end of the Grand Canyon at Lake Mead requires a big commitment in time and gear, so you'll want to plan carefully. You can go either on your own—if suitably equipped and experienced—or with a river company. See the "Running the Colorado River" section.

Bicycling

To be fully alive to the land, skies, sounds, plants, and birds of Arizona, tour on a bicycle. Gliding across the desert or topping out on a mountain pass are experiences beyond words. Some effort, a lightweight touring or mountain bicycle, and awareness of your surroundings are all that's required.

In Grand Canyon National Park, cyclists have the big advantage of being able to ride the West Rim Drive when it's closed to cars. Although hiking trails in the park are closed to bicycles, the Kaibab National Forest on both rims features some excellent mountain biking through the forest and to overlooks. The North Rim offers the most possibilities, including the road out to Point Sublime for perhaps the best views in the entire park. The regions surrounding the Grand Canyon have good riding too, both for mountain biking and long-distance touring.

Start with short rides if you're new to bicycle touring, then work up to longer cross-country trips. By learning to maintain and repair your steed, you'll seldom have trouble on the road. An extra-low gear of 30 inches or less will take the strain out of long mountain grades. The performance of mountain bikes for touring can be improved by using road tires (no knobs) and handlebar extenders (for a variety of riding positions). Bookstores and bicycle shops provide good publications on bicycle touring. As when hiking, always carry rain and wind gear and plenty of water. Also, don't forget to wear a bicycling helmet.

Fishing

Rainbow trout thrive in the cold water that flows from Glen Canyon Dam, upstream of the Grand

Canyon. Lees Ferry offers the easiest fishing access, either from the shore or on a boat. Fishing downstream from here requires the effort of hiking into the Grand Canyon or taking a river rafting trip. Trout also lurk in permanent tributaries such as Bright Angel Creek. Other popular fishing areas in the region include vast Lake Powell above the Grand Canyon and Lake Mead at its lower end.

The trout, catfish, carp, and other species exotic to the river here could not have survived before the dam was in place. Before the early 1960s, the warm river water had so much silt and such irregular flows that only a handful of specially adapted fish swam in the Colorado. The native Colorado Squawfish, humpback chub, bonytail chub, and humpback or razorback sucker are now endangered; fishermen and women should know what they look like and return any they catch to the water.

Skiing
Grand Canyon National Park doesn't have developed ski areas or trails, but the North Rim area offers limitless backcountry skiing. On the South Rim, cross-country ski loops lie just a few miles south of Grandview Point in the Kaibab National Forest. Flagstaff features the best downhill facilities of the region and a large Nordic center. Williams offers a smaller downhill area and a couple of cross-country areas too.

COURTESY: AISLINN RACE

GRAND CANYON NATIONAL PARK

Most people head first to the South Rim, entering at either the South Entrance Station near Grand Canyon Village or the East Entrance Station near Desert View. A 26-mile scenic drive along the rim connects these entrances.

The South Rim features great views, a full range of accommodations and restaurants, and easy access—it's just 58 miles north of I-40 from Williams. Roads and most facilities stay open all year. Attractions include views from Yavapai Observation Station and other points near Grand Canyon Village, West Rim Drive to Hermit's Rest (eight miles), and East Rim/Desert View Drive to Desert View (25 miles). Some remarkable architecture lines the South Rim, including a series of unique stone structures designed by Mary Colter. The South Rim also features most of the Canyon's easily accessible viewpoints and trails. It's not surprising, then, that large crowds of visitors, especially in summer, are the main draw-

back of this part of the Canyon. Park staff have big plans to relieve the congestion by adding a light-rail system, more shuttles, bike paths, and foot trails; see the Special Topic "Shuttling Out to the South Rim."

The park collects an admission fee of $20 per private vehicle ($10 per pedestrian or bicyclist) that's good for seven days at the south and east entrances of the South Rim and at the main entrance of the North Rim. Once in the park, the visitor centers, exhibits, programs, and day hiking are free. Budget travelers can save money by stocking up on groceries and camping supplies at Flagstaff, Williams, or other towns away from the Canyon; prices at Tusayan and within the park run up to 25% higher.

Only about one in 10 visitors makes it to the North Rim, but that visitor is rewarded with pristine forests, rolling meadows, splendid wildflower displays, and superb panoramas. View-

GRAND CANYON HIGHLIGHTS

Dramatic Views: Many easily accessible viewpoints line both rims of the Grand Canyon.

Amazing Hiking: Trails on the rims and into the depths draw people of all abilities.

Mule Trips: You can descend into the Canyon just as the first tourists did, letting the animals do most of the work.

Grand Canyon Railway: Passenger trains once again steam into the Grand Canyon depot on a nostalgic ride from Williams.

Kaibab Plateau: Alpine meadows and forests with summer wildflowers lie just back from the North Rim.

Toroweap: Dizzying views of the Colorado River from cliffs nearly 3,000 feet high amidst a volcanic landscape lie at the end of a long, unpaved road on the North Rim.

River Running: The mighty Colorado River will sweep you through the heart of the Canyon on one of the world's greatest adventures.

points here are about 1,500 feet higher than those at the South Rim and provide a dramatically different perspective of the Canyon. The North Rim area offers lodging, dining, and camping facilities similar to the South Rim's, though on a smaller scale. Unless you ski in (backcountry permit required), the North Rim's high country is open only from mid-May to late October, depending on the arrival of the first big winter storm. Although the rims stand just 10 miles apart, motorists on the South Rim must drive 215 miles to get here.

Adventurous travelers on the North Rim willing to tackle 61 miles of dirt road (each way; impassable when wet) can head west over to **Toroweap Overlook,** a 140-mile, three-and-a-half-hour drive from the Bright Angel Point area. This perch sits a dizzying 3,000 feet directly above the Colorado River—one of the Canyon's most spectacular viewpoints. Don't expect any facilities other than the road and outhouses. Bring all supplies, including water. Low elevations (4,500-5,000 feet) allow access most of the year; check road conditions first with a ranger, tel. (520) 638-7888.

SOUTH RIM SIGHTS

GRAND CANYON VILLAGE AREA

Mather Point

This overlook provides the first view of the Grand Canyon if you come in from the south. Below Mather Point (elev. 7,120 feet) lie Pipe Creek Canyon, the Inner Gorge of the Colorado River, and countless buttes, temples, and points eroded from the rims. Stephen Mather served as the first director of the National Park Service and was in office when the Grand Canyon joined the national park system on February 26, 1919. The south entrance road curves west here to Grand Canyon Village.

Visitor Center

A stop here will inform you about what's happening in the park. The bulletin board in the lobby lists ranger-guided rim walks, Canyon hikes, talks, photography workshops, campfire programs, and evening presentations. Kids have presentations

just for them (and their parents) in summer, and they can learn skills in the Junior Ranger Program year-round. *The Guide,* published by the park, lists programs and sightseeing suggestions, though you'll have to call or drop in at the Visitor Center to find out the topic of each program. Rangers at the desk will answer your questions and provide maps and brochures.

The Grand Canyon Association's bookstore offers a great selection of Canyon-related books (including ones for kids), posters, topo maps, videos, slides, and postcards. The Visitor Center is open daily 8 a.m.-5 p.m., extended in summer. Call (520) 638-7888 to reach the automated switchboard with recordings of scheduled programs and offices. (People with hearing impairments can call the TDD, tel. 520-638-7804.) The Visitor Center is on the east side of Grand Canyon Village, three miles in from the South Entrance Station. This Visitor Center will close about 2002, when the new light-rail system goes into operation and exhibits move to other areas of the park.

A cloud inversion "fills" the Grand Canyon at Mather Point, December 1977.

ROBERT M. BUTTERFIELD AND GRAND CANYON NATIONAL PARK (NEG #6725)

Yavapai Observation Station

Set on the brink of the Canyon, this overlook makes a great spot to take in the panorama or watch sunsets. Panels identify the many buttes, temples, points, and tributary canyons seen through the windows. A few geology exhibits are on display too. It's open daily 8 a.m.-5 p.m., with extended summer hours. Grand Canyon Association sells books, maps, videos, slides, and postcards. The road to Yavapai Observation Station turns off between Mather Point and the Visitor Center, or you can hike one mile in via the Rim Trail from either place.

Rim Trail

People of all ages enjoy a walk along this easy trail. The 2.9-mile section from the Yavapai Observation Station past the El Tovar Hotel to Maricopa Point is paved and nearly level. A 0.4-mile connector trail from the Visitor Center goes out to the rim. Pick up biology and geology brochures for the trail at the Visitor Center, at Yavapai Observation Station, or outside Verkamp's Curios (near El Tovar Hotel). Start anywhere you like, as there are no keyed trail numbers. You'll enjoy views from many different vantage points. Pinyon pine, juniper, cliffrose, and smaller plants grow on exposed areas of the rim; ponderosa pines stick to more protected areas below the rim or farther back.

The Rim Trail continues west 6.7 miles as a dirt path to Hermit's Rest, at the end of West Rim Drive. Another unpaved segment heads east one mile from Yavapai Observation Station to Mather Point. Shuttle buses stop at both ends of the trail and many places along the way; they're free and run about every 15 minutes except in winter, when they don't operate.

Hopi House

Designed by Mary Colter to resemble an Indian Pueblo, this unusual building opened in 1905. She patterned it after structures in the Hopi village of Old Oraibi with a stone and adobe exterior, thatched ceilings, and corner fireplaces. Hopi Indians not only helped in the construction, but lived inside on the upper floors, worked as craftsmen, displayed their work, and performed nightly dances. Today Hopi House has an outstanding collection of Indian art and crafts for sale on two floors. Indian dances by various tribes take place outside in the warmer months (donation). It's near the Canyon rim just east of El Tovar.

Verkamp's Curios

Just east past Hopi House, this venerable institution is also worth a look for Indian crafts and Canyon souvenirs. John Verkamp failed in his first attempt at a curio shop out of a tent in 1898, but he returned in 1905 and built on the present site. The family continues to run the business.

Lookout Studio

The inspiration and materials of this Mary Colter building came from the Grand Canyon itself. Early visitors, after the 1914 completion, could relax by the fireplace in the lounge, purchase art and postcards in the art room, or gaze into the Canyon depths with a high-power telescope. It's open today with a gift shop and view platform. The studio stands on the Canyon's edge, just west of Bright Angel Lodge.

Kolb Studio

Perched on the rim near Lookout Studio and the Bright Angel Trailhead, this building began in 1904 as a photo studio of the Kolb brothers. Emery Kolb expanded and operated it until his death in 1976 at the age of 95. Canyon visitors could watch movies taken by the Kolbs on an early river-running expedition along with movies and stills of other Canyon subjects. The Grand Canyon Association now has a bookstore inside where you can still see some of the Kolb photography on computer screens; the Association also sells a CD-ROM of the Kolbs' work. The auditorium where Emery showed his movies now hosts visiting art exhibitions.

WEST OF GRAND CANYON VILLAGE

West Rim Drive

The Santa Fe Railroad built this eight-mile-long road from Grand Canyon Village to Hermit's Rest in 1912. Stops along the way allow visitors to walk to the rim and enjoy the views. Highlights include a great overlook of the Bright Angel Trail from Trailview, the copper and uranium Orphan Mine from Maricopa Point, some of the best views and a large historic marker at Powell Memorial, the Colorado River from Hopi and Mohave Points, the 3,000-foot sheer drop of the Abyss, and views of Granite Rapid and foundations of an old hotel below from Pima Point. Your map will help identify Canyon features: Bright Angel Trail switchbacking down to the grove of trees at Indian Garden; Plateau Point at the end of a short trail from Indian Garden; long, straight Bright Angel Canyon on the far side of the river; the many majestic temples rising to the north and east; and the rapids of the Colorado River.

Hermit's Rest—with restrooms, gift shop, and drinking water—marks the westernmost viewpoint and end of the drive. Mary Colter designed the imaginative stone building and its Great Fireplace according to what she thought a hermit might like. During the warmer months a free shuttle bus runs the length of the drive; at other times you can take your own vehicle. Bicyclists enjoy this drive too, and they aren't affected by the shuttle-season ban on cars.

If you've walked to Hermit's Rest on the Rim Trail, you'll probably want to rest too. Louis Boucher, the Hermit, came to the Canyon in 1891 and stayed 21 years; he lived at Dripping

SILENCE IN THE CANYON

Wilderness can provide a refuge from the ever busier worlds that we create. Just being out in the canyons turns out to be a delightful experience. Part of this delight seems to come from the space and the silence, which then reflects back on our own minds. "Preserving the power of presence," as Jack Turner terms in his book *The Abstract Wild*, is far more complex than just looking after the biodiversity. Rather than presence being something that we can add on to make the wilderness whole, he states that "the loss of aura and presence is the main reason we are losing so much of the natural world." Turner believes that by viewing wilderness as amusement and resource, we lose sight of the magic, holiness, and sacred nature of it.

In the Grand Canyon, this value of presence or silence has come under assault from a steady stream of aircraft circling over the heart of the Canyon. No topic has become as heated or difficult to resolve. Pilots and passengers enjoy flying so much that they refuse to consider a ban on flights. Proponents of presence will not be satisfied until the skies over the park become silent. Congress first addressed the noise problem in 1987, which banned non-emergency flights below the rims and required the designation of flight-free zones. The current compromise of restricted flight paths reduces the noise over some parts of the park, but it comes far short of the tranquility that early tourists to the park must have experienced. Only public opinion, expressed to representatives in Congress and to the Grand Canyon National Park administration, will determine how much natural silence future visitors will have in the Canyon.

Springs and built the Boucher Trail to his mining claims in Boucher Canyon.

Hermit Trail, built by the Fred Harvey Company after Louis Boucher departed, begins beyond Hermit's Rest at the end of a gravel road. It descends to the Tonto Trail, then continues down to the river at Hermit Rapids. Visitors who took this trail between 1912 and 1930 could stay at a tourist camp partway down on the Tonto Platform; only foundations remain today. A branch in the upper trail goes to Dripping Springs and Boucher Canyon.

EAST OF GRAND CANYON VILLAGE

East Rim/Desert View Drive
Outstanding overlooks line this 25-mile drive between Grand Canyon Village and Desert View.

Each has its own character and is worth a stop, but many people consider the aptly named Grandview Point one of the best. It's 12 miles east of Grand Canyon Village (14 miles before Desert View), then 0.8 mile north. Sweeping panoramas take in much of the Grand Canyon from this commanding site above Horseshoe Mesa. The vastness and intricacies of the Canyon show themselves especially well here.

Other major viewpoints on East Rim/Desert View Drive include Yaki Point, Moran Point, Lipan Point, and Desert View. At Lipan, by looking both up- and down-canyon, you can see the entire geologic sequence of the Canyon.

Tusayan Ruin
Prehistoric ancestral pueblo people built this village in A.D. 1185-1190, according to tree-ring dating.

POINT-AND-SHOOT POINTERS

Compact cameras can take wonderful pictures—if their pea-sized electronic brain isn't too heavily relied upon! The small size of compacts makes it easy to keep your camera ready for those "magic moments." Here's a checklist of ideas to obtain rewarding results:

• Moving in close to your subject gives striking results! Too often people step back and try to take a photo of their sweetheart AND the Grand Canyon without doing justice to either. A closer snap of the sweetheart with a bit of Canyon background would have made a better shot. Simple backgrounds give a sense of place without distracting from the subject.

• To zoom or not to zoom? Wide-angle settings often work best for landscapes and in confined spaces. Normal or telephoto lens settings do well for portraits.

• People busy enjoying themselves make for memorable photos.

• The early photographer gets the greatest shots. Morning's warm, soft, misty light creates wonderful effects for both landscapes and portraits. Evening's light is almost as good.

• Foregrounds add depth and interest to scenics. The infinity or spot button on many cameras ensures that the camera focuses on the distant scenery—not a nearby tree.

• To flash or not to flash? Cameras optimistically think their flash will illuminate the entire Grand Canyon for that evening shot! Then it's best to turn off the flash, prop the camera up on something (a tripod if you're lucky enough to have one handy), and use the self-timer or remote to release the shutter without jarring the camera; you can obtain surprisingly good night and interior shots this way. Some cameras have a "night scene" mode that illuminates near objects with flash, then leaves the shutter open to expose the distant background; again, you'll need to prop up the camera. Flash can work well in daytime to "fill in" dark shadows. You can dust off the camera's instruction manual to see what flash modes, flash ranges, and shutter-speed range you have.

• Flash ranges: If you copy the flash-range distances out of the instruction manual for the film speeds you use and write it on a label on the back of the camera, you'll always know when you're "in the light." Typically compact camera flashes work from the minimum focusing distance up to about 16 feet at wide angle (most non-zoom cameras), decreasing to about 9 feet at telephoto settings with ISO 100 films; distances double with ISO 400 and double again at ISO 1600.

• Steady cameras get the sharp shots. If you hold the camera securely but not tightly, and let out half of your breath and hold it while clicking the shutter, you'll get the best results. In low light or

Perhaps 30 people lived here, contending with poor soil, little rain, and scarce drinking water. After staying 35-40 years, they moved on. Archaeologists who excavated the site in 1930 named it Tusayan, a Spanish term for Hopi Indian territory.

A small museum introduces the ancestral pueblo people with artifacts and illustrations of dwellings. An archaic exhibit has some split-twig figures dating as far back as 4,000 years; other exhibits introduce modern tribes of the region. Outside, a short, self-guided trail leads to the plaza and ruins of living quarters, storage rooms, and two kivas. A leaflet (pick one up at the trailhead) and interpretive signs describe how the ancestral pueblo people farmed and obtained some of their wild foods. You can also take a free guided 45-minute tour, check *The Guide* for times. Related books can be purchased.

The museum is open daily 9 a.m.-5 p.m., except in winter when it may close some days, but the trail stays open even in winter, weather permitting. It's on the East Rim/Desert View Drive, 23 miles east of Grand Canyon Village and three miles west of Desert View, tel. (520) 638-2305.

Desert View
This overlook presents a stunning view at the end of East Rim/Desert View Drive. Although the surrounding pinyon pines and junipers suggest a lower elevation, this is the highest viewpoint on the South Rim at an elevation of 7,500 feet. Far to the east lies the multi-hued Painted Desert that gave the viewpoint its name. Below, to the north, the Colorado River flows out of Marble Canyon, then curves west.

---

with telephoto settings, you might consider propping the camera up.

• Prints or slides? The old adage "take print film for prints, slide film for slides" is fine, but if you'd really like both, great prints can be made from slides, though at a higher cost.

• What film speed? ISO 100 gives very sharp, fine-grained pictures if you have steady hands. ISO 200 or 400 makes a good alternative for low light, fast-moving subjects, and telephoto shots.

• 35mm, APS, or digital? Despite its age, 35mm has yet to be surpassed as the most efficient format for compact cameras. APS offers quality similar to 35mm, but with a bit more convenience (smaller size and easier film loading), three selectable formats (normal, wide, and panoramic on some models), and minor enhancements (strips store processing and picture information on more expensive models). APS has a smaller format than 35mm, so slide photographers may want to stick with 35mm. Digital photography has made a big splash with its instant results (you can see the photo immediately on cameras with preview screens!) and ease of hooking to a computer to do all kinds of "darkroom" modifications; you can then e-mail the photo to friends or see it emerge from an inexpensive color printer. Digital photography can be lots of fun, though you'll have to pay more for cameras and printing supplies than for film cameras. Results may not be quite as good as with film, and prints may have a shorter

life. You can almost have your cake and eat it too by using a film camera, then scanning prints into your computer; some scanners go for less than $100.

• Out in the weather or on a spashy river-rafting trip, you'll find a water-resistant camera handy to have. A camera like the Pentax 90WR features weatherproofing, a glass lens protector (can't jam), and a zoom lens with only a slightly higher cost and weight than unprotected models. Waterproof disposable cameras provide a low-cost alternative.

• A critical look at professional photos in *Arizona Highways* magazine will provide a wealth of ideas—you can see how lighting, camera angle, foreground, background, and placement of subjects lead your eye into and around each photo for a delightful experience.

• Books and websites offer examples and tips. *Arizona Highways* reveals how its photographers get such great results in the book *Photographing Arizona: Practical Techniques to Improve Your Pictures.* Kodak has many how-to books; its website features picture-taking advice at http://www.kodak.com/US/en/. The independent Sun Spot Photography site offers picture-taking instruction at www.sunspotphoto.com. The author of www.photo.net/photo provides lots of how-to and equipment advice. Curtin's Short Courses at www.shortcourses.com claims to be the number-one site for digital photography.

MARY COLTER, ARCHITECT OF THE SOUTHWEST

In an early 20th-century world dominated by male architects, Mary Colter (1869-1958) succeeded in designing many of the Grand Canyon National Park's most notable structures. After her father died in 1886, her mother gave Colter permission to attend the California School of Design in San Francisco in order to learn skills to support the remaining members of the family. Upon graduation, Colter moved to St. Paul, Minnesota, and began teaching mechanical drawing. She later applied for work with the Fred Harvey Company and, in 1901, obtained a contract to decorate the Indian Building, a new museum and sales gallery of Indian crafts between the Alvarado Hotel and depot in Albuquerque. Her association with the Fred Harvey Company spanned more than 40 years.

Colter's keen interest and research in Native American architecture led to a remarkable series of buildings along the Grand Canyon's South Rim, beginning with the Hopi House that opened in 1905. She used Southwestern themes and simple designs with careful attention to detail—interiors had to have just the right colors and furnishings, for example. So much thought went into the design of each building that it tells a story about its history or setting. Colter gave the stone Lookout Studio, perched on the Canyon rim, a jagged roof to blend into the scenery; it opened in 1914. In the same year she

Mary Colter shows blueprints to Mrs. Ickes, wife of the secretary of the Interior, in 1935.

GRAND CANYON NATIONAL PARK [NEG #16940]

The strange-looking Desert View Watchtower, designed by Mary Colter, incorporates design elements from both prehistoric and modern Indian tribes of the region. The Fred Harvey Company built the 70-foot structure in 1932, using stone around a steel frame. The interior contains reproductions of Hopi paintings and petroglyphs; stairs lead to several levels inside and to an outdoor terrace. You enter the watchtower through a room shaped like a Navajo hogan with a traditional log ceiling.

Desert View has a small information center/bookstore, gift shop, snack bar, general store, service station, and campground. There is a $10 fee for the campsites, which have drinking water but no hookups; they're open mid-April to the end of October, weather permitting; no reservations taken.

Vicinity of Desert View

Highway AZ 64 continues east 33 miles from Desert View to Cameron on US 89. On the way you'll pass two impressive overlooks of the **Little Colorado River**—signed Scenic View—on the Navajo Indian Reservation. The sheer 800-foot cliffs of the Little Colorado create a spectacular sight. The first overlook, 16.5 miles from Desert View, requires a half-mile walk out to the best

GRAND CANYON NATIONAL PARK (NEG #8307)

Hopi artist Fred Kabotie worked with Mary Colter on the Desert View Watchtower's interior artwork.

completed Hermit's Rest at the end of the West Rim Drive; its Great Fireplace and cozy interior seem much like a place that a hermit prospector might inhabit. She sought the "lived-in look" and had workmen smear soot on the new fireplace to enhance the atmosphere. Colter's work also extended to the bottom of the Grand Canyon, where in 1922 she

designed the stone lodge and four cabins of Phantom Ranch. In 1932 she finished the Desert View Watchtower using a variety of prehistoric and modern Indian themes; it's the most intriguing of her buildings to explore. After settling on a watchtower patterned after those of ancestral pueblo people, Colter wrote, "First and most important was to design a building that would . . . create no discordant note against the time eroded walls of this promontory." She not only designed the 1935 Bright Angel Lodge, intended to provide accommodations for tourists with moderate incomes, but incorporated the 1890s Buckey O'Neill Cabin and Red Horse Station into it. Without her interest in these historic structures, they would have been torn down. She also designed the unusual geologic fireplace in the lodge's lounge.

La Posada Hotel, which opened in 1930 beside the railroad tracks in downtown Winslow, might be her most exotic commission—a fantasy of arches, halls, and gardens in a Spanish Colonial Revival style. La Posada nearly suffered demolition, the fate of the Alvarado Hotel, but it has recently been saved and restored; Winslow visitors are welcome to tour the public areas. Train travelers at the Union Station in Los Angeles, built in 1939, can admire interior design that brings a Southwestern style into the geometry of Art Deco. Colter enjoyed her professional life—she never married and was reportedly rarely at home. Only in recent times has the public taken note of Colter's work. Perhaps her working as "house architect" on a relatively small number of major buildings, some in remote areas, led to her relative obscurity. That's changed now, with books, exhibits, and documentaries out on her life. Five Colter structures have become National Historic Landmarks.

viewpoints. The second overlook, 5.2 miles farther east, offers a large Indian market of jewelry, pottery, and other crafts with just a short walk to the views.

Cape Solitude, directly above the confluence of the Little Colorado and Colorado Rivers, lives up to its name and features amazing views of both canyons. The jeep road has been closed to vehicles, but adventurous drivers with 4WD can take back roads on the Navajo Reservation (tribal permit needed) to the Park boundary, then walk the last 6.7 miles. When the Little Colorado isn't in flood, you'll see blue waters from mineral-rich springs in its canyon. Hikers can

reach Blue Springs on a very rough route, estimated at 1.5 miles and an elevation change of 2,100 feet each way; it's on the Navajo Reservation (tribal permit required) and approached on 4WD roads from Desert View via Cedar Mountain or from the Kaibab National Forest farther east. The Little Colorado offers a challenging hiking route between Cameron and the Colorado River; conditions constantly change, and it should be avoided when in flood. Hiking books describe some of these routes. Ask around at Desert View, Tusayan Ruins, and the Backcountry Office to find a ranger knowledgeable in these areas. See **Cameron** (northeastern Ari-

Desert View Watchtower

zona section) for details on obtaining Navajo tribal permits to explore this remote country east of the Grand Canyon.

KAIBAB NATIONAL FOREST (TUSAYAN RANGER DISTRICT)

Tusayan Bike Trails
Three interconnected loops for mountain bikers begin from a trailhead on the west side of AZ 64 between Moqui Lodge and Tusayan. Trail 1 is three miles (it takes about half an hour); Trail 2 goes eight miles (just over an hour); and Trail 3 runs nine miles (about an hour and a half).

Grandview Lookout
Some of the prettiest country of the Tusayan Ranger District surrounds the lookout. You can climb the 80-foot steel tower, built by the Civilian Conservation Corps in 1936, for a panorama of the region. The tower is easily reached from the

East Rim/Desert View Drive, two miles east of the Grandview Point turnoff; turn south at the sign for "Arizona Trail" between Mileposts 252 and 253 and proceed 1.3 miles. You can also drive east 15 miles on Forest Road 302 from the south edge of Tusayan.

Cross-country ski loops begin one-third of a mile north of Grandview Lookout; the Forest Service grooms trails here in the snow season, beginning about late December.

The historic **Hull Cabin** and outbuildings, two miles from the lookout by road, once belonged to a sheep ranch. You're welcome to visit the grounds. The Kaibab Forest Map (Tusayan District) shows the roads in.

Hikers have several options at the trailhead beside Grandview Lookout. **Vishnu Trail** does a 2.2-mile loop from which a spur trail goes out to some Grand Canyon viewpoints; interpretive signs on local history are planned. The trail heads northeast from the tower, then loops back on the Arizona Trail. Whether you're setting out on a months-long expedition or just a short stroll, the **Arizona Trail** offers some scenic hiking and mountain biking. The first mile southeast from the trailhead has interpretive signs about mistletoe. Altogether, the Arizona Trail runs 22.3 miles in three segments on the Tusayan Ranger District. The northern Coconino Rim Trail segment follows the top of 500-foot cliffs southeast of Grandview Lookout; it's 9.4 miles long with views of the Painted Desert, moderate grades, and some switchbacks. The 8.3-mile Russell Wash segment farther south is mostly level in a forest changing from ponderosa in the north to pinyon pine and juniper in the south. The Moqui Stage Trail segment is 4.6 miles long and follows the old stage route (1892-1901) between the station site and the south forest boundary.

Red Butte Trail
Few hikers know about this mountain south of Tusayan, despite the good trail and fine views. It's a remnant of the red-colored Moenkopi Formation, protected from erosion by a thick lava cap. You can visit the lookout tower for the best 360-degree panorama. The large meadows just to the north once hosted Grand Canyon's original airport; a bit farther north stands the green tower of a uranium mine, currently inactive due to

low ore prices. A long stretch of the North Rim rises farther to the north, Grandview Lookout can just be seen on the wooded ridge to the northeast, and the San Francisco Peaks and Volcanic Field lie to the south. From Tusayan, head nine miles south on AZ 64 to between Mileposts 226 and 227, then turn east 4.3 miles on Forest Roads 305, 340, and 340A. From the south, you can take AZ 64 to Milepost 224, then turn east 2.7 miles via Forest Roads 320, 340, and 340A to the trailhead.

VALLE

Highways US 180 from Flagstaff and AZ 64 from Williams meet at this road junction 28 miles south of Grand Canyon Village. The tiny community has an excellent aviation museum, a simple theme park based on the cartoon Flintstones, two motels, a campground, convenience stores,

GRAND CANYON NATIONAL PARK (NEG #8801)

Hopi artist Fred Kabotie explains the snake legend painting in Desert View Watchtower, 1932.

gift shops, and a gas station. The desolate high-desert spot isn't a place to linger, except for the museum. The motels are poor value compared with those in Flagstaff or Williams, and the motel restaurant lacks a smoke-free area. The campground at the theme park is exposed to winds, and the cafe here also lacks a smoke-free area.

Planes of Fame Air Museum
Outstanding aircraft of the past, along with some oddities and replicas, reside beside Valle's airport on the south side of town. During the Korean War, General Douglas MacArthur flew aboard the Lockheed Constellation C-121A named "Bataan," which has been beautifully restored and opened for tours. Replicas represent a few famous WW I aircraft. The 1928 Ford Trimotor, said to have been a personal aircraft of Henry Ford, still flies; it's a type of plane used in early tourist flights over the Grand Canyon. World War II highlights include a Fuji Ohka 11 piloted suicide rocket, a Messerschmitt Bf 109G Gustav fighter plane, and an early P-51A Mustang. Newer fighters represent the dawn of the jet age. Some homebuilts and other light aircraft, a Link Trainer Model C-3 ("the sweat box"), and a timeline of women in aviation round out the collection. The museum, open daily except Thanksgiving and Christmas, is part of the Planes of Fame Air Museum based in Chino, California; some planes rotate between the two collections. The website www.planesoffame.org has information on both, or call (520) 635-1000 for information. Admission is adults $5, children 5-12 $2, and "Bataan" tours cost an extra $3.

On the last weekend in May, the museum sponsors the **High Country Warbirds Air Display** with flybys of vintage aircraft and ground displays.

Flintstones Bedrock City
Fans of the cartoon series *The Flintstones* may enjoy walking around this life-size town. It has the houses of Fred and Barney and their families, businesses, dinosaur statues (one is a kid's slide), a little ride through a "volcano," and a theater where the cartoons play. The park, tel. (520) 635-2600, is open year-round; admission is $5 for ages two and up. There's also a campground here (see below for details).

SOUTH RIM PRACTICALITIES

SOUTH RIM ACCOMMODATIONS

The Grand Canyon offers too much to see in one day. In Grand Canyon Village you can stay right on the rim at Bright Angel Lodge, Thunderbird Lodge, Kachina Lodge, or El Tovar Hotel. Other lodges lie back in the woods. The town of Tusayan, just outside the park nine miles south of Grand Canyon Village, provides additional places to stay. One can usually find a place to stay anytime, but reservations from six up to 23 months in advance will give the best choice of rooms. If planning a late arrival, you might consider either a reservation or staying in one of the towns surrounding the park.

Grand Canyon Village

Grand Canyon National Park Lodges operates all the lodges here, as well as Moqui Lodge just outside the South Entrance Station, and the lodge and cabins at the North Rim's Bright Angel Point. All the lodges have non-smoking rooms and totally smoke-free public areas. Make reservations at 14001 E. Iliff Ave., Suite 600, Aurora, CO 80014; tel. (303) 297-2757 (advance reservations) or (520) 638-2631 (same-day reservations), or fax (303) 297-3175; Internet: www.amfac.com.

One of the grand old hotels of the West, **El Tovar** has offered the Canyon's finest accommodations and food since 1905. This national historic landmark offers rooms—no two alike—with modern conveniences, yet it retains an old-fashioned lodge ambience; guests enjoy a restaurant, lounge, and concierge service. Four suites have Canyon views. Room rates run $112 d for a standard double, $126 d for a standard queen, $169 d for a deluxe, and $192-277 for a suite. Premium.

Kachina and **Thunderbird** Lodges, on the rim between El Tovar and Bright Angel Lodge, offer modern rooms for $107 d back side or $117 d canyon side. Expensive-Premium.

Historic 1935 **Bright Angel Lodge** sits on the rim a short distance from the Bright Angel trailhead. Hikers and other visitors gather in the lobby, patio, restaurant, and lounge of this popular place. Rates for standard cabins are $58 d, historic cabins $68 d, rim cabins $94 d, and rim cabins with fireplace $114 d. Moderate-Expensive. Rooms in the lodge cost $42 with sink, $48 with toilet, $58 d with shower (other facilities are down the hall). Inexpensive. The Buckey O'Neill Suite dates from the early 1890s and is one of the oldest historic structures in the park; it costs $227 d. Luxury. The Bright Angel History Room displays memorabilia from early tourist days and a "geological fireplace" in which Canyon rocks have been laid, floor to ceiling, in the proper stratigraphic sequence. The transportation desk in the lobby organizes scheduled bus service, bus and air tours, mule trips, and Phantom Ranch accommodations. The lodge also features a restaurant, steak house, snack bar, lounge, and beauty/barber shop.

Maswik Lodge, two blocks south of Bright Angel Lodge, has a cafeteria and cozy cabins for $59 d and modern rooms for $72 d in the south section, $112 d in the north section. Moderate-Expensive. **Yavapai Lodge,** one mile east of Bright Angel Lodge, then one-third mile south, offers modern rooms for $83 d in the west section and $98 d in the east section; there's also a cafeteria here. Expensive.

Tusayan

Motels, restaurants, a campground, an IMAX Theater, and other tourist services line AZ 64 in this compact town, nine miles south of Grand Canyon Village. They're all well-signed. Prices run on the high side for accommodations, though they drop a bit in winter or anytime business is slow. New motels under construction will ease the room shortage at busy times. You won't find any rooms in the Budget or Inexpensive ranges.

Moderate: In the $60-85 category, there's the **Seven Mile Lodge** with rooms at $79 d in summer, less in winter; tel. (520) 638-2291.

Expensive: In the $85-110 category, the **Moqui Lodge,** one mile north of Tusayan and just outside the South Entrance Station, offers rooms at $89 s, $94 d from April 1 to October 31 (closed in winter); tel. (520) 638-2424 or (303)

297-2757 (central reservations). The lodge has a restaurant open daily for a breakfast buffet and à la carte dinner, an information desk where you can arrange tours and horseback riding, a gift shop, and a service station.

Red Feather Lodge/Rodeway Inn has standard rooms at $99 d in the annex and deluxe rooms at $119 d in the new building with lower rates off season; guests can enjoy an outdoor pool and spa, fitness room, game room, and adjacent restaurant; tel. (520) 638-2414, (800) 538-2345, or (800) 228-2000 (Rodeway reservations).

Best Western Grand Canyon Squire Inn features a restaurant, lounge, outdoor pool, jacuzzi, sauna, exercise room, tennis courts, bowling alley, beauty salon, and gift shop. Rooms cost $99-150 d and the few suites are $175-225 d; tel. (520) 638-2681 or (800) 622-6966.

Premium: Moving up to the $110-150 category, you'll find the **Grand Canyon Quality Inn & Suites** which features a huge atrium, restaurant, outdoor pool and hot tub, 18-foot spa (in the atrium), Wintergarten Lounge (in the atrium), and a gift shop. Standard rooms are $118-135 d, and suites go for $168-185 d from March 25 to October 31, less off season; tel. (520) 638-2673 or (800) 221-2222.

Grand Canyon Suites next door has a different theme for each suite; from mid-May to September, the "Juniors" cost $145 d, "Canyons" (with a sofabed in the living area) are $165 d, and the two-bedroom "Grands" run $225; tel. (520) 638-3100 or (888) 538-5353.

Holiday Inn Express includes a continental breakfast with its rooms, which run $119-129 d in summer; tel. (520) 638-3000 or (800) HOLIDAY.

The Grand Hotel presents a dinner theater, Native American programs, restaurant, and an indoor pool and spa on the south side of town; rooms go for $138 d ($79 d November-mid-March); tel. 638-3333 or (888) 634-7263.

Valle
You'll pass through this little town, 28 miles south of Grand Canyon Village, if coming on the direct routes from Williams or Flagstaff. **Grand Canyon Inn** (Moderate at $79 d) and the nearby **Grand Canyon Motel** (Inexpensive at $49-59 d) are under the same management, tel. (520) 635-9203. Both close January to mid-February, and the inn has a smoky restaurant and a gift shop.

SOUTH RIM CAMPGROUNDS

Grand Canyon Village
Campgrounds tend to be crowded in the warmer months. It's best to have a reservation then; otherwise, try to arrive before noon to look for a site. Rangers enforce the "No Camping Outside Designated Sites" policy with stiff fines. Backpackers inside the Canyon or in backcountry areas atop the rim need a permit from the Backcountry Office. RVs have a dump station near the road to the campgrounds.

Mather Campground is south of the Visitor Center in Grand Canyon Village. It's open year-round with drinking water but no hookups for $15 per night, $7.50 with a Golden Age or Access pass; tel. (520) 638-7851. Reservations, highly recommended in the summer months, can be made for family and group sites with National Park Reservations Service; tel. (800) 365-2267 (365-CAMP); Internet: reservations.nps.gov. Backpackers and bicyclists can camp at a walk-in area for $4 per person, no reservations needed; it has space even when the campground is signed "FULL." **Camper Services** offers nearby showers, laundromat, and ice for a small charge. Campfire programs are held during the warmer months.

Trailer Village, just east of Mather Campground, has RV sites for $19 with hookups all year. Reservations are highly recommended from the week before Easter to the end of October; you can make them with Grand Canyon National Park Lodges, 14001 E. Iliff Ave., Suite 600, Aurora, CO 80014, tel. (303) 297-2757 (advance reservations) or (520) 638-2631 (same-day reservations), fax (303) 297-3175, Internet: www.amfac.com. No showers, but those in Camper Services lie within walking distance. Trailer Village may be temporarily taken over by construction crews while all of the planned transportation and new building projects are under way, so you might have to go elsewhere then.

Desert View
This campground, near the East Entrance Station (25 miles east of Grand Canyon Village), has sites in a pinyon pine-juniper forest with drinking water but no hookups. It's open May to October, weather permitting, for $10; no reservations taken.

Tusayan

Grand Canyon Camper Village offers sites in the ponderosa pines for tents ($15) and RVs ($18-22 with hookups) year-round and in tepee tents ($18) during the warmer months with coin showers and a playground. Reservations can be made only for the hookup sites, though spaces are usually available; tel. (520) 638-2887.

Ten X Campground in the ponderosa pines of the Kaibab National Forest has drinking water but no hookups or showers; it's open May-Sept. for $10 per vehicle and usually has room. Amphitheater programs take place many nights, and a nature trail provides an introduction to the natural history of the area. From Tusayan, go south two miles (between Mileposts 233 and 234), then turn east a quarter mile. **Charley Tank Group Site** nearby can be reserved; tel. (520) 638-2443 (Tusayan Ranger Station).

Dispersed camping in the Kaibab National Forest south of the park is another possibility—just practice no-trace camping, carry your own drinking water, and stay at least a quarter mile from the nearest paved road and a quarter mile from any surface water. Check with the ranger station, on the right one mile north of Tusayan, to learn whether campfires are permitted; staff can also make suggestions for dispersed camping. The Kaibab Forest map (Williams and Tusayan Districts) shows the back roads.

Valle

Flintstones Bedrock City campsites in Valle, 28 miles south of Grand Canyon Village on AZ 64, cost $12 for tents or RVs ($16 w/hookups). It has coin showers, a store, snack bar (smoky), and theme park. The campground is open March-October, weather permitting, and self-contained vehicles can park in winter; tel. (520) 635-2600.

SOUTH RIM FOOD

Grand Canyon Village Area

El Tovar Hotel offers elegant continental and American dining daily for breakfast, lunch, and dinner at moderate to expensive prices; you'll need to make reservations for dinner, tel. (520) 638-2631. Bright Angel Lodge features two moderately priced restaurants, the **Bright Angel Restaurant** serving breakfast, lunch, and dinner daily, tel. (520) 638-2631, and the **Arizona Steakhouse,** offering steaks, fish, chicken, and ribs nightly for dinner, tel. (520) 638-2631. **Maswik Lodge,** two blocks south of Bright Angel Lodge, and **Yavapai Lodge,** one mile east of Bright Angel Lodge, then one-third mile south, both have large cafeterias open daily for breakfast, lunch, and dinner at inexpensive prices.

A **general store** near the Visitor Center has a supermarket and a deli counter with tables. **Bright Angel Fountain** serves ice cream and other snacks on the Canyon rim behind Bright Angel Lodge; it's closed in the winter. You can also buy groceries at general stores in Desert View and Tusayan.

Tusayan

Moqui Lodge's restaurant serves a breakfast buffet and dinner (steak, chicken, fish, and a few Mexican items) daily during the April-October season; tel. (520) 638-2424. The spacious atrium and greenery in the **Grand Canyon Quality Inn & Suites'** restaurant provides an enjoyable setting. Diners have a choice of a la carte or buffets daily for breakfast, lunch, and dinner. The large selection of salads and fruit in the buffets will appeal to vegetarians; non-veggies will appreciate steak and seafood on the menu as well as a variety of meat dishes in the buffet; tel. (520) 638-2673. The new **Canyon Star** of the Grand Hotel plans dinner theater and Native American programs as well as serving breakfast, lunch, and dinner daily; tel. (520) 638-3333. **Denny's,** next to the Red Feather Lodge, features American favorites daily for breakfast, lunch, and dinner; tel. (520) 638-2150. The **Grand Canyon Squire Inn's** Coronado Room offers fine dining of steak, barbecued ribs, prime rib, seafood, pasta, and some Mexican items nightly for dinner. The Canyon Room serves a la carte meals (year-round) and buffets (summer only) daily for breakfast, lunch, and dinner; tel. (520) 638-2681. **The Steak House** serves up steak, chicken, shrimp, and even a few veggie options; it's open daily for lunch (summer only) and dinner; tel. (520) 638-2780. **We Cook Pizza & Pasta** offers pizza, pasta, calzones, and sandwiches daily for lunch and dinner; tel. (520) 638-2278. **Grand Canyon Soup & Subs** next door does lunches daily;

tel. (520) 638-2224. **Pizza Hut** and **Taco Bell** can be found in the Grand Canyon IMAX Theater complex. **McDonald's** is nearby across the highway. **Subway** has inexpensive subs on the south side of town just in from the south airport entrance; it's open daily for breakfast lunch, and dinner; tel. (520) 638-3385.

SOUTH RIM SERVICES

Entertainment

Rangers present **evening programs** and **campfire talks;** see *The Guide* listings for times and places, check the bulletin board at the Visitor Center, or call (520) 638-7888 for the day's topics. Chamber music comes to the Grand Canyon in September during the **Grand Canyon Music Festival,** held at Shrine of the Ages auditorium on the South Rim. The **Grand Canyon IMAX Theatre** in Tusayan projects an impressive movie, *The Grand Canyon—The Hidden Secrets,* on a 70-foot screen with six-track stereo sound. The 34-minute presentation portrays prehistoric Indians, explorers, wildlife, river running, and flying with spectacular photography. Showings take place every day on the half hour 8:30 a.m.-8:30 p.m. March-October, then 10:30 a.m.-6:30 p.m. in winter. Admission is $7.75 adults, $5.50 children 3-11; tel. (520) 638-2468/2203. You'll also find fast-food restaurants, gift shops, ATM, and tourist information here.

The **Wintergarten Lounge** has piano music most evenings in the atrium of the Grand Canyon Quality Inn & Suites in Tusayan; tel. (520) 638-2673. **Bright Angel Lodge** may have music in its lounge; tel. (520) 638-2631. The weekly *Grand Canyon News* lists special performances and events.

Shopping

Grand Canyon Association has excellent selections of regional books, children's books, topo maps, posters, and videos in its shops at the Visitor Center, Kolb Studio, Yavapai Observation Station, and Desert View. Tusayan Ruins has a small stock of related books; Internet: www. thecanyon.com/gca. **General stores,** just south of the Visitor Center in Grand Canyon Village, at Tusayan, and at Desert View, sell groceries, camping and hiking supplies, clothing, books, maps, souvenirs, and offers one of the best selections of camera film. The Grand Canyon Village store is the largest and has a deli; the Tusayan store also has video rentals. There's a gift shop almost everywhere you turn in the developed areas of the South Rim! El Tovar, other lodges, most motels, the helicopter terminals, and the airport have them. **Hopi House,** the Indian pueblo replica just east of El Tovar, has an impressive array of Indian crafts and art from the Southwest; it's worth a visit to see both the architecture—interior and exterior—and the high-quality merchandise. A bit farther east is **Verkamp's Curio** with Indian crafts and souvenirs. **Lookout Studio,** on the rim's edge near

Hopi dancer Chester Dennis (right) leads other Indian dancers at the dedication of the Desert View Watchtower, 1933. These days you can see Indian dancers at Hopi House in Grand Canyon Village.

Bright Angel Lodge, features curios and books in a picturesque stone building. Other places to shop in the park include Hermit's Rest and Desert View Lookout Tower at opposite ends of the South Rim drives.

Other Services
Backpackers can stow their bags with staff in the Bright Angel Lodge lobby. The **post office,** near the general store south across the road from the Visitor Center, opens Mon.-Fri. 9 a.m.-4:30 p.m. and Saturday 11 a.m.-1 p.m.; tel. (520) 638-02512. **Bank One** next door has a 24-hour ATM. The bank can exchange foreign currency and give cash advances on Visa and MasterCard, but it cannot cash out-of-town checks; open Mon.-Thurs. 10 a.m.-3 p.m. and Friday 10 a.m.-5 p.m.; tel. (520) 638-2437. The **general store** in Tusayan also includes a **post office** and an ATM, and there's another ATM at the IMAX Theater across the highway. **Western Union** does wire transfers at National Park Lodges general offices in Grand Canyon Village and at Canyon Store in Tusayan; tel. (800) 325-6000. **Print film processing** is offered at the general stores and several places in Tusayan. **Grand Canyon Garage** fixes ailing cars and provides 24-hour emergency service; tel. (520) 638-2631. **Grand Canyon Clinic** offers medical (tel. 520-638-2551 or 520-638-2469) and dental (tel. 520-638-2395) services and a pharmacy (tel. 520-638-2460). For an ambulance or other emergency, dial 911.

National Park Service staff provide wheelchairs, an *Accessibility Guide,* Braille literature, and other services for visitors with special needs; ask at the Visitor Center or write ahead to the park, Box 129, Grand Canyon, AZ 86023.

The **Pet Kennel** houses the furry companions who won't be welcome in the park lodges or permitted on the inner-canyon trails; tel. (520) 638-2631, ext. 6549. Reservations are suggested at the kennel. Leashed pets may walk the rim trails in developed areas and may be able to stay in some of the motels in Tusayan. You'll find a coin-operated **laundromat** and **showers**—a welcome sight to any traveler who's been a long time on the road or trail—near Mather Campground.

Theft has become a problem at the Canyon—be sure to keep valuables hidden or keep them with you. Park rangers patrol the park, serving as law enforcement officers and firefighters; see them if you have difficulties.

SOUTH RIM INFORMATION

Visitor Center
You can stop here for exhibits, slide shows, the bookshop, a bulletin board of scheduled events, and information desks. It's open daily 8 a.m.-5 p.m. with extended hours in summer. Look for the Visitor Center on the east side of Grand Canyon Village, six miles from the South Entrance Station. The planned **Canyon View Information Center** at Mather Point will replace the Visitor Center in about 2002; see the special topic "Shuttling Out to the South Rim." Pick up a copy of *The Guide* newspaper for the latest visitor information; it lists the hours and locations of programs, places to stay and eat, and other visitor services. The park's mailing address is Box 129, Grand Canyon, AZ 86023.

You can obtain a **weather forecast** and many other recordings and reach all park offices through the **automated switchboard,** tel. (520) 638-7888. **Hearing-impaired** people can use the TDD number for park information, tel. (520) 638-7804.

Tusayan's tourist information counter offers local and regional information daily 9 a.m.-5 p.m. beside the IMAX Theater's ticket office.

The airport at the south end of Valle served as a training field in WW II; the new terminal here has Arizona tourist information but seems to get few visitors; tel. (520) 638-0116.

Backcountry Office
For trail information and backcountry camping permits, drop by this office in the Maswik Transportation Center, open daily 8 a.m-noon and 1-5 p.m.; tel. (520) 638-7875. Call between 1 and 5 p.m. to speak with someone in person. Day-hikers don't need a permit.

Kaibab National Forest
Though often ignored in the shadow of Grand Canyon National Park, the Kaibab offers hiking, mountain biking, and both developed and primitive camping. Stop by the **Tusayan Ranger Station** for handouts on hiking and biking trails, scenic drives, and other attractions. The Kaibab

National Forest map (Williams and Tusayan Districts) shows the trails and back roads. Staff can also provide directions for hiking the Red Butte Trail, the prominent butte 12 miles south of Tusayan, as well as 22 miles (one-way) of the Arizona Trail just south of the park. In winter, cross-country skiers can glide along loops near the Grandview Lookout. The station, open Mon.-Fri. 8 a.m.-5 p.m., is in the Tusayan Administrative Site, across and 0.2 miles south from Moqui Lodge just outside the South Entrance Station. Contact the station at Box 3088, Grand Canyon, AZ 86023, tel. (520) 638-2443, Internet: www.fs.fed.us/r3/kai/.

Internet Sites
A "virtual tour" can give you ideas of things to do on your visit. The "Unofficial Grand Canyon National Park Home Page" is an especially good source at www.kaibab.org. The National Park Service site contains news, visiting tips, hiking information, and regulations for river runners at www.thecanyon.com/nps or www.nps.gov/grca. The Grand Canyon Chamber of Commerce site offers a good introduction to the park and links to surrounding towns at www.thecanyon.com.

Grand Canyon Community Library
This small collection resides in an old schoolhouse tucked behind the garage and general office for the lodges in Grand Canyon Village. It offers general and Southwestern reading and periodicals; tel. (520) 638-2718.

SOUTH RIM TOURS

Most of the lodges in the park, along with Moqui Lodge just outside, have a Transportation Services desk where you can arrange tours. You'll also see signs for reservations agencies in Tusayan, such as **South Rim Travel,** which offers a free booking service for rooms, flights, and tours; tel. (800) 682-4393.

Mule Rides
Sure-footed mules have carried prospectors and tourists in and out of the Canyon for more than a century. These large animals, a crossbreed of female horses and male donkeys, depart daily year-round on day and overnight trips. Although easier than hiking, a mule ride should still be considered strenuous—you need to be able to sit in the saddle for long hours and control your mount. These trips are definitely not for those afraid of heights.

Day-trips go down the Bright Angel Trail to Indian Garden and out to Plateau Point, a spectacular overlook above the river; the 12-mile, seven-hour roundtrip costs $106.60 per person. The overnight trip follows the Bright Angel Trail all the way to the river, crosses a suspension bridge to Phantom Ranch, spends the night in a cabin, then comes out the next day via the South Kaibab Trail. This costs $272.51 for one person, $480.31 for two, and $218.89 each additional person including meals and cabin. Three-day, two-night trips of-

COURTESY: AISLINN RACE

ready to provide a mule ride on Hance's Trail, late 19th century

fered mid-November to March 31 cost $385.21 for one, $640.64 for two, and $277.77 each additional person. Mules will also carry hikers' overnight gear to Phantom Ranch, $46.13 each way (30-pound limit). All these rates include tax.

Enforced requirements for riders include good health, weight under 200 pounds (91 kilograms), fluency in English, height over four feet seven inches (138 cm), and ability to mount and dismount without assistance. No pregnant women are allowed. A hat, tied under the chin, long pants, a long-sleeved shirt, and sturdy shoes (no open-toed footwear) are necessary. Don't bring bags, purses, or backpacks, but you can carry a camera or binoculars. A bota (water carrier), which ties on the saddle horn, is supplied.

Reservations should be made 9-12 months in advance for summer and holidays. Also be sure to claim your reservation at least one hour before departure. Without a reservation, there's a chance of getting on via the waiting list, especially off-season; register in person between 6 and 10 a.m. the day before you want to go.

For information and reservations less than four days in advance, see the Bright Angel transportation desk, tel. (520) 638-3283. To make reservations more than four days in advance, contact Grand Canyon National Park Lodges at 14001 E. Iliff Ave., Suite 600, Aurora, CO 80014, tel. (303) 297-2757, Internet: www.amfac.com.

Trail Rides

Apache Stables offers mule and horse rides through the Kaibab National Forest for one hour ($26.45), two hours ($42.32), and all the way to the South Rim and back in four hours ($68.77) from the stables near Moqui Lodge, one mile north of Tusayan. Campfire trips ($31.74) ride out and take a hay wagon back, or you can take the hay wagon both ways. You may bring your own food, if you like. Riding season runs March-December depending on the weather. You can make reservations, recommended two weeks ahead in summer or two days the rest of the season—though last-minute openings are possible—at Moqui Lodge, tel. (520) 638-2424; when the lodge is closed, call the stables direct at (520) 638-2891.

Bus Tours

Fred Harvey Transportation Co. will show you the sights of the South Rim and narrate the

Canyon's history, geology, and wildlife. Hermit's Rest Tour visits viewpoints on West Rim Drive (two hours, $12.50). Desert View Tour travels along East Rim/Desert View Drive (just under four hours, $23.50 or $25 including Hermit's Rest Tour). Sunset Tour heads over to Mohave or Yaki points (hour and a half, $9, May-October only).

Railroad Express takes you to Williams early in the morning to catch the train ride back to Grand Canyon Village. A river raft excursion runs the smooth-flowing Colorado River in Glen Canyon from the dam to Lees Ferry; stops on the drive there point out highlights of the East Rim/Desert View Drive and the Navajo Indian Reservation (12 hours, $96, April to early November). Tours in the park leave daily (twice a day in summer for the Hermit's Rest and Desert View tours). Lodge transportation desks have tickets; children under 16 (under 12 for tours out of park) go at half price. No reservations needed; contact Box 699, Grand Canyon, AZ 86023, tel. (520) 638-2401.

Jeep Tours

Grand Canyon Jeep Tours in Tusayan visits backcountry historic and scenic spots in the Kaibab National Forest and the Grand Canyon. The two-hour Canyon Pines Tour runs mid-day for $48 adult ($30 age 12 and under). The two-and-a-half-hour Grand Sunset Tour goes late in the afternoon—a good time to spot wildlife—and includes a stop to watch the sunset for $53 ($35 age 12 and under). The Indian Cave Paintings Tour visits a site with petroglyphs and pictographs in the Kaibab National Forest at $30 adult ($20 age 12 and younger). Make reservations at tel. (520) 638-5337 or (800) 320-5337.

Grand Canyon Field Institute

Small groups explore the Grand Canyon with day-hikes, backpacking, river-running trips, van tours, and classroom instruction. You can pick up a schedule at the Grand Canyon Association bookstores in the park or write the institute at Box 399, Grand Canyon, AZ 86023, tel. (520) 638-2485, Internet: www.thecanyon.com/fieldinstitute.

Air Tours

Flights over the Canyon provide breathtaking views and a look at some of the park's more remote areas. About 40 scenic flight companies operate helicopters or fixed-wing aircraft here, mostly out of Las Vegas. The 50,000-plus flights a year sometimes detract from the wilderness experience of backcountry users—Tusayan's airport is the third busiest in the state. However, restrictions on flight routes and elevations help minimize the noise.

Scenic flights depart all year from Tusayan Airport. Helicopters fly near rim-level and offer the novelty of their takeoffs and landings, but they cost more. Fixed wing aircraft fly about 1,000 feet higher and provide more air time for your dollar; they also offer better children's discounts. Most fixed-wing aircraft leave from the main terminal, while Grand Canyon Airlines and the helicopter companies fly from separate terminals nearby.

Grand Canyon Airlines started flying here in 1927 with Ford Trimotors. Today the company uses high-wing, twin-engine planes on a 45- to 55-minute loop over the South Rim, Little Colorado River, and back over the North Rim ($75 adult, $45 children under 12). Planes leave from just north of the main terminal; tel. (520) 638-2407 or (800) 528-2413; Internet: www.grand-canyonairlines.com.

Air Grand Canyon's high-wing Cessnas offer three loops: a 30- to 35-minute flight over the eastern Canyon ($58.90 adult, $36.90 children

under 12); a 50- to 60-minute trip over the eastern Canyon and North Rim ($74.90 adult, $42.90 children under 12); and a 80- to 85-minute grand tour of the Grand Canyon from Havasupai to Marble Canyons ($127.90 adult, $106.90 children under 12). Grand Canyon Railway/flight combinations to Williams, charters, and other tours can be arranged too; tel. (520) 638-2686 or (800) 247-4726; Internet: www.airgrandcanyon.com.

Windrock Airlines offers tours similar to Air Grand Canyon's. Other flights journey to Monument Valley, Bryce Canyon, Zion, Lake Powell, Sedona, Prescott, Bullhead City, and Flagstaff; tel. (800) 24-ROCKY.

AirStar Airlines flies high-wing Cessnas on a 50-minute tour to the eastern Grand Canyon and over the North Rim ($71 adult, $51 children under 15); tel. (520) 638-2139 or (800) 962-3869; Internet: www.airstar.com.

Papillon Grand Canyon Helicopters flies across the Canyon to the North Rim (25-30 minutes, $94 adult, $76 children 2-11) and over the eastern Grand Canyon and North Rim (40-45 minutes, $154 adult, $124 children 2-11). You can also arrange to land at Supai village in Havasu Canyon and visit the waterfalls on day and overnight excursions. Helicopters fly from a site north and across the street from the main terminal; there's a gift shop and photo lab here; tel.

GRAND CANYON NATIONAL PARK (NEG #2435)

the first train to carry passengers to the Grand Canyon, 1901

(520) 638-2419 or (800) 528-2418; Internet: www.papillon.com.

AirStar Helicopters will take you across the Canyon to the North Rim and back (25-30 minutes, $94), around the eastern Grand Canyon (40-45 minutes, $131), and over both the eastern and North Rim areas (50-55 minutes; $161) from the hill just east of the main terminal; tel. (520) 638-2622 or (800) 962-3869; Internet: www.airstar.com.

Kenai Helicopters heads across the Canyon to the North Rim (25-30 minutes, $94 adult, $85 children 2-12) and over the eastern Grand Canyon and North Rim (45-55 minutes, $160 adult or children) from the hill just east of the main terminal; tel. (520) 638-2412 or (800) 541-4537.

SOUTH RIM TRANSPORTATION

Shuttle Services
The park service runs three free shuttle services during the warmer months to reduce traffic congestion. During this period the West Rim Drive and Yaki Point/S. Kaibab Trailhead are closed to private vehicles. Handicapped people can obtain a permit at the Visitor Center to drive their own vehicles in the shuttle-only areas.

The **Village Loop Shuttle** connects the Visitor Center, Yavapai Observation Station, campgrounds, lodges, shops, and offices of Grand Canyon Village; the service operates daily about every 15 minutes from early morning to late at night.

The **West Rim Drive Shuttle** leaves from the West Rim Interchange near Bright Angel Lodge and goes to Hermit's Rest with stops at eight overlooks; it operates daily every 15 minutes from about 7:30 a.m. to before sunset. The trip out and back takes 90 minutes if you don't get off.

The Yaki Point/S. Kaibab Loop connects these spots east of Grand Canyon Village with Bright Angel Lodge, Maswik Transportation Center, and Yavapai Lodge from one hour before sunrise to one hour after sunset about every 30 minutes. In the off-season, Fred Harvey Co. runs a shuttle to the South Kaibab trailhead for a charge.

Airport Tusayan Shuttle connects Bright Angel Lodge and other places in Grand Canyon

---

SHUTTLING OUT TO THE SOUTH RIM

The park will be using increased public transit to ease the vehicle congestion in the popular Grand Canyon Village area. Officials plan to have a light rail system in operation by the year 2002 with service as often as every five minutes at peak times. New parking areas in Tusayan, just outside the park, are planned to replace the inadequate spaces in Grand Canyon Village. Visitors will be able to park and quickly check out a menu of sightseeing options before hopping on a light rail shuttle to the Canyon View Information Plaza at Mather Point, with its new information center and bookstore. Also in the works here are outdoor exhibits introducing the geology, history, and culture of the Canyon and kiosks illustrating things to see and do, practicalities, and weather. Another branch of the light rail will transport visitors to Mather Transportation Center in Grand Canyon Village, where shuttles will convey people to other points in the Village and out along the West Rim/Hermit Drive. Lodge and campground guests can still drive into Grand Canyon Village on a new road. Once in the park, everyone will walk, cycle, or use shuttles. Cyclists and walkers can use a new Greenway Trail from Tusayan to the park and along the Rim. The East Rim/Desert View Drive will continue to be open to motorists for at least the near future, though private vehicles may not be able to go all the way out to some overlooks.

The **Heritage Education Campus** in central Grand Canyon Village will have exhibits on natural and cultural aspects of the park, current issues, and Native American cultures.

Village with Tusayan and the airport all year for a small charge; check the schedule with lodge transportation desks or call (520) 638-0821.

Trans-Canyon Shuttle offers daily roundtrip van service to the North Rim from May to October; contact any lodge transportation desk or call (520) 638-2820.

Auto Rentals and Taxi
No rentals were operating at press time, but you could ask at the Tusayan airport. For a taxi, call

Fred Harvey Transportation Dispatch at (520) 638-2822.

Bus
Nava-Hopi buses connect Bright Angel Lodge with Flagstaff ($12.50 each way) and Williams ($9 each way). See lodge transportation desks for schedules, but no reservations are needed; tel. (520) 774-5003 (Flagstaff) or (800) 892-8687.

Train
Passenger trains rolled into the railroad station at the Grand Canyon from 1901 to 1968. Twenty-one years later, steam locomotives of the **Grand Canyon Railway** began a new service pulling vintage railway cars from downtown Williams to the historic 1909 log depot in Grand Canyon Village.

Trains run daily except December 24th and 25th out of Williams; see the Williams section for the many options and entertainment provided;

tel. (800) THE-TRAIN; Internet: www.thetrain.com. Transportation Services desks in the lodges have a tour that combines a bus to Williams with the train back to the Grand Canyon.

Air
The airport just southwest of Tusayan has both north and south entrances from AZ 64. The main terminal offers scheduled flights, fixed-wing scenic tours, a Harveycar Excursions desk (ground tours), and a gift shop. A Subway restaurant one block east on the south entrance road is open daily for breakfast, lunch, and dinner.

Scenic Airlines flies large F-27 and some smaller aircraft from Las Vegas six to seven times daily in summer, and two or three times a day in winter. Fares run $134 one-way, $222 roundtrip; tour packages are offered out of Las Vegas; tel. (520) 638-2617 (Grand Canyon), (702) 740-8300 (Las Vegas) or (800) 446-4584; Internet: www.eagleair.com.

NORTH RIM SIGHTS

The North Rim offers an experience very different from that of the South Rim. Elevations 1,000 to 1,500 feet higher result in lower temperatures and nearly 60% more precipitation. Rain and snowmelt have cut deeply into the North Rim so that it is now about twice as far back from the Colorado River as the South Rim. Dramatic vistas from the north inspired early explorers to choose names like Point Sublime, Cape Royal, Angel's Window, and Point Imperial.

Even away from the viewpoints, the North Rim displays great beauty. Spruce, fir, pine, and aspen forests thrive in the cool air. Wildflowers bloom in blazes of color in the meadows and along the roadsides.

You'll find visitor facilities and major trailheads near Bright Angel Point, a 45-mile drive south on AZ 67 from Jacob Lake in the far north of Arizona. The road to Bright Angel Point opens in mid-May, then closes after the first big winter storm, anytime from early October to the end of November.

In winter, a deep blanket of snow covers the Kaibab Plateau's rolling meadow and forest country. The snow cover typically reaches a depth of

four to 10 feet, and during the winter of 1994-95 it was more than 19 feet deep. Cross-country skiers and snowshoers find the conditions ideal. The park itself has no facilities open on the North Rim in winter; you can camp here, however, with a permit from the Backcountry Office.

BRIGHT ANGEL POINT AND VICINITY

Bright Angel Point
Park at the end of the highway, near Grand Canyon Lodge, and follow the paved foot trail to the tip of Bright Angel Point, an easy half-mile roundtrip walk. Shells and other fossils can be spotted in the outcrop of Kaibab limestone on your right, just after a stone bridge. Roaring Springs Canyon on the left and Transept Canyon on the right join the long Bright Angel Canyon below. John Wesley Powell's expedition camped at the mouth of this canyon and gave the name Bright Angel Creek to its crystal-clear waters. Listen for Roaring Springs far below on the left and you'll see where the springs shoot out of the cliff. A pumping station at the base supplies

drinking water to both North and South rims. Roaring Springs makes a good day-hike or mule-back-ride destination via the North Kaibab Trail. (See the "Maintained Trails of the Inner Canyon" section later in the book.) The volcanic summits on the horizon to the south are, from left to right, O'Leary, San Francisco Peaks, Kendrick, and Sitgreaves. Red Butte, on the right and closer, preserves a remnant of Moencopi Formation under a lava cap.

Transept Canyon

You can enter the mouth of this canyon, which usually has only a small flow, from the North Kaibab Trail; it's best done as an overnight trip, when you can stay at nearby Cottonwood Campground. Up on top, **Transept Trail** (1.5 miles one-way) winds along the canyon rim between Grand Canyon Lodge and the campground.

Cape Royal Scenic Drive

This paved road leads to some of the North Rim's most spectacular viewpoints. **Point Im-**

Mt. Hayden, from Point Imperial

perial (elev. 8,803 feet) offers picnic tables and the highest vantage point from either rim. Views encompass impressive geology in the park's eastern section. You can see Nankoweap Creek below, Vermilion Cliffs on the horizon to the north, rounded Navajo Mountain on the horizon in Utah to the northeast, the Painted Desert far to the east, and the Little Colorado River Canyon to the southeast. Hikers can descend to Nankoweap Creek and the Colorado River on the difficult Nankoweap Trail; the trailhead lies northeast of here near Saddle Mountain. (See the "Unmaintained Trails of the Inner Canyon" section later in the book.) You can hike to Saddle Mountain Trailhead on a four-mile trail through the forest from Point Imperial; it begins on the far side of the road loop from the overlook. You can also drive there. Point Imperial is 11 miles from Grand Canyon Lodge; head north three miles from the lodge, turn right 5.3 miles on Cape Royal Road (there's a picnic area 3.8 miles in), then left 2.7 miles to the parking area.

Cape Royal Road continues beyond the Point Imperial turnoff past **Vista Encantadora** (with picnic tables), **Roosevelt Point, Walhalla Overlook,** and other viewpoints to a parking area and a few picnic tables at the end of the road, just before Cape Royal. Total driving distance from Grand Canyon Lodge is 23 miles one-way. A trail, paved and level, continues south 0.6 mile from the parking lot to Cape Royal. Signs along the way identify plants growing on this high, arid ridge. On the way you'll see **Angel's Window,** a massive natural arch, which you can walk out on via a short side trail. **Cape Royal** (elev. 7,865 feet) features a fantastic panorama; it's the southernmost viewpoint of the North Rim in this part of the Grand Canyon. Signs point out Freya Castle to the southeast, Vishnu Temple and the distant San Francisco Peaks to the south, and a branch of Clear Creek Canyon and flat-topped Wotans Throne to the southwest.

Cliff Spring Trail

Hikers enjoy pretty scenery on this trail, which descends into a forested ravine, passes a small Indian ruin, and travels under an overhang to the spring in half a mile. The canyon walls open up impressively as you near the spring. It's possible to continue on a rougher trail another half mile for more canyon views. Cliff Spring Trail begins from

Angel's Window Overlook, a small pullout on a curve of Cape Royal Road, 1.1 miles past Walhalla Overlook and 0.6 mile before road's end.

Cape Final

An easy two-mile (each way) hike leads east from the Cape Royal Road to a unique perspective at the east edge of the Kaibab Plateau above Unkar Creek Canyon. The trailhead at a small unpaved parking area on the north side of the road can be difficult to spot; it's 5.5 miles past Roosevelt Point, one mile before Walhalla Overlook, and 2.5 miles before road's end at Cape Royal. Other scenic vistas on the North Rim can be reached on back-road hikes on the Walhalla Plateau; consult a ranger for suggestions.

Walhalla Ruins

Ancestral pueblo people, known by archaeologists as Kayenta Anasazi, farmed more than 300 sites on the plateau, most of them near the rim where warm air currents extended the growing season. The Indians probably occupied the pueblo at Walhalla (elev. 8,000 feet) in summer and wintered at Unkar Delta (visible from Walhalla Overlook); they departed from the Grand Canyon about 1150. A 100-yard walk across the road from Walhalla Overlook leads to this site.

Widforss Trail

Gently rolling terrain, fine Canyon views, and a variety of forest types attract hikers to the Widforss Trail. From the edge of a meadow, the trail climbs a bit, skirts the head of Transept Canyon, then leads through ponderosa pines to an overlook near Widforss Point. The trail and point were named to honor Swedish artist Gunnar Widforss, who painted the national parks of the West between 1921 and 1934.

Haunted Canyon lies below at trail's end, flanked by The Colonnade on the right and Manu Temple, Buddha Temple, and Schellbach Butte on the left; beyond lie countless more temples, towers, canyons, and the cliffs of the South Rim.

Widforss Trail is 10 miles roundtrip and takes about five hours to hike. Many people enjoy going just partway. You'll often see mule deer along the trail. From Grand Canyon Lodge, go 2.7 miles north on the highway, then turn left and go one mile on a dirt road; the turnoff is 0.3 mile south of the Cape Royal Road junction.

Ken Patrick Trail

This 10-mile trail offers forest scenery and views across the headwaters of Nankoweap Creek. From Point Imperial, the Ken Patrick winds about three miles along the rim to Cape Royal Road, then continues seven miles through forest to the North Kaibab trailhead, with an elevation drop of 560 feet. Allow six hours for the entire hike, one-way.

Trailheads lie at the following places: near the south end of the Point Imperial parking area; on Cape Royal Road one mile east of the Point Imperial junction; and at the upper end of the North Kaibab trailhead parking area, two miles north of Grand Canyon Lodge.

Ken Patrick worked as a ranger on the North Rim for several seasons in the early 1970s. He was shot and killed by escaped convicts while on duty at California's Point Reyes National Seashore in 1973.

Uncle Jim Trail

The first mile follows the Ken Patrick Trail—from the North Kaibab trailhead—then turns southeast to make a loop around Uncle Jim Point. Allow three hours for the five-mile roundtrip. Views from the point include Roaring Springs Canyon and North Kaibab Trail. James "Uncle Jim" Owens served as the Grand Canyon Game Reserve's first warden from 1906 until establishment of the national park.

THE WESTERN KAIBAB PLATEAU

Kanab Creek Wilderness

Kanab Creek has the largest canyon system in the Grand Canyon's North Rim, with headwaters 100 miles north on the Paunsaugunt Plateau in Utah. The wilderness area protects 77,100 acres along the Kanab and its tributaries. Springs in Kanab Canyon nourish large cottonwood trees and lush growths of desert willow, tamarisk, maidenhair fern, and grass. From Hack Canyon, a popular entry point on the west, hikers can descend 21 miles down Kanab Creek to the Colorado River; allow three days for the one-way trip. Hack Canyon and a bit of the wilderness lie on BLM land; the office in Kanab, Utah, has information on trailhead access and hiking. You'll need a Grand Canyon backcountry permit to camp below the junction with Jumpup Canyon. Other trailheads lie on the Kaibab National Forest; contact the Fredonia or Kaibab Plateau Visitor Center offices for road and trail information. The easy to moderate, 17-mile **Ranger Trail** wraps around the base of Jumpup Point in the heart of the wilderness. You can reach it on the west side via the easy, 21.5-mile **Snake Gulch-Kanab Creek Trail #59,** as well as from Kanab or Hack Canyons. On the east side, Jumpup Cabin Trailhead and the difficult, six-mile **Jumpup-Nail Trail #8** provide access.

Jumpup Point
An amazing canyon panorama greets the rare visitor who ventures out along the rough road on this long point in the western Kaibab Plateau. Five miles before the end of the point, the vast Jumpup Canyon first appears on the left, along with its tributaries Sowats Canyon and Indian Hollow. Much of this canyon country belongs to the Kanab Creek Wilderness, which almost completely surrounds Jumpup Point. Although there's no trail access to the canyons from here, Ranger Trail can be seen far below, where it's joined by Jumpup-Nail Trail, which descends from Sowats Point across to the east. You might even spot a bighorn sheep on one of their precarious ledges. At road's end, a short walk reveals more views. Lower Kanab and the Grand Canyon seem almost lost in the vastness. Kanab Canyon and the broad Hack Canyon lie to the west. Mt. Trumbull stands as the highest of the volcanoes across Kanab Canyon. The summit of Mt. Logan, identified by its cliff profile, is just to the left and farther back. Vermilion Cliffs and other high points of Utah lie to the northwest and north.

High-desert pinyon pine, juniper, sage, and cactus sparsely cover the point at an elevation of 5,650 feet. The Kaibab National Forest map (North Kaibab District) shows the ways in. From Jacob Lake, go south 0.3 mile on AZ 67, turn west on Forest Road 461, and take Forest Roads 462, 22, 423, 235, 423, then 201 to its end. Forest Road 22 provides access from either the east edge of Fredonia (US 89A between Mileposts 607 and 608) or DeMotte Park (0.8 mile south of the North Rim Store on AZ 67), then you'll follow Forest Roads 423, 235, 423, and 201. A high-clearance vehicle will be needed for the rocky sections of the last 10 miles of road. Mountain bikers enjoy this ride too.

Sowats Point
This viewpoint of Jumpup Canyon lies east across from Jumpup Point at an elevation of 6,200 feet. **Jumpup-Nail Trail #8** descends into the depths here, six miles and a drop—steep in places—of 2,000 feet to Ranger Trail #41 in Kanab Creek Wilderness. You can start on the same roads as to Jumpup Point, but take Forest Roads 425 and 233 off Forest Road 22. High-clearance vehicles will be needed for the last several miles.

Cream-colored blossoms of the cliffrose (Cowania stansburiana), an evergreen member of the rose family, festoon canyon rims in early summer and then transform into long, white plumed seeds.

Indian Hollow and
Thunder River Trailhead

A tiny campground with an outhouse and tables is 0.4 mile before the end of Forest Road 232 at an elevation of 6,300 feet. Ponderosa pine start to thin out closer to the rim, where pinyon pine, juniper, and Gambel oak predominate. At the rim, a short walk from road's end, you'll have a view of the Deer Creek drainage of the Grand Canyon. Great Thumb Mesa lies directly across to the south. The full length of the Powell Plateau presents itself to the southeast. Downcanyon, Mt. Sinyala stands near the mouth of Havasu Canyon.

Thunder River Trail drops steeply from the rim for the first few hundred yards, then contours west half a mile to a break in the cliffs, a good day-hike destination. (See the "Inner Canyon Hiking" section for a description of the hike to Thunder River and Deer Creek Falls.) Forest Road 22 provides access either from the east edge of Fredonia (US 89A between Mileposts 607 and 608) or from DeMotte Park (0.8 mile south of the North Rim Store on AZ 67), then you'll follow Forest Roads 425 and 232 to the end of 232. Cautiously driven cars might be able to make it; check with Kaibab National Forest staff.

Crazy Jug Point

This point features great views and good access roads at an elevation of 7,500 feet. Pinyon pine, cliffrose, and some ponderosa grow here. A walk of a few hundred feet from the parking area leads to the overlook. The Colorado River comes out from behind the Powell Plateau, wraps around Great Thumb Mesa, then winds far downstream. Dark, forested volcanoes of Mt. Trumbull and the rest of the Uinkaret Mountains rise to the west. Directly below are Crazy Jug Canyon, Tapeats Amphitheater, and other tributaries of Tapeats Creek. The lineup of Fence, Locust, North Timp, Timp, and Fire Points marks the Kaibab Plateau to the southeast; all of these points can be reached by road for a variety of perspectives of this part of the Grand Canyon. Directions are the same as for Indian Hollow except that you continue south on Forest Road 425 and 292B, following signs. Cars can do this trip in dry weather.

Monument Point and Bill Hall Trailhead

Bill Hall Trail climbs west up along the rim nearly a mile before plunging steeply to the Thunder River Trail. The ridge just above the trail has a sweeping panorama up Tapeats Canyon and down the Grand Canyon. Near the trailhead area (elev. 7,050 feet), you'll see effects of the Bridger Burn of 1996. This fire affected 54,000 acres—a large portion of the western Kaibab Plateau—but pinyon pine, juniper, and lots of cliffrose and wildflowers grow here. Follow directions for Crazy Jug Point until the junction half a mile before the point, then keep straight 1.7 miles on Forest Road 292A; it's okay for cars in dry weather.

Timp, North Timp, and
Parissawampitts Point

Walk about one-third mile out on Timp Point from the parking area for the best panoramas and to see Thunder River emerge from the north wall of Tapeats Canyon and drop in two large cascades amidst lush cottonwoods. You can also spot the trail that climbs from Thunder River to the top of cliffs and over into Surprise Valley. Binoculars give the best view. Nearby North Timp and Parissawampitts Points also provide good perspectives.

Rainbow Rim Trail #10 follows the convoluted rim between Timp and Parissawampitts for 18 miles one-way. Mountain bikers can make many pleasant loops on this trail and on forest roads in the area. Forest Road 250 connects roads to these points, though you'll need a high-clearance vehicle or mountain bike. Cars can easily reach Timp Point (elev. 7,600 feet) in good weather by turning off AZ 67 at DeMotte Park (0.8 mile south of the North Rim Store on AZ 67), then following Forest Roads 22, 270, 222, 206, and 271. Forest Road 271A branches to North Timp Point from 271. Parissawampitts Point may also be okay for cars; take Forest Roads 22, 270, 222, 206, then 214 to its end.

Fire Point

The panorama here takes in Tapeats Amphitheater, Steamboat Mountain, and Powell Plateau (you can spot the trail to its top); Great Thumb Mesa lies across the river. You can walk 100 feet out on the rocks for an even better look. A fine stand of ponderosa pine grows on the point. Careful drivers can negotiate the roads with cars in good weather.

Turn west two miles on Forest Road 22 from AZ 67 in De Motte Park (0.8 mile south of the

North Rim Country Store), head south two miles on Forest Road 270, then turn west 13 miles on Forest Road 223 to the end of the road. The last mile is within Grand Canyon National Park and will probably be closed to vehicles.

Point Sublime

This well-named overlook and picnic area, southeast of Fire Point and west of Bright Angel Point, lies at the end of a rugged 17-mile dirt road negotiable by high-clearance vehicles, mountain bicycles, on horseback, or on foot. Point Sublime extends far into the Grand Canyon for awesome views. You can scan a great length of both North and South Rims and spot a section of Colorado River. The South Rim can be traced from below Bass Canyon upcanyon nearly to Desert View. With binoculars, parts of the Tonto, Hermit, and South Kaibab Trails can be seen along with Grand Canyon Village and Hermit's Rest. On the North Rim, the Powell Plateau lies to the northwest, Confucius and Mencius Temples to the southeast, and Tiyo Point and Cape Royal to the east, truly sublime. Closer in, cliffs drop into the Tuna Creek drainage. Point Sublime makes a great place to camp, but you'll need a backcountry permit to do so.

The route is bumpy and not always passable; check at the North Rim Backcountry Office or the North Rim Visitor Center. You can enter from the Kaibab National Forest by turning west two miles on Forest Road 22 from the AZ 67 turnoff in De Motte Park (0.8 mile south of the North Rim Country Store), head south two miles on Forest Road 270, turn west six miles on Forest Road 223, then south 1.5 miles on Forest Roads 268 and 268B to the park boundary, where the road becomes rougher and less well signed on the last 15 miles to Point Sublime. Keep left at the junction 0.2 mile inside the park (the right fork goes to Swamp Point), then keep right past the junctions for Kanabownits Lookout and the road to AZ 67. The North Kaibab National Forest map (North Kaibab District) is essential for navigating these back roads.

Tiyo Point has been closed to vehicles, but you can hike or go by horseback. Turn south 6.3 miles from Point Sublime Road at a large meadow, 4.2 miles in from AZ 67.

THE EASTERN KAIBAB PLATEAU

Saddle Mountain Wilderness

This 40,610-acre wilderness protects part of the densely forested Kaibab Plateau, along with sheer cliffs and narrow canyons. Mountain lions, bears, and mule deer roam the area. North Canyon Wash is noted for its pure strain of native Apache trout. Saddle Mountain (elev. 8,424 feet) stands northeast of the Bright Angel Point area on the Grand Canyon's North Rim; you can see Saddle Mountain from the Point Imperial viewpoint. Three trails cross the wilderness between the top of the Kaibab Plateau and House Rock Valley: Nankoweap, South Canyon, and North Canyon.

East Rim Viewpoint

Expansive vistas across the Marble Canyon area greet visitors at this overlook on the east edge of the Kaibab Plateau. The site (elev. 8,800 feet) lies on Kaibab National Forest land several miles north of Grand Canyon National Park. Cars and small RVs can easily travel the gravel roads in good weather. East Rim Viewpoint features great sunrises and sunsets; colors reflect off the distant Vermilion Cliffs and Painted Desert. The Forest Service offers some outhouses but no other facilities. Camping may be restricted at the viewpoint, but good places for primitive camping lie in the conifer and aspen forests nearby; no camping permit or fee is required. From AZ 67 in De Motte Park (0.8 mile south of the North Rim Country Store), turn east about four miles on Forest Road 611. Another fine panorama lies farther north at the end of Forest Road 611, 6.9 miles from AZ 67 (keep right at the fork 6.5 miles in; this last 0.4 mile is too rough for cars); walk a few hundred feet beyond road's end for the views. Still farther north in the area, **Dog Point** also features a fine view; head east 1.2 miles on Forest Road 611 from AZ 67, then turn left (north) 7.2 miles on Forest Road 610 to its end; keep right at the fork 6.4 miles in.

Hikers can wander some of the Kaibab Plateau/Arizona Trail #101 along the rim or descend into North Canyon in the Saddle Mountain Wilderness from East Rim Overlook. East Rim Trail #7 descends from a trailhead 300 feet north of the overlook, and North Canyon Trail #4 descends from the rim two miles south. Together, these three trails make a loop of about six miles into the valley below. North Canyon Trail #4 continues down North Canyon to House Rock Valley, a total of seven miles one-way.

Marble Viewpoint

This overlook, southeast of East Rim Viewpoint, provides another perspective. From AZ 67 in De Motte Park (0.8 mile south of the North Rim Country Store), turn east 1.3 miles on Forest Road 611, right 6.7 miles on 610, then left 4.6 miles on 219 to its end.

Saddle Mountain Trailhead

The drive out Forest Road 610 is worthwhile for the spectacular views of Marble Canyon, Nankoweap, and House Rock Valley areas. From the trailhead (elev. 8,800 feet), Nankoweap Trail #57 drops down several hundred feet to the best viewpoints; this trail continues to the Nankoweap Trailhead (three miles) and on to Road 8910/445G (five-six miles) in House Rock Valley. From the AZ 67 turnoff in De Motte Park, 0.8 mile south of the North Rim Country Store, head east 1.3 miles on 611, then turn right 12 miles on 610 to the trailhead. Cautiously driven cars should be able to do this in dry weather. A trail to Point Imperial begins on the right 0.2 mile before Saddle Mountain Trailhead; it follows a former fire road about four miles through the forest. The national park border is just south of 611, so do not camp here without a backcountry permit. The Kaibab National Forest has many spots suitable for dispersed camping.

Although not shown on the Kaibab Forest map, the road continues 1.4 miles past Saddle Mountain Trailhead to another great viewpoint of Marble Canyon, House Rock Valley, and far beyond. Use a high-clearance vehicle or hike in.

House Rock Valley

Rolling hills of grasslands and pinyon-juniper woodlands of this valley separate cliffs of the Kaibab Plateau above and Marble Canyon below. Viewpoints provide intimate and detailed views of Marble Canyon. The turnoff for House Rock Buffalo Ranch Road (Road 8910/445) from AZ 89A is between Mileposts 559 and 560, 20 miles east of Jacob Lake and 21.5 miles west of Marble Canyon Lodge. About 90 **buffalo** roam freely across 67,000 acres of the valley; you're most likely to see them in summer, least likely during hunting season in autumn.

For **Buck Farm Overlook,** head south 23.5 miles from US 89A to a fork; take the left fork east two miles, then turn left three miles on Forest Road 445H to its end.

Triple Alcoves Overlook features a different panorama; go 2.5 miles south on Forest Road 445 from the 445-445H junction, then hike east a half mile on an old jeep road to the overlook. Signs mark the trailhead. House Rock Buffalo Ranch Road provides nearly year-round access to these and other viewpoints as well as to Saddle Mountain Wilderness.

the view east from Forest Road 610 at Saddle Mountain Trailhead

The very scenic Forest Roads 213 and 220 connect the Kaibab Plateau with House Rock Valley. You'll need a high-clearance vehicle for the steep and winding sections. Turnoff from AZ 67 is between Mileposts 601 and 602, about three miles north of the North Rim Country Store. Forest Road 213 crosses the Arizona Trail 2.6 miles in, then begins the descent on short switchbacks seven miles in from AZ 67. The road skirts the north edge of Saddle Mountain Wilderness before ending after 8.6 miles at the East Side Game Road (Forest Road 220). Turn right 8.2 miles to continue down to House Rock Valley, following Tater Canyon part of the way to a T-junction with Road 8910/445, 17 miles south of US 89A. Turn left for US 89A or turn right for Buffalo Ranch, Saddle Mountain trailheads, and Marble Canyon overlooks.

TOROWEAP

This little-visited area of the North Rim lies between Kanab Canyon to the east and the Pine Mountains (Uinkaret Mountains) to the west. An overlook (elev. 4,552 feet) provides awesome Canyon views from sheer cliffs that drop nearly 3,000 feet to the river below. Toroweap, also known as Tuweap or Tuweep, lies 140 road miles west of the developed North Rim area of Bright Angel Point. The views, many hiking possibilities, and solitude reward visitors who make it here. No park entry or campground fee was charged here at presstime, though user fees may be forthcoming. Obtain hiking information, backcountry permits, and emergency help at the Tuweep Ranger Station, open all year (though the ranger does take a few days off now and then). If you'll be needing a backcountry permit, it's safer to obtain it beforehand, though you could try for a last-minute permit here or at Pipe Spring National Monument. (See "Practicalities" section below.)

Pinyon pine, juniper, cactus, and small flowering plants cover the plateau. Watch for rattlesnakes. Hikers can enjoy many easy rambles near the rim, a descent to the river near Lava Falls, a scramble up Vulcan's Throne, or multi-day trips on the Tuckup Trail.

Sinyala Butte
Sinyala Butte, 25 miles east of the overlook, marks the mouth of Havasu Canyon. Most of

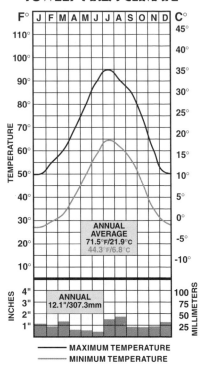

TUWEEP AREA CLIMATE

ANNUAL
AVERAGE
71.5°F/21.9°C
44.3°F/6.8°C

ANNUAL
12.1"/307.3mm

—— MAXIMUM TEMPERATURE
—— MINIMUM TEMPERATURE

the Havasupai Indians who live on the reservation dwell in Supai village, nine miles up Havasu Canyon. The **Hualapai Indian Reservation** lies directly across the Colorado River from the overlook. Lava Pinnacle, also known as Vulcan's Forge or Thor's Hammer, rises in the middle of the river directly below. This 50-foot-high lava neck is all that remains of an extinct volcano.

Lava Falls
Lava Falls, visible 1.5 miles downstream, roars with a vengeance. You can see it from a point just one-eighth mile to the right from the overlook at road's end. Debris from Prospect Canyon on the South Rim forms the rapids, perhaps the roughest water in the Grand Canyon. Water flowing between 12,000 and 20,000 cubic feet per second drops abruptly, then explodes into foam and spray. River-runners commonly rate these rapids a 10-plus on a scale of 1-10. Lava

Falls Route is a steep hike that leads down to the rapids from a nearby trailhead.

Saddle Horse Canyon Trail
The trailhead for this easy hike lies beside the main road 5.7 miles south of the ranger station. The path heads east to a Colorado River overlook, then north with views of wonderfully weathered rock near Saddle Horse Canyon; it's about 1.6 miles roundtrip.

Esplanade Loop Trail
Both hikers and mountain bikers may do this 2.9-mile trail. It begins from the nine-site campground, 5.4 miles south of the ranger station.

Vulcan's Throne
Vulcan's Throne, the 600-foot-high rounded cinder cone west of the overlook, is one of the youngest volcanoes in the area. The hike to the top (no trail) is about 1.5 miles roundtrip with a 500-foot elevation gain; it's most easily reached by road via normally dry Toroweap Lake. Between 30,000 and 1.2 million years ago, eruptions of red-hot lava built about 60 volcanic cones here, even forming dams across the Colorado River. One of the dams towered nearly 2,000 feet, but the river washed it away long ago.

More adventurous hikes in the area include Lava Falls Route or Tuckup Trail (see "Inner Canyon Hiking" below).

NORTH RIM PRACTICALITIES

The road from Jacob Lake to the Rim is usually open earlier in the spring and later in the fall than Grand Canyon Lodge, restaurants, gas station, and campground. A sign at Jacob Lake near the turnoff for the North Rim lists the services available.

BRIGHT ANGEL POINT

Accommodations and Campgrounds
Grand Canyon Lodge, overlooking Transept Canyon near Bright Angel Point, offers the only accommodations within the park on the North Rim. Lodging comes in four types: Frontier Cabins, $62 d; Western Cabins, $85 d; Pioneer Cabins, $79 for one-four people; and modern motel rooms, $71 d. Four cabins are available that are so close to the edge you can see the canyon from the porch, $95 d. Each additional person costs $5 in both cabins and rooms. The season runs mid-May to mid-October, when reservations and a deposit are recommended. Call (303) 297-2757 for advance reservations or (520) 638-2631 for same-day reservations, or fax (303) 297-3175; the lodges can also be reached at 14001 E. Iliff Ave., Suite 600, Aurora, CO 80014; Internet: www.amfac.com. Moderate.

North Rim Campground, 1.5 miles north and west of Grand Canyon Lodge, provides drinking water but no hookups. It's open mid-May to mid-October at $10 per night, $5 with Golden Age pass; reservations are required. Four rim sites have views—and winds—at a cost of $20. Backpackers and bicyclists can camp at a walk-in area for $4 per person; a "FULL" sign at the campground means that all drive-in spaces are taken but spaces will be available for walk-ins. Coin-operated showers, a laundromat, store, and ice are available next to the campground. Reservations for family and group sites can be made one day to three months in advance at tel. (800) 365-2267 (365-CAMP); Internet: reservations.nps.gov.

Food and Services
Grand Canyon Lodge serves moderately priced breakfasts, lunches, and dinners in a huge rustic dining room with Canyon views; open daily mid-May to late October. Reservations are suggested for breakfast and required for dinner; tel. (520) 638-2611. A cafeteria style **snack bar,** also part of the lodge, offers faster service and lower prices but no atmosphere; it's open in season (May-Oct.) for breakfast, lunch, and dinner. The **Saloon** in the lodge serves gourmet coffees as well as more potent beverages.

You'll find a **post office** and **gift shop** in Grand Canyon Lodge. A **service station** is near the campground, along with a small **general store/snack bar** offering camping supplies, groceries, and cooked food. In **emergencies,** see a ranger or call 911. For recorded **weather forecasts,** dial (520) 638-7888.

Information

The new **North Rim Visitor Center** next to the lodge has an information desk, book sales, and a few exhibits; it's open daily 8 a.m.-8 p.m. Signs list times of nature walks, talks, and children's programs.

Obtain overnight camping permits and trail information from the **Backcountry Office** (Box 129, Grand Canyon, AZ 86023) on the South Rim or at the ranger station on the North Rim. The North Rim Backcountry Office is open daily 8 a.m.-noon and 1-5 p.m. from May 15 to October 15, weather permitting. The turnoff from the highway is a quarter mile north of the campground turnoff, then go around to the window on the side of the building. The park's automated telephone switchboard has recorded information and will connect you to any office; tel. (520) 638-7888.

Mule Rides, Tours, and Transportation

Mule rides take you along the rim and into the Canyon. One-hour rim rides cost $15 (minimum age five), half-day trips down the North Kaibab Trail to the tunnel are $40 (minimum age eight), and full-day rides to Roaring Springs are $95 including lunch (minimum age 12). Requirements for riders are similar to those for South Rim trips, including good health, weight under 200 pounds (91 kilograms), fluency in English, height over four feet seven inches (138 cm), and ability to mount and dismount without assistance. Reservations with the mule rides desk in the Grand Canyon Lodge lobby are a good idea; call (520) 638-9875 at the lodge, or (801) 679-8665 before June 1.

Trans-Canyon Shuttle offers daily roundtrip van service between the South and North Rims from May to October; tel. (520) 638-2820.

NORTH OF THE PARK

Accommodations, Campgrounds, and Services

Moderately priced **Kaibab Lodge** lies 18.5 miles north of Bright Angel Point and 26 miles south of Jacob Lake at the edge of a large meadow just west of AZ 67. Guests stay in cabins ($68 d to $95 for a cabin that sleeps four-five people) and dine at the restaurant (breakfast and dinner daily) during the mid-May to September season; tel. (520) 526-0924 or (800) 525-0924; Internet: www.canyoneers.com. Across the highway, **North Rim Country Store** sells groceries, camping and auto supplies, and gas and diesel; open mid-May to mid-November.

De Motte Park Campground, just south of Kaibab Lodge, is open early June to late September with drinking water and interpretive programs but no showers or hookups; $10 per night. Try to arrive before noon for the best chance of getting a space—no reservations are taken.

Jacob Lake Inn, 45 miles north of the North Rim at the junction of AZ 67 and US 89A, stays open all year with basic motel rooms ($82-85 d to $91-97 four persons), cabins (April to November only, $66-84), restaurant (American food daily for breakfast, lunch, and dinner), grocery store, Indian crafts shop, and service station; tel. (520) 643-7232; Internet: www.jacoblake.com. Moderate.

Jacob Lake Campground has sites in the ponderosa pines with drinking water but no hookups or showers from mid-May to late October; $10 per night. It's often filled by late afternoon; campers can enjoy summer interpretive programs and nearby hiking trails; tel. (520) 643-7770. Head west 0.1 mile on US 89 A from AZ 67, then turn right at the sign. Only groups can reserve sites with Recreation Resource Management at tel. (520) 204-5528.

Jacob Lake RV Park overlooks the little lake just 0.3 mile south on AZ 67 from US 89A, then west 0.7 mile; it's open May 15 to October 15 with a modem hookup but no showers. Tent spaces cost $10, dry RV sites run $12, and sites with hookups are $22; tel. (520) 643-7804. Tent sites are usually available, though RVers should make reservations or arrive by noon.

Allen's Outfitters offers trail rides of one and two hours in the forest, half- and full-day trips to overlooks, and pack trips from about mid-May to early September at their stables 0.3 mile south on AZ 67 and year-round in Kanab; tel. (435) 644-8150 or (435) 689-1979.

Information

Foresters in the **Kaibab Visitor Center** in Jacob Lake provide information on the many viewpoints, trails, campgrounds, and historic sites in the Kaibab National Forest along the North Rim;

they also sell books and maps. Exhibits include a 3-D model of the Grand Canyon and wildlife displays. It's open daily 8 a.m.-5 p.m., though it may close in winter; tel. (520) 643-7298.

TOROWEAP

Campgrounds
A small campground in a scenic setting is 5.4 miles past the ranger station and 0.9 mile before the overlook at the end of the road. The overlook itself is now a day-use area. There's no water, no camping charge, no reservations accepted, and no permit needed for the established sites; an eight-person, two-vehicle limit per site applies. If all campsites are full, you must obtain the expensive backcountry permit for other areas in the park or simply drive north and find an undeveloped spot on BLM land. Bring lots of water, extra food, and camping gear.

Getting There
Three roads lead in to the area. The most popular one begins from AZ 389, nine miles west of Fre-

donia; turn south 40 miles on Road 109 at the sign for Toroweap and Mt. Trumbull, continue straight seven miles on Road 5, and straight on Road 115. These dirt roads are usually in good condition when dry but have washboard sections. Watch for livestock and take it slow through washes and cattleguards. The last few miles are a bit rocky, but careful drivers should make it through fine. The Tuweep Ranger Station is on the left 6.3 miles before the overlook. Beyond the ranger station, Toroweap Point (summit elev. 6,393 feet) towers on the left; dumpy Vulcan's Throne (summit elev. 5,102 feet) sits on the right.

You can also drive to Toroweap on a 85-mile dirt road from St. George (Roads 1069 and 5 for 78 miles, then right seven miles on Road 115) or a 54.5-mile road from Colorado City (Road 5 for 47 miles, then right 7.5 miles on Road 115). Avoid driving these roads after heavy rain or snow, especially the route from Colorado City. Snows usually block the road from St. George between October and May. Water, food, and gas are not available in this country. Bring a map—the BLM's Arizona Strip one is best, as signs may be missing at some junctions.

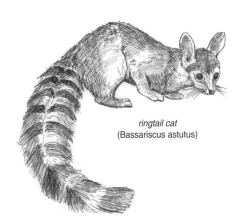

ringtail cat
(Bassariscus astutus)

LOUISE FOOTE

INNER CANYON HIKING

The wonders of the Canyon reveal themselves best to those who enter its depths. Just remember that the Inner Canyon is a wilderness area, subject to temperature extremes, flash floods, rockslides, and other natural hazards. You can have a wonderful trip in the Canyon by taking enough food, water, and other supplies.

Always carry—and drink—water. All too often people will walk merrily down a trail without a canteen, and then suffer terribly on the climb out. Only the Bright Angel and North Kaibab trails have sources of treated water. In summer, carry one quart or liter of water for each hour of hiking; half a quart per hour should be enough in the cooler months. Electrolyte-replacement drinks may be helpful too.

Canyon trails offer little shade—you'll probably want a hat, sunglasses, and sunscreen. Footgear should have good traction for the steep trails; lightweight boots work well. During winter and early spring, instep crampons—metal plates with small spikes—greatly improve footing on icy trails at the higher elevations. Rain gear will keep you dry during rainstorms; ponchos, on the other hand, provide poor protection against wind-driven rain. Be careful when rock-scrambling—soft and fractured rocks predominate in the Canyon. Don't swim in the Colorado River—its cold waters and swift currents are simply too dangerous.

Information and Permits

Rangers are the best source of up-to-the-minute information about trails and permit procedures. On the South Rim, the **Backcountry Office** at Maswik Transportation Center is open daily 8 a.m.-noon and 1-5 p.m. all year. The **Backcountry Information Line** is answered Mon.-Fri. 1-5 p.m.; tel. (520) 638-7875. The Backcountry Office at the North Rim Ranger Station is open daily 8 a.m-noon and 1-5 p.m. from May 15 to October 15, weather permitting. Bookstores sell hiking guides and topo maps at the Visitor Center and other shops in the park. Also see the Booklist at the back of this book for suggested titles.

You'll need a permit for all overnight camping trips in the backcountry, but not for day-hikes or stays at Phantom Ranch. Permits can be requested in person or by mail through the Backcountry Office, Grand Canyon National Park, P.O. Box 129, Grand Canyon, AZ 86023 or by fax at (520) 638-2125. Ask for the *Backcountry Trip Planner,* which includes regulations, a map, and a permit request form, or obtain the information over the Internet at www.kaibab.org or www.thecanyon.com/nps/. Permits will be sent through the mail.

Each permit costs a nonrefundable $20 plus $4 per person per night. If you plan on doing a lot of trips, the 12-month Frequent Hiker member-

Hikers Yvonne Arntzen and Greg Jones, two of the first people to hike all of the Arizona Trail from Mexico to Utah, Grandview Lookout, July 1998

ARIZONA TRAIL: THE GRAND CANYON SECTION

The Grand Canyon section of the Arizona Trail presents one of the biggest challenges for trail users. Besides the deep descent into the chasm and the even longer climb out the other side, hikers must plan ahead to obtain the required backcountry permit or make a reservation to stay at Phantom Ranch. The rim-to-rim distance is just too great to hike and enjoy in one day. If you don't get a permit or reservation ahead of time, you can show up at the Backcountry Office for a camping permit or at the Bright Angel Lodge Transportation Desk for a Phantom Ranch bed and hope that a space is available. This may delay transcanyon hikers for several days.

Bicyclists face a long detour. Not even the most experienced mountain biker will be permitted to ride down any of the trails into the Canyon because of dangers to the cyclist and other trail users. The Park Service won't allow cyclists to carry their bikes across the Canyon on pack frames because a wide load could knock hikers off the trail. So cyclists will have to follow the same route as cars—adding more than 200 miles to the route. Cyclists who dislike riding next to motor traffic can ride sections of old Hwy. 64 through the Kaibab National Forest; a few sections are even paved—although one quarter-mile section has been converted into a cistern collection spillway and is fenced off. Cyclists planning to camp in the Navajo Nation should obtain permission from the local landowner first.

The Arizona Trail arrives at Grandview Lookout Tower from the south. This area has some good day-hiking, too (see "Kaibab National Forest"). The Arizona Trail turns west to Half Way Trick Tank,

then will continue into the park (this section is not scheduled to be completed until 2002—you can call the Grand Canyon Backcountry Info Line at 520-638-7875 for updates) and descend the 9.3-mile Bright Angel Trail. One could also hike the short distance of road from Grandview Lookout to Grandview Trailhead, then take the Grandview, Tonto, and either South Kaibab or Bright Angel Trails down to the Colorado River. From the Colorado, North Kaibab Trail climbs 14 miles to the top of the North Rim. From here one could continue north 9.9 miles on the Ken Patrick Trail to Point Imperial. A former road turns north four miles from the Point Imperial Road, opposite the viewpoint, and parallels the rim to the Kaibab National Forest and the Saddle Mountain Trailhead near the end of FR 610.

From the Saddle Mountain Trailhead, one could hike west 7.5 miles along the park boundary on FR 610 to the trailhead for Kaibab Plateau/Arizona Trail 101, which goes north seven miles to East Rim View and on to AZ 89A. If driving to the south end of Trail 101, take the AZ 67 turnoff in De Motte Park, 0.8 mile south of the North Rim Country Store, and head east 1.3 miles on 611, then turn right 4.8 miles on 610 to the trailhead, marked by log fences and an outhouse. The North Kaibab Ranger District office has handouts and advice for this part of the Arizona Trail at 430 S. Main St. in Fredonia, open Mon.-Fri. 7 a.m.-5 p.m., or write Box 248, Fredonia, AZ 86022; tel. (520) 643-7395. You can also stop by the Kaibab Visitor Center at Jacob Lake, open daily 8 a.m.-5 p.m., though it may close in winter; tel. (520) 643-7298.

ship of $50 will let you purchase permits for just the $4 per person per night fee. The park service limits the number of campers in each section of the Canyon to provide visitors with a quality wilderness experience and to protect the land from overuse. Try to submit your choices early, especially for holidays and the popular months of March to May. Requests are not accepted more than four months in advance, starting with the first day of the month of that four-month period. Small groups (fewer than six people) have a greater chance of getting a permit, because the backcountry has only a few spots for larger ones; 11 is the maximum group size.

Permits can sometimes be obtained from rangers on duty at Tuweep, Meadview, and

Lees Ferry Ranger Stations. However, rangers are often hard to find because patrol duties have priority. Do not depend on obtaining a permit on a walk-in basis. Another option in the Arizona Strip area is Pipe Spring National Monument, which can issue last-minute permits if space is available.

If you arrive without a permit, show up at the Backcountry Office by 8 a.m. to find out what's available, or get on a waiting list. If you're flexible and have extra days, there's a good chance of getting into the Canyon.

Other Areas

Not all of the Grand Canyon lies within the park. The Havasupai Indian Reservation contains Havasu Canyon, famous for its waterfalls, travertine pools, and blue-green waters. The Hualapai Indians have the only road access to the bottom of the Grand Canyon via Diamond Creek and some spectacular rim viewpoints. The Arizona Strip has trailheads and some amazing views from the North Rim; these places—some easy to reach, some very remote—lie on lands of the Kaibab National Forest, Bureau of Land Management, and Lake Mead National Recreation Area.

MAINTAINED TRAILS OF THE INNER CANYON

You have the option of three types of hikes in the Inner Canyon. You can follow maintained trails, unmaintained trails, or routes. Park Service rangers usually recommend that first-time visitors try one of the maintained trails to get the feel of Canyon hiking. These trails are wide and well-signed. Rangers and other hikers will be close by in case of problems.

Camping along maintained trails is restricted to established sites at Indian Garden, Bright Angel, and Cottonwood. Mice and other small varmints at these campgrounds have voracious appetites for campers' food—keep yours in the steel ammo boxes provided or risk losing it.

Phantom Ranch, on Bright Angel Creek at the bottom of the Canyon, offers dormitory beds ($22.34), cabins ($64.89 d, $11.17 each extra person), meals (breakfast $12.64, box lunch $7.94, stew dinner $17.62, steak dinner $28.14), drinks, snacks, and souvenirs. You must make reservations for meals and accommodations with transportation desks in the lodges or contact Grand Canyon National Park Lodges, 14001 E. Iliff Ave., Suite 600, Aurora, CO 80014, tel. (303) 297-2757 in advance or (520) 638-3283 if four days or less in advance, Internet: www.amfac.com. If you'd rather have your gear carried by someone else, mules are available for $46.13 in or out with a weight limit of 30 pounds. Mules will carry you, too (see **mule rides**).

Bright Angel Trail

Havasupai Indians used this route from the South Rim to reach their fields and the spring at Indian Garden. Prospectors widened the trail in 1890, later extending it to the Colorado River.

FUN ON THE TRAIL CHECKLIST

- In summer, it's well worthwhile to hit the trail at first light, before 7 a.m. at the latest—or start after 4 p.m.; a lightweight flashlight provides the option of hiking after dark.

- Keep your body humming with frequent water and food (carbohydrate) breaks. All water and no food can lead to water intoxication—a dangerous condition caused by low electrolytes.

- Water and sun protection will come in handy even on short hikes, as the grand scenery will try to draw you in farther than you'd planned!

- Rangers recommend one gallon of water for an eight-hour hike in hot weather.

- Drinking water *before* you get thirsty will prevent the 10-20% loss of efficiency caused by even slight dehydration.

- If it's hot, try soaking your clothing in water for refreshing coolness.

- An easy pace allows the body to function more efficiently and feel better.

- Kicking back and putting your legs up for a five-to-seven-minute break once or twice an hour will refresh your leg muscles.

- Best to ignore that temptation to try a rim-to-river-to-rim hike unless you're sure you can do it AND the weather is cool.

- The Canyon Rule is to allow one-third of the time and energy on the descent and the rest for the climb back up.

- Wind and rain can cause hypothermia even in summer, so raingear can save the day year-round.

- Traveling light increases the fun; food and water should be the heaviest items. You might be able to replace a heavy tent with a tarp and ground sheet, a heavy sleeping bag with a lightweight blanket, and the Walkman with sounds of the Canyon.

- Rangers will be happy to advise you on your trip plans and possible difficulties that may lie ahead.

Now it's the best-graded and most popular trail into the Canyon.

The trailhead lies just west of Bright Angel Lodge in Grand Canyon Village. Resthouses one and a half miles and three miles below the rim contain emergency telephones and usually offer water from May 1 to September 30. Pipeline breaks commonly occur, so it's best to check that water is available by asking at the Visitor Center or Backcountry Office. One-way distances from the top are 4.6 miles to Indian Garden (campground, water, and ranger station), 7.7 miles to the Colorado River, and 9.3 miles to Bright Angel Creek (campground, water, ranger station, and Phantom Ranch). Allow four to five hours for the descent to the river and 8-10 hours coming out (elevation change 4,500 feet).

Plateau Point makes a good all-day hike. Perched 1,300 feet directly above the swirling Colorado River, you'll enjoy a 360-degree panorama of the Canyon. To reach Plateau Point, take the Bright Angel Trail to Indian Garden, then follow the signs. This strenuous dayhike is 12.2 miles roundtrip from the rim; elevation change is 3,080 feet.

River Trail

This short, 1.7-mile trail parallels the river in the twisted rocks of the Inner Gorge, connecting the bottoms of the Bright Angel and South Kaibab trails. There's little elevation change. Two suspension bridges cross the river to Bright Angel Creek.

South Kaibab Trail

Hikers enjoy sweeping views up and down the Canyon on this trail. From the trailhead near Yaki Point, 4.5 miles east of Grand Canyon Village, the South Kaibab drops steeply, following Cedar Ridge toward the river and Bright Angel Creek (6.4 miles one way). There's an emergency telephone at the Tipoff, 4.4 miles below the rim, where the trail begins to descend into the Inner Gorge.

Lack of shade and water and the steep grade make this trail especially difficult in summer. Allow three to five hours for the descent and six to eight hours coming out (elev. change 4,800 feet). Cedar Ridge, partway down, is a good day-hike destination—three miles roundtrip and an elevation change of 1,160 feet. Strong hikers

enjoy continuing down to the nearly level Tonto Trail (4.4 miles from the rim), turning left 4.1 miles on the Tonto to Indian Garden, then 4.6 miles up the Bright Angel Trail. Except in winter, the park's shuttles connect the trailheads for this 13.1-mile hike. Very strong hikers can make it all the way from rim to river and back in one day. During summer, however, this is grueling and dangerous for *anyone* and isn't recommended.

North Kaibab Trail

Few other Canyon trails compare in the number of interesting side trips and variety of scenery. Hikers on this trail start in the cool forests of the North Rim, descend through the woods into Roaring Springs Canyon, then follow rushing Bright Angel Creek all the way to the Colorado River. Look for the trailhead at the lower end of the parking lot, two miles north of Grand Canyon Lodge. Snows close the road from some time in October or November until mid-May, but you can reach the lower end of the North Kaibab at Bright Angel Campground year-round on trails from the South Rim. A long section of trail between the rim and Roaring Springs has been cut into sheer cliffs; waterfalls cascade over the rock face in spring and after rains. A picnic area near Roaring Springs makes a good destination for day-hikers; it's 9.4 miles roundtrip from the North Rim and has an elevation change of 3,160 feet. Water is available from May to September.

Cottonwood Campground, 6.9 miles below the rim, is a good stopping point for the night or a base for day-trips—it has a ranger station and, from May to September, water; winter campers must obtain and purify water from the creek. **Ribbon Falls** pours into a miniature paradise of travertine and lush greenery, nestled in a side canyon 1.5 miles from Cottonwood Campground. **The Transept,** a canyon just upstream and across the creek, offers good exploring too.

The North Kaibab Trail continues downstream along Bright Angel Creek, entering the dark contorted schists and other rocks of the ancient Vishnu Group. Near the bottom you'll walk through Phantom Ranch, then Bright Angel Campground. Most people can descend the 14.5-mile North Kaibab in eight to nine hours of steady hiking (elev. change 5,700 feet). Climbing out requires 10-12 hours and is best attempted over two days. Anglers are often successful in pulling rainbow trout from Bright Angel Creek, especially in winter.

UNMAINTAINED TRAILS AND ROUTES OF THE INNER CANYON (SOUTH RIM)

These trails and routes lead to some beautiful corners of the park, offering solitude and new Canyon perspectives. Hikers here must be self-reliant—know where water sources are, how to use map and compass, and how to handle emergencies. Most trails follow prehistoric Indian routes or game trails that miners improved in the late 1800s. Conditions vary widely; some trails are in excellent condition, while others are dangerous or require careful map reading. Although the Park Service calls these trails "unmaintained," Hermit and Grandview get some maintenance, and other trails may receive attention if they become impassable. Hermit Trail and parts of the Tonto Trail have designated camping areas, which you're required to use.

The Canyon offers thousands of possible routes for the experienced hiker. Harvey Butchart, master of Canyon off-trail hiking, describes many routes in his books (see the "Booklist" at the back of the book). Staff at the Backcountry Office will suggest interesting routes as well, and they'll give you an idea of current conditions. You'll no doubt come up with route ideas of your own while hiking through the Canyon and studying maps.

Just keep in mind that much of the Canyon's exposed rock is soft or fractured—a handhold or foothold can easily break off. The Colorado River presents a major barrier, as the water is too cold, wide, and full of treacherous currents to cross safely.

The following trails and routes are listed from west to east.

Great Thumb Mesa

Although practically unknown, this viewpoint is considered by some aficionados the best in the Canyon. Routes drop down to the Esplanade for loop hike possibilities. The trick, as usual for remote corners of the Canyon, is getting there! You'll need a difficult-to-obtain permit to cross Havasupai Indian lands, a permit from the Backcountry Office, a 4WD vehicle, and good weather—and then you still won't be able to drive all the way out to the end of the mesa due to road closures. There have been some nasty encounters between Havasupai Indians and tourists who treated this area as public land. If you're determined, contact the Havasupai Tourist Enterprise for the latest word on the road and permit situation at Box 160, Supai, AZ 86435, tel. (520) 448-2141. The Backcountry Office can

Prospector and tourist guide William Bass, dog Shep, and burro Joe, circa 1899

GRAND CANYON NATIONAL PARK (NEG #833)

also advise on roads and routes. The drive out begins from Tusayan on Forest Road 328 near Moqui Lodge, though the 328 road is often better approached via Rowe Well Road from Grand Canyon Village if there's been any rain.

Tonto Trail

Canyon views change continually along this 92-mile trail as it contours along the Tonto Platform, winding in and out of countless canyons and sometimes revealing spectacular panoramas from the edge of the Inner Gorge. The Tonto connects most of the trails below the South Rim between the mouth of Red Canyon at Hance Rapids and Garnet Canyon far downstream. Average elevation on the gently rolling trail is 3,000 feet. You might lose the trail occasionally, but with attention to rock cairns and the map, you'll soon find it again. The sun bears down relentlessly in summer, when it's best to hike elsewhere.

South Bass Trail

William Bass learned about this route from the Havasupai Indians in the 1880s, then used it to start a small tourist operation. Bass also built a trail up to the North Rim, crossing the river by boat and later by a cage suspended from a cable. No crossing exists today.

The South Bass Trail is generally in good condition and easy to follow. It drops to the Esplanade, a broad terrace, then down to the river. You'll need a high-clearance vehicle to reach the trailhead, four miles north of Pasture Wash Ranger Station; ask at the Backcountry Office for directions. Hiking the nine-mile trail to the river takes about five hours down and nine hours up, with an elevation change of 4,400 feet. No reliable water is available before the river.

Boucher Trail

Louis Boucher, the Hermit, came to the Canyon in 1891 and mined copper along the creek that bears his name until 1912. Steep terrain and rockslides can make the trail difficult—it's best for experienced hikers with light packs.

Take Hermit and Dripping Springs trails to Boucher Trail, which contours along the base of the Hermit shale, high above the west side of Hermit Canyon with excellent views. You'll reach Tonto Trail just before Boucher Creek.

Dripping Springs

The route down the creek to Boucher Rapids on the Colorado River is an easy 1.5 miles. From the Hermit trailhead on West Rim Drive, it's 11 miles to Boucher Creek; allow seven to eight hours down and nine to 10 hours coming up, with an elevation change of 3,800 feet. The Boucher, Tonto, and Hermit Trails make a fine three- or four-day loop hike. Boucher and Hermit Creeks have water year-round.

Hermit Trail

Although named for Boucher, the trail was actually built for tourists by the Santa Fe Railroad in 1912. Visitors took this route to Hermit Camp, which operated until 1930. Most of Hermit Trail is in good condition; the few places covered by rockslides can be easily crossed. The trail begins just beyond Hermit's Rest, at the end of eight-mile West Rim Drive. Water is available at Santa Maria Spring (two miles one way) and Hermit Creek (seven miles one way). Hermit Rapids on the Colorado River is an easy 1.5-mile walk down the bed of Hermit Creek; a sign on the

Tonto Trail points the way down to Hermit Creek. The elevation change from rim to river is 4,300 feet, so allow five to six hours going down and eight to 10 hours climbing out.

Hermit Trail also connects with Waldron, Dripping Springs, and Tonto Trails. Day-hikers can head to Dripping Springs, a six-mile roundtrip hike requiring four to six hours with an elevation change of 800 feet. Descend the Hermit Trail 1.5 miles, then turn left 1.5 miles on Dripping Springs Trail. Carry water for the entire trip, as the springs offer only a tiny flow. The 22.5-mile Hermit Loop hike, which follows the Hermit, Tonto, and Bright Angel Trails, is quite popular. You can find water on this loop year-round at Monument Creek and Indian Garden. Hikers can easily descend the bed of Monument Creek to Granite Rapids, 1.5 miles one way.

Grandview Trail

Day-hikers frequently use this steep but scenic trail to Horseshoe Mesa. The trailhead lies at Grandview Point on the East Rim/Desert View Drive. Miners improved an old Indian route in 1892 so they could bring out high-grade copper ore from Horseshoe Mesa. Mining ceased in 1907, but mine shafts, machinery, and ruins of buildings remain.

Cave of the Domes, a limestone cavern on the west side of the mesa, has some good passages; look for a trail fork west of the butte atop the mesa. Three trails descend Horseshoe Mesa

to the Tonto Trail. Bring water, as the springs are either unreliable or difficult to reach. Allow two hours down and three up for the six-mile roundtrip hike to Horseshoe Mesa, with an elevation change of 2,600 feet.

New Hance Trail

John Hance, one of the first prospectors to switch to the tourist business, built this trail down Red Canyon in 1895. The unsigned trailhead lies about one mile southwest of Moran Point turnoff on the East Rim/Desert View Drive; obtain directions from a ranger. Suited for more experienced hikers, the trail—with poor footing in places—descends steeply to the river at Hance Rapids. Most of the trail is easy to follow, especially when you're descending. No reliable water is available before the river. The eight-mile trail takes about six hours to descend and eight to 10 hours to ascend, with an elevation change of 4,400 feet.

Escalante Route

The Tonto Trail's upper end gives out at Hance Rapids, but you can continue upstream to Tanner Rapids and the Tanner Trail. Cairns mark the 15-mile Escalante Route. Expect rough terrain and a difficult time finding the route in some sections. The Colorado River, easily accessible only at the ends of the route, provides the only reliable source of water. The route is somewhat easier to hike in the downstream direction, Tanner to Hance.

Capt. John Hance (1835?-1919) was one of the first to promote tourism on the South Rim. He spent the last 40 years of his life entertaining Canyon visitors with wild tales.

GRAND CANYON NATIONAL PARK (NEG #825)

Tanner Trail

Seth Tanner improved this Indian trail in the 1880s to reach his copper and silver mines along the Colorado River. Although in good condition and easy to follow, the Tanner Trail is long—10 miles one-way—and dry, and best attempted in the cooler months. Hikers often cache water partway down for the return trip.

The trailhead lies about 100 yards back down the road from Lipan Point, off the East Rim/Desert View Drive. Allow six to eight hours for the descent and an eight- to 10-hour return, with an elevation change of 4,700 feet.

Beamer Trail

This slim path begins at Tanner Canyon Rapids (lower end of Tanner Trail) and follows the river four miles upstream to Palisades Creek, then climbs to a high terrace for the remaining five miles to the Little Colorado River confluence. No camping is allowed within a half mile of the confluence.

UNMAINTAINED TRAILS AND ROUTES OF THE INNER CANYON (NORTH RIM)

Whitmore Wash Trail

Although little known or used, this three-quarter-mile-long trail offers the park's easiest hike from trailhead to river. The trick is reaching the trailhead! You'll need a high-clearance 4WD vehicle and lots of time. Follow County 5 and other dirt roads on the Arizona Strip from Toroweap, Fredonia, Colorado City, or St. George to the four-way intersection at Mt. Trumbull Schoolhouse, turn south 1.8 miles on BLM Road 257, then bear left 21.7 miles on BLM Road 1045 its end. The last 7.5 miles are rough, as the road crosses lava flows from Mt. Emma. This lava acts as a ramp for the road to descend deep into the Grand Canyon. The trail appears to drop off the rim where the road ends, but that's not the real trail. Instead, climb up above the barbed-wire fence to the trail.

You'll drop about 850 feet as the trail switchbacks, then skirts the base of a massive cliff of columnar basalt before ending on a sandy beach. Lava remnants of ancient dams can be seen on both sides of the river. A small trail near the bottom leads a half mile downstream to Whitmore Rapids and lower Whitmore Canyon, which you can explore for about a half mile upstream.

Lava Falls Route

The Colorado River explodes in a fury of foam and waves at Lava Falls, reached by this short but steep route from the Toroweap area. Cairns mark the way down a lunarlike landscape of volcanic lava. Barrel cacti thrive on the dark, twisted rock. Although the route is only 1.5 miles one way, it's considered difficult because of steep grades and poor footing. It is not a developed or maintained trail. Summer temperatures get *extremely* hot; elevation at the river is only 1,700 feet. Summer hikers should start at dawn and carry plenty of water.

From Toroweap Overlook, backtrack on the road 2.5 miles and look for a dirt track on the left (3.5 miles south of Tuweep Ranger Station); follow it 2.5 miles across normally dry Toroweap Lake and around the west side of Vulcan's Throne. The route is too rough for cars and impassable for any vehicle when the lake contains water. At road's end, the route descends to a hill of red cinders about two-thirds of the way down; the last part of the descent follows a steep gully. Lava Falls lies 0.3 mile downstream. Camping is allowed along the river with a permit. Allow two hours going down and three to six hours coming out, with an elevation change of 2,500 feet.

Tuckup Trail

Experienced Canyon hikers looking for solitude and expansive vistas can try this faint trail. It follows the Esplanade of the North Rim for more than 70 miles between the Toroweap Point area and Hundred and Fifty Mile Canyon. Back roads lead to trailheads near these two areas and to upper Tuckup Canyon, about the halfway point on the trail.

The trailhead is reached by a 3.5-mile jeep road; turn east at a fork 4.6 miles south of the ranger station, 1.4 miles north of the overlook. You can wander off on a variety of jaunts in this remote area. Hikers have followed the Tuckup Trail from Toroweap Point to Cottonwood Canyon, descended Cottonwood and Tuckup canyons to the Colorado River (rope needed), hiked the shore downstream to Lava Falls Route, and ascended back to Toroweap in a week or so of travel. Springs of varying reliability may provide water along the Tuckup Trail. Talk with rangers knowledgeable about the area for trailhead, spring, and hiking conditions.

Thunder River Trails

Thunder River blasts out of a cave in the Muav limestone, cascades a half mile, then enters Tapeats Creek. It's not only the world's shortest river but suffers the humiliation of being a tributary to a creek!

Deer Creek Falls, another area attraction, plummets more than 100 feet onto the banks of the Colorado River. Cottonwood trees, willows, and other cool greenery grace the banks of Thunder River and both creeks. Trails are generally good and easy to follow, though spring runoff and rains can make Tapeats Creek too high to cross safely.

Two trails descend from the North Rim: the **Thunder River Trail** from the end of Forest Road 232 (just past Indian Hollow Campground) and the **Bill Hall Trail** from the east side of Monument Point at the end of Forest Road 292A. The Bill Hall Trail saves five miles of walking but the steep grade can be slippery and hard on the knees.

Reach the trailheads by turning west on Forest Road 22 from AZ 67 in De Motte Park, 0.8 mile south of the North Rim Store and 17.5 miles north of Bright Angel Point; consult a Kaibab National Forest map (North Kaibab Ranger District). It's about 35 miles of dirt road and an hour and a half from AZ 67 to either trailhead. Cars can negotiate the roads in good weather, but winter snows bury this high country from about mid-November to mid-May. Thunder River and Bill Hall Trails both drop to the Esplanade, where they meet. The Esplanade could be used for dry camping, and you may wish to cache some water here for the climb back out. Thunder River Trail then switchbacks down to Surprise Valley, a giant piece of the rim that long ago slumped thousands of feet to its present position. The valley turns into an oven in summer and lacks water; it's about eight miles from the Bill Hall Trailhead.

In another two miles, **Thunder River Trail** goes east across Surprise Valley, drops to Thunder River, and follows it to Tapeats Creek. Except at high water, Tapeats Creek can be followed 2.5 miles upstream to its source in a cave. The Colorado River is a 2.5-mile hike downstream from the junction of Thunder River and Tapeats Creek. If the creek runs too deep to cross, you can stay on a west-side trail all the way to the Colorado. Upper Tapeats Campsite is just below the Thunder River-Tapeats Creek confluence; Lower Tapeats Campsite lies downstream on the Colorado River. Good fishing attracts anglers to Tapeats Creek and perhaps always has—prehistoric Cohonina Indians left ruins here. The trek from Bill Hall trailhead at Monument Point to Tapeats Rapids is about 12.5 miles one way, with an elevation change of 5,250 feet. Figure seven hours to reach the upper campsite on Tapeats Creek, nine hours to hike all the way to Tapeats Rapids, and return times are nearly double. Thunder River, 9.5 miles from the Bill Hall trailhead, is the first source of water.

Deer Creek Trail, marked by a large cairn in Surprise Valley, splits off to the west and drops about 1.5 miles to Deer Creek (Dutton) Spring, another cave system gushing a waterfall. You can hike up to the falls for a closer look or take the path that goes higher and behind the falls. The creekside trail winds down one mile past some remarkable Tapeats narrows, then drops to the base of Deer Creek Falls at the river. Watch out for poison ivy here. Campsites lie along Deer Creek between Deer Creek Springs and the head of the narrows. Distance from the Bill Hall Trailhead to the Colorado River is about 11 miles one way with a descent of 5,400 feet; Deer Creek Springs, 9.5 miles in, is the first water source. Allow about seven hours to reach Deer Creek and 45 minutes more to descend to the Colorado River, then almost double that to return.

North Bass Trail

This long and faint trail drops from Swamp Point on the North Rim to Muav Saddle, where there's a 1925 Park Service cabin. The trail makes a sharp left toward Muav Springs, drops steeply to White Creek in Muav Canyon, follows a long bypass to a safe descent through the Redwall, winds down White Creek to Shinumo Creek, continues to Bass Camp, then cuts over a ridge to the left and drops down to a fine beach on the Colorado River. The trail reaches the Colorado about 0.3 mile below where the South Bass Trail comes down on the other side. No crossing exists today, though people occasionally hitch rides to the far shore with river-rafters. A waterfall blocks travel down Shinumo Creek just before the river, so the trail climbs over the ridge. The Muav and Shinumo drainages create their own canyon worlds—you're not really exposed to the Grand Canyon until you reach the ridge above the Colorado River near trail's end.

Once at the Colorado River via the main trail, you can loop back to Bass Camp on another trail; it begins at the downstream end of the beach and crosses over to lower Shinumo Creek, which you can then follow upstream back to Bass Camp and the North Bass Trail. Many routes off the North Bass Trail invite exploration, such as the Redwall Narrows of White Creek above the trail junction, Shinumo Creek drainage above White Creek, and Burro Canyon.

Muav Saddle Springs offers water just off the trail. White Creek has intermittent water above and below the Redwall. Shinumo Creek's abundant flow supports some small trout. Shinumo can be difficult to cross in spring and after summer storms; at other times you can hop across on rocks. Allow three to four days for the 28-mile roundtrip to the river, with an elevation change of 5,300 feet; the trail is best suited for experienced hikers.

With a high-clearance vehicle you can reach the trailhead at Swamp Point from AZ 67 in DeMotte Park via Forest Roads 22, 270, 223, 268, 268B, and Swamp Point Road. You'll need the current Kaibab Forest map, as old ones may not show these roads correctly. The drive from DeMotte Park to Swamp Point takes nearly two hours due to the rough condition of Swamp Point Road.

Powell Plateau Trail

A good trail from Swamp Point connects this isolated "island" that lies within the vast reaches of the Grand Canyon. Once part of the North Rim, the plateau has been completely severed from the rim by erosion, except for the Muav Saddle connection. The trail is about 1.5 miles one way; you drop 800 feet to Muav Saddle on the North Bass Trail, then continue straight across the saddle and up another set of switchbacks to a ponderosa pine forest on the Powell Plateau. Here the trail fades out. Many places on the seven-mile-long plateau offer outstanding views. Travel is

cross-country, so you'll need a map and compass; expect to do some bushwhacking.

The easiest viewpoint to reach lies to the northwest; just follow the northern edge of the plateau (no trail) to a large rock cairn about one mile from where the trail from Swamp Point tops out on the plateau. You can camp on the Powell Plateau with a backcountry permit; all water must be carried in from the trailhead or Muav Saddle Springs. See **North Bass Trail** for directions to Swamp Point.

Clear Creek Trail

This trail, in very good condition and easy to follow, is the North Rim's version of the Tonto Trail. It begins 0.3 mile north of Phantom Ranch and climbs 1,500 feet to the Tonto Platform, which it follows—winding in and out of canyons—until dropping at the last possible place into Clear Creek, nine miles from Phantom Ranch. Carry water—there's no source before Clear Creek—and be prepared for very hot weather in summer. The best camping sites lie scattered among the cottonwood trees where the trail meets the creek.

Day-hikers enjoy the first mile or so of Clear Creek Trail for its scenic views of the river and Inner Gorge. Strong hikers can walk all the way to Clear Creek and back in a long day. Better still would be a trip of several days.

The route to **Cheyava Falls,** the highest in the Canyon, takes six to eight hours roundtrip up the long northeast fork of Clear Creek. The falls put on an impressive show only in spring and after heavy rains. Other arms of the creek offer good hiking as well. The canyon that branches east about a half mile downstream from the end of Clear Creek Trail cuts through a narrow canyon of quartzite. You can also walk along Clear Creek to the Colorado River, a five- to seven-hour roundtrip hike through dark and contorted granite and schist, a dark, easily split metamorphic rock with closely spaced bands of mica. The 10-foot-high waterfall a half mile from the river is bypassed by clambering around to the right.

Nankoweap Trail

Thrilling ledges on the Nankoweap Trail discourage hikers afraid of heights. But if you don't mind tiptoeing on the brink of sheer cliffs, this trail will open up a large section of the park for your exploration. The trailhead lies at Saddle

Mountain Saddle, 2.4 crow-flying miles northeast of Point Imperial. You can't drive to the trailhead, however; it must be approached on foot, either three miles one way from House Rock Buffalo Ranch Road (south from US 89A), or three miles one way from near the end of Forest Road 610 (east off AZ 67). Both access roads are dirt, passable by cars, but House Rock Buffalo Ranch Road lies at a lower elevation and is less likely to be snowed in.

The Nankoweap Trail drops several hundred feet, then contours along a ledge all the way to Tilted Mesa before descending to Nankoweap Creek. Some care in route-finding is needed between Tilted Mesa and the creek. Nankoweap Creek, 10 miles from the trailhead, is the first source of water; you should cache water partway down to drink on your return. The remaining four miles to the river is easy. Allow three to four days for a roundtrip, with an elevation change of 4,800 feet.

RUNNING THE COLORADO RIVER

Running the Colorado River through the Grand Canyon provides the excitement of roaring rapids and the tranquility of gliding in silent passages. It rates as one of the world's greatest adventures! A journey through the Canyon by river with some side hikes might be the single best way to see and appreciate the grandeur and beauty here. Many beautifully sculptured side canyons, some with lush vegetation, can be easily reached only

from the river. Just being at the bottom of the Canyon is a delight, whether you're riding atop the waves, strolling past the convoluted walls of an unnamed side canyon, or enjoying life at camp.

Although explorers of the 19th century feared this section of the river, rendering it in dark and gloomy drawings, boating the Canyon has become a safe and enjoyable experience. It opens some of the most grand and remote corners of

running a rapid

THE EXPLORATION OF THE COLORADO RIVER AND ITS CANYONS

the Canyon. River parties stop frequently to explore the twisting side canyons, old mining camps, and Indian ruins along the way. Within the Grand Canyon, the Colorado River flows 277 miles, drops 2,200 feet, and thunders through 70 major rapids.

A river trip through the Grand Canyon requires a large commitment in time, whitewater experience, equipment, expense, and permit procedures. About one-third of river runners do it themselves with a noncommercial river trip permit from the park. The easier option, taken by most people, simply involves setting aside the time for the trip and paying a river company to handle the many details.

YOUR OPTIONS

Boats

Both oar-powered and motor-powered craft run the river. Motor-powered rafts can zip through the entire Canyon in six days, or zoom from Lees Ferry to Phantom Ranch in two days. The oar-powered boat trips take half again as much time but provide a quieter and more natural experience. On these smaller boats, passengers have the advantage of being able to talk easily with the crew and one another. Whether in a little or a big rig, you can be assured that the crew will work hard to provide a safe and enjoyable trip.

All but two of the tour companies use rafts of various sizes; the exceptions are Grand Canyon Dories and Grand Canyon Expeditions, which employ sturdy, hard-shelled boats with upturned ends. The dories ride high in the water as they dance through the waves. They're small—16-18 feet long—with one person at the oars and just four passengers. Only the most skilled boaters can handle dories because, unlike rafts, they can't bounce off rocks without damage.

Small rafts typically measure 18 feet and carry four or five passengers plus one crew member to do the rowing. Some companies provide a paddle-boat option—not a Mississippi-type paddlewheeler, but a small raft in which everyone has a paddle! The guide sits at the stern to steer and give instructions, but it's up to the passengers to succeed in running each rapid.

The motor-powered rigs can be 30 feet long or more and have pontoon outriggers for extra sta-

bility. A small outboard motor near the stern provides steering and speed. Some people dislike the use of motors in a wilderness, but these boats do allow more people to run the Colorado than would be possible if everyone went in non-motorized rigs.

Routes

Most tours put in at Lees Ferry, just upstream from the park, and end downstream at Diamond Creek or Pearce (also spelled Pierce) Ferry on Lake Mead. You can also travel just half the distance by combining river travel to Phantom Ranch (at the bottom of the Canyon) with a hike to the rim. You can leave or join the lower section of river via a helicopter ride to Hualapai Indian land near Whitmore Wash. If you'd like just a taste of river-running, try a one-day smooth-water trip from Glen Canyon Dam to Lees Ferry, just above Grand Canyon National Park, with **Wilderness River Adventures,** based in Page. Or you can visit the lowermost part of the Grand Canyon and run a few rapids with **Hualapai River Runners,** based in Peach Springs.

A typical commercial oar trip takes 12-16 days from Lees Ferry to Diamond Creek, covering 226 miles. The upper half takes five or six days from Lees Ferry to Phantom Ranch, 87.5 miles; the lower half requires eight or nine days from Phantom Ranch to Diamond Creek, 138.5 miles. Continuing to Pearce Ferry on Lake Mead adds just a day or two. Equivalent motorized trips typically run eight days from Lees Ferry to Diamond Creek or Pearce Ferry with three or four days from Lees Ferry to Phantom Ranch and five days from Phantom Ranch to Diamond Creek or Pearce Ferry.

Those preferring shorter trips can end a trip or begin a two- or three-day run in the lowermost Grand Canyon at Whitmore Wash, at Mile 187 below Lava Falls. Although there's a trail from the North Rim here, river parties use helicopters between the river (on Hualapai Indian land) and the Bar 10 guest ranch, where small planes shuttle people to Las Vegas or other destinations.

Other combinations are available too. Extra days may be added to some trips for hiking or layovers, especially early or late in the season. Expect to pay $200 or more per day; discounts may be available for groups, children under 14, early booking, and off-season journeys.

paddle rafters

If you have children in tow, check for minimum age requirements. Sometimes these are left up to the passenger; at other times operators require minimum ages of anywhere between 8 and 16 years. Trips usually include land transportation, and most depart from Flagstaff, Page, St. George, or Las Vegas. Meals, camping gear, and waterproof bags are usually included in the price. Experienced kayakers can tag along with many tours, paying a lower rate.

Seasons

The river-running season normally lasts April-Oct., with only nonmotorized craft departing mid-September to mid-December. When you choose to go makes a big difference in the river experience. Most people go during summer because that's when they take their vacations. The Canyon gets very hot then, but a little splash of river water will always be cooling. Hiking at this time is limited to shady side canyons with water. Spring—April to early June—offers many advantages. The redbud trees and many plants bloom in beautiful colors, hiking weather will be near perfect, days get long, trip operators often add a couple of extra days for long hikes or layovers, and it's much easier to get a reservation for a trip. The downside is the possibility of cold weather, even sleet, which the author woke up to on one April morning in the upper Canyon! Some boaters think that early June offers the best weather for a boat trip, though hiking can get hot then. Autumn brings shorter days, along with

cooler temperatures. The Canyon quiets after mid-September, when all the motorized rigs have left the river. Heavy-duty rain gear with sweaters underneath can keep spring and autumn boaters warm during cool spells.

Rafting the Lower Grand Canyon

This last section, beginning at Diamond Creek, offers beautiful Canyon scenery and some rapids. You can get on a trip here much more easily than in the upper Canyon, either with Hualapai River Runners or on your own. The Park Service gives free permits for up to two private parties (16 people maximum in each) per day. River runners will need to pay for a Hualapai permit to use the Diamond Creek Road and launch. Summers get very hot here, so spring, autumn, or even winter offer better weather for exploring side canyons.

Boating into the
Lower Grand Canyon from Lake Mead

Boats may go up as far as Separation Canyon from Lake Mead National Recreation Area without a permit. Primitive camping is also allowed on the Park's shore in this section without permits, though high lake levels can flood all the spots. Campers may be required to carry portable toilet systems. South Cove offers the closest paved boat ramp, reached by the paved road via Dolan Springs from US 93. Pearce Ferry nearby is closer with a primitive boat ramp and camping, but the last four miles in are unpaved.

Canoeing the Lower Grand Canyon

Canoes in the Grand Canyon? Yes, indeed, in the last 40 miles within the park. You'll need a powerboat to carry the canoes from Lake Mead to Separation Canyon (Mile 240 on the river). Most of the southern shore on this trip belongs to the Hualapai Indians, so obtain tribal permits if you plan to camp or hike on their land.

Private River Trips

Step One is to read Grand Canyon National Park's regulations and procedures! Obtain them from the River Trips Office, Box 129, Grand Canyon, AZ 86023, tel. (520) 638-7884 or (800) 959-9164, or online at www.thecanyon.com/nps/gcgovregs.htm. Step Two—getting the permit—will be the hard part. Unfortunately, you'll be at the end of a very long line. So many groups have applied that the waiting list extends for more than 12 years. Cancellations do occur during this lengthy wait, so flexible and lucky groups might get on sooner, even the same year. The River Permits Office has worked out a system for applications that's as fair as possible to everyone during this waiting period. To get on the waiting list, carefully follow the instructions for making an initial application ($100 at press time) and annual renewals, all of which you must make within specified date ranges.

RIVER COMPANIES

The following companies offer a wide variety of trips through the Canyon, ranging from one- or two-day introductions to adventurous 19-day expeditions. Write Grand Canyon National Park for the latest list of companies (Box 129, Grand Canyon, AZ 86023), ask at the visitor center, or check listings on the Internet at www.thecanyon.com. The Internet works best because you not only get a list, but also links to most of the companies, many of which have colorful and informative sites. If possible, make reservations (with deposit) six months to a year in advance. It's possible to get on a trip with short notice, especially if there are just a few in your group and you're going early or late in the season. **Rivers and Oceans** specializes in river trips; it will supply information about companies, make reservations, and let you know about last-minute openings at Box 40321, Flagstaff, AZ

86004, tel. (520) 526-4575 or (800) 473-4576; Internet: www.grand-canyon.az.us/R&O.

All of the companies put in at Lees Ferry except for Wilderness River Adventure's day-trips, which start from Glen Canyon Dam, and Hualapai River Runners trips, which begin at Diamond Creek in the lower Grand Canyon. The following rates apply for 1999; prices will be lower if you start or leave from Phantom Ranch or Whitmore Wash.

Arizona Raft Adventures goes to Diamond Creek on 12- to 15-day oar ($2,240-2,460) and eight- or 10-day motorized trips ($1,600-1,900), most with the option of ending or starting at Phantom Ranch. It offers paddle raft trips too, either in combination with oar-powered rafts or all by themselves. Contact 4050 E. Huntington Dr., Flagstaff, AZ 86004, tel. (520) 526-8200 or (800) 786-7238, Internet: www.azraft.com.

Arizona River Runners offers a 13-day oar trip to Diamond Creek ($2,210) with an option to end or start at Phantom Ranch and an eight-day motorized run to Pearce Ferry with options to end or start from Phantom Ranch or Whitmore Wash. Contact Box 47788, Phoenix, AZ 85068-7788, tel. (602) 867-4866 or (800) 477-7238, Internet: www.raftarizona.com.

Canyon Explorations/Expeditions uses oar boats on trips to Diamond Creek of 13-16 days ($2,310-2,825); a paddle raft comes along too. Some trips have a Phantom Ranch exit/entry option. Contact Box 310, Flagstaff, AZ 86002, tel. (520) 774-4559 or (800) 654-0723, Internet: canyonx.com.

Canyoneers runs motorized rafts to Pearce Ferry in seven days for $1,500 ($1,100 in April) with the option of ending/starting at Phantom Ranch. Contact Box 2997, Flagstaff, AZ 86003, tel. (520) 526-0924 or (800) 525-0924, Internet: www.canyoneers.com.

Colorado River & Trail Expeditions goes to Pearce Ferry in 12 days by oar-powered raft ($2,495) and eight or nine days in motorized rafts ($1,725); a paddleboat goes along on the oar raft trips. You can leave or join at Phantom Ranch on both trips. Contact Box 57575, Salt Lake City, UT 84157-0575, tel. (801) 261-1789 or (800) 253-7328, Internet: www.crateinc.com.

Diamond River Adventures offers 12-day oar trips ($2,255) and eight-day motorized trips ($1,705) to Diamond Creek with options of leaving or joining at Phantom Ranch; an excursion just to Whitmore Wash from Lees Ferry takes 10 days by oar and seven days by motor. Contact Box 1316, Page, AZ 86040, tel. (520) 645-8866 or (800) 343-3121, Internet: www.diamondriver.com.

Grand Canyon Dories features dories on 16-day trips ($3,482) to Pearce Ferry; 19-day trips also run in spring and autumn ($3,556). You can join or leave the trip at Phantom Ranch or Whitmore Wash. Contact Box 67, Angels Camp, CA 95222, tel. (209) 736-0805 or (800) 877-3679, Internet: www.oars.com.

Grand Canyon Expeditions Co. runs dories, too, on 14-day trips to Pearce Ferry ($2,480); motorized rafts do this run in eight days ($1,770). All trips go straight through without any passenger exchanges. Contact Box O, Kanab, UT 84741, tel. (435) 644-2691 or (800) 544-2691, Internet: www.gcex.com.

Hatch River Expeditions runs motorized rafts to Whitmore Wash in six and a half days for $1,450. Contact Box 1200, Vernal, UT 84078, tel. (435) 789-3813 or (800) 433-8966; www.hatchriver.com.

High Desert Adventures offers oar rafts to Whitmore Wash in 12 days ($2,285) with an exchange option at Phantom Ranch, and motorized rafts to Pearce Ferry ($1,620) in eight days without passenger exchanges. Contact Box 40, St. George, UT 84771-0040, tel. (435) 673-1200 or (800) 673-1733, Internet: funboat.com.

Hualapai River Runners travels just the lower Grand Canyon on motorized rafts, putting in at Diamond Creek and coming out one ($221) or two ($321) days later at Pearce Ferry. Contact Box 246, Peach Springs, AZ 86434, tel. (520) 769-2210 or (800) 622-4409, Internet: www.arizonaguide.com/grandcanyonwest.

Moki Mac River Expeditions heads down to Pearce Ferry in 14-day oar trips ($2,317), with an option to end or begin from Phantom Ranch, and eight-day motorized rafts ($1,572) without a passenger exchange option. Contact Box 71242, Salt Lake City, UT 84171, tel. (801) 268-6667 or (800) 284-7280, Internet: www.mokimac.com.

O.A.R.S. offers oar rafts to Diamond Creek in 13 days for $2,966 and 14- to 17-day runs all the way to Pearce Ferry for $3,151-3,484 with options to leave or join at Phantom Ranch (or Whitmore Wash, for the Pearce Ferry trips). Contact Box 216, Altaville, CA 95221, tel. (209) 736-0805 or (800) 346-6277, Internet: www.oars.com.

Outdoors Unlimited goes to Pearce Ferry on oar rafts in 13 days ($2,395) with an option to leave or join at Phantom Ranch; a paddle raft comes along too, and some trips are all paddle rafts. Contact 6900 Townsend Winona Road, Flagstaff, AZ 86004, tel. (520) 526-4546 or (800) 637-7238, Internet: www.outdoorsunlimited.com.

Tour West runs oar rafts to Whitmore Wash in 12 days ($2,120) without any passenger exchanges; paddle rafts can be added on request. Motorized rafts go to Whitmore Wash in six days, then another three days to Pearce Ferry. Contact Box 333, Orem, UT 84059, tel. (801) 225-0755 or (800) 453-9107, Internet: www.twriver.com.

Western River Expeditions offers just one oar trip, to Whitmore Wash in 12 days ($2,500); motorized rafts go to Pearce Ferry in eight days ($2,060 March-April, $2,300 May-Sept.) with a passenger exchange at Whitmore Wash. Contact 7258 Racquet Club Dr., Salt Lake City, UT 84121, tel. (801) 942-6669 or (800) 453-7450, Internet: www.westernriver.com.

Wilderness River Adventures goes to Whitmore Wash on 12-day oar trips for $2,416 with a Phantom Ranch end or start option. Motorized trips take eight days for $1,902; seven-day and Phantom Ranch end or start trips are also available. The company also offers a day-trip from Glen Canyon Dam to Lees Ferry, a scenic ride on smooth water. Contact Box 717, Page, AZ 86040, tel. (520) 645-3296 or (800) 992-8022, Internet: www.riveradventures.com.

DOWN THE COLORADO THROUGH THE GRAND CANYON

This miniguide of river-running highlights contains just a sampling of the sights along the river. Even so, it would be tough to fit them all into one trip. Experienced river guides know far more places, including some "secret" ones they may share with you. Weather, schedules, and where other river parties have stopped will affect which places your group will decide to take in. Rapids with ratings of five or more on the 1-10 scale are listed in parentheses. The 1-10 scale is unique to the Colorado River; other rivers are rated on a 1-6 scale.

The place descriptions come from the author's experience on two river trips and advice from river guides and National Park Service staff. Geology information is mostly from the book *River Runner's Guide to the Canyons of the Green and Colorado Rivers: With Emphasis on Geologic Features, Vol. III* by George C. Simmons and David L. Gaskill (Northland Publishing, 1969).

Mile 0: Lees Ferry
This historic site along the Colorado River, once the only easily accessible crossing for hundreds of miles upstream or down, now marks the beginning of river voyages into the Grand Canyon. Most boaters have only one thing on their minds here—getting on the river and embarking on their adventure. Yet it's worthwhile to come early or at another time to explore Lonely Dell Ranch, other historic buildings, and remnants of past mining attempts at Lees Ferry. Spencer Trail beckons hikers from the rim of the Canyon and the far more gentle Cathedral Wash route offers a pleasant walk to the river below. The Paria Canyon hike, one of the finest in the region, ends here after four to six days of twisting through its wonderful sandstone walls from a trailhead north across the Utah border. Then some people come just to relax or fish by the cold, clear, trout-filled river. See the **Lees Ferry** section later in this book for details on the area, including lodging, camping, and restaurant information.

You're now at an elevation of 3,116 feet. A descent of 1,936 vertical feet lies ahead as you plummet deep within the Grand Canyon through more than a dozen geologic formations before meeting the Canyon's last riffles near Separation Canyon, where the Colorado River meets Lake Mead. Note how the types of rock affect the river and thus your ride—wide and smooth through the soft shales, then narrower and bumpier in the sandstone, limestone, granite, and schist—but be ready for surprises where tributaries have dumped huge piles of rocks into the river!

Rock layers visible near Lees Ferry formed during the Triassic and Jurassic periods, roughly 240-140 million years ago, when the dinosaurs first appeared and walked this land. Rocks of this age actually once lay atop the older layers seen on the much higher rims of the Grand Canyon, but there they've been reduced by erosion to just a few remnants, such as Cedar Mountain, visible from Desert View. Dramatic folding and faulting downstream have raised the Colorado Plateau thousands of feet, which you'll soon plunge into. The sights mentioned below follow the convention of "river right" and "river left" facing downstream.

Mile 0.8: Kaibab Formation
Look on the left for the emergence of the Kaibab Formation, the cream-colored, weather-resistant limestone that caps much of the Grand Canyon rims. Scientists have found fossils of marine invertebrates and some fish. You've now crossed a major geologic time boundary into the Permian period (290-240 million years ago) of the Paleozoic era.

Mile 1: Paria Riffle
The Colorado gets some of its namesake reddish color here if the Paria River (on the right) is flowing. Marble Canyon begins downstream from here. Major John Wesley Powell and his men saw the sheer, polished walls from here down to the Little Colorado confluence and named this section Marble Canyon, although no marble is actually present.

Mile 2: Toroweap Formation
This silty limestone, formed near the sea's edge, was also deposited during the Permian period. The Toroweap has thinner beds and less chert than the Kaibab.

Mile 4: Coconino Sandstone
Tilted crossbedding, reptile tracks, and even imprints of raindrops indicate windblown deposits—ancient sand dunes built up during the middle of the Permian period. By comparing the angles of the crossbedding with those of modern sand dunes, geologists have concluded that winds had blown the sand from the north.

Mile 4.5: Navajo Bridge
The bridge, recently built beside its 1929 cousin, connects the Canyon rims 470 feet above the river. In 1937, river runner Buzz Holmstrum stopped near here to get supplies at what looked on his map like the nearby Marble Canyon store. He did make it up and down the cliff somehow and then went on to make the first intentional solo run through the Grand Canyon.

GEOLOGIC CROSS SECTION OF THE GRAND CANYON REGION

Mile 7: Hermit Shale
Fossils of ferns, other plants, and even some insects have been collected from this soft reddish shale. The rock formed in a vast river floodplain in the early part of the Permian period.

Mile 8: Badger Creek Rapid (5-8)
River runners rate this, your first of many exciting rapids, at five to eight, depending on flow. The outwash from ephemeral streams of Badger Canyon on the right and Jackass Canyon on the left creates the rapid. A rough, three-mile trail connects the river to US 89A via Jackass Canyon; Navajo sometimes come down this way to fish. Hikers can scramble up Badger Canyon about a mile. Badger and nearby Soap Creek got their names when 19th-century Mormon explorer Jacob Hamblin shot a badger, took it back to camp, stewed it overnight, and then found that the alkaline water had turned the fat in his breakfast into soap!

Mile 11.2: Soap Creek Rapid (5-6)
Soap Creek comes in from the right. This rapid marks the beginning of a series of tragic sites for the 1889 Stanton-Brown survey, which came to study a proposed railroad route through the Grand Canyon. Despite having portaged the rapid, Frank M. Brown, the organizer of the Denver, Colorado Canyon, and Pacific Railroad Company, drowned below here. Five days later, two other members drowned before the group abandoned its work and climbed out of the Canyon. The following year, Robert B. Stanton and a team returned equipped with lifejackets and better gear to complete the survey.

The Supai Group exposed here comprises four formations that contain fossils of plants deposited in ancient deltas. Tracks of primitive reptiles occur in the upper half of the group. First, you'll see reddish-brown sandstone from the early part of the Permian period (about 280 million years ago) with thinner layers of ripple-marked siltstone and shale. The rock commonly weathers into ledges. Below are rocks of the Pennsylvanian period (330-290 million years ago)—crossbedded sandstone in the middle part of the group, then thin-bedded sandstone with much interbedded siltstone and mudstone in the lower part.

Mile 12: Salt Water Wash
A rough route on the left climbs about four miles to US 89A; lots of boulders in the lower half make for slow going.

Mile 16.9: House Rock Rapid (7-9)
Rider Canyon comes in from the right. Robert B. Stanton used this difficult canyon route during his second expedition in 1890 to carry out an injured photographer who had fallen from a 20-foot cliff.

Mile 20.5: North Canyon Rapid (5)
You've now entered the "Roaring 20s"—a lively section of rapids in Marble Canyon. North Canyon, on the right, offers beautiful hiking. It's less than a mile to where cliffs block the way; you may see pools and small waterfalls.

Mile 21.2: 21 Mile Rapid (5)

Mile 23: Redwall Limestone
Perhaps the most distinct layer in the Grand Canyon, the Redwall forms long, unbroken cliffs. Here it makes up much of the impressive walls of Marble Canyon. The Redwall challenges skills of trailbuilders and hikers who attempt rim-to-river routes. The upper Redwall contains many caves; sometimes you'll even see matching caves on both sides of the river. The namesake color comes not from the limestone itself, but from

CANYON ROCKS

With 94 types of rock discovered in the Grand Canyon, how does one remember even the major formations? All you have to do is remember "Know the canyon history. See rocks made by time very slowly."

Know	Kaibab limestone
the.	Toroweap
canyon	Coconino sandstone
history.	Hermit shale
See	Supai Group
rocks	Redwall limestone
made	Muav limestone
by.	Bright Angel shale
time	Tapeats sandstone
very slowly	Vishnu schist

stains of the Hermit shale above. Fossils of nautiloids (straight and spiraled), corals, brachiopods, crinoids, and sponges show that the limestone was deposited on the floor of a shallow sea in the Mississippian period (360-330 million years ago).

Mile 23.3: 23 Mile Rapid (4-6)

Mile 24.2: 24 Mile Rapid (6-8)

Mile 24.5: 24¹/2 Mile Rapid (5-6)

Mile 24.9: 25 Mile Rapid (5-7)
It's also known as Hansbrough-Richards Rapid in memory of two members of the trouble-plagued Stanton-Brown railroad survey expedition of 1889. They drowned when their boat capsized just after they lined it through the rapid.

Mile 25.3: Cave Springs Rapid (5-6)

Mile 26.6: Tiger Wash Rapid (4-5)
Tiger Wash is on the left.

Mile 29.2: Silver Grotto and Shinumo Wash
In warm weather, boaters clamber up into the narrow canyon of lower Shinumo Wash on the left and swim several icy pools to Silver Grotto. You can also see Silver Grotto from above by pulling over on the left at Mile 30.1 and hiking back upstream on the Fence Fault Route. Shinumo Altar rises from the south side of Shinumo Wash; the name comes from the Paiute word for the former inhabitants (ancestral pueblo people) of the area.

Mile 30: Redwall Dam Site
This spot is remarkable for what you *don't* see. Recognized as one of a series of potential dam sites by government surveys in the 1920s, it was later proposed by the Bureau of Reclamation as the site for a dam that would have raised the water 222 feet in a lake stretching nearly to Lees Ferry.

Mile 31.6: South Canyon
South Canyon, on the right, provides hikers a route from the rim.

Mile 31.8: Stanton's Cave
High up (150 feet) and to the right in the Redwall

you'll see a large cave entrance. The name honors Robert B. Stanton, chief engineer of the 1889 and 1890 Brown-Stanton railroad expeditions, who used the cave to store gear when the demoralized first expedition walked out South Canyon. Archaeologists value the cave for the split-twig figurines left behind thousands of years ago and for more recent pottery and granaries left by the ancestral pueblo people. The Park Service has closed it to the public.

Mile 31.9: Vasey's Paradise
Springs transform the right shore into a beautiful oasis of flowers, maidenhair fern, mosses, and poison ivy. The Park Service recommends that visitors don't enter the vegetated area because of endangered Kanab ambersnails, found only here and at one spot in southern Utah. George W. Vasey worked as a botanist with Major Powell on an 1868 expedition to what's now the state of Colorado.

Mile 33: Redwall Cavern
Major Powell thought that this giant alcove on the left could serve as a theater seating 50,000 people, but he allowed that "at high water the floor is covered with a raging flood." Today it's a popular stop, though camping isn't permitted.

Mile 34.8: Nautiloid Canyon
On the left stop to see large fossils of chambered shells, from an animal related to squid, embedded in the floor of the canyon.

Mile 35: Muav Limestone
and The Bridge of Sighs
The contact between the Redwall and the underlying Muav (river level) can be difficult to see; at some places a small slope or a bench marks the line. The Muav was deposited in a sea about 535 million years ago during the Cambrian period and has very few fossils. The Bridge of Sighs, a natural arch, appears high on the right.

Mile 43: Point Hansbrough and Anasazi Bridge
A log bridge high on the right survives from a prehistoric trail of ancestral pueblo people. The river begins a big loop to the right around the point. The second Stanton expedition found the skeleton of Peter Hansbrough here six months after he had drowned at 25 Mile Rapid.

Redwall Cavern

Mile 43.7: President Harding Rapid
A U.S. Geological Survey expedition, led by Claude Birdseye, came through in 1923 to make the first detailed maps of the Canyon and to survey potential dam sites. The expedition carried the first radio receiver into the Canyon. Having heard earlier on the radio of the president's death, the group stopped here for a day in observance of the president's funeral. Eminence Break Trail on the left beside the rapid climbs out to the rim; you'll enjoy great panoramas on the way up. You can reach the upper trailhead (difficult to find) by road (difficult to navigate); see **Tatahatso Point** in Western Navajo Country.

Mile 46.6: Triple Alcoves
The alcoves appear on the right.

Mile 47: Saddle Canyon
Hike up this canyon on the right one mile, past redbud trees flowering in the spring in the shady recesses of the canyon, to pools and a little waterfall.

Mile 50: Bright Angel Shale
This purple and green shale formed in the sea during the Cambrian period about 550 million years ago.

Mile 51.9: Little Nankoweap Creek
Like many tributaries, this canyon on the right becomes prettier as you head upstream; cliffs eventually block the way. Redbud trees and pools add to the beauty.

Mile 52.2: Nankoweap Area
Nankoweap Rapid (3) offers a long ride, but hiking in the area draws more attention. The Nankoweap and Little Nankoweap form a large delta with many places to camp and explore. A short, steep hike leads to an impressive row of granaries constructed by ancestral pueblo people. In the period between 900 and 1150, they built many structures on the section of river between here and Unkar Delta (Mile 72.5). Hikers could spend days exploring Nankoweap Canyon and its tributaries or even hike out to the North Rim on the Nankoweap Trail. Most river runners prefer shorter explorations in the area. A good loop day-trip begins by hiking up the Nankoweap about two miles, then turning south up the first major draw and going down the other side to Kwagunt Creek, and then following Kwagunt back to the river, where you could either meet the other boaters in your party or hike up the Colorado back to Nankoweap. Bring plenty of water and a sun hat for this spring or autumn trek.

Mile 56: Kwagunt Rapid (6)
You can explore Kwagunt Creek on the right on foot.

Mile 60: Tapeats Sandstone
The brown, medium- to coarse-grained sandstone formed about 570 million years ago during the Cambrian period.

Mile 61.4: Little Colorado River
This major tributary of the Colorado flows from the left in two colors. During spring snowmelt or summer storms in the mountains of eastern Arizona, the Little Colorado carries a heavy load of brown silt. In dry periods, the only flow comes from mineral-laden Blue Spring, 12.5 miles upstream. The water becomes a beautiful aqua-

ENDANGERED FISH OF THE COLORADO RIVER

Colorado squawfish (Ptychocheilus lucius)
Native only to the Colorado and its tributaries, this species is the largest minnow in North America. It has been reported as weighing up to 100 pounds and measuring six feet long. Loss of habitat due to dam construction has greatly curtailed its size and range. Fisherman often confuse the smaller more common roundtail chub (Gila robusta) with the Colorado squawfish; the chub is distinguished by a smaller mouth extending back only to the front of the eye.

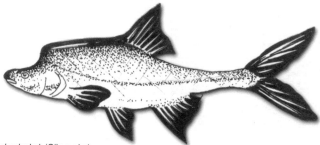

humpback chub (Gila cypha)
Scientists first described this fish only in 1946 and know little about its life. The small fish usually weighs in under two pounds and under 13 inches. Today the humpback chub hangs on the verge of extinction; it has retreated to a few small areas of the Colorado River where the water still runs warm, muddy, and swift. The bonytail chub (Gila robusta elegans) has a similar size and shape, but without a hump; its numbers are also rapidly declining.

humpback or razorback sucker (Xyrauchen texanus)
This large sucker grows to weights of 10-16 pounds and lengths of about three feet. Its numbers have been slowly decreasing, especially above the Grand Canyon. They require warm, fast-flowing water to reproduce. Mating is done as a bizarre ritual in the spring. When the female has selected a suitable spawning site, two male fish press against the sides of her body. The female begins shake her body until the eggs and spermatozoa are expelled simultaneously. One female can spawn three times, but she uses a different pair of males each time.

marine because of salts and calcium carbonate; it's not drinkable. Endangered fish hang out near the confluence, so no fishing or camping is permitted here.

You can hike up the Little Colorado nearly a mile to see Ben Beamer's stone-slab cabin on the south bank. Beamer came here in 1889 to prospect and do a bit of farming; he likely "borrowed" stones from ruins left by ancestral pueblo people to build his cabin. Beamer's Trail still connects the confluence with Tanner Rapid downstream and the Tanner Trail to the South Rim.

Back on the Colorado River, you'll spot some salt deposits along the left bank in the next three miles. Hopi Indians once made long pilgrimages from their villages to collect this salt. The salt mines remain sacred to the Hopi; hence, Park Service rangers prohibit others from visiting them. Instead, wait until Mile 119.8, where you can stop and take a close look at a salt deposit.

Mile 63.4: The Great Unconformity
About 250 million years have been lost from the geologic record at this unconformity between the Tapeats sandstone above and the Unkar Group of the Precambrian period below. The Unkar contains five formations of about 1,250 to 825 million years ago. From the oldest (lowermost), they are the Bass limestone, Hakatai shale, Shinumo quartzite, Dox sandstone, and the Cardenas Lavas. You'll also hear the term "Grand Canyon Supergroup," which includes the Unkar Group and three formations of roughly the same time range that occur in the Colorado River's tributaries, but not at river level: Nankoweap Formation (Nankoweap and Basalt Canyons); Chuar Group (Nankoweap, Carbon, and Lava Canyons); and Sixtymile Formation (Nankoweap Butte and upper Sixtymile Canyon). Faults have tilted these formations and caused large offsets between one side of the Canyon and the other.

Mile 64.7: Carbon Creek
For a look at the complex geology in this part of the Canyon, you can hike up Carbon Creek (on the right), cut south over a pass, and then descend Lava Canyon to the river, where you should arrange to be picked up. The pass has especially fine views of the Unkar Group and lava flows. On the way down Lava Canyon, look

for a trail to the left that passes a dry fall.

Mile 65.6: Lava Canyon (Chuar) Rapid (3-5)
Lava Canyon is on the right, Palisades Creek on the left. A park naturalist found a moonshine still in Lava Canyon in 1928, but you'd be safer to carry your own liquid refreshment on hikes here.

Mile 68.5: Tanner Canyon
Hikers descend from the South Rim on the Tanner Trail to the beach and the small rapid at the river. The Beamer Trail goes upstream to the Little Colorado. The Escalante Route winds downstream to connect with the Tonto and New Hance (Red Canyon) Trails.

Mile 71: Cardenas Creek
You can scramble south up the ridge for a wonderful panorama of the Canyon and a look at a stone structure left by ancestral pueblo people; it may have been a watchtower. Spanish explorer García López de Cárdenas arrived on the South Rim in 1540 as the first white man to see the Grand Canyon; his group tried but failed to reach the river.

Mile 72.5: Unkar Rapid (6-7)
Ancestral pueblo people once farmed the Unkar delta on the right. You can stop to look at foundations of their pueblo village.

Mile 75.5: Nevills Rapid (6)
Norm Nevills led the first commercial river trip through the Grand Canyon in 1938.

Mile 76.8: Hance Rapid (8-10)
Rock gardens in the river present a real challenge, especially to the hard-shelled dories. Red Canyon on the left is the start of the long Tonto Trail that heads downstream and the Hance (Red Canyon) Trail that climbs to the South Rim. John Hance arrived at the Grand Canyon in 1883, built the first lodge on the South Rim two years later, made trails, did some mining, and guided tourists. All the while he entertained his tour guests with amazing yarns, such as the time the Canyon filled with clouds and he just strapped on his snowshoes and walked across. On stretches where trails parallel the river, the difference in time between foot and boat travel is amazing. A lazy day on the river with just an

"Lily dipping,"
or effortless paddling,
is a sure recipe for
disaster once rafters
hit the rapids.

oar-powered boat can cover as much distance as several hard days on the trail.

Mile 77: Upper Granite Gorge
Another Great Unconformity marks the boundary between the Unkar Group and rocks even more ancient, perhaps 1.7 billion years old in the Lower Precambrian period. Unimaginable extremes of time, pressure, and heat have folded, twisted, and crystallized these rocks, which probably once lay underneath a mountain range. Despite the gorge's name, you'll find mostly gneiss (a coarse-grained metamorphic rock with bands of visibly different minerals) and schist (a dark, easily split metamorphic rock with closely spaced bands of mica). Pink pegmatite (a coarse-grained igneous rock) was injected into these rocks. You'll see milky quartz too. The Upper Granite Gorge extends about 48 miles downstream. The Canyon's character changes dramatically as the dark walls close in, constrict the river, and speed up the water's flow.

Mile 78.7: Sockdolager Rapid (8-9)
Major Powell's second expedition used a slang word meaning "knockout blow" for this one. Powell's men weren't able to portage their frail craft here, so they ran the rapid with the loud roar of the waves reverberating off the Canyon walls.

Mile 81.5: Grapevine Rapid (8)
Grapevine Creek comes in from the left, Vishnu Creek from the right. Many of the rock "temples" and canyons below the North Rim bear names of

Eastern gods and philosophers. The Hindu god Vishnu preserves the world. Geologist Clarence Dutton started the "heroic nomenclature" for Grand Canyon features.

Mile 83.5: 83 Mile Rapid (3-5)

Mile 84: Clear Creek Canyon
You wouldn't think such a small stream and canyon could drain a large area of the North Rim. It's worth making the short hike of about half a mile up to a small waterfall. You could also climb around the waterfall and continue far upstream. Clear Creek Trail connects the creek with the North Kaibab Trail near Phantom Ranch.

Mile 84.6: Zoroaster Rapid (5-8)
Zoroaster Creek on the right descends from the south side of Zoroaster Temple. About 700 B.C., the Persian philosopher Zoroaster founded what became a major religion of that region.

Mile 85: 85 Mile Rapid (2-6)

Mile 87.5: Kaibab Bridge
The South Kaibab Trail from the South Rim crosses the river here on its way to Phantom Ranch after a very scenic descent of 6.8 miles to Bright Angel Camp via Cedar Ridge. The bridge warns you that a touch of civilization lies just ahead. River trips put in at the beach on the right past the bridge to exchange passengers leaving or joining at this point. You can wander over to Phantom Ranch to use a telephone, mail

your postcards via mule train, buy snacks or souvenirs at the store, or ogle at a flush toilet, which you won't have seen for days.

If you have time for a hike, try part of the North Kaibab or climb the Clear Creek Trail for views. Or leave the crowds and head up Phantom Creek to lush greenery and small waterfalls; walk about one mile up the North Kaibab Trail until you see the creek on the other side of Bright Angel Creek, which you'll have to ford.

Mile 87.8: Bright Angel Rapid
and Bright Angel Bridge
Major Powell named the swift and clear-flowing Bright Angel Creek to honor the forces of good, after earlier naming the muddy Dirty Devil River upstream in Utah. Much of the Bright Angel's flow comes from Roaring Springs, which blasts out of caves in the Redwall limestone below the North Rim. Hikers can reach the North Rim on the 14.2-mile North Kaibab Trail.

Mile 89: Pipe Springs Rapid (4-5)
The Bright Angel Trail turns up Pipe Creek Canyon on its well-graded, 7.8-mile-long ascent to the South Rim.

Mile 90.2: Horn Creek Rapid (8-10)
Horn Creek comes in on the left. Two boulders near midstream give the rapid its name.

Mile 93.5: Granite Rapid (9)
Monument Creek on the left offers an easy walk up to the Tonto Trail.

Mile 95: Hermit Rapid (8-9)
Hermit Creek on the left provides a scenic walk up the Tonto Trail. Louis Boucher, the Hermit, mined copper and guided tourists in the area during his stay from 1891 to 1912. He wore a white beard, rode a white mule, and told only "white lies."

Mile 96.8: Boucher Rapid (3-5)
The route along Boucher Creek on the left is an easy walk to the Tonto and Boucher Trails.

Mile 98.2: Crystal Rapid (10)
This fierce rapid has weakened the knees of many a river-runner scouting it from the shore. Places in the Grand Canyon may stay nearly unchanged for more than a century, only to be turned topsy-turvy by a single storm. That happened here in 1966, when a massive flood tore through Crystal Creek (on the right), washing many huge boulders into the Colorado and forcing the river into the left wall. Now boaters must pick out a route that stays clear of the rocks, the wall, and giant, boat-flipping holes. If you're camping near here, Crystal Creek offers a pleasant stroll up its relatively open canyon.

Mile 99.2: Tuna Creek Rapid (6)

Mile 101.3: Sapphire Rapid (7)
One of a series of rapids here called "The Jewels." Sapphire Canyon is on the left.

Mile 102: Turquoise Rapid (3-6)
Turquoise Canyon is on the left.

*the boat-flipping
Crystal Rapid*

Shinumo Creek

Mile 103.9: 104 Mile Rapid (5-7)

Mile 104.6: Ruby Rapid (6-7)
Ruby Canyon is on the left.

Mile 106: Serpentine Rapid (6-8)
Serpentine Canyon is on the left. Serpentine (an ornamental stone) and asbestos (sought by Hance, Bass, and other prospectors) occur in the Canyon where molten volcanic rock subjected the Bass limestone to intense heat.

Mile 107.8: Bass Rapid (3-6)
Bass Canyon on the left and the South Bass Trail, just upstream of the rapid, provide access to the Tonto Trail and South Rim. William Bass arrived in the 1880s, did some prospecting, raised a family, and ran a tourist operation until he left the area in 1923. He built tourist camps and constructed trails to both South and North Rims. Boats, and in 1908 a cableway with a cage big enough for horses, connected his trails. The Park Service cut the cable in 1968, so there's no crossing today. A metal boat, the *Ross Wheeler,* lies on the left bank just above the rapid, where it was abandoned about 1914.

Mile 108.2: Beach and
Trailhead for Bass's Camp
From this popular campsite on the right, a trail climbs high over a ridge (blazing with yellow brittlebush in spring), drops to Shinumo Creek, and then winds upstream to Bass's Camp. You'll discover relics of his camp and small farm along the swift, sparkling creek. Cottonwood trees shade the banks. Be sure to carry lots of water and a sun hat for this hike of two miles each way. The North Bass Trail continues another 12 miles upcanyon to the pine-forested North Rim.

Mile 108.7: Shinumo Rapid
Boats can pull in at lower Shinumo Creek on the right so that you can take a short walk to a pool and waterfall. The waterfall blocks hikers from continuing upstream to Bass's Camp.

Mile 112.2: Waltenberg Rapid (6-9)
John Waltenberg worked with William Bass in developing copper and asbestos mines in the area during the early 20th century.

Mile 112.6: 112$^1/_2$ Mile Rapid (1-6)

Mile 113.1: Rancid Tuna Rapid (6)
One can only assume that this rapid was named by an early boating expedition that discovered the terrible truth about its food situation here.

Mile 114.4: Garnet Canyon
The Tonto Trail ends its 92-mile meandering at this canyon on the left.

Mile 116.5: Elves Chasm
Royal Arch Creek creates this beauty spot on the left with a waterfall, greenery and flowers, and extensive travertine deposits.

Mile 116.9: Stephen Aisle

This straight section of Canyon runs about two miles. The Upper Granite Gorge ends in this section at a fault where the river cuts into Tapeats sandstone. From here until the start of the Middle Granite Gorge at Mile 126.6, you'll be seeing stretches of Tapeats sandstone, Precambrian gneiss, and Bright Angel shale.

Mile 119.8: Salt Deposits

Look on the right for alcoves filled with salty stalactites, stalagmites, and columns. It's possible to stop here or walk back from the Blacktail Canyon camp 0.3 mile farther.

Mile 120.1: Blacktail Canyon and Conquistador Aisle

Blacktail Canyon on the right offers a short hike into Tapeats sandstone narrows. Conquistador Aisle, another two-mile straight section of canyon, lies downstream.

Mile 121.7: 122 Mile Rapid (4-6) and Bright Angel Shale

Mile 122.8: Forster Rapid (6)

Forster Canyon is on the left.

Mile 125: Fossil Rapid (6-7)

Fossil Canyon is on the left.

Mile 126.6: Middle Granite Gorge

Schist and quartzite make up most of the low walls of this narrow, 3.9-mile gorge. Sheetlike dikes of igneous pegmatite (coarse-grained rock) and amphibolite (dark rock composed mostly of the mineral hornblende) have cut into the older rocks. You'll see salt deposits on the left.

Mile 129: Specter Rapid (5-8)

Specter Chasm is on the left.

Mile 130.5: Bedrock Rapid (8) and Unkar Group

Bedrock Canyon and the "Doll's House" are on the right. Middle Granite Gorge ends just below, where the river cuts into the Unkar Group. Bass limestone, with its igneous intrusions, predominates over the next five miles.

Mile 131.7: Deubendorff Rapid (7-9), Galloway Canyon, and Stone Creek

Galloway Canyon, on the right just above the rapid, and Stone Creek, on the right just below, invite exploration. Galloway is dry, but Stone Creek features pools, waterfalls, greenery, flowers, and a magical narrows. Stone Creek makes a great spot for a layover day. The whole walk up offers pretty scenery, so just tramp as far as the spirit moves you. Look for a bypass trail on your right around the first high waterfall about one mile up; another mile of climbing will take you to the short narrows that end in a waterfall.

In 1909, Julius Stone earned the distinction of being the first to boat through the Grand Canyon for the fun of it. A president of a gold-dredging company, he had met pioneering boatman Nathaniel Galloway in Glen Canyon and hired him to supervise construction of four wooden, flat-bottomed boats. Galloway had devised not only superior riverboat designs but also a better way of rowing them in the rapids. He found that it made no sense to row blindly into the dangerous rapids when one could simply turn the boat around, face the rapids, and pull upstream to give more time and control to make a safe descent. The new boats, $16^1/2$ feet long and four feet wide, featured sealed compartments and lightweight construction. Stone and four companions, including Galloway and helper Seymour Deubendorff, pushed off from Green River, Wyoming, and reached Needles, California, just over two months later. Galloway became the first to make two complete transits of the canyons, and his rowing technique endures today. Deubendorff capsized here, much to his embarrassment at the time.

Mile 133.7: Tapeats Rapid (5-8), Tapeats Creek, and Thunder River

Two sets of voluminous springs feed crystal-clear Tapeats Creek, on the right just above the rapid. Thunder Spring rates as one of the Grand Canyon's top hiking destinations—you're not likely to be disappointed! Trails run up both sides of Tapeats Creek from the Colorado. In spring, when the creek can be too high and swift to ford easily, it's best to get off the boats on the down-river side of the creek. In 2.5 miles you'll reach Thunder River, which suffers the indignity of both being short and serving as a tributary to a creek.

A trail climbs steeply half a mile to good vantage points of Thunder Spring as it blasts out of a cave system in the Muav limestone. Large Fremont cottonwood trees provide shade. In spring or autumn, you can continue 1.5 miles up the trail past Thunder Spring and down into the gently sloping Surprise Valley, renowned for its ovenlike heat in summer. A cairn marks the junction of the Thunder River Trail to the North Rim, but continue west 1.5 miles on the Deer Creek Trail, which drops to Deer Creek (Dutton) Spring, another cave system gushing a waterfall. You can hike up to the falls for a closer look or take the path that goes higher and behind the falls. The creekside trail winds down one mile past the remarkable Tapeats narrows, then drops to the base of Deer Creek Falls at the river. Watch out for poison ivy here. If it's hot or you can't arrange to be met by boats, Deer Creek makes a great stop on its own.

Mile 134.7: 135 Mile Rapid (5) (Helicopter Eddy)

Mile 135.4: Granite Narrows
The Colorado constricts to just 76 feet in the Granite Narrows, its smallest width in the Grand Canyon.

Mile 136.2: Deer Creek Falls
See the Mile 133.7: Tapeats Creek/Thunder River entry at above for hiking details on the Deer Creek Trail (on the right).

Mile 136.6: Unconformable Contact of Precambrian rocks and overlying Tapeats Sandstone
Tapeats predominates for the next 3.5 miles; you'll also see some Precambrian quartzite and spring-deposited travertine.

Mile 137.7: 137 1/2 Mile (Doris) Rapid (5-7)
Doris, wife of Norm Nevills, took a swim here after getting washed overboard on one of the early commercial river trips in 1940.

Mile 139: Fishtail Rapid (5-7)
Fishtail Canyon is on the right.

Mile 140.1: Conformable Contact (no gap in the geologic record) between the underlying Tapeats Sandstone and Bright Angel Shale
The river cuts through Bright Angel shale for the next seven miles.

Mile 143.5: Kanab Rapid and Kanab Canyon
A major canyon system with many tributaries of its own, Kanab Creek on the right extends far north into Utah past the town of Kanab to the Paunsaugunt Plateau, 100 miles from the Grand Canyon. Kanab means "willows" in Paiute. Major Powell ended his second river expedition here in 1872 and walked out Kanab Canyon. Whispering Falls makes a good hiking destination; walk up about four miles from the river and turn right into the first tributary.

Mile 145.6: Olo Canyon
The overhanging cliff to the left with a waterfall doesn't look promising for hikers, but some groups will send a rock climber on a bypass just downriver to put in a cable ladder at the pour-off. Two other steep sections a little farther upstream can be rigged with ropes to aid hikers. The climb is worthwhile to view the water-sculpted canyon full of pools. Upstream, the canyon widens a bit, and vegetation finds soil to take root. Olo is Havasupai for "little horse."

climbing a ladder at the mouth of Olo Canyon

climbing lower narrows of Matkatamiba Canyon

Mile 147.1: Conformable Contact between the
Bright Angel Shale and overlying Muav Limestone
The river flows through the Muav for the next
18.6 miles.

Mile 147.9: Matkatamiba Canyon
"Matkat" on the left presents a beautiful show
of rock sculpture and pools similar to those in
Olo Canyon. Agile hikers should be able to make
it up Matkat without ropes. As in Olo, you can
hike a long way in, limited mainly by the time
you have. Matkatamiba is an Indian family name.

Mile 149.7: Upset Rapid (6-9)
and 150 Mile Canyon
The 1923 Birdseye (U.S. Geological Survey)
River Expedition had made it this far when the
head boatman, Emery Kolb, performed the
group's first flip; 150 Mile Canyon is on the right.

Mile 156.8: Havasu Canyon
The turquoise-blue waters and Shangri-La reputation of this canyon on the left put it at the top
of many river runners' favorite hikes. Trees,
grass, and flowers fill the canyon floor. Havasupai Indians live in their secluded Supai village
about nine miles upcanyon; *havasu* means "blue
water" and *pai* means "people." Everyone wants
to visit Havasu Canyon, yet there's no beach to
land boats. So boaters have to tie up in the
canyon mouth—an amazingly complex network
of interconnected ropes at times.

The trail upstream crosses the creek many
times, but has little elevation gain to Beaver
Falls, four miles away, the most popular destination for river runners. Here you can swim in
large pools enclosed by travertine terraces. Fleet-
of-foot hikers can continue two more miles to
see 196-foot Mooney Falls, the most impressive in Havasu Canyon. No camping is allowed
in the lower canyon, so boaters are limited to
day-trips. For a longer visit, it's best to hike in
from the top at another time to visit Supai Village and the other waterfalls; see the **Havasupai
Indian Reservation** section later in this book.

Mile 165.7: Contact of Muav Limestone
and the underlying Bright Angel Shale
The river flows through Bright Angel shale for
the next 10.2 miles.

Mile 166.5: National Canyon
The canyon on the left, sometimes with a small
stream, is an easy one-mile walk; after that point
you'll need a rope.

Mile 168: Fern Glen Rapid (3)
and Fern Glen Canyon
A worthwhile hike of about half a mile through the
canyon on the right takes you to seeps that support expanses of maidenhair fern.

Mile 175.9: Contact of Bright Angel Shale
and the underlying Tapeats
The river flows through Tapeats for the next 3.2
miles.

Mile 178: Vulcan's Anvil
The Anvil, a neck of an extinct volcano, rises in
the middle of the river. The Anvil marks the beginning of a long stretch of volcanic features in
the Grand Canyon. A series of eruptions took
place over the last million years, burying the
countryside under lava and cinders and even

filling the Grand Canyon with massive lava dams. Much of the basaltic lava formed columnar jointing. The fractures developed as the basalt cooled; cooler spots commonly formed three radial fracture planes (120 degrees apart) that grew outward and intersected other fracture planes to create the columnar joints—usually hexagons. The faster the basalt cooled, the more fractures occurred, so you'll sometimes see cross-sections of fanlike columns near the surface branching out from larger "trunks" below.

Toroweap Overlook stands high above on the North Rim with some classic Canyon views. Lava Falls Route connects the river and the Toroweap area, though it's probably best to come by road at another time to explore this region; see **Toroweap** earlier in this book.

Mile 179.1: Crossing the Toroweap Fault
The downstream side of the fault has dropped 580 feet, so you go from Tapeats sandstone to the younger Muav limestone without seeing the intervening Bright Angel shale; look for the fault on the left (the right side is covered by lava). From here to the head of the Lower Granite Gorge at Mile 215.1, you'll be in one of these three formations or some Precambrian rocks at river level.

Mile 179.3: Lava Falls Rapid (10)
Boaters may discuss whether Crystal or Lava Falls is the more difficult, but there's no denying that both are BIG and receive lots of respect. After a lengthy scout of the rapid from shore, you're in the boats and into the wild waves for an exhilarating ride.

Mile 183: Plugged Channel
An old river channel on the right is filled with lava.

Mile 187: Whitmore Wash
When lava filled the mouth of Whitmore Wash on the right, the stream cut a new channel farther downriver. You can easily hike about a half mile up this new canyon. Whitmore Trail climbs from river to rim in only three-quarters of a mile—the shortest access trail within Grand Canyon National Park—but you're still a very long and bumpy road from the nearest town. Some river parties do a passenger exchange here, not by trail, but by helicopter using a pad on Hualapai Indian land across the river.

The helicopter flies to the North Rim's Bar 10 guest ranch, where a day of activities is usually included; small planes then take departing guests to Las Vegas or other destinations.

Mile 205.5: 205 Mile (Kolb) Rapid (7-8)
205 Mile Creek is on the left.

Mile 208.5: Granite Park
The large beach on the left makes an attractive campsite. Nearby canyons invite exploration. The river splits around a large, low island just downstream.

Mile 212.2: Little Bastard Rapid (1-7)

Mile 214.3: ShadyLedges
(below 214 Mile Creek)
The lower Canyon can get mighty hot even in spring and autumn. These ledges on the right provide a shady lunch spot.

Mile 215.1: Entering Lower Granite Gorge
The Tapeats sandstone makes an unconformable contact with the underlying Precambrian granite.

Mile 217.4: 217 Mile Rapid (6-7)
217 Mile Canyon is on the left.

Mile 225.6: Diamond Creek Rapid (4)
and Diamond Creek
The name comes from the distinctive 3,512-foot peak that you see long before reaching the creek; the summit is only 400 feet higher in elevation than Lees Ferry. This left side of the Colorado River belongs to the Hualapai Indians, who maintain a 21-mile gravel road from here to Peach Springs on old Route 66.

If you were to stay on the Colorado, there's only one day's river running remaining, and then a long stretch of lake to Pearce Ferry, the next road access. Still, this last section offers great beauty, well worth seeing if you can take the time to do it. You can also start river trips here; contact the Hualapai River Runner's office in Peach Springs.

Mile 229: Travertine Rapid (3)
and Travertine Canyon
A bit of steep scrambling (a rope is handy) up some travertine on the left will take you into a large cavelike room with a refreshing waterfall.

Mile 230.6: Travertine Falls
A waterfall near the river splashes thousands of sparkling drops off large travertine deposits on the left.

Mile 230.8: 231 Mile Rapid (4-7)

Mile 232.2: 232 Mile Rapid (4-7)

Mile 233.5: 234 Mile Rapid (4-6)

Mile 235.3: Bridge Canyon Rapid (3-6)
Bridge Canyon, with a spring and a natural bridge, is on the left.

Mile 236: Gneiss Canyon Rapid (3-6)
Gneiss Canyon is on the left.

Mile 237.2: 237 Mile Rapid (3-6)

Mile 239.6: Separation Canyon
On August 28, 1869, during Major Powell's first river expedition, the hardships of the unknown, the rapids, and dwindling food supplies brought three of the crew to the breaking point; they decided to hike out here through this canyon on the right. Rapids roared just downstream, and what lay beyond, Powell and the men could only guess. When they separated here, each group assumed the other to be embracing the greater danger. Powell and his remaining party safely negotiated the last rapids and left the Grand Canyon at noon on the following day. The three who climbed out never made it home. Powell later personally investigated and concluded that the men met their deaths at the hands of Shivwits Indians.

Today there's not much more than riffles where rapids once terrified Powell's men. You're on Lake Mead now, though the Colorado still provides a current and the Canyon still reveals magnificent views. Most groups start motoring out or arrange to be met by motorboats somewhere below Separation, even if they've been rowing so far.

Mile 259.3: End of the Lower Granite Gorge
Exposures of Tapeats sandstone and Bright Angel shale appear at lake level, though they're likely to be covered by silt. In pre-dam days, intermittent exposures of Precambrian rocks reportedly extended all the way to the end of the Grand Canyon.

Mile 266.3: Bat Cave and Guano Point
U.S. Guano sank a lot of money to develop a deposit of bat guano (dung used as fertilizer) in a cave during the late 1950s. Cables suspended from the towers once carried the guano from Bat Cave high on the north side across the Canyon to Guano Point high on the Hualapai Plateau. The Park Service discourages visits to the cave because it disturbs the bats. You can visit Guano Point by road or air for spectacular views and a close look at one of the towers; see **Grand Canyon West** in the Hualapai Indian Reservation section below.

Mile 277.7: Grand Wash Fault
and End of the Grand Canyon
The Canyon abruptly ends at Grand Wash Fault because rock layers on the west side have dropped several thousand feet—the Colorado never had a chance to carve a canyon in them. You're now on the vast expanse of water in Lake Mead National Recreation Area.

Mile 280: Pearce Ferry
Takeout and the road home.

THE EXPLORATION OF THE COLORADO RIVER AND ITS CANYONS

WESTERN GRAND CANYON AND THE ARIZONA STRIP
HAVASUPAI AND HUALAPAI INDIAN RESERVATIONS

VISITING HAVASU CANYON

The towering cliffs of Havasu Canyon enclose a land of blue-green waters, breathtaking waterfalls, and lush vegetation. Havasu Creek rushes through the canyon past the Indian village of Supai before beginning its wild cascade down to the Colorado River. The canyon and its creek, about 35 air miles northwest of Grand Canyon Village, belong to the Havasupai Indians (*havasu* means "blue water," and *pai* means "people").

Havasupai lived here long before the first white people arrived. The tribe farmed the fertile canyon floor each summer, then moved to the plateau after harvest to gather abundant wild foods and firewood during winter. Spanish missionary Francisco Tomás Garcés visited the Havasupai in 1776 and thought them a peaceful and industrious tribe. However, as was often the case, white settlers grabbed their tribal lands over the following years. The Havasupai protested, and the tribe's winter homelands were finally returned in 1975. The Havasupai Reservation now spans 188,077 acres and houses 500-600 tribal members, most of whom live in Supai village.

Getting There

The tribe wisely decided against allowing road construction in the canyon, so most residents and tourists enter by mule, horse, or on foot. Helicopters provide another option, though the noisy machines seem out of place here.

The eight-mile trail from Hualapai Hilltop to Supai is the usual way in. From Seligman on I-40, take AZ 66 northwest for 28 miles (between Mileposts 110 and 111), then turn right and go 63 miles on signed Indian 18, paved all the way to Hualapai Hilltop. If coming from the west, take AZ 66 northeast out of Kingman for 60 miles, then turn left and drive the 63 miles. Fill up with gas before leaving AZ 66, as no water, supplies, or stores are available after the turnoff. The road to Hualapai Hilltop climbs into forests of ponderosa pine that give way to pinyon and juniper, then desert grasslands close to the rim. Parking areas and stables mark road's end. Various dirt-road shortcuts to Hualapai Hilltop suffer from poor signing and rough surfaces.

Hiking In
You *must* obtain reservations to camp or to stay in the lodge. From Hualapai Hilltop (elev. 5,200 feet), the trail descends at a moderate grade into Hualapai Canyon for the first 1.5 miles, then lev-

els off slightly for the remaining 6.5 miles to Supai village (elev. 3,200 feet). About 1.5 miles before the village, the trail joins the sparkling waters of Havasu Canyon. Avoid the heat of the day in summer when temperatures soar past 100° F, and always carry drinking water. All visitors must pay a $15 entrance fee ($12 in winter) on arrival at Supai. The tribe asks you to leave pets, alcohol, and firearms at home. To preserve the canyon floor, no fires or charcoal are allowed, so campers need to bring stoves if planning to cook.

Riding In
If you'd rather ride than walk, local families will take you and your gear on horses or mules from the parking lot at Hualapai Hilltop to Supai ($55 one way or $80 roundtrip) or all the way to the campground ($55 each way), 2.75 miles farther. One animal can carry about four backpacks. Try to get an early start from Hualapai Hilltop, especially in the warmer months; a small surcharge is added for departures after 9 a.m. A sightseeing ride from Supai to the falls and back can be arranged too. You must make reservations at least six weeks in advance and pay a 50% deposit to Havasupai Tourist Enterprise, Box 160, Supai, AZ 86435, tel. (520) 448-2141. Also call two days before arrival to make sure your animal is available. Visitors may also bring their own horses if they take along feed and pay a $15 trail fee.

Sights
The famous waterfalls of the canyon begin 1.5 miles downstream from Supai. Three cascades plunge over cliffs of Redwall Limestone in a space of just two miles.

You'll first come to 75-foot-high **Navajo Falls,** featuring several widely spaced branches. It's named after a 19th-century Havasupai tribal chief kidnapped by Navajo Indians as an infant and raised as a Navajo. Not until he grew to manhood did he learn of his true origin and return to the Havasupai.

A bit farther, spectacular **Havasu Falls** drops 100 feet into a beautiful turquoise-colored pool rimmed by travertine deposits. Clear, inviting waters make this a perfect spot for swimming or picnicking.

Mooney Falls, most awe-inspiring of all, plummets 196 feet into a colorful pool one mile beyond Havasu Falls. The Havasupai named this

---

WESTERN GRAND CANYON AND ARIZONA STRIP HIGHLIGHTS

Havasu Canyon: Waterfalls and travertine pools in this beautiful canyon create a "Shangri-La" setting for an Indian village.

Diamond Creek: You can drive along this creek all the way to the bottom of the Grand Canyon on an unpaved road on the Hualapai Indian Reservation.

Grand Canyon West: Spectacular panoramas take in the lower Grand Canyon from viewpoints few people have visited.

Arizona Strip: Adventurous travelers who love wilderness and solitude seek out the canyons and mountains of this vast area.

Pipe Spring National Monument: You can experience life on a ranch straight out of the Old West.

Paria Canyon and Coyote Buttes: Exquisitely sculptured rock awaits hikers in the Paria Canyon-Vermilion Cliffs Wilderness.

the steep descent to the base of Mooney Falls

most sacred of waterfalls Mother of the Waters. The present name comes from a prospector who died here in 1880. When assistants lowered Daniel Mooney down the cliffs next to the falls, the rope jammed and Mooney hung helpless as the rope frayed and broke. He fell to his death on the rocks below, and 10 months passed before his companions could build a wooden ladder down the falls to reach and bury the travertine-encrusted body. A rough trail descends beside the falls along the same route hacked through the travertine by miners in those months after Mooney's death. You'll pass through two tunnels and then ease down with the aid of chains and iron stakes. At the bottom—as soon as your knees stop shaking—you can enjoy a picnic or swim in the large pool. Miners extracting silver, lead, zinc, and vanadium drilled these holes high on the canyon walls.

Beaver Falls, two miles downstream from Mooney, makes a good day hike from the campground or Supai village. You pass countless inviting travertine pools and small cascades, of which Beaver Falls is the largest. The trail, rough in places, crosses the creek three times, climbs high up a cliff, then descends and crosses a fourth time below Beaver Falls. The trail continues downstream along Havasu Creek four more miles to the Colorado River. Travel fast and light if going to the river, as camping is prohibited below Mooney Falls. Photographing the falls can be a challenge; the best time to snap them in full sunlight is in May, June, and July.

Havasu Campground
Most visitors prefer to camp, listening to the sounds of the canyon and enjoying the brilliant display of stars in the nighttime sky. Havasu Campground begins a quarter mile below Havasu Falls (or 10.75 miles from Hualapai Hilltop) and provides spring water, picnic tables, litter barrels, and pit toilets. It's recommended that campers treat or filter the spring water. Most campers don't realize that the campground extends three-quarters of a mile along Havasu Creek to the brink of Mooney Falls. You'll enjoy more solitude if you walk to the far end. Theft is a serious problem in the campground, so don't leave valuables in your tents or lying around.

To camp, you must have reservations and pay $10 per person per night ($9 in winter). Camping outside the established campground is prohibited. Call (520) 448-2141 or write Havasupai Tourist Enterprise, Box 160, Supai, AZ 86435. Try to make reservations far ahead, especially for holidays, weekends, and all of May, June, and July. The tribe now accepts Visa and MasterCard.

Accommodations and Food
The village of Supai offers the modern **Havasupai Lodge,** featuring rooms with air-conditioning, two double beds, and private bath for $75 s, $80 d (rates drop Nov.-Mar. to $45 s, $50 d). Obtain the required reservations—recommended three months in advance in spring and autumn—from Havasupai Lodge, Supai, AZ 86435, tel. (520) 448-2111. Moderate. A cafe nearby serves breakfast, lunch, and dinner daily 7 a.m.-7 p.m. (8 a.m.-5 p.m. in winter) Try the Indian taco—red beans, beef, cheese, onion, and lettuce on Indian fry bread. Ice cream prices are high, though not so bad when you consider what it takes to bring the frozen dessert to such a remote area. A store across the street, open daily, sells meat, groceries, and cold drinks.

Services

Send your postcard home via pack train—the only such mail service in the country—with a postmark to prove it. The **post office** is open weekdays 9 a.m.-4 p.m., next to the store. A **health clinic** in Supai provides emergency medical care.

VISITING THE HUALAPAI INDIAN RESERVATION

The Hualapai (Pine Tree People) once occupied a large area of northwestern Arizona. In language and culture, the Hualapai are closely related to the Havasupai and Yavapai tribes. Though the Hualapai were friendly to early white visitors, land seizures and murders by the newcomers eventually led to open warfare. Army troops forced the Hualapai south onto the Colorado River Reservation, where many died. Some of the survivors fled back to their traditional lands, part of which later became the 993,000-acre Hualapai Indian Reservation, now housing about half the tribe's 1,500 members. Much of the lower Grand Canyon's South Rim belongs to the Hualapai. Highlights for visitors include the drive into the Grand Canyon to Diamond Creek, Colorado River trips, and spectacular viewpoints in the lowermost Grand Canyon. Respect the privacy of the tribal residents and obtain permits for sightseeing or other activities off the main highway.

Peach Springs

This community, 54 miles northeast of Kingman on AZ 66, is the only town on the reservation. Peach Springs offers neither charm nor anything to see, but it does have lodging and offices where you can obtain required permits for back-road drives and outdoor recreation. Moderately priced **Hualapai Lodge** opened in 1997 with comfortable rooms ($75 d, less in winter) and a restaurant that serves breakfast, lunch, and dinner daily; tel. (520) 769-2230 or (888) 216-0076.

The lodge's front desk sells permits to drive into the Grand Canyon via Diamond Creek Road, detailed below. Grand Canyon West permits, also described below, can be obtained when you arrive there. For other areas, you'll need to contact the tribe's Wildlife office, across the highway from the lodge and several doors to the west; open Mon.-Fri. 8 a.m.-4:30 p.m.; tel. (520) 769-2227. **Hualapai Office of Tourism** has a desk open Mon.-Fri. 9 am.-6 p.m. in the lobby of Hualapai Lodge, where you can arrange one- and two-day rafting trips through the lower Grand Canyon and get information about visits to Grand Canyon West; contact Box 359, Peach Springs, AZ 86434, tel. (888) 255-9550. A grocery store and post office lie across the highway and a few doors west.

Frontier Motel, nine miles southwest in Truxton, has motel rooms ($25 s, $30 d), an RV park ($10 w/hookups; self-contained only), and a smoky cafe; tel. (520) 769-2277. Budget. **Grand**

Farlee Hotel near Diamond Creek, built in 1884 and in ruins when this picture was taken, circa 1914

MOJAVE COUNTY HISTORICAL SOCIETY

Canyon Caverns Inn also offers year-round accommodations ($38 s, $46 d, lower rates in winter), an RV park for self-contained vehicles ($5), and snack bar 13 miles southeast on Route 66; tel. (520) 422-3223. Inexpensive.

Diamond Creek Road

This scenic 21-mile gravel road winds north from Peach Springs to the Colorado River at Diamond Creek, providing the only road access to the river within the Grand Canyon. You'll see fine canyon views, though not as spectacular as those in the developed areas of Grand Canyon National Park. Except for river-runners, who use the road to take out or put in boats, few people visit this spot. Yet the very first organized groups of tourists to the Canyon rode down to Diamond Creek in 1883. A hotel built here and used in 1884-89 was the first in the Grand Canyon.

If the weather has been dry for several days, cars with good ground clearance can traverse the road. Summer rains in July and August may wash out sections and necessitate use of a truck. A camping area near the Colorado River has some picnic tables and an outhouse or two. Hikers can explore Diamond Creek and other canyons; see Stewart Aitchison's *A Naturalist's Guide to Hiking the Grand Canyon* for ideas. Before turning down Diamond Creek Road, you must stop at the Hualapai Lodge front desk to obtain permits; hikers may also need to visit the Wildlife office for a hiking permit. Staff at either place can advise on road conditions. Sightseeing

permits cost $5 per day per person (ages 6 and over). Camping is $8 per day per person and includes the sightseeing fee. Fishing is an extra $8 per day per person. Diamond Creek Road turns off AZ 66 opposite the Hualapai Inn.

River-Running

Hualapai River Runners does motorized-raft trips down the lower Grand Canyon between Diamond Creek and Pearce Ferry on Lake Mead for $221 (one day) or $321 (two days). This is the only company to offer a day-trip within the Grand Canyon. Rates during the March-Oct. season cover food, waterproof bag for personal gear, and transportation from Peach Springs. Contact the office at Box 246, Peach Springs, AZ 86434, tel. (520) 769-2210 or (800) 622-4409; or ask at the Hualapai Office of Tourism in the lobby of Hualapai Lodge, tel. (888) 255-9550.

Grand Canyon West

The Hualapai tribe offers a 4.5-mile tour along the rim of the western Grand Canyon to Guano Point, where visitors enjoy a great panorama of this little-visited part of the Canyon. The Colorado River, placid now that it has met the waters of Lake Mead, lies nearly 4,000 feet directly below. Sheer, terraced cliffs rise even higher on the North Rim. The Canyon remains grand to the end, as you'll see. The Grand Wash Cliffs, which lie just out of sight downstream, mark the western end of both the Grand Canyon and the Colorado Plateau. One of the towers and some of its ma-

view down Grand Canyon from Guano Point

chinery once used in a guano mining operation still stand on the point, and another tower is visible below. When in use, a tram carried guano from a bat cave located across the river; a third tower once at the cave has been dismantled. The tour also makes a short stop at an overlook of Eagle Point, an exceptionally long and narrow neck of land extending out into the Canyon.

Cost for the bus tour and a barbecue lunch at Guano Point runs $27.50 adult, $18 children 3-18; the lunch contains enough vegetables to satisfy most vegetarians too. Prices without lunch are only slightly lower. Tour buses depart frequently during the day year-round; the first is at 10 a.m. and the last about 3:30 p.m.; tours are about an hour and a half long. Tickets, Quartermaster Point permits, and a gift shop are in the terminal building at the Grand Canyon West airport. It's a good idea to call ahead and allow plenty of time, since this is such a long drive out. Contact the Hualapai Office of Tourism for information (see Peach Springs above).

While at Grand Canyon West, you can also enjoy a visit to **Quartermaster Point,** another outstanding panorama of the Grand Canyon farther upstream. A quarter-mile trail from road's end leads down to the best views at the top of sheer cliffs. Quartermaster Canyon lies to your right, and Burnt Canyon is across the river. The long Twin Point stands above Burnt Canyon. Farther upcanyon, Kelly Point extends even farther out from the North Rim. (Both of these can be visited via jeep roads; see the Arizona Strip section for access.) You can also picnic or camp at Quartermaster Point, staying as long as you like; the spot has a few tables and an outhouse. The turnoff is 1.1 miles before the Grand Canyon West Terminal, then 2.3 miles in at the sign to the rim. First, however, obtain a permit from the Grand Canyon West Terminal; day-use costs $10 per person (less if you also take a tour) and camping runs an extra $10 per person. Bring water.

Getting to Grand Canyon West is an adventure too. Allow at least two hours for any of the driving routes. Four roads allow loop possibilities, or you can fly from Las Vegas. Buck and Doe Road stays within the reservation all the way. This dirt road is passable by cars when the weather has been dry, but it can be rough—ask about road conditions before you leave. When it's wet, even 4WD vehicles should avoid it. Buck and Doe turns north from AZ 66 between Mileposts 100 and 101, several miles west of Peach Springs; at its end, turn right 4.3 miles on paved Diamond Bar Road. Antares Road, also dirt but likely to be better graded, turns north off AZ 66 farther west from Peach Springs, between Mileposts 74 and 75; follow it 33 miles, turn right 7 miles on Pearce Ferry Road (paved), then go right 21 miles on Diamond Bar Road. The first 14.4 miles on Diamond Bar Road is dirt but very scenic, as you pass Joshua trees and enter a canyon through the Grand Wash Cliffs. Another back-road route is to head north 40 miles on Stockton Hill Road from Kingman, then right 7.1 miles on Pearce Ferry Road and right 21 miles on Diamond Bar Road. The best road in approaches from the west; take US 93 from Kingman or Las Vegas to paved Pearce Ferry Road, near Milepost 42, follow it 29 miles east, then turn right 21 miles on Diamond Bar Road.

Hualapai Lodge in Peach Springs runs a shuttle to Grand Canyon West at low cost (free for guests). Several fixed wing and helicopter companies offer tours from Las Vegas; check with operators there for the many options. Some helicopters fly into the Grand Canyon and land either near the river or on a bench part way down on Hualapai land. Heli USA also offers five-minute helicopter rides from Grand Canyon West into the Canyon, lands, then picks up passengers later for the flight back to the top; tel. (800) 359-8727; Internet: www.heliusa.com.

THE ARIZONA STRIP

Lonely and vast, the Arizona Strip lies north and west of the Colorado River. This land of forests, desert grasslands, mountains, and canyons covers 14,000 square miles, yet supports only 3,200 people. The Grand Canyon presents a formidable barrier between these citizens and the rest of the state; all highway traffic has to follow a circuitous route around the mighty chasm. To cover 140 miles as the crow flies, residents of Moccasin in the Arizona Strip must drive 357 miles to the Mohave County seat at Kingman, detouring through Utah and Nevada before reentering Arizona at Hoover Dam.

Historically, the Strip has far more in common with Utah, as Mormon pioneers established the first settlements here. Today, this country appeals to those who love wilderness and solitude. Travelers can wander the canyons, back roads, and trails here without meeting another soul. Other attractions include fishing and boating on Lake Powell, historic Lees Ferry (15 river miles below Lake Powell), and Pipe Spring National Monument, an early Mormon ranch.

Some beautiful canyon and mountain country await the adventurous traveler. In addition to Grand Canyon National Park and Glen Canyon National Recreation Area, nine designated wilderness areas totaling nearly 400,000 acres protect some of the most scenic sections. Several tiny communities in the Arizona Strip offer food and accommodations; more extensive facilities lie just outside in Mesquite across the Nevada border to the west, in St. George and Kanab across the Utah border to the north, and in Page across the Colorado River to the east.

Information

For hiking and access information for public lands on the Arizona Strip and into Utah, contact the **Interagency Visitor Center,** 345 E. Riverside Dr., St. George, UT 84790; open Mon.-Fri. 7:45 a.m.-5 p.m. (best times for reaching someone with first-hand travel experience) and Saturday and holidays 9 a.m.-5 p.m.; tel. (435) 688-3246; Internet: azstrip.az.blm.gov. Take I-15 Bluff Street Exit 6 and turn southeast one-third mile; the office is on your left.

The BLM's **Kanab Resource Area** office takes care of the Paria Canyon-Vermilion Cliffs Wilderness at 318 N. 100 East, Kanab, UT 84741; open Mon.-Fri. 7:45 a.m.-4:30 p.m.; tel. (435) 644-2672.

The U.S. Forest Service manages Saddle Mountain Wilderness and most of the Kanab Creek Wilderness; the **North Kaibab Ranger District** office, at 430 S. Main St. in Fredonia (Box 248, Fredonia, AZ 86022), is open Mon.-Fri. 8 a.m.-5 p.m.; tel. (520) 643-7395; Internet: www.fs.fed.us/r3/kai/.

The BLM's *Arizona Strip District* map shows topography, roads with numbers, and land ownership at 1:168,960 scale. The St. George Interagency office, Kanab Resource Area office, and most regional bookstores have the map; you can also order it online from the Interagency Internet address. The more detailed USGS 1:100,000- and 1:24,000-scale topo maps will be handy for hikers.

Exploring the Arizona Strip

Paved highways lead to the Virgin River gorge in the northwest corner, Pipe Spring National Monument in the north, the Grand Canyon's North Rim, and Lees Ferry. Elsewhere, high-clearance 4WD vehicles are recommended in this remote and rugged land. Three roads—from St. George, Colorado City, and near Fredonia—can be driven by cautiously driven 2WD vehicles to the Trumbull and Toroweap areas in dry weather. Parts of these roads are so smooth that one can drive at high speeds, often too fast to spot that washout or rough cattle guard! Drivers of 2WD vehicles need to take extra care not to become stuck on steep or washed-out roads. Mountain bikers can do some wild trips in the mountains and out to Grand Canyon viewpoints. For these cyclists, the BLM has marked the Dutchman Trail, an "easy" nine-mile loop near Little Black Mountain (south of St. George) and the "more difficult" 8.5-mile Sunshine Loop southeast of St. George. The Arizona Trail farther east is another riding possibility.

All visitors must respect the remote location, lack of water, and absence of facilities here. Be sure to carry camping gear, extra food and water, tools, and a first-aid kit in case of breakdown. Distances can be great—make sure you have enough gas. Some roads shown on maps will be very difficult, hazardous, or completely closed; learn of current conditions from the BLM or Forest Service. Major junctions have signs and most roads also have a number, which helps with navigation. Some critical intersections lack signs, however, so it's highly recommended to have the BLM's Arizona Strip District map and to make frequent reference to it. Leave an itinerary with a reliable person in case you don't emerge on time. Some people live seasonally on the Arizona Strip, but you cannot count on being able to find anyone in case of trouble. Ranchers run cattle on the

strip, so gates should be left as you found them. Drivers need to keep an eye out for endangered desert tortoises that might wander across the road on the Mohave Desert, west of the Grand Wash Cliffs and the Virgin Mountains.

WILDERNESS AND SCENIC AREAS ON THE WESTERN ARIZONA STRIP

Little Black Mountain Petroglyph Site
Impressive groups of rock art, most believed to have ceremonial or calendar functions, cover boulders at the base of this mesa just south into Arizona from St. George. Archaeologists have discovered more than 500 individual designs. A

THE DESERT TORTOISE

A threatened species, the desert tortoise survives the harsh climate of western Arizona by burrowing underground for about 95% of its lifetime. Here it escapes the 140-degree surface temperatures in summer and freezing conditions of winter. It also seeks out catchment basins, where it will lie waiting when the rare rains seem likely. A tortoise's bladder can store a cup of liquid for later use, and they've been known to expel the bladder's contents at intruders. Wastes are excreted in a nearly dry form. Tortoises can withstand dehydration, then increase their weight 43% by drinking after a storm. Growth and sexual maturity depend much on availability of food and moisture. Several growth rings may appear each year. The female reaches maturity when about seven to eight inches long (mid-carapace), perhaps at 15 years old. Mating peaks in late summer/early autumn, though egg laying won't take place until May-June, when tortoises lay two or three batches of two to nine eggs. Babies emerge three to four months later. Oddly, experiments have shown that eggs incubated at 79-87 degrees F turn out to be all males, at 88-91 degrees all females.

The tortoise's diet includes grasses, herbs, flowers, and new cactus growth. Males may fight each other for territory until one flees or gets flipped onto its back. If the defeated rival cannot right itself, it will die in the sun. Because the tortoise needs sand or gravel to burrow, you're most likely to see them in washes and canyon bottoms. Life span may be 70 years or more. The male has a longer protruding plate (used in jousting matches) under its neck and a size of up to 14 inches long and 20 pounds; the female is a bit smaller. Habitat loss and people collecting them have left the tortoise's future in doubt. Laws forbid disturbing or collecting a wild tortoise. The western box turtle *(Terrapene ornata),* sometimes confused with the desert tortoise, is much smaller at about five inches long and has distinctive light and dark striping on its shell.

the desert tortoise
(Gopherus agassizii)

short trail winds past the petroglyphs, where signs describe some of their features. At St. George, take the I-15 Bloomington Exit 4, head east 1.8 miles (becomes Brigham Road), turn south 3.8 miles on River Road to the Arizona border and continue 0.4 mile on unpaved Quail Hill Road (#1069), turn east 4.5 miles to a T-junction (there's a gate on the way), then left into the parking area, which has a picnic table and outhouse.

Virgin River Canyon Recreation Area
Picnic and campsites overlook the Virgin River at this scenic spot just south off I-15 Exit 18. It's open year-round with water but no showers or hookups; expect hot weather in summer. Campsites cost $6, picnic areas $2, or you can reserve group day and camp areas with the BLM's Arizona Strip office in St. George, Utah; tel. (435) 688-3200. A one-fifth-mile nature trail leads to hilltop views, where interpretive signs explain the unusual geology of the canyon at this transition between the Colorado Plateau and the Basin and Range Province. Trailhead parking is on the left where the picnic and campground roads divide; other trails drop from the picnic and camping areas to the river.

River Running on the Virgin
Experienced whitewater boaters prepared for changing conditions can tackle the Virgin River. A minimum of about 1,000 cubic feet per second (cfs) is needed, which doesn't occur every year;

spring, and especially May, offer the best chance of sufficient flow. No permits are needed. The Interagency Visitor Center in St. George can advise on river travel and possibly on local boat rentals and shuttle services. River runners can put in at the Man of War Road bridge in Bloomington, just south of St. George. Take-out can be at the last I-15 bridge or farther down on slow water near the Arizona town of Beaver Dam.

Littlefield and Beaver Dam
These two farming communities lie near the Virgin River on opposite sides of I-15 in Arizona's extreme northwest corner. Turn north 0.6 mile from Exit 8 for the **Beaver Dam Inn,** a historic hotel on old highway 91; Fri.-Sat. rates run $40-50 d, weekday rates $30-40 d, and monthly rates are $350-400 d. Inexpensive. The restaurant serves breakfast, lunch, and dinner daily (summer dinners are served at the bar); tel. (520) 347-5080. A gas station/grocery store is nearby. Mesquite, Nevada, has motels, restaurants, and supermarkets just eight miles west on I-15.

Beaver Dam Mountains Wilderness
This 19,600-acre wilderness includes alluvial plains and the rugged mountains of extreme northwestern Arizona and part of adjacent Utah. Desert bighorn sheep, desert tortoises, raptors, the endangered woundfin minnow, Joshua trees, and several rare plant species live here. There are no trails, but hikers enjoy traveling cross-country through the beautiful Joshua tree forest

Beaver Dam Mountains

or exploring canyons. Unpaved BLM Road 1005, 10 miles long, follows a corridor through the wilderness, providing easy access. The east end begins at I-15 Exit 18, opposite the Virgin River Recreation Area, 20 miles southwest of St. George. The west end (unsigned) turns off between Mileposts 14 and 15 of Hwy. 91, 5.5 miles north of I-15 Beaver Dam Exit 8.

Paiute Wilderness

This 84,700-acre wilderness lies south of I-15 and the Virgin River in the northwest corner of Arizona. The jagged Virgin Mountains contain a wide variety of plant and animal life, from desert country at 2,400 feet to pine and fir forests surrounding Mt. Bangs, 8,012 feet high.

Several hiking trails wind through the rugged terrain. Cougar Spring Trailhead at the wilderness boundary provides the easiest route to the summit. Follow an old road up one mile through the wilderness to a saddle, then turn left one more mile up another old road toward the top. When the road ends, you'll need to bushwhack through some chaparral (look for cairns and wear long pants) and rock scramble the last quarter mile to the top; the climb takes about four and a half hours roundtrip. Despite the high elevations, only a few pines grow on the upper slopes; you'll see mostly manzanita, jojoba, Gambel oak, and some hedgehog and prickly pear cactus. Surrounding ridges have forests, however.

Other hiking options from Cougar Spring Trailhead area include the ridge north of Mt. Bangs and the Sullivan Trail. The 15-mile Sullivan Trail crosses the wilderness from Cougar Spring Trailhead or Black Rock Road to the Virgin River via Atkin Spring and Sullivan Canyon; expect some rough and poorly defined sections. The lower trailhead lies 1.5 miles downstream and across the Virgin River from Virgin River Campground, near I-15, 20 miles southwest of St. George; check the water depth of the Virgin River carefully and turn back if it's too high to cross safely.

Hikers have a choice of approaching Cougar Spring Trailhead from the east via Black Rock Road (#1004), a pretty route through ponderosa pines on Black Mountain (good camping and a few picnic tables); from the south via Lime Kiln Canyon (#242) and other roads; or from the west on the very steep Elbow Canyon Road (#299; best driven downhill). From Mesquite, Nevada,

turn south 0.9 mile on Riverside Road (just east of Oasis Casino), then turn left onto Lime Kiln Canyon Road #242 (just after crossing the Virgin River bridge). In 0.9 mile you'll see the road to Elbow Canyon on the left, but keep straight 16 miles for Lime Kiln Canyon, cross over a pass and descend past some pretty red sandstone outcrops, then turn left 22 miles on BLM Road 1041 to Cougar Spring Trailhead.

From St. George, head south on Quail Hill Road (#1069), as described under Little Black Mountain Petroglyph Site above, and continue 28 miles past St. George, turn right 25 miles on Black Rock Road (#1004), then right 0.5 mile to the trailhead.

If coming from Toroweap, take County 5 to Mt. Trumbull Schoolhouse, turn north 40 miles on County 5, then left 25 miles on Black Rock Road (#1004) and right 0.5 mile to the trailhead. If you're feeling adventurous and have a high-clearance 4WD vehicle, Elbow Canyon Road (#299) is an option—head west from the trailhead, climb a bit to a pass, then plummet down the rough road to the desert plains below. Loose rock makes this drive much easier going downhill. Mesquite is about 18 miles from the trailhead. Lots of other very scenic roads head toward the Virgin Mountains too; see the Arizona Strip District Map.

Cottonwood Point Wilderness

The 6,860-acre wilderness contains part of the multicolored 1,000-foot Vermilion Cliffs, jagged pinnacles, and wooded canyons. Springs and seeps in the main canyon east of Cottonwood Point support a world of greenery surrounded by desert. The wilderness lies on the Utah border near Colorado City, west of Fredonia. Dirt roads from AZ 389 and Colorado City provide access; check with the BLM for trailhead directions.

Grand Wash Cliffs Wilderness

Grand Wash Cliffs mark the west edge of the Colorado Plateau, forming a major landmark of the western Grand Canyon. The wilderness protects 36,300 acres along a 12-mile section of the cliffs in an extremely remote portion of Arizona. Desert bighorn sheep and raptors live in the high country; desert tortoises forage lower down. **Grand Wash Bench Trail,** a 10-mile gated road along a bench between upper and lower cliffs, can be reached on the north and south wilderness boundaries. The trail follows a bench between the upper (1,800 feet high) and lower (1,600 feet high) cliffs. Hikers can also head out cross-country to the cliffs from BLM Road 1061 along the west boundary of the wilderness.

An exceptionally scenic jeep road through Hidden Canyon crosses the Grand Wash Cliffs north of the wilderness. To reach the east end of this drive from County 5 (11.5 miles north of Mt. Trumbull Schoolhouse and 48 miles south of St. George), follow Parashant Road (#103) southwest 16.6 miles, then turn right on BLM Road 1003 at the sign for Hidden Canyon. Small canyon cliffs appear four miles in, then become higher and higher as the road winds downstream along the canyon floor, repeatedly crisscrossing the normally dry streambed. Juniper and pinyon pine on the Shivwits Plateau in the upper canyon give way to Joshua trees in the desert country below. After about 20 miles, you leave the canyons. BLM Road 1061 turns south for the west face of the Grand Wash Cliffs Wilderness; you can continue on BLM Road 1003 for Grand Wash Bay of Lake Mead. Other roads turn north to the Virgin Mountains. Due to numerous sandy washes, a high-clearance 4WD vehicle is required for Hidden Canyon and most other roads in the Grand Wash Cliffs area.

Mount Dellenbaugh

This small volcano atop the Shivwits Plateau offers a great panorama of the Arizona Strip. Vast forests of juniper and pinyon and ponderosa pine spread across the plateau. A long line of cliffs marks the Grand Canyon to the south. Beyond rise the Hualapai Mountains near Kingman. You can see other mountain ranges in Arizona, Nevada, and Utah as well. Frederick Dellenbaugh served as artist and assistant topographer on Major John Wesley Powell's second river expedition through the Grand Canyon in 1871-72.

From Mt. Trumbull Schoolhouse, go north 11.5 miles on County 5, then turn southwest 42 miles on Parashant Road (#103), following signs. Note that this road is *not* the one into Parashant Canyon. From St. George, Utah, it's 48 miles to the junction, then 42 miles to Mt. Dellenbaugh. The last five miles can be negotiated only when dry; high-clearance vehicles are recommend-

ed. The trailhead lies just past the BLM's Shivwits Ranger Station; follow an old jeep road, now closed to motor vehicles. The trail is an easy four miles roundtrip, climbing 900 feet to the 7,072-foot summit.

Twin Point

The beautiful views here take in the lower Grand Canyon, Surprise Canyon, Burnt Canyon, and Sanup Plateau. Follow Parashant Road 103 south 37 miles, keep straight where the road to Mt. Dellenbaugh turns left, and continue south another 14 miles. You'll pass Parashant Field Station on the left two miles beyond the Mt. Dellenbaugh turnoff. Ponderosa pine gives way to juniper and pinyon pine as you near the point. Stay left at a fork three miles past the field station—the right fork goes one mile to an overlook of upper Burnt Canyon, perhaps named for the colorful yellow and red rock layers. The main road continues south 2.7 miles, then skirts the west rim, offering many fine views into Burnt Canyon. Just before the road ends, it forks left for Twin Point and right for a trailhead to Sanup Plateau. Ranchers run cattle down this trail for winter grazing. Twin Point offers plenty of places to camp, no permit needed.

Kelly Point

Located east of Twin Point, this point extends much farther south than any other on the North Rim. Road conditions have deteriorated to such an extent that the route is now extremely rough, rocky, and slow—figure 5 m.p.h. on the last 20 miles. Follow Parashant Road (#103) toward Mt. Dellenbaugh and continue south to road's end.

Whitmore Point

Spectacular views of the Grand Canyon, Parashant Canyon, Mt. Logan, and Uinkaret Mountains greet those who ascend this 5,500-foot perch. Volcanoes and massive lava flows between here and the Toroweap area to the east can be seen clearly. There are plenty of good places to camp, with no permit needed.

From Mt. Trumbull Schoolhouse, head west, then south 22.2 miles on BLM Road 1063. Some junctions feature signs, but you'll need to refer frequently to a map. At 9.9 miles in, a jeep road to the right heads down Trail Canyon to Parashant Canyon, a good area for adventurous hikers. Continue straight (south) for Whitmore Point. As with most roads on the Arizona Strip, conditions get rougher as you move closer to the Grand Canyon; a high-clearance vehicle is necessary. Whitmore Point and other areas north of the western Grand Canyon are the responsibility of the Lake Mead National Recreation Area; the agency could improve its road maintenance and signing efforts, as you'll see.

Whitmore Wash Road

Lava flows from Mt. Emma in the Uinkaret Mountains enable you to drive a high-clearance, 4WD vehicle deep into the Grand Canyon, though the last part of the drive is very rough. A short trail at road's end leads down to the Colorado River. See "Whitmore Wash Trail" under "Visiting Grand Canyon National Park" for directions and hiking information.

Bar 10 Ranch lies along this road about nine miles from the rim. It offers miles of open country, cowboy-style meals, and an informal Western atmosphere. Activities include horseback riding, pack trips, cattle drives, hiking, scenic flights, river trips, cookouts, and entertainment. Many visitors spend a day here when shuttling in or out from a river trip by helicopter and flying by small plane to Las Vegas or other destinations. You can also drive here, though high-clearance vehicles are recommended. Make the required reservations with Bar 10 at Box 910088, St. George, UT 84791-0088, tel. (435) 628-4010 or (800) 582-4139, Internet: www.infowest.com/bar10.

Mt. Trumbull School

Homesteaders arrived in this remote valley about 1917 to farm and raise livestock. Population peaked at 200-250 in the 1930s, when a drier climate forced residents to switch their livelihood from crops to cattle and sheep. People gradually drifted away until the last full-time resident departed in 1984. Abandoned houses stand empty, along with some houses that are inhabited seasonally. No trespassing is allowed on private lands, but you can get some good photos from the main roads. Dedicated teachers taught at the well-preserved one-room schoolhouse from 1922 until the bell rang for its last class in 1968. Volunteers restored it in 1984; it's often open with photo and document exhibits that show what life was like here. Donations are appreciated.

Mount Trumbull Wilderness

Forests cover the basalt-rock slopes of Mt. Trumbull (8,028 feet), the centerpiece of this 7,900-acre wilderness. Oak, pinyon pine, and juniper woodlands grow on the lower slopes; ponderosa pine, Gambel oak, and some aspen are found on the higher and more protected areas. Kaibab squirrels, introduced in the early 1970s, flourish in the forests. You might see or hear a turkey, too. The 5.4-mile roundtrip climb to the summit makes an enjoyable forest ramble with some views through the trees. From the marked trailhead at an elevation of 6,500 feet on the southwest side of Mt. Trumbull, the wide path climbs around to the south side, with some good views across Toroweap Valley, the Grand Canyon, and the San Francisco Peaks. The trail then turns north and becomes faint, but cairns show the way to the summit, marked by a survey tower and some viewpoints. You can reach the trailhead by County Road 5 from Toroweap, Fredonia, Colorado City, or St. George; you'll know that you're close when ponderosa pines appear. The buildings and trailers across the field belong to a BLM site; if staff are in, they may be able to help with local information.

Mormon pioneers built a steam-powered sawmill just west of the trailhead in 1870 to supply timbers for the St. George Temple. A historic marker tells about the sawmill operation; you can explore the site for the scant remnants. Water from Nixon Spring, higher on the slopes, once supplied the sawmill. A faucet near the road between the historic site and trailhead usually has water from the spring—a handy resource for travelers in this arid land. Mount Trumbull and nearby Mt. Logan lie northwest of the Toroweap area of the Grand Canyon. John Wesley Powell named both peaks after U.S. senators.

Nampaweap Petroglyph Site

Archaic, ancestral pueblo, and Paiute Indians have pecked thousands of glyphs into boulders near Mt. Trumbull. Nampaweap means "foot canyon" in Paiute, perhaps referring to it being on a travel corridor dating back to prehistoric times. From the Mt. Trumbull Trailhead, go east three miles on County Road 5 (or west 3.5 miles from the Toroweap Road), turn south 1.1 miles on BLM Road 1028 toward the private Arkansas Ranch, turn east into the parking area, and then walk three-quarters of a mile to the head of a small canyon. The rock art is on the canyon's north side.

Mount Logan Wilderness

Scenic features of this 14,600-acre volcanic region include Mt. Logan (7,866 feet), other parts of the Uinkaret Mountains, and a large natural amphitheater known as Hell's Hole. Geology, forests, and wildlife resemble those of Mt. Trumbull, a short distance to the northeast. A road climbs the east side of Mt. Logan to within a half mile of the summit; the rest of the way is an easy walk—just continue north along the side of the ridge. On top you can peer into the vast depths of Hell's Hole, a steep canyon of red and white rock. The sweeping panorama takes in much of the Arizona Strip and beyond to mountains in Nevada and Utah. Trees block views to the south.

From County 5, just southeast of the Mt. Trumbull trailhead, turn southwest 4.2 miles on BLM Road 1044, then right 2.2 miles on BLM Road 1064 until it becomes rough and steep at its end. Many fine spots in the ponderosa pines suitable for camping line the roads in.

A rough jeep road follows a corridor through the wilderness, from which hikers can turn south onto the old Slide Mountain Road (closed to vehicles) or enter Hell's Hole from below You'll need to follow a map closely as none of these destinations will be signed; roads also branch off to other unsigned destinations, adding to the navigational challenge. Loose rock and erosion of the corridor road necessitate use of a high-clearance 4WD; it's slow going, but the road continues all the way down to the Whitmore Wash Road (#1045), one mile north of the Bar 10 Ranch.

PIPE SPRING NATIONAL MONUMENT

Excellent exhibits in Winsor Castle, an early Mormon ranch southwest of Fredonia, provide a look into frontier life. The abundant spring water here first attracted prehistoric Basket Maker and Pueblo Indians, who settled nearby more than 1,000 years ago, then moved on. Paiute Indians, who believe they're related to the ancestral pueblo people, arrived more recently and now live on the surrounding Kaibab-Paiute Indian Reserva-

tion; in earlier times, they spent summers on the Kaibab Plateau and winters near Pipe Spring. Mormons discovered the spring in 1858. They began ranching five years later despite Navajo raiders who occasionally stole stock and were suspected of having killed two Mormon men who tried to pursue them. Raids ended after 1870 when Mormons and Navajo signed a treaty.

Mormon leader Brigham Young then decided to move the church's southern Utah cattle herd to Pipe Spring. A pair of two-story stone houses went up with walls connecting the ends to form a protected courtyard; workers added gun ports just in case, but the settlement was never attacked.

The structure became known as Winsor Castle—the ranch superintendent, Anson P. Winsor, possessed a regal bearing and was thought to be related to the English royal family. Winsor built up a sizable herd of cattle and horses and oversaw farming and the ranch dairy.

A telegraph office—the first in Arizona—opened in 1871, bringing Utah and the rest of the

visiting Winsor Castle

world closer. Eventually, so many newlyweds passed through after marriage in the St. George Temple that the route became known as the Honeymoon Trail. In the 1880s, the Mormon Church came under increasing assault from the U.S. government, primarily over the practice of polygamy. Fearing the feds would soon seize church property, the church sold Winsor Castle to a non-Mormon.

President Harding proclaimed Pipe Spring a national monument in 1923 "as a memorial of Western pioneer life." Today, National Park Service staff keep the frontier spirit alive by maintaining the ranch much as it was in the 1870s. Activities such as gardening, weaving, spinning, quilt-making, cheese-making, and butter-churning still take place, albeit on a smaller scale. At times you can hear a real cowboy or a Paiute speaker tell of life on the Arizona Strip. Short guided tours of Winsor Castle relate how people lived here in the early days, and you can explore the outbuildings and gardens on your own. A half-mile-loop Rim Trail climbs the small ridge behind the ranch to a viewpoint, where signs describe the history and geology of the area.

Visitor Center

Historic exhibits are open daily 8 a.m.-5 p.m. year-round with extended hours in summer; $2 per person admission (16 and under free); tel. (520) 643-7105; Internet: www.nps.gov/pisp. A short video and historic artifacts introduce the monument. Demonstrations, talks, and walks take place in summer. Produce from the garden is oftentimes given away. A gift shop has a good selection of regional books, maps, and Southwestern Indian arts and crafts, and the snack bar has fast food. Hikers may be able to obtain last-minute backcountry permits for the Grand Canyon National Park, a useful service for some North Rim destinations. Pipe Spring National Monument lies just off AZ 389, 14 miles southwest of Fredonia.

The Paiute tribe operates a **campground** one quarter mile northeast of the monument. It has showers and is open all year at a bargain-priced $3 tent or $5 RV with hookups; tel. (520) 643-7245 (tribal office). A new gas station/convenience store is at the highway turnoff. Colorado City (not on the highway) and Fredonia also sell gas. The nearest restaurants and motels are in

Fredonia, but Kanab has more extensive services, including supermarkets.

KANAB AND VICINITY

Striking scenery surrounds this small Utah town just north across the Arizona border. The Vermilion Cliffs to the west and east glow with a fiery intensity at sunrise and sunset. Streams have cut splendid canyons into surrounding plateaus. The Paiute Indians knew the spot as Kanab, meaning "Place of the Willows," which still grow along Kanab Creek. Mormon pioneers arrived in the mid-1860s and tried to farm along the unpredictable creek. Irrigation difficulties culminated in the massive floods of 1883, which in just two days gouged a section of creekbed 40 feet below its previous level. Ranching proved better suited to this rugged and arid land.

Hollywood discovered the dramatic scenery in the 1920s and has filmed more than 150 movies and TV series here, including *The Outlaw Josey Wales* and *Rin Tin Tin*. Film crews have constructed several Western sets near Kanab, but most lie on private land. The Pahreah set east of town, however, is on BLM land and open to the public. A couple sites at Best Friends Animal Sanctuary can be toured too (see below for a detailed description). Ask at the visitor center for advice on visiting other sets.

Travelers find Kanab (pop. 3,500) a handy stopover on trips to Bryce, Zion, and Grand Canyon National Parks and to the Glen Canyon National Recreation Area. A good selection of motels and restaurants lines US 89, which zigzags through town. Short detours on many of the side streets reveal 19th-century houses from Kanab's pioneer days.

Kanab Heritage House

This 1895 Queen Anne-style Victorian house reflects the prosperity of two of Kanab's early Mormon residents. Henry Bowman built it, but he lived here only two years before going on a mission. He sold the property to Thomas Chamberlain, who led a busy life serving as a leader in the Mormons' United Order and caring for his six wives and 55 children. (There's a family photo in the sitting room.) A guide will show you around the house and explain its architectural details.

Photos, furnishings, and artifacts give an idea of what life was like in early Kanab. The town had no stores when the house was built, so each family grew its own vegetables and fruit. The grape arbor, berry bushes, and trees here represent what was grown during pioneer times; fruit is free for the picking to visitors. The house is usually open for tours in summer Mon.-Sat. 10 a.m.-5 p.m.; admission is free. You might be able to visit at other times by appointment; call the number posted on the front of the house. It's located one block off US 89 at the corner of Main and 100 South.

Frontier Movie Town

The owners assembled this movie-set replica in Kanab to show tourists a bit of the Old West. Some of the buildings have seen actual use in past movies and TV shows. Many small exhibits display Western and movie memorabilia; there's a photo studio where you can dress up in Old West costumes. Shops sell handicrafts and snacks. Local tour information is available too.

Admission to Frontier Movie Town is free. On most nights from Memorial Day to Labor Day weekends there's a Dutch-oven cookout here along with Western entertainment for about $25. The town is open April 1 to October 31 about 9 a.m.-10 p.m. Turn in off W. Center between Brandon Motel and Gift City; tel. (435) 644-5337.

Best Friends Animal Sanctuary

Located in Angel Canyon just north of Kanab, this is one of the more unusual destinations in Utah. The scenic canyon was formerly the set for several Western movies and TV shows, including *Rin Tin Tin,* and several of the sets are still standing. However, the canyon is now home to Best Friends Animal Sanctuary, the largest no-kill animal shelter in the country. Best Friends takes in unwanted or abused "companion animals"— pets, farm animals, or other abandoned or neglected creatures—and gives them a permanent home. Around 1,800 animals live at the sanctuary at any given time.

Tours of the facility visit the movie sets and can include a short talk on the natural history of the canyon; a hike to ancestral pueblo ruins can be arranged, too. Call ahead for tour times and when you depart leave a donation; tel. (435) 644-2001; Internet: www.bestfriends.org.

towers of the Vermilion Cliffs

THE EXPLORATION OF THE COLORADO RIVER AND ITS CANYONS

Squaw Trail

This well-graded trail provides a close look at the geology, plant life, and animals of the Vermilion Cliffs just north of town. Allow about an hour on the moderately difficult trail to reach the first overlook (two miles roundtrip with a 400-foot elevation gain) or one and a half hours to go all the way up (three miles roundtrip with an 800-foot elevation gain). Views to the south take in Kanab, Fredonia, Kanab Canyon, and the vast Kaibab Plateau. At the top, look north to see the White, Gray, and Pink Cliffs of the Grand Staircase. Some maps show the trail continuing across the mesa to Hog Canyon, but the BLM has not completed that part of the tail. The trailhead is at the north end of 100 East near the city park. Pick up a trail guide at the visitor center. Brochures may also be available at the trailhead or BLM office. Bring water, and try to get a very early start in summer.

Moqui Cave

This is a tourist attraction with a large collection of Indian artifacts. Most of the arrowheads, pottery, sandals, and burials have been excavated locally. A diorama re-creates a ruin located five miles away in Cottonwood Wash. Fossils, rocks, and minerals are exhibited, too, including what's claimed to be one of the largest fluorescent mineral displays in the country. The collections and a gift shop lie within a spacious cave that stays pleasantly cool even in the hottest weather. Open daily except Sunday from early March to mid-November, with summer hours of 9 a.m.-7 p.m., shorter hours in spring and autumn; admission costs $4 adults, $3.50 seniors, $3 children 13-17, and $2 ages 6-12. The cave is five miles north of Kanab on US 89; tel. (435) 644-2987.

Accommodations

All of the motels and campgrounds lie along US 89, which follows 300 West, Center, 100 East, and 300 South through town. Reservations are a good idea during the busy summer months. The summer rates listed may drop in winter.

Budget: Canyonlands International Youth Hostel is a great place to meet other travelers, many from foreign countries. Guests stay in simple dorm-style accommodations with a free breakfast buffet and use of the kitchen, laundry, TV room, patio, lawn, locked storage, and a reference library of regional maps and books. Open year-round; check-in is all day; $10 per person (no hostel card required). It's centrally located a half-block off US 89 at 143 E. 100 South, tel. (435) 644-5554.

Inexpensive: Treasure Trail Motel, 150 W. Center, tel. (435) 644-2687 or (800) 603-2687, has a pool and rooms for $40-48 s, $48-56 d.

Aiken's Lodge National 9 Inn is at 79 W. Center, tel. (435) 644-2625 or (800) 524-9999, with a pool and rooms for $40 s, $43 d; Aiken's Lodge may close in January and February.

Sun-N-Sand Motel has a pool, spa, and four kitchenettes at 347 S. 100 East, tel. (435) 644-5050 or (800) 654-1868; rooms start at $38 s, $40 d.

Brandon Motel has a pool, eight kitchenettes, and accepts pets at 223 W. Center, tel. (435) 644-2631 or (800) 839-2631; rooms go for $35 s, $38 d (slightly more for kitchenettes).

Riding's Quail Park Lodge has a pool and accepts pets at 125 N. US 89, tel. (435) 644-2639; rooms run $40-55 d or $65-85 (family).

The **Four Seasons Motel** has a pool and accepts pets at 36 N. 300 West, tel. (435) 644-2635; rooms start at $45 s, $50 d.

Inexpensive to Moderate: You can stay where the stars stayed at **Parry Lodge,** 89 E. Center, tel. (435) 644-2601 or (800) 748-4104. Rooms cost $43 s, $46-73 d; room doors have names of the movie stars who stayed there and you'll see their photos in the lobby and restaurant. There's also a pool here.

Moderate: Red Hills Motel (Best Western) has a pool at 125 W. Center, tel. (435) 644-2675 or (800) 528-1234; the rate is $84 d.

Rooms at the **Super 8,** 70 S. 200 West, tel. (435) 644-5500 or (800) 800-8000, cost $67 s, $72 d.

Holiday Inn Express offers a nine-hole golf course, free breakfast bar, pool, and hot tub one mile east of downtown at 815 E. US 89, tel. (435) 644-8888 or (800) HOLIDAY; rooms are $89 d.

Campgrounds

Kanab RV Corral has sites with hot showers, pool, and laundromat open all year at 483 South 100 East, tel. (435) 644-5330. Tents cost $16, RVs with hookups $20.

Hitch'n Post RV Park has sites with showers open all year at 196 E. 300 South, tel. (435) 644-2142; rates are $10 tents, $12 RVs no hookups, $16 with hookups including tax.

Crazy Horse RV Campark, 625 E. 300 South, tel. (435) 644-2782, has sites with pool, store, game room, and showers; open mid-April to late October. Spaces cost $9.50 tents or RVs without hookups, $15 RVs with hooksups.

Food

Parry's Lodge features steak, prime rib, seafood, and chicken and dumplings at 89 E. Center, tel. (435) 644-2601; open daily for breakfast and dinner. Photos of movie-star guests decorate the walls.

Chef's Palace Restaurant, 176 W. Center, tel. (435) 644-5052, is open daily for breakfast, lunch, and dinner. Dinner fare includes steak, prime rib, and seafood.

For Mexican food, including steak and seafood, try **Fernando's Hideaway** in the west end of town at 332 W. 300 North, tel. (435) 644-3222, open daily for lunch and dinner, and **Nedra's Too,** 310 S. 100 East in Heritage Center, tel. (435) 644-2030, open daily for breakfast, lunch, and dinner.

Houston's Trail's End Restaurant serves up steak, seafood, and some Mexican items with a western atmosphere at 32 E. Center, tel. (435) 644-2488, open daily for breakfast, lunch, and dinner.

Pizza Hut, 421 S. 100 East, tel. (435) 644-2513, cooks pizza daily for lunch and dinner.

The **Wok Inn,** 86 S. 200 West, tel. (435) 644-5400, serves Hunan and Szechuan cuisine. It's open Mon.-Fri. for lunch and nightly for dinner and is closed in winter.

Entertainment and Events

In summer, there are free musical concerts at the city park gazebo, in the center of town. **Kanab Theatre** has movies at 29 W. Center, tel. (435) 644-2334.

The town hosts the **Kanab 10K** run in May. **Kanab West Fest** features a rodeo, Western art, and festivities in October.

Shopping and Services

Gift City, 288 W. Center across from Four Seasons Motel, specializes in "Kanab Wonderstone" slabs; this natural sandstone, found nearby, has curious patterns (possibly caused by deposits from mineral springs) that resemble scenic landscapes. Prices range from a few dollars for a pocket-sized piece to $1,000 for a five-foot by two-and-a-half-foot specimen. Several other shops sell Indian crafts and assorted souvenirs. **Alderman & Son Photo,** 19 W. Center, tel. (435) 644-5981, supplies film and camera needs (including repairs) beyond what you would expect in a town this size. The shop almost qualifies as an antique camera museum.

Denny's Wigwam, 78 E. Center, tel. (435) 644-2452, is a landmark Old West trading post with lots of quality Western jewelry, cowboy hats and boots, and souvenirs.

The **city park** has picnic tables, playground, tennis courts, and a baseball field at the north end of 100 West; the trailhead for Squaw Trail also starts here (see **Squaw Trail,** above). An outdoor **swimming pool** opens in summer at 44 N. 100 West (behind the State Bank); tel. (435) 644-5870. **Coral Cliffs Golf Course** has nine holes and a driving range on the east edge of town; tel. (435) 644-5005. You can arrange

trail rides from an hour to a day or more through Frontier Movie Town; tel. (435) 644-5337.

The **post office** is at 34 S. Main; tel. (435) 644-2760. **Kane County Hospital** provides emergency care at 355 N. Main St.; tel. (435) 644-5811. The **public library** is at 13 S. 100 East; tel. (435) 644-2394.

Information

Staff at the **Kanab Visitor Center** offer literature and advice for services in Kanab and travel in Kane County; they're in the center of town at 78 S. 100 East (Kanab, UT 84741), tel. (435) 644-5033 or (800) 733-5263 (SEE KANE), Internet: www.kane.com. The visitor center is open Mon.-Fri. 8 a.m.-5 p.m. all year with extended hours and Saturday hours in summer. Visit the **BLM** office to learn about hiking and back roads in the Kanab area; it's open Mon.-Fri. 7:45 a.m.-4:30 p.m. at 318 N. 100 East, Kanab, UT 84741, tel. (435) 644-2672.

Tours

Lake Mead Air will take you over the Grand Canyon on a 40- to 45-minute flight for $89 per person or a 60- to 90-minute flight for $119 per person. Flights require a two-person minimum and leave from the airport three miles south of town on US 89A, toward Fredonia; tel. (435) 644-2299.

FREDONIA TO MARBLE CANYON ON US 89A

Fredonia

Though just a tiny town, Fredonia (pop. 1,220) is the largest community on the Arizona Strip. Mormon polygamists, seeking refuge from federal agents, settled here in 1885. They first called the place Hardscrabble but later chose the name Fredonia, perhaps a contraction of the words "freedom" and "doña" (Spanish for wife).

Five modest places to stay, listed south to north, lie along Main St. (US 89A). All are Budget-Inexpensive. **Crazy Jug Motel** at 465 S. Main St. runs $35-45 d; tel. (520) 643-7752. The **Blue Sage Motel and RV** is located at 330 S. Main St.; rates are $15 RV with hookups, $33 s, $40 d. The Blue Sage may close in winter; tel. (520)

643-7125. The **Ship Rock Motel (National 9)** is across the highway at 337 S. Main St.; rates are $30-37 d. The Ship Rock closes in winter; tel. (520) 643-7355 or (800) 524-9999. The **Grand Canyon Motel** at 175 S. Main St. offers a choice of motel rooms at $32.50-38 d and hotel rooms at $27.50-32.50 with no extra charge for tax or kitchenettes; tel. (520) 643-7646. **Jackson House** offers rooms and use of the kitchen in a 1913 house at 90 N. Main St.; rates run $30-35 d for regular rooms and $45-50 for the family room (sleeps up to eight); tel. (520) 643-7702. The town of Kanab, seven miles north, offers a much larger selection of accommodations (including a hostel), restaurants, shopping, and recreation.

For Mexican and American food, dine at **Nedra's Cafe**, 165 N. Main St., tel. (520) 643-7591. It's open daily for breakfast, lunch, and dinner but may close some days in winter.

Crazy Jug Restaurant, next to the motel at 465 S. Main St., has American food daily for breakfast, lunch and dinner; tel. (520) 643-7712.

Traveler's Inn Restaurant serves steak, seafood, and other fare three miles north of town Tues.-Sat. for dinner with reduced service in winter; tel. (520) 643-7402.

Fredonia is building a welcome center at the north end of town to offer information about local services and area attractions; tel. (520) 643-7241 (town office). Folks at the **North Kaibab Ranger District** office will tell you about hiking, Grand Canyon viewpoints, and the back roads of the national forest north of the Grand Canyon; the Kaibab National Forest map (North Kaibab Ranger District) sold here is a must for exploring the Kaibab Plateau. The office is open Mon.-Fri. 8 a.m.-5 p.m. and possibly summer Saturdays; 430 S. Main St. (Box 248, Fredonia, AZ 86022). tel. (520) 643-7395; Internet: www.fs.fed.us/r3/kai/.

Jacob Lake

High in the pine forests at an elevation of 7,925 feet, this tiny village is on US 89A at the AZ 67 turnoff for the Grand Canyon North Rim. The nearby lake honors Mormon missionary and explorer Jacob Hamblin. A **1910 forest cabin** that overlooks the lake has been restored and opened to visitors; check hours at the Kaibab Visitor Center. From US 89A, head south 0.3 mile on AZ 64, turn right and go 0.6 mile, then go south 0.2 mile on Forest Road 282. **Jacob Lake**

Lookout has views of plateaus and mountains in Utah to the north; it's one mile south on AZ 64, between Mileposts 580 and 581, from US 89A. **Dry Park Lookout** features great views from a 125-foot tower southwest of Jacob Lake. These and other lookouts welcome visitors when they're staffed; check the Kaibab National Forest map.

Jacob Lake Inn stays open all year with basic motel rooms ($82-85 d to $91-97 four persons), cabins (April to November only, $66-84), restaurant (American food for daily breakfast, lunch, and dinner), grocery store, Indian crafts shop, and service station; tel. (520) 643-7232; Internet: www.jacoblake.com. Moderate.

Jacob Lake Campground has sites in the ponderosa pines with drinking water but no hookups or showers from mid-May to late October at $10 per night; it's often filled by late afternoon. Campers can enjoy summer interpretive programs and nearby hiking trails; tel. (520) 643-7770. Groups (only) can reserve sites with Recreation Resource Management at tel. (520) 204-5528. **Jacob Lake Picnic Area** is on the left just 0.1 mile south on AZ 64; you can also picnic at Jacob Lake Campground for a $3 fee.

Jacob Lake RV Park overlooks the little lake just 0.3 mile south on AZ 67 from US 89A, then west 0.7 mile; it's open May 15 to October 15 with a modem hookup but no showers. Tent spaces cost $10, dry RV sites run $12, and sites with hookups are $22; tel. (520) 643-7804. Tent sites are usually available, though RVers should make reservations or arrive by noon.

Allen's Outfitters offers trail rides of one and two hours in the forest, half- and full-day trips to overlooks, and pack trips from about mid-May to early September at its stables 0.3 mile south on AZ 67 and year-round in Kanab; tel. (435) 644-8150 or (435) 689-1979.

The Forest Service's **Kaibab Visitor Center** near Jacob Lake Inn is open daily 8 a.m.-5 p.m., though it may close in winter; tel. (520) 643-7298. Staff offer handouts on viewpoints, trails, campgrounds, and historic sites, as well as books and maps for sale. A 3-D model shows features of the Grand Canyon. Wildlife exhibits illustrate creatures living in the forests.

Vermilion Cliffs

These sheer cliffs, a striking red, appear to burst into flames at sunset. The cliffs dominate the

THE EXPLORATION OF THE COLORADO RIVER AND ITS CANYONS

the heart of Marble Canyon

Lodge is located on US 89A, nine miles west of Marble Canyon and 32 miles east of Jacob Lake; tel. (520) 355-2228. Moderate.

Lees Ferry Lodge
The lodge has motel rooms ($45 s, $50 d) and a smoky restaurant (American food for breakfast, lunch, and dinner daily). Inexpensive. **Lee's Ferry Anglers, Guides, & Flyshop** next door caters to fishermen. The lodge is on US 89A, three miles west of Marble Canyon and 38 miles east of Jacob Lake; tel. (520) 355-2231.

Marble Canyon Lodge
Major John Wesley Powell named the nearby section of Colorado River canyon for its smooth, marblelike appearance. The lodge, on US 89A at the turnoff for Lees Ferry, offers motel rooms ($50 s, $60-65 d), a cottage ($80 with four beds), and two-bedroom apartments ($125). Moderate. Other amenities are a smoky restaurant (American food for breakfast, lunch, and dinner daily), store (Indian crafts, regional books, and supplies for camping, river-running, and fishing), post office, laundromat, coin showers, gas station, convenience store, and paved airstrip; tel. (520) 355-2225 or (800) 726-1789.

northern horizon for many miles; a hilltop pullout 11 miles east of Jacob Lake on US 89A offers the best view. John Wesley Powell described them as "a long bank of purple cliffs plowed from the horizon high into the heavens."

San Bartolome Historic Site
Markers tell the story of the Dominguez-Escalante Expedition, which camped near here in 1776. Returning from a failed attempt to reach Monterey, California, the group struggled to find a route through the forbidding terrain to Santa Fe. The site is signed on the north side of US 89A between Mileposts 557 and 558, about midway between Marble Canyon and Jacob Lake.

Cliff Dweller's Lodge
About 1890, white traders built an unusual trading post underneath a giant boulder. The old buildings are still visible along the highway beside modern Cliff Dweller's Lodge. The lodge offers rooms ($57 d and $67 d, less in winter), a smoky restaurant (American food for breakfast, lunch, and dinner), small store, and gas station. The

LEES FERRY

The Colorado River cuts one gorge after another as it crosses the high plateaus of southern Utah and northern Arizona. Settlers and travelers found the river a dangerous and difficult barrier until well into the 20th century. A break in the cliffs above Marble Canyon provided one of the few places where a road could be built to the water's edge. Until 1929, when Navajo Bridge finally spanned the canyon, vehicles and passengers had to cross by ferry. Zane Grey expressed his thoughts about this crossing, known as Lees Ferry, in *The Last of the Plainsmen* (1908):

I saw the constricted rapids, where the Colorado took its plunge into the box-like head of the Grand Canyon of Arizona; and the deep, reverberating boom of the river, at flood height, was a fearful thing to hear. I could not repress a shudder at the thought of crossing above that rapid.

The Dominguez-Escalante Expedition tried to cross at what's now known as Lees Ferry in 1776, but without success. The river proved too cold and wide to swim safely, and winds frustrated attempts to raft across. The Spaniards traveled 40 miles upriver into present-day Utah before finding a safe ford.

About 100 years later, Mormon leaders eyed the Lees Ferry crossing as the most convenient route for expanding Mormon settlements from Utah into Arizona. Jacob Hamblin led a failed rafting attempt in 1860, but he returned four years later and that time made it safely across.

Although Hamblin first recognized the value of this crossing, it now bears the name of John D. Lee, a dubious character who gained notoriety in the 1857 Mountain Meadows Massacre. One account of this chain of events relates that Paiute Indians, allied to the Mormons, attacked an unfriendly wagon train; Lee and fellow Mormons then joined in the fighting until all but the small children, too young to tell the story, lay dead.

When a federal investigation some years later uncovered Mormon complicity in the slaughter, the Mormon Church leaders, seeking to move Lee out of sight, asked him to start a regular ferry service on the Colorado River. This he did in 1872. One of Lee's wives remarked on seeing the isolated spot, "Oh, what a lonely dell," and thus Lonely Dell became the name of their ranch. Lee managed to succeed with the ferry service despite boat accidents and sometimes hostile Navajo, but eventually his past caught up with him. In 1877, authorities took Lee back to Mountain Meadows, where a firing squad and casket awaited.

Miners and farmers came to try their luck along the Colorado River and its tributaries. Charles Spencer, manager of the American Placer Company, brought in sluicing machinery, an amalgamator, and drilling equipment. In 1910 his company tried using mule trains to pack coal from Warm Creek Canyon, 15 miles upstream. When the mules proved inadequate, company financiers shipped a 92-foot-long steamboat, the *Charles H. Spencer,* in sections from San Francisco. The boat performed poorly, burning almost its entire load of coal in just one roundtrip, and was used only five times. The boiler, decking, and hull can still be seen at low water on the shore upstream from Lees Ferry Fort. Although Spencer's efforts to extract fine gold particles

NAVAJO BRIDGE~ THE OLD AND THE NEW

A new, wider bridge for traffic has replaced the old Navajo Bridge across Marble Canyon. The old bridge, admired for its design and beauty, has been preserved as a pedestrian path just upstream from the new one. Now you can enjoy a walk 470 feet above the water on the old bridge's 909-foot length. Do not throw anything off the bridge, as even a small object can pick up lethal velocity from such a height and hurt boaters below. A 1930s stone shelter built by the Civilian Conservation Corps and a new visitor center stand just west of the bridges. Indoor and outdoor exhibits illustrate the history and construction details of both structures. You'll find local travel information for the Grand Canyon and Glen Canyon National Recreation Area and a large selection of books, maps, videos, music (Indian and Southwest), and posters in the Navajo Bridge Interpretive Center; it's open daily 9 a.m.-5 p.m. Navajo Indians sell crafts on the old bridge's east end. Both ends of the old bridge have parking.

proved futile, he persisted in his prospecting here as late as 1965 and made an unsuccessful attempt to develop a rhenium mine.

The ferry service continued after Lee's departure, though fatal accidents occurred from time to time. The last run took place in June 1928, while the bridge was going up six miles downstream. The ferry operator lost control in strong currents and the boat capsized; all three people aboard and a Model-T were lost. Fifty-five years of ferryboating had come to an end. Navajo Bridge opened in January 1929, an event hailed by the Flagstaff *Coconino Sun* as the "Biggest News in Southwest History."

Today, the Lees Ferry area and the canyon upstream belong to the Glen Canyon National Recreation Area. Grand Canyon National Park begins just downstream. Rangers of the National Park Service administer both areas.

Lonely Dell Ranch and Lees Ferry

You can tour old buildings, mining machinery, a wrecked steamboat, the ferry site, and trails in these historic districts. A self-guided tour booklet, available on site, as well as at the Carl Hayden

Visitor Center, identifies historic features and traces their backgrounds. A log cabin thought to have been built by Lee, root cellar, blacksmith shop, ranch house, orchards, and cemetery survive at Lonely Dell Ranch, a short distance up the Paria River. Historic buildings on the Colorado River include Lees Ferry Fort (built in 1874 to protect settlers from possible Indian attack, but used as a trading post and residence), a small stone post office (in use 1913-23), and structures occupied by the American Placer Company and the U.S. Geological Survey. A trail along the Colorado leads about one mile upstream to the main ferry site, now marked by ruins of ferrymen's stone houses.

A paved road to Lees Ferry turns north from US 89A just west of Navajo Bridge. Follow the road in 5.1 miles and turn left 0.2 mile for Lonely Dell Ranch Historic District or continue 0.7 mile on the main road to its end for Lees Ferry Historic District. The **ranger station** offers boating, fishing, and hiking information and sells some books and maps but is open irregular hours; it's on the left 0.4 mile after the campground turnoff; tel. (520) 355-2234.

Entry now costs $5 per vehicle or $3 per cyclist or hiker for seven days unless you have Golden Eagle, Golden Age, or Golden Access card.

Spencer Trail

Energetic hikers climb this unmaintained trail for fine views of Marble Canyon from the rim 1,500 feet above the river. The ingenious route switchbacks up sheer ledges above Lees Ferry. It's a moderately difficult hike to the top, three miles roundtrip; you should carry water. From Lees Ferry parking lot at the end of the road, follow the path through the historic district to the steamboat wreck, then take the trail leading to the cliffs.

Cathedral Wash Route

This 2.5-mile roundtrip hike follows a narrow canyon to Cathedral Rapid and back. Park at the second pullout, overlooking the wash, on the road to Lees Ferry, 1.4 miles in from US 89A and three miles before the campground.

Boating and Fishing

Rainbow trout flourish in the cold, clear waters released from Lake Powell through Glen Canyon Dam. Special fishing regulations apply here and

are posted. Anglers should be able to identify and must return to the river any of the endangered native fish—the Colorado squawfish, bonytail chub, humpback chub, and razorback sucker. There's a fish-cleaning station and parking area on the left just before the launch areas. At road's end, there's a paved upriver launch site used by boaters headed toward Glen Canyon Dam; Grand Canyon river-running groups use the unpaved downriver launch area. Powerboats can travel 14.5 miles up Glen Canyon almost to the dam. The Park Service recommends a boat with a minimum 10-hp motor to negotiate the swift currents. Boating below Lees Ferry is prohibited without a permit from Grand Canyon National Park. Kayakers and canoeists can arrange for Wilderness River Adventures rafts to take them from Lees Ferry upstream to the dam; contact the company at 50 S. Lake Powell Blvd., tel. (520) 645-3279 or (800) 528-6154, Internet: www.visitlakepowell.com.

Fishing guides include Ambassador Guide Service, tel. (800) 256-7596, and Arizona Reel Time, tel. (520) 355-2222 or (888) 533-7337.

Campground

The $10 sites at Lees Ferry Campground have drinking water but no hookups or showers; there's usually space available. Campers can use showers and laundry facilities beside Marble Canyon Lodge. From US 89A, take Lees Ferry Road in 4.4 miles and turn left at the sign. A dump station is on the right on the main road, 0.4 miles past the campground turnoff. The National Park Service allows boat camping on the Colorado River above Lees Ferry only at developed campsites. These plentiful sites lack piped water but are free. Remember to purify river water before drinking and pack out what you pack in.

PARIA CANYON~ VERMILION CLIFFS WILDERNESS

The wild and twisting canyons of the Paria River and its tributaries offer a memorable adventure for experienced hikers. Silt-laden waters have sculpted the colorful canyon walls, revealing 200 million years of geologic history. You enter the 2,000-foot-deep gorge of the Paria in southern Utah, then hike 38 miles downstream to Lees

the Narrows inside Paria Canyon

Paria Canyon. Though outlaws used it and prospectors came in search of gold, uranium, and other minerals, much of the Paria Canyon remained little visited.

In the late 1960s, the Bureau of Land Management (BLM) organized a small expedition whose research led to protection of the canyon as a primitive area. The Arizona Wilderness Act in 1984 designated Paria Canyon a wilderness, together with parts of the Paria Plateau and Vermilion Cliffs.

Hiking

Allow four to six days to hike Paria Canyon—there are many river crossings and you'll want to take side trips up some of the tributary canyons. The hike is considered moderately difficult. Hikers should have enough backpacking experience to be self-sufficient, as help may lie days away. Flash floods can race through the canyon, especially from July to September. Rangers will advise if they think danger exists, but they no longer close the canyon when storms threaten. The upper end contains narrow passages, particularly between Miles 4.2 and 9.0. Rangers suggest all hikers obtain up-to-date weather information.

You must register at White House, Buckskin, Wire Pass, or Lees Ferry Trailheads when entering or exiting the canyons. Backpackers also need to purchase a permit at $5 per person per day, but day-hikers do not need one. Backpackers have to fork over the same $5 fee on behalf of their dogs, too. Permits, weather forecasts, and up-to-date information are available from BLM rangers at the Paria Information Station near the trailhead, open daily 8:30 a.m.-5 p.m. March-Oct. and intermittently the rest of the year; get permits by mail by writing Paria Permits, NAU Box 15018, Flagstaff, AZ 86011. Information and permits are also available from the Kanab Area Office, 318 N. 100 East, Kanab, Utah 84741, tel. (435) 644-2672, open Mon.-Fri. 7:45 a.m.-4:30 p.m. year-round. An interactive website shows available dates and gives reservation procedures at paria.az.blm.gov. You can check dates by phone and obtain permits from the Arizona Strip Interpretive Association in St. George, Utah; tel. (435) 688-3246. The BLM state offices in Phoenix and Salt Lake City may also be able to issue permits. The Paria Information Station posts weather forecasts and offers drinking water. The

Ferry in Arizona, where the Paria empties into the Colorado River. Besides the canyons, this 110,000-acre wilderness area protects colorful cliffs, giant natural amphitheaters, sandstone arches, and parts of the Paria Plateau. Wonderful swirling patterns in sandstone hills, known as the "Coyote Buttes," enthrall visitors on top of the plateau. The 1,000-foot-high, rosy-hued Vermilion Cliffs meet the mouth of Paria Canyon at Lees Ferry. The river's name, sometimes spelled Pahreah, is Paiute for "muddy water."

History

Ancient petroglyphs and campsites indicate that Pueblo Indians traveled the Paria more than 700 years ago. They hunted mule deer and bighorn sheep while using the broad lower end of the canyon to grow corn, beans, and squash.

The Dominguez-Escalante Expedition stopped at the mouth of the Paria in 1776 and were the first white people to gaze upon the river. After John Lee began his Colorado River ferry service in 1872, he and others farmed the lower

BLM's *Hiker's Guide to Paria Canyon* book ($8) has detailed maps and information.

All visitors need to take special care to minimize impact on this beautiful canyon. Check the BLM "Visitor Use Regulations" before you go. Rules include no campfires in the Paria and its tributaries, a pack-in/pack-out policy (including toilet paper!), and a latrine location at least 100 feet away from river and campsites. Hiking parties may not exceed 10 people.

The best times to travel along the Paria are mid-March to June, and late September to November. May, especially Memorial Day weekend, is the most popular time. Winter hikers often complain of painfully cold feet. Wear shoes suitable for frequent wading; light fabric and leather boots or jungle boots work better than heavy leather hiking boots.

You can draw good drinking water from springs along the way—see the BLM's book *Hiker's Guide to Paria Canyon*. It's best not to use river water because of possible chemical pollution from farms and ranches upstream. Normally the river flows only ankle deep, but can rise to waist-deep levels in the spring or after rainy spells. During thunderstorms, the river can roar up to 20 feet deep in the Paria Narrows, so heed weather warnings. Floods usually subside within 12 hours. Quicksand, most prevalent after flooding, is more a nuisance than a danger—rarely more than knee deep. Still, many hikers carry a walking stick for probing the opaque waters before crossing.

Wrather Canyon Arch

One of Arizona's largest natural arches lies about one mile up this side canyon. The massive structure has a 200-foot span. Veer right (southwest) at Mile 20.6 on the Paria hike. The mouth of Wrather Canyon and other points along the Paria are unsigned; you need to follow your map. No camping is allowed in this canyon.

Trailheads and Shuttle Services

The BLM's Paria Information Station is in Utah, 30 miles northwest of Page on US 89 near Milepost 21, on the south side of the highway just east of the Paria River. The actual trailhead lies two miles south on a dirt road near an old homestead site called White House Ruins. You may camp here (pit toilets and picnic tables) for a $5

fee with up to five persons. The exit trailhead is at Lonely Dell Ranch near Lees Ferry, 44 miles southwest of Page via US 89 and 89A.

The hike requires a 150-mile roundtrip car shuttle. You can make arrangements for someone else to do it for you, using either your car (about $50-90), or theirs (about $100-150). Staff at the Arizona Strip Interpretive Association, Paria Information Center, or BLM Kanab Resource District can supply you with an up-to-date list of shuttle services.

Buckskin Gulch

This amazing Paria tributary features convoluted walls hundreds of feet high, yet narrows to as little as four feet in width. In some places the walls block out so much light you'll think you're walking in a cave. Be *very* careful to avoid times of flash floods. Hiking can be strenuous, with rough terrain, deep pools of water, and log and rock jams that sometimes require the use of ropes.

You can descend into Buckskin from two trailheads, Buckskin and Wire Pass, both approached by a dirt road not always passable by cars. The hike from Buckskin trailhead to the Paria River is 16.3 miles one-way and takes six to eight or more hours. From Wire Pass trailhead it's 1.7 miles to Buckskin Gulch, then 11.8 miles to the Paria. You can climb out to a safe camping place on a hazardous route—extremely hazardous if you're not an experienced climber—about halfway down Buckskin Gulch; this way out should not be counted on as an escape route. Carry enough water to last until you reach the mouth of Buckskin Gulch. Wire Pass also makes a good day-hike; it's even narrower than Buckskin and an easy 1.7-mile walk.

Coyote Buttes

The secret is out on this colorful swirling sandstone atop the Paria Plateau! You've probably seen photos of these wonderful ridges, but not directions on how to reach them. The BLM has opened Coyote Buttes for day use only with a $5 fee and the same permit procedures as for the Paria River. The area, just south of Wire Pass, has been divided into Coyote North and Coyote South with a limit of 10 people per day in each. The famous "wave" is in the north, so this region is the most popular; staff will give you a map and directions to the wave, but you're then on your own, as the wilderness lacks signs. Permits are more difficult to obtain in spring and autumn—the best times to visit—and on weekends. The fragile sandstone can break if climbed on, so it's important to stay on existing hiking routes and wear soft-soled footwear. Lightning storms occur most often in late summer but can appear at any time of year.

Hikers also need to carry water and keep an eye out for rattlesnakes. BLM staff can advise on road conditions. You can reach Coyote North from the Notch Access, about two miles south of Wire Pass Trailhead. Coyote South requires 4WD for Paw Hole Access and Cottonwood Cove Access; deep sand may make these areas impassable during summer.

PAGE

Until 1957, only sand and desert vegetation lay atop Manson Mesa, 130 miles north of Flagstaff. In that year the U.S. Bureau of Reclamation decided to build a giant reservoir in Glen Canyon on the Colorado River. Glen Canyon Dam became one of the largest construction projects ever undertaken: the 710-foot-high structure created a lake covering 250 square miles with a shoreline of nearly 2,000 miles. Workers hastily set up prefabricated metal buildings for barracks, dining hall, and offices. Trailers rolled in, one serving as a bank, another as a school. And thus was born the town of Page. The Bureau of Reclamation named it for John C. Page, who served as the bureau's commissioner from 1937 to 1943.

The remote desert spot (elev. 4,300 feet) gradually turned into a modern town with schools, businesses, and churches. Streets were named and grass and trees planted so that Page took on the appearance of an American suburb. Today, the town still looks new and clean. Though small (pop. 8,500), it's the largest community in far northern Arizona and offers travelers a variety of places to stay and eat.

Wedged between the Arizona Strip to the west, Glen Canyon National Recreation Area to the north, and the Navajo Reservation to the east and south, Page makes a useful base for visiting all of these areas. The townsite overlooks Lake Powell and Glen Canyon Dam; the large Wahweap Resort and Marina lies just six miles away.

SIGHTS AND RECREATION

Powell Museum
This collection honors scientist and explorer John Wesley Powell. In 1869 Powell led the first expedition down the Green and Colorado River canyons, then ran the rivers a second time in 1871-72. It was he who named the most splendid section the Grand Canyon.

Old drawings and photographs illustrate Powell's life and voyages. Fossil and mineral displays interpret the thick geologic sections revealed by the canyons of the Colorado River system. Other exhibits contain pottery, baskets, weapons, and tools of Southwestern Indian tribes, as well as memorabilia from early pioneers and the founding of Page. Staff offer travel information, Lake Powell boat tours, all-day and half-day float trips, Corkscrew/Antelope Canyon tours, scenic flights, and a regional bookstore.

In summer (May-Sept.), the museum is open daily 8 a.m.-6 p.m.; during April and October the hours are Mon.-Sat. 8 a.m.-5 p.m.; and from mid-February through March and November to mid-December the hours are Mon.-Fri. 9 a.m.-5 p.m.; it's closed mid-December to mid-February. A $1 donation is appreciated. The museum is in downtown Page at the corner of 6 N. Lake Powell Blvd. and N. Navajo Drive, tel. (520) 645-9496, fax (520) 645-3412, e-mail: museum@page-lake-powell.com.

Diné Bí Keyah Museum (Big Lake Trading Post)
The small collection of prehistoric and modern Indian artifacts on the second floor is open daily 8 a.m.-7 p.m.; tel. (520) 645-2404. Admission is free. Big Lake Trading Post lies 1.3 miles southeast of downtown at the corner of Coppermine Road and AZ 98. The post offers Indian crafts and groceries for sale.

The Best Dam View
An excellent panorama of Glen Canyon Dam and the Colorado River can be enjoyed just west

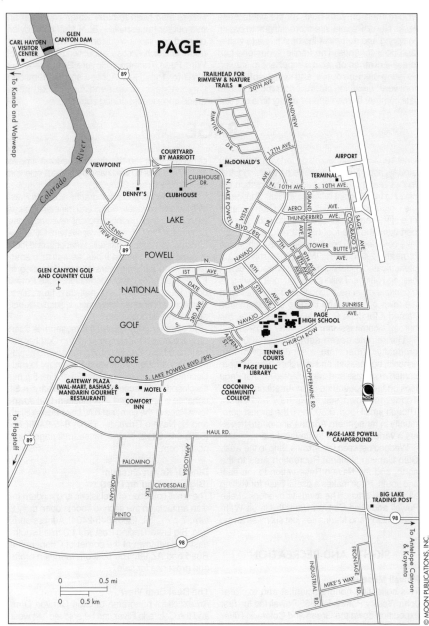

PAGE

CARL HAYDEN VISITOR CENTER

GLEN CANYON DAM

To Kanab and Wahweap

Colorado River

89

TRAILHEAD FOR RIMVIEW & NATURE TRAILS

20TH AVE.

GRANDVIEW

RIMVIEW DR.

12TH AVE.

AIRPORT

COURTYARD BY MARRIOTT

McDONALD'S

TERMINAL

VIEWPOINT

CLUBHOUSE DR.

N. 10TH AVE.

S. 10TH AVE.

DENNY'S

CLUBHOUSE

N. LAKE POWELL BLVD.

VISTA DR.

89L

AERO

GRAND VIEW AVE.

SAGE AVE.

LAKE

THUNDERBIRD AVE.

COLORADO ST.

POWELL

NAVAJO

7TH ST.

TOWER AVE.

9TH AVE.

BUTTE AVE.

SCENIC VIEW RD.

89

NATIONAL

1ST AVE.

N.

6TH AVE.

8TH AVE.

SUNRISE AVE.

GLEN CANYON GOLF AND COUNTRY CLUB

DATE

ELM

5TH AVE.

DR.

GOLF

3RD AVE.

NAVAJO

PAGE HIGH SCHOOL

S.

COURSE

ASPEN ST.

CHURCH ROW

COPPERMINE RD.

TENNIS COURTS

S. LAKE POWELL BLVD./89L

PAGE PUBLIC LIBRARY

GATEWAY PLAZA (WAL-MART, BASHAS', & MANDARIN GOURMET RESTAURANT)

MOTEL 6

COCONINO COMMUNITY COLLEGE

COMFORT INN

To Flagstaff

89

HAUL RD.

PAGE-LAKE POWELL CAMPGROUND

PALOMINO

APPALOOSA

MORGAN

ELK

CLYDESDALE

BIG LAKE TRADING POST

PINTO

98

98

To Antelope Canyon & Kayenta

FRONTAGE RD.

INDUSTRIAL RD.

MIKE'S WAY

0   0.5 mi

0   0.5 km

of town. It's reached via Scenic View Road behind Denny's Restaurant off US 89; turn west at the junction of US 89 and N. Lake Powell Blvd. or west beside the Glen Canyon N.R.A. headquarters building and turn at the sign for "scenic overlook." A short trail leads down to the best viewpoint.

Rimview Trail

An eight-mile trail for walkers, joggers, and cyclists encircles Page with many views of the surrounding desert and Lake Powell. The unpaved route has some sandy and rocky sections that will challenge novice bike riders. If you find yourself more than 30 vertical feet below the mesa rim, you're off the trail. You can pick up a map from the chamber office. A popular starting point is at the short nature trail loop near Lake View School at N. Navajo Dr. and 20th Ave. in the northern part of town. Other access points allow for excursions of different lengths.

Corkscrew/Antelope Canyon

You'll see photos around town of the beautifully convoluted red rock in this canyon, so narrow in places that you have to squeeze through. Sunshine reflects off the smooth Navajo sandstone to create extraordinary light and colors. It's also very dim. Photographers don't wish to spoil the effect with a flash, so most bring a tripod to help capture the infinite shapes and patterns. Beams of light enter the canyons at midday, further entrancing visitors.

Antelope Canyon has a wider upper section known as "Corkscrew" and a narrower lower section. The shallow wash in between that you see from the highway gives no hint of the marvels up or downstream. Both can easily be reached from Page by driving south on Coppermine Road or east on AZ 98 to Big Lake Trading Post, then continuing east one mile on AZ 98 toward the power plant. Turn right into the parking area for the upper canyon, or stay on AZ 98 just 0.15 mile farther and then turn left half a mile at the sign on paved Navajo Route N22B (Antelope Point Road) for the lower canyon. At either place you'll pay $5 for a tribal entry permit plus shuttle or tour fees. The upper section has a $10 shuttle charge for the 3.5-mile drive to the trailhead and a one-hour visit; no walk-ins or private drive-ins are permitted. The shuttle cost increases to $15 for a two-hour visit, $20 for three to four hours, and $30 for all day. The lower canyon can be visited only on guided hikes of $12.50 for one hour, $15 for two hours, $20 for three to four hours, or $30 for all day. Children pay less. Sightseers can tour either section easily in an hour; photographers will probably wish to spend more time. As captivating as the forms and patterns may be, photographers need to be careful not to block passages for other canyon visitors!

Both sections are open daily 8 a.m.-5 p.m. April-Sept. and daily 9 a.m.-3 p.m. the rest of the year; closed Thanksgiving. It's a good idea to check first with the chamber office or call the An-

arch in Lower Antelope Canyon

telope Canyon Navajo Tribal Park at (520) 698-3347. From early April to late October, the canyon hours run on the Navajo Reservation's daylight saving time (when it's 4 p.m. in Page, it's 5 p.m. at Antelope). Late starts also run the risk of the canyons closing early if business is slow. In winter (Dec.-March) you may need to telephone ahead to arrange a visit; phone numbers are on the gates. You can also take a guided excursion from Page; see "Tours" under "Page Practicalities." Check the weather forecast before heading out, as slot canyons be deadly during a flash flood. Escape netting is planned in the lower canyon, after 11 hikers who were warned not to go in perished during an August 1997 flood there.

Horseshoe Bend View

The Colorado River makes a sharp, 180-degree bend below this spectacular viewpoint. Look for the parking area just west of US 89, 0.2 mile south of Milepost 545; it's 2.5 miles south of the Gateway Plaza in Page. A three-quarter-mile trail leads from the parking to the overlook. Photographers will find a wide-angle lens handy to take in the whole scene. Mornings have good light for pictures; afternoons can be dramatic if the sky is filled with clouds.

Water Holes Canyon

A Navajo guide takes visitors into the scenic narrows of this canyon near Milepost 542 on US 89, about six miles south of Page. It has three slot sections. Listed hours (Navajo Reservation time) are daily 8 a.m.-1 p.m. and 3-7 p.m., but it's a good idea to check with the chamber office first.

More Recreation

Page High School features a year-round indoor **swimming pool** near the corner of S. Lake Powell Blvd. and AZ 98; tel. (520) 608-4100. Play **tennis** at the courts on S. Lake Powell Blvd. (Church Row).

Lake Powell National Golf Course offers an 18-hole championship golf course that wraps around the west side of the mesa; turn in on Clubhouse Drive adjacent to the Courtyard by Marriott; tel. (520) 645-2023. **Glen Canyon Golf and Country Club** has a nine-hole golf course west across US 89 from the 18-hole course; tel. (520) 645-2715.

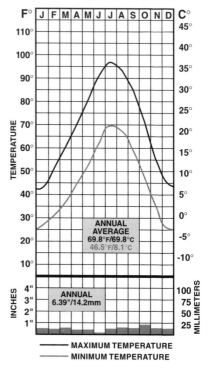

PAGE AREA CLIMATE

ANNUAL AVERAGE
69.8°F/69.8°C
46.5°F/8.1°C

ANNUAL
6.39"/14.2mm

—— MAXIMUM TEMPERATURE
········· MINIMUM TEMPERATURE

Twin Finn Diving Center offers a variety of diving activities and classes and rents diving equipment and kayaks at 811 Vista Ave.; tel. (520) 645-3114. There are several places in Page and the surrounding area that rent boats and personal watercraft; consult the telephone yellow pages.

PAGE ACCOMMODATIONS

Nearly all Page motels lie on or near Lake Powell Blvd./Hwy 89L, a 3.25-mile loop that branches off the main highway. The summer rates listed here drop in winter (Nov.-March). Prices run on the high side in town—you're unlikely to find anything under $35 in season except for the hostel. The Eighth Avenue places lie in Page's "historic district," a quiet residential area two blocks off Lake Powell Boulevard. These apartments date way back to 1957 when they housed the higher-ranking workers at the dam; today some have been fixed up as pensions and motels.

Budget
Lake Powell International Hostel & Pension at 141 Eighth Ave., tel. (520) 645-3898, offers the lowest rates in Page. Dorm rooms run $15 ($12 in winter, mid-October to mid-April); pension rooms with shared bath cost $35-40 d ($25 d in winter), while suites with private bath and kitchen go for $45-70 (four people). It's a great place to meet people from around the world—guests gather in the backyard for evening barbecues, volleyball, and basketball. Amenities include common rooms, kitchens, and laundry facilities.

Inexpensive
Uncle Bill's Place next to the hostel at 117 Eighth Ave. features a quiet garden in back; rooms with shared bath and kitchen run $36-39 d, private suites start at $59-69 d and go up to $109-119 (six people); tel. (520) 645-1224.

Lu Lu's Sleep EZZe Motel has Eighth Avenue's most luxurious rooms, all with private bath, at 105 Eighth Ave., tel. (520) 608-0273 or (800) 553-6211; rates run $39-54 d.

Red Rock Motel has private baths and some kitchens at 114 Eighth Ave., tel. (520) 645-0062; rates start at $39 s, $49 d.

KC's Motel is nearby at 126 Eighth Ave., tel. (520) 645-2947; rooms have private bath and cost $49 d.

Bashful Bob's Motel around the corner at 750 S. Navajo Dr. offers mostly two-bedroom apartments, all with kitchens, at $39-45 d; tel. (520) 645-3919; Internet: www.page.az.net/bashfulbobsmotel.

Page Boy Motel and its swimming pool can be found at 150 N. Lake Powell Blvd., tel. (520) 645-2416; rates are $40.50 s, $45.50 d.

Navajo Trail Motel has rooms at two downtown locations and on the southern outskirts; contact the office for all three places at 800 Bureau, where rooms are $35 s, $39 d; tel. (520) 645-9508. The nearby motel unit at 630 Vista, behind Glen Canyon Steak House, costs $39 s, $44 d; the third unit is at 524 Haul Road, where rooms go for $35 s, $39 d.

Moderate
Econo Lodge at 121 S. Lake Powell Blvd. near downtown offers rooms for $64 s, $69 d; tel. (520) 645-2488 or (800) 553-2666.

Weston's Empire House Motel features a swimming pool at 107 S. Lake Powell Blvd; rates are $54 s, $60 d.; tel. (520) 645-2406.

Super 8 Motel, at 75 S. Seventh Ave., furnishes accommodations for $66 d; tel. (520) 645-2858 or (800) 800-8000.

Holiday Inn Express has a pool, spa, and continental breakfast at 751 S. Navajo Dr.; rooms with two beds go for $79 d; tel. (520) 645-9000 or (800) HOLIDAY.

The **Best Western Weston Inn & Suites** offers a swimming pool at 207 N. Lake Powell Blvd.; rooms cost $63 s, $68 d; tel. (520) 645-2451 or (800) 637-9183.

Best Western at Lake Powell has a pool, spa, and exercise room at 208 N. Lake Powell Blvd.; rates are $69-139 d; tel. (520) 645-5988 or (800) 528-1234.

The nearby **Best Western Arizona Inn** provides fine views, swimming pool, and adjacent restaurant; rates are $60 s, $70 d ($70 s, $90 d for lakeview) at 716 Rim View Dr. and Lake Powell Blvd. (across from Ramada Inn); tel. (520) 645-2466 or (800) 826-2718.

Heading south from downtown, you'll find the new **Motel 6** with a pool at 637 S. Lake Powell Blvd.; rooms go for $49 s, $59 d; tel. (520) 645-5888 or (800) 4MOTEL6.

Comfort Inn, also new, is next door at 649 S. Lake Powell Blvd. with a pool and spa; rooms are $79-89 d; tel. 645-5858 or (800) 228-5150.

Day's Inn & Suites lies on the south edge of town beside US 89 with an outdoor pool and jacuzzi; rates are $79 d and up; tel. (520) 645-2800 or (877) 525-3769.

Expensive to Premium
Ramada Inn features a swimming pool, restaurant, and fine views over Lake Powell from 287 N. Lake Powell Blvd.; rooms cost $105 d ($115 d lakeside); tel. (520) 645-8851 or (800) 261-6702.

Courtyard by Marriott offers great views, a restaurant, a pool, spa, exercise room, and adjacent 18-hole golf course at 600 Clubhouse Dr. for $149 d; tel. (520) 645-5000 or (800) 321-2211.

Bed and Breakfasts

These include **Ammie Ann's,** tel. (520) 645-5505; **Canyon Colors,** tel. (520) 645-5979 or (800) 536-2530; **The Captain's Rest,** tel. (520) 645-2342; **Edie's,** tel. (520) 645-2754; **Des Jardines,** tel. (520) 645-5900; **Talbot's,** tel. (520) 645-3819; and **Thatcher's,** tel. (520) 645-3898.

Campgrounds

Page-Lake Powell Campground offers sites for tents ($15) and RVs ($17-20 w/hookups) with an indoor pool and spa, store, laundry, and showers; non-guests may use the showers or dump station for a small fee. The campground is 0.7 mile southeast of downtown on Coppermine Road; tel. (520) 645-3374. Other campgrounds, an RV park, and motels are in the Wahweap area.

MORE PAGE PRACTICALITIES

Food and Entertainment

M Bar H Cafe is a handy place for breakfast and does American lunches too; open daily 5 a.m.-3 p.m. at 819 N. Navajo Dr., tel. (520) 645-1420. **Dam Bar & Grill** serves up steak, barbecue, seafood, pasta, and sandwiches daily for lunch and dinner at 644 N. Navajo Dr. in the Dam Plaza, tel. (520) 645-2161; it also has a sports bar. The adjacent **Gunsmoke Saloon** features country bands and a variety of other music Wed.-Sat.; tel. (520) 645-2161.

Family Tree Restaurant in the Ramada Inn offers a varied menu daily for breakfast, lunch, and dinner; in summer, you can choose a buffet for breakfast daily, lunch on Sunday, and dinner (seafood on Friday). The Ramada is located at 287 N. Lake Powell Blvd., tel. (520) 645-8853. **Butterfield Stage Co. Restaurant** serves American food daily for breakfast, lunch, and dinner at 704 Rim View Dr. next to Best Western Arizona Inn; dinner choices include steak, prime rib, and seafood; tel. (520) 645-2467. **Pepper's Restaurant** at the Courtyard by Marriott offers American and continental cuisine with a Southwestern touch and is open daily for breakfast (a buffet is also available), lunch, and dinner at 600 Clubhouse Dr., tel. (520) 645-1247. **Denny's** serves popular American fare daily for break-

fast, lunch, and dinner at 169 Scenic View Dr. (turn west at the US 89-N. Lake Powell Blvd. junction), tel. (520) 645-3999.

For Chinese cuisine, try **Mandarin Gourmet Restaurant,** open daily for lunch and dinner in Gateway Plaza; tel. (520) 645-5516. **Padre Bay Cafe & Grill** does Mexican food, steaks, seafood, and sandwiches; it's open daily for lunch and dinner at 635 Elm St., tel. (520) 645-9058. **Bella Napoli** offers fine Italian cuisine daily for dinner in summer and Mon.-Sat. for dinner the rest of the year; the restaurant closes completely from late December to mid-February; 810 N. Navajo Dr., tel. (520) 645-2706. **Strombolli's Pizza** is open daily for lunch and dinner at 711 N. Navajo Dr., where diners have a choice of indoor seating or the outdoor deck, a popular gathering spot for boaters in the summer; tel. (520) 645-2605. Pizza, spaghetti, and other Italian fare are also served daily for lunch and dinner by **Pizza Hut,** 6 S. Lake Powell Blvd. in Dam Square, tel. (520) 645-2455, and **Little Caesar's** (carry-out only), Page Plaza near the corner of S. Lake Powell Blvd. and Elm St., tel. (520) 645-5565.

You can buy **groceries** at Safeway (Page Plaza at corner of S. Lake Powell Blvd. and Elm St.), Bashas' (Gateway Plaza), or at Mrs. C's Health Food Center (32 S. Lake Powell Blvd.).

Cultural Dinner Theater

An Evening with the Navajo begins with a horse-drawn wagon ride to a Navajo village, then participants enjoy a dinner with traditional foods, stories, and demonstrations (cooking, weaving, and silversmithing). The five-hour evening presentations cost $55 adults, $40 children 6-13; tel. (520) 660-0304 (pager) or contact the Page/Lake Powell Chamber of Commerce; tel. (520) 645-2741 or Powell Museum; tel. (520) 645-9496.

Events

In March, anglers test their skills in the Bullfrog Open bass tournament. In late April-early May, women's pro basketball players compete in an invitational tournament. Also in May, Page and regional firefighters have a competition on the first weekend. Cowboy Days & Indian Nights, a Native American Pow Wow on the second weekend in May, has amazing dances, drumming, and music.

rafting the Colorado River through Glen Canyon

On July 4th, fireworks light the sky over Glen Canyon Dam. Mr. Burfel's Softball Tournament plays on the fourth weekend of September. In October, Air Affaire lifts off over Page with hot air balloons, airplane acrobatics, and parachutists on the first weekend.

Scenic Southwest Art and Photography Competition and Show comes to town on the second weekend of November, while Bullfrog's Festival of Lights Parade takes place on the Saturday after Thanksgiving. In December, the Here Comes Santa Parade marks the holiday season in Page. Wahweap Festival of Lights Parade on Lake Powell glides by on the first Saturday.

For more information on Lake Powell events, ask at the marina. To learn about other events, contact Page/Lake Powell Chamber of Commerce, tel. (520) 645-2741.

Services and Information

The **post office** is at 44 Sixth Ave., tel. (520) 645-2571. Catch movies at **Mesa Theatre**, 42 S. Lake Powell Blvd., tel. (520) 645-9565. **Page Hospital** stands at the corner of Vista Ave. and N. Navajo Dr., tel. (520) 645-2424. In **emergencies**—police, fire, medical—dial 911.

The **Page/Lake Powell Chamber of Commerce** offers information about area sights and services and books lake and river tours, Corkscrew/Antelope Canyon tours, and scenic flights. It's open Mon.-Sat. 8 a.m.-8 p.m. and Sun. 9 a.m.-6 p.m. from May 16 to October 16, then Mon.-Sat. 8 a.m.-5:30 p.m. the rest of the year. The office is at 644 N. Navajo Dr. in the Dam Plaza (Box 727, Page, AZ 86040), tel. (520) 645-2741 or (888) 261-PAGE, e-mail: chamber@page-lakepowell.com.

The new semi-circular **Page Public Library** rises impressively from the mesa rim at 479 S. Lake Powell Blvd.; it has an Arizona/Native American collection, internet computers, and fine views. It's open Mon.-Thurs. 10 a.m.-8 p.m. and Fri.-Sat. 10 a.m.-5 p.m.; tel. (520) 645-4270. **Front Page** has regional titles, general reading, and office supplies at 48 S. Lake Powell Blvd., tel. (520) 645-5333.

Tours

You can get information and make reservations for many area tours through the Page/Lake Powell Chamber of Commerce or Powell Museum.

Lake Powell Jeep Tours offers regular and photographer's tours to Corkscrew Canyon in Antelope Wash year-round, weather permitting; 104 S. Lake Powell Blvd., tel. (520) 645-5501, Internet: www.jeeptour.com. **Roger Ekis' Photographic Tours** goes to both upper and lower Antelope Canyon; tel. (520) 645-8579 or (435) 675-9109. **Scenic Tours** does 90-minute excursions to Corkscrew Canyon; tel. (520) 645-5594. **J&C Outfitters** takes visitors on guided ATV tours in the Page and Kaibab Plateau areas; beginners receive instruction; tel. (520) 645-9557.

Wilderness River Adventures offers raft trips down the Colorado River from just below Glen Canyon Dam to Lees Ferry, traveling over

15 miles of smooth-flowing water through the beautiful canyon of Navajo Sandstone. You'll stop to inspect some fine petroglyphs, and you're likely to see condors, blue herons, ducks, and other birds. Half-day trips leave once or twice daily March-Oct., weather permitting; the cost is $49 adults, $39 children 12 and under. All-day trips have more time on the water and include a lunch buffet; they run May 15 to Sept. 15 and cost $68.50 adults, $59.25 children 12 and under. Kayakers and canoeists can arrange for rafts to take them from Lees Ferry upstream to the dam. Contact the company at 50 S. Lake Powell Blvd.; tel. (520) 645-3279 or (800) 528-6154; Internet: www.visitlakepowell.com.

Sun Air offers a number of flightseeing trips, including journeys over Lake Powell and Rainbow Bridge (half-hour, $71), Lake Powell and Escalante River (one hour, $119), Grand Canyon (hour and a half, $159), Monument Valley (hour and a half, $150, $190 with ground tour), and Bryce Canyon (hour and a half, $149). A two-person minimum applies to most tours, and children 2-11 fly at a discount; tel. (520) 645-2494 or (800) 245-8668. **Classic Helicopter Tours** takes to the air with 10-minute Tower Butte ($39), 15-minute Tower Butte & Antelope Creek ($59), 25- to 30-minute Rainbow Bridge ($95), and 50- to 55-minute Rainbow Bridge and Escalante ($160) tours; there's a four-person minimum; tel. (520) 645-5356. Boat tours to Rainbow Bridge and other destinations leave from nearby Wahweap Marina; see "Glen Canyon National Recreation Area" below.

Transportation

Wahweap Lodge operates **Page Shuttle** frequently to Page and the airport; tel. (520) 645-2433. Most area motels also provide transportation for guests to and from the airport. From the Page Airport on the east edge of town, **Sun Air** offers several flights daily to Phoenix at $150 one way, $170-219 roundtrip; charters can be arranged; tel. (520) 645-2494 or (800) 245-8668. **Avis,** which meets incoming flights, rents cars; tel. (520) 645-2024 or (800) 331-1212.

Adventure Network for Travelers (ANT) buses make a one-way loop through the Southwest from Los Angeles with hop-on, hop-off service; tel. (415) 399-0880 or (800) 336-6049; Internet: www.TheANT.com.

GLEN CANYON NATIONAL RECREATION AREA

This vast recreation area covers 1.25 million acres, most of which spreads northeast into Utah. Lake Powell is the centerpiece, surrounded by beautiful canyon country. Just a handful of roads approach the lake, so the visitor must boat or hike to truly explore this unique land of water and rock. The recreation area also includes a beautiful remnant of Glen Canyon in a 15-mile section of the Colorado River from Glen Canyon Dam to Lees Ferry. As big as the lake is, it comprises only 13% of the vast Glen Canyon National Recreation Area—there's much to discover!

Rainbow Bridge National Monument—50 miles uplake from the dam—contains the world's largest natural bridge; it's easily reached on boat tours from Wahweap or Bullfrog or by your own boat. You can also hike in on a spectacular trail. See below. The Carl Hayden Visitor Center has information on the monument.

Entry Fees
Visits to most areas now cost $5 per vehicle or $3 per cyclist or hiker for seven days unless you have a Golden Eagle, Golden Age, or Golden Access card; an annual pass to the recreation area is $15. Motorized boats are an extra $10, then $4 for each additional; an annual boat pass runs $20. Admission to the Carl Hayden Visitor Center is still free.

Climate
Summer, when temperatures rise into the 90s and 100s F, is the busiest season for swimming, boating, and water-skiing. Visits during the rest of the year can be enjoyable, too, though more conducive to sightseeing, fishing, and hiking. Spring and autumn are the best times to enjoy the backcountry. Winter temperatures drop to highs in the 40s and 50s, with freezing nights and the possibility of snow. Lake surface temperatures range from a comfortable 80° in August to a chilly 45° in January. Chinook winds can blow day and night from February to May. Thunderstorms in late summer bring strong, gusting winds with widely scattered rain showers. Annual precipitation averages about seven inches.

Geology, Flora, and Fauna
The colorful rock layers rising above the lake's surface are the remains of deposits from ancient deserts, oceans, and rivers. Uplift of the Colorado Plateau, beginning about 60 million years ago, started a cycle of erosion that has carved canyons and created delicately balanced rocks and graceful natural arches and bridges.

The desert comes right to the edge of the water, because fluctuating lake levels prevent plant growth along the shore. Common plants of this high-desert country include prickly pear and hedgehog cacti, rabbitbrush, sand sagebrush, blackbrush, cliffrose, mariposa and sego lilies, globemallow, Indian paintbrush, evening primrose, penstemon, and Indian rice grass. Pinyon pine and juniper trees grow on the high plateaus. Springs and permanent streams support sandbar willow, tamarisk, cattail, willow, and cottonwood. Look for hanging gardens of maidenhair

black-tailed jackrabbit
(Lepus californicus)

fern, columbine, and other water-loving plants in small alcoves high on the sandstone walls.

Most animals are secretive and nocturnal; you're most likely to see them in early morning or in the evening. Local mammals include desert bighorn sheep, pronghorns, mule deer, mountain lions, coyotes, red and gray foxes, ringtail cats, spotted and striped skunks, bobcats, badgers, river otters, beavers, prairie dogs, Ord kangaroo rats, black-tailed jackrabbits, several species of squirrels and chipmunks, and many species of mice and bats. Types of lizards you might spot sunning on a rock include collared, side-blotched, desert horned, and chuckwalla. Snake species include the common kingsnake, gopher snake, striped whipsnake, western rattlesnake, and western diamondback rattlesnake.

Birds stopping by on their migratory routes include American avocet, Canada goose, and teal. Others, such as blue heron, snowy egret, and bald eagle, come for the winter. Birds in residence all year are American merganser, mallard, canyon wren, pinyon jay, common raven, red-tailed and Swainson's hawks, great horned and long-eared owls, peregrine and prairie falcons, and the golden eagle. The giant California condors, recently released in the area, have been spotted in Glen Canyon downstream of the dam.

Recreation at Lake Powell

If you don't have your own craft, Wahweap and other marinas will rent you a boat for fishing, skiing, or houseboating. Boat tours visit Rainbow Bridge and other destinations from Wahweap, Bullfrog, and Halls Crossing Marinas. Sailboats find the steadiest breezes in Wahweap, Padre, Halls, and Bullfrog Bays, where spring winds average 15-20 knots. Kayaks and canoes can be used in the more protected areas. All boaters need to be alert for approaching storms that can bring wind gusts up to 60 mph. Waves on open expanses of the lake are sometimes steeper than ocean waves and can exceed six feet from trough to crest. Marinas and bookstores sell Lake Powell navigation maps.

You'll need an Arizona fishing license for the southern five miles of Lake Powell and a Utah license for the rest. Get licenses and information from marinas on the water or from sporting goods stores in Page. Anglers can catch largemouth, smallmouth, and striped bass; northern and walleye pike; catfish; crappie; and carp. Smaller fish include bluegill, perch, and sunfish. Wahweap has a swimming beach (no lifeguards), and boaters can seek out their own remote spots. **Fishing guides** know many of the angles on where and how to find the elusive fish. In the Page-Lake Powell area, you can contact Bubba's Guide Service at tel. (520) 645-5785 and Lake Powell Charter at tel. (520) 645-5505.

Hikers can choose between easy day-trips or long wilderness backpack treks. The canyons of the Escalante in Utah rate among America's premier hiking areas. Other good areas within or adjacent to Glen Canyon N.R.A. include Rainbow Bridge National Monument, Paria Canyon, Dark Canyon, and Grand Gulch. You'll find descriptions of these last two places as well as Escalante in Moon Publications' *Utah Handbook*. National Park Service staff at the Carl Hayden Visitor Center and the Bullfrog Visitor Center can suggest trips and supply trail descriptions. Several guidebooks to Lake Powell offer detailed hiking, camping, and boating information. Most of the canyon country near Lake Powell remains wild and little explored—hiking possibilities are limitless. Be sure to carry plenty of water.

Mountain bikers can head out on many back roads. The Visitor Center has a list of possibilities.

Scuba divers can visit the canyon cliffs and rock sculptures beneath the surface. Visibility runs 30-40 feet in late Aug.-Nov., the best season; there's less boat traffic then, too. In other seasons, visibility can drop to 10-20 feet.

Packing It Out

Much of the revenue from the new fees has gone toward improving water quality and cleaning up the shore. Visitors can help by packing out all trash. Also, anyone camping within one-quarter mile of the lake must have a container (not plastic bags) for solid human wastes unless a toilet is available on the beach or on your own boat. Eight "restrooms/pump-outs/dump stations" are located along the lake between Warm Creek Bay (13 miles from the dam) and Forgotten Canyon (106 miles from the dam).

LAKE POWELL

Conservationists deplore the loss of remote and beautiful Glen Canyon, buried today beneath Lake Powell. Only words, pictures, and memories remind us of its lost wonders.

Lake Powell is the second-largest artificial lake in the United States. Only Lake Mead, farther downstream, has a greater water-storage capacity. Lake Powell boasts a shoreline of 1,960 miles and holds enough water to cover the state of Pennsylvania a foot deep. Bays and coves offer nearly limitless opportunities for exploration by boaters. Only the lower portion—Glen Canyon Dam, Wahweap Resort and Marina, Antelope and Navajo Canyons, and the lower parts of Labyrinth, Face, and West Canyons—extend into Arizona. Lake Powell's surface elevation fluctuates an average of 20-30 feet through the year (fluctuation has reached 59 feet), peaking in July; it's at an elevation of 3,700 feet when full. The Carl Hayden Visitor Center, perched beside the dam, offers tours of the dam, related exhibits, and an information desk covering the entire Glen Canyon National Recreation Area.

GLEN CANYON DAM

Construction workers labored from 1956 to 1964 to build this giant concrete structure. It stands 710 feet high above bedrock, the top measuring 1,560 feet across. Thickness ranges from 300 feet at the base to just 25 feet at the top. As part of the Upper Colorado River Storage Project, the dam provides water storage (its main purpose), hydroelectricity, flood control, and recreation on Lake Powell. Eight giant turbine generators churn out a total of 1,150,000 kilowatts at 13,800 volts. Vertigo victims shouldn't look down when driving across Glen Canyon Bridge, just downstream of the dam; the cold green waters of the Colorado River glide 700 feet below.

Carl Hayden Visitor Center

Photos, paintings, movies, and slide presentations in the visitor center present various features of the Glen Canyon National Recreation Area, including Lake Powell and the construction of the dam. A giant relief map helps you visualize the rugged terrain surrounding the lake; look closely and you'll spot Rainbow Bridge. Guided one-hour tours visit the top of the dam, tunnels, the generating room, and the transformer platform; they depart daily every 30 minutes from mid-April to mid-October with the first tour at 8:30 a.m. and the last at 3:30 p.m. (5:30 p.m. Memorial to Labor Day). Senator Carl Hayden, a major backer of water development in the West, served as Arizona member of Congress 1912-1969, a record 57 consecutive years.

National Park Service staff operate an information desk where you can find out about boating, fishing, camping, and hiking in the immense Glen Canyon National Recreation Area, or you can write Box 1507, Page, AZ 86040, tel. (520)

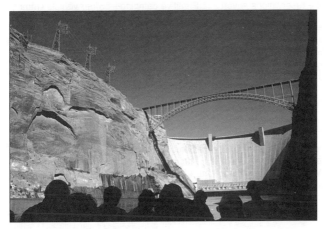

Glen Canyon Dam from the Colorado River

608-6404, Internet: www.nps.gov/glca. In case of emergency only, dial (520) 608-6300 or just 911. Staff also offer short talks on a variety of topics relevant to the Glen Canyon area. The Glen Canyon Natural History Association sells a variety of books on the recreation area and its environs. A Navajo rug exhibit illustrates one of the many different weaving patterns used. Another exhibit depicts prehistoric mammals that roamed the Glen Canyon area during the Ice Age. Souvenirs, snacks, and postcards are available at a gift shop in the visitor center building.

The Carl Hayden Visitor Center is open daily 7 a.m.-7 p.m. in summer and 8 a.m.-5 p.m. the rest of the year. Tours, exhibits, and movies are free. In summer, you can attend an evening program most nights at nearby Wahweap Campground amphitheater.

MARINAS

The **National Park Service** provides public boat ramps and ranger offices at most of the marinas. Rangers know current boating and backroad conditions, primitive camping areas, and good places to explore. **Lake Powell Resorts & Marinas** operates marina services, boat rentals, boat tours, accommodations, RV parks, and restaurants; for information and reservations (strongly recommended in summer) write Box 56909, Phoenix, AZ 85079, call (800) 528-6154 or (602) 278-8888 in greater Phoenix, or fax (602) 331-5258. To make reservations seven days or fewer in advance, contact each marina or resort directly. All the marinas stay open year-round; you can avoid crowds and peak prices by arriving in autumn, winter, or spring. Private or chartered aircraft can fly to Page Airport, Bullfrog's small airstrip, and Halls Crossing's large airstrip.

Wahweap

The name means Bitter Water in the Ute Indian language. Wahweap Lodge and Marina, Lake Powell's largest, offers complete boaters' services and rentals, guided fishing trips, deluxe accommodations, an RV park, and fine dining. Wahweap lies seven miles northwest of Page, five miles beyond the visitor center.

Wahweap Lodge offers swimming pools and several types of rooms—many with lake views—at $139 d ($149 d lake view) in summer and $97 d ($107 d lake view) the rest of the year. Premium. The lodge's fine-dining restaurant features a panoramic view for its daily breakfast, lunch, and dinner; in summer there's live entertainment and dancing. The nearby Itza Pizza does pizza, subs, and salads daily. A boat tour desk and a large gift shop (books, Indian crafts, and souvenirs) lie just off the lobby. Contact Lake Powell Resorts & Marinas for reservations at Box 56909, Phoenix, AZ 85079, tel. (800) 528-6154 or (602) 278-8888 in greater Phoenix, fax (602) 331-5258. You can also reach Wahweap Lodge & Marina at Box 1597, Page, AZ 86040, tel. (520) 645-2433.

Lake Powell Motel features less expensive rooms at nearby Wahweap Junction, four miles northwest of Glen Canyon Dam on US 89; rooms cost $77 d. The motel is closed in winter; call (520) 645-2477 or contact Lake Powell Resorts & Marinas for reservations. Moderate.

An **RV park** with coin showers and laundry costs $23 with hookups ($16 in winter). **Wahweap Campground** is operated first-come, first-served by the concessionaire; the $13 sites have drinking water but no showers or hookups. Evening **interpretive programs** take place here most days in the summer. Campers may use the pay showers and laundry at the RV park. The campground, RV park, and a picnic area lie between Wahweap Lodge and Stateline, 1.3 miles northwest of the lodge.

Primitive camping—$6 per vehicle with no water available—is available at **Lone Rock** in Utah, six miles northwest of Wahweap off US 89. Boaters may also camp along the lakeshore, but not within one mile of developed areas. A free picnic area and fish-cleaning station are just west of Wahweap Lodge. You'll find public boat ramps adjacent to the lodge and at Stateline. During summer (June 1 to September 30), you can obtain maps and brochures from the **Wahweap Ranger Station** near the picnic area; at other times see the staff at Carl Hayden Visitor Center.

The marina offers seven **lake tours,** ranging from an hour-long paddle-wheel cruise around Wahweap Bay ($10 adults, $7 children 2-12) to an all-day trip to Rainbow Bridge, 50 miles away ($88 adults, $58 children 2-12). Half-day trips to Rainbow Bridge cost $63 adults, $43 children 2-12. The other tours are a 90-minute Antelope Canyon cruise, two-and-a-half-hour Canyon Explorer/Navajo Tapestry tour, two-hour sunset cruise, and three-hour dinner cruise. **Boat rentals** at Stateline include a 14-foot skiff with small motor at $116 ($70 off season) per day, an 18-foot powerboat with 115-hp motor at $226 ($136 off season) per day, personal watercraft for $209 per day, and six sizes of houseboats starting at $851 ($511 off season) for three days. You can rent fishing gear and waterskis, too.

Dangling Rope

This floating marina lies 42 miles uplake from Glen Canyon Dam. The only access is by boat. Services include a ranger station, store, minor boat repairs, gas dock, and sanitary pump-out station. A dangling rope left behind in a nearby canyon, perhaps by uranium prospectors, prompted the name. The Rainbow Bridge dock lies 10 miles farther uplake in Bridge Canyon, a tributary of Forbidding Canyon.

San Juan

You can hand-launch boats at **Clay Hills Crossing** at the upper end of the San Juan Arm. An unpaved road that requires a high-clearance vehicle branches 11 miles southwest from UT 276 to the lake; don't attempt the road after rains. River-runners on the San Juan often take out here, but no facilities are provided. Boat access to the lake is sometimes blocked at low water by a bar of sediment dropped by the San Juan River as it enters Lake Powell. At high water the bar is covered.

Halls Crossing-Bullfrog Ferry

The *John Atlantic Burr* ferry can accommodate vehicles of all sizes as well as passengers for the short 20-minute crossing between these marinas. Halls Crossing and Bullfrog Marinas lie on opposite sides of Lake Powell about 95 lake miles from Glen Canyon Dam, roughly midway up the length of the lake. Highway UT 276 connects both marinas with UT 95. The ferry's daily schedule has six roundtrips from May 15 to September 30 and four roundtrips the rest of the year, no reservations needed. You can pick up a schedule at either marina. Service is sus-

pended for a brief time annually in winter for maintenance; signs at the UT 276 turnoffs warn you when the ferry is closed.

Halls Crossing

In 1880, Charles Hall built the ferry used by the Hole-in-the-Rock pioneers, who crossed the river to begin settling in southeast Utah. The approach roads were so bad, however, that in 1881 Hall moved the ferry 35 miles upstream to present-day Halls Crossing. Business remained slow, and Hall quit running the ferry in 1884.

Arriving at Halls Crossing by road, you first pass a small store offering three-bedroom **Family Units** ($149 up to six persons in summer, $104 off season), an **RV park** ($23 with hookups in summer, $16 off season), and gas pumps. The store may close in winter, but services are still available—ask at the trailer office next door. Coin-operated showers and laundry at the RV park are also open to the public. The separate campground just beyond and to the left offers sites with good views of the lake, drinking water, and restrooms for $12. A half mile farther down the main road are the boat ramp and **Halls Crossing Marina.** The marina features a larger store with groceries and fishing and boating supplies, tours to Rainbow Bridge, a boat rental office, a gas dock, slips, and storage. The ranger station is nearby, though rangers are usually out on patrol; look for ranger vehicles in the area if the office is closed.

Contact Lake Powell Resorts & Marinas for accommodations, boat rental, and tour reservations at Box 56909, Phoenix, AZ 85079, tel. (800) 528-6154 or (602) 278-8888 in greater Phoenix, fax (602) 331-5258. You can also reach the marina at Box 5101, Lake Powell, UT 84533, tel. (435) 684-7000.

Stabilized ancestral pueblo ruins at **Defiance House** in Forgotten Canyon make a good boating destination 12 miles uplake; a sign marks the beginning of the trail to the ruins.

Bullfrog

Before the days of Lake Powell, Bullfrog Rapids offered boaters a fast and bumpy ride. Today, Bullfrog Marina rivals Wahweap in its extensive visitor facilities. When arriving, you'll come first to the **visitor center** on the right, open daily 8 a.m.-5 p.m. (may be closed in winter); tel. (435) 684-

7400. The **clinic** is here too; it's open mid-May to mid-October 9:30 a.m.-6 p.m.; tel. (435) 684-2288. Next you'll see a large **campground** on the left; the $13 sites include drinking water and restrooms. Continue on the main road to a junction, where a service station offers repairs and supplies. Continue straight at the junction for a picnic area and the boat ramp, or turn right at the service station for Defiance House Lodge and Restaurant, Trailer Village, Bullfrog Painted Hills RV Park, and Bullfrog Marina.

Defiance House Lodge offers luxury accommodations and the **Anasazi Restaurant** (open daily for breakfast, lunch, and dinner). The front desk at the lodge also handles boat tours and three-bedroom **family units** (trailers) and an **RV park,** both nearby with the same rates as at Halls Crossing. Showers, laundry, a convenience store, and post office are at **Trailer Village.** The RV park also has showers. Ask rangers for directions to primitive camping areas at Upper Bullfrog and Stanton Creek near Bullfrog Bay; these cost $6 per vehicle.

All-day **Rainbow Bridge tours** usually leave daily from April 15 to October 31 and stop on request to pick up passengers at Halls Crossing Marina; call for dates in winter. The cost is $88 adults, $58 children 2-12. **Canyon Explorer/Navajo Tapestry tours** spend two and a half hours in nearby canyons during the same season from both marinas at $32 adults, $24 children 2-12. **Escalante Canyon excursions** visit this canyon on half-day trips from both marinas for $63 adults, $43 children 2-12. **Bullfrog Resort & Marina** offers boat rentals, gas dock, slips, storage, and a store. Contact Lake Powell Resorts & Marinas for accommodations, boat rental, and tour reservations at Box 56909, Phoenix, AZ 85079; tel. (800) 528-6154 or (602) 278-8888 in greater Phoenix, fax (602) 331-5258. Contact Bullfrog Resort & Marina at Box 4055-Bullfrog, Lake Powell, UT 84533, tel. (435) 684-3000.

Hite

In 1883, Cass Hite came to Glen Canyon in search of gold. He found a few nuggets at a place later named Hite City, setting off a small gold rush. Hite and some of his relatives operated a small store and post office, the only services available for many miles.

Travelers wishing to cross the Colorado River here faced the difficult task of swimming their animals across. Arthur Chaffin put through the first road and opened a ferry service in 1946. The Chaffin Ferry served uranium prospectors and adventurous motorists until the lake backed up to the spot in 1964. A steel bridge now spans the Colorado River far upstream; Cass Hite's store and the ferry site lie underwater about five miles downlake from Hite Marina.

The uppermost marina on Lake Powell, Hite lies 141 lake miles from Glen Canyon Dam. From here boats can continue uplake to the mouth of Dark Canyon in Cataract Canyon at low water or into Canyonlands National Park at high water. Hite tends to be quieter than the other marinas and is favored by anglers. The turnoff for the marina from UT 95 lies between Hanksville and Blanding. On the way in, you'll find a small **store** with gas pumps, three-bedroom **family units** (trailers, same rates as at Halls Crossing), and a primitive **campground** (no drinking water, $6). Primitive camping is also available nearby off UT 95 at Dirty Devil, Farley Canyon, White Canyon, Blue Notch, and other locations for $6. **Hite Marina,** at the end of the access road, features boat rentals (fishing, ski, and houseboat), slips, storage, gas dock, and a small store. Hikers can make arrangements with the marina for drop-offs and pick-ups at Dark Canyon. A **ranger station,** tel. (435) 684-2457, is occasionally open.

Contact Lake Powell Resorts & Marinas for accommodations and boat rentals at Box 56909, Phoenix, AZ 85079; tel. (800) 528-6154 or (602) 278-8888 in greater Phoenix, fax (602) 331-5258. Reach Hite Marina at Box 501-Hite, Lake Powell, UT 84533, tel. (435) 684-2278.

RAINBOW BRIDGE NATIONAL MONUMENT

Rainbow Bridge forms a graceful span 290 feet high and 275 feet wide; the Capitol building in Washington, D.C., would fit neatly underneath. The easiest way to Rainbow Bridge is by boat tour on Lake Powell from Wahweap, Bullfrog, or Halls Crossing Marinas.

The more adventurous can hike to the bridge from the Cha Canyon Trailhead (just north across the Arizona-Utah border on the east side of Navajo Mountain) or from the Rainbow Lodge ruins (just south of the Arizona-Utah border on the west side of Navajo Mountain). Rugged trails from each point wind through highly scenic canyons, meet in Bridge Canyon, then continue two miles to the bridge. The hike on either trail, or a loop with both (a car shuttle is needed), is 26-28 miles roundtrip. Hikers must be experienced and self-sufficient, as these trails cross a wilderness. Because the trails are unmaintained and poorly marked, hikers should consult a Navajo Mountain (Utah) 15-minute topo map or the newer 7¹/₂-minute Navajo Begay and Chaiyahi Flat maps.

No camping is allowed at Rainbow Bridge and no supplies are available. You may camp a half mile east of the bridge at Echo camp. The

Dangling Rope Marina and National Park Service ranger station are 10 miles away, by water only. The best times to go are April to early June, September, and October. Winter cold and snow discourage visitors, and summer is hot and can bring hazardous flash floods. The National Park Service offers "Hiking to Rainbow Bridge" trail notes; write Glen Canyon N.R.A., Box 1507, Page, AZ 86040, tel. (520) 608-6404; Internet: www.nps.gov/rabr.

The National Park Service cannot issue hiking permits to Rainbow Bridge. Obtain the required tribal hiking permit ($5 for one person, $10 group of 2-10, $20 group of 11 or more) and camping permit ($2 per person per night) from the Cameron Visitor Center/Ranger Station at Box 459, Cameron, AZ 86020, tel. (520) 679-2303, fax (520) 679-2330; or from the Navajo Parks and Recreation Department, Box 9000, Window Rock, AZ 86515, tel. (520) 871-6647, 871-6635, or 871-6636. Both offices are open Monday to Friday about 8 a.m.-5 p.m.; the Cameron office may extend its hours to daily 7 a.m.-6 p.m. from Memorial Day to Labor Day weekends. Allow six weeks for permit processing.

The only road access to the Navajo Mountain area is Indian Route 16 from AZ 98, between Page and Kayenta. To reach the east trailhead, drive north 32 miles on Indian Route 16 past Inscription House Trading Post to a road fork, and then turn right six miles to Navajo Mountain Trading Post. Continue on the main road 6.5 miles (go straight at the four-way junction) to an earthen dam. Drive straight across the dam, take the left fork after a half mile, and then go 1.6 miles to Cha Canyon Trailhead at the end of the road.

You can reach the west trailhead by driving north 32 miles on Indian Route 16 then turning left and driving about another six miles from the road fork to the Rainbow Lodge ruins. Always lock vehicles and remove valuables at trailheads. Because Navajo Mountain is sacred to the Navajo, you probably won't get permission to climb it; check with the Navajo Parks Department in Window Rock.

Rainbow Bridge

THE EXPLORATION OF THE COLORADO RIVER AND ITS CANYONS

INDIAN COUNTRY OF NORTHEASTERN ARIZONA

INTRODUCTION

This is Indian country, a place made special by the ancient cultural traditions of Native Americans—traditions that have survived to the present. The hardworking Hopi have lived here longest. Ruins, occupied by their ancestors as long ago as 1,500 years, lie scattered over much of northeastern Arizona and adjacent states. The once warlike and greatly feared Navajo came relatively late, perhaps 500-700 years ago. Today, Native Americans welcome visitors who respect tribal customs and laws. Here you'll have an opportunity to glimpse a unique way of life in a land of rare beauty.

THE LAND

Multihued desert hills, broad mesas, soaring buttes, vast treeless plains, and massive mountains give an impression of boundless space. Northeastern Arizona sits atop the Colorado Plateau, ranging in elevation from 4,500 to 7,000 feet. Several pine-forested ranges rise above the desert near Arizona's borders with Utah and New Mexico. Navajo Mountain, just across the border in Utah, is the highest peak in the area at 10,388 feet. Nearby you'll find Rainbow Bridge,

the world's highest natural stone span over water. You can reach the bridge by boat on Lake Powell or by a spectacular 26- to 28-mile roundtrip hike. The beautiful canyons in Navajo and Canyon de Chelly National Monuments also offer excellent scenery and hiking.

Climate

Expect warm to hot summers and moderate to cold winters. Spring and autumn are the ideal times to visit, especially for hiking, though winds in March and April can kick up dust and sand. Afternoon thunderstorms frequently build up from early July to early September. Showers usually pass quickly, but flash floods pose a danger in low-lying areas.

HISTORY

Indian Reservations

In 1878 the federal government began ceding to the Navajo land that has since grown into a giant reservation spreading from northeastern Arizona into adjacent New Mexico and Utah. The Navajo Nation, with more than 200,000 members, ranks as the largest Native American tribe in the country. In 1882 the federal government also recognized the Hopi's age-old land rights and began setting aside land for them. Approximately 10,000 Hopi live today on a reservation completely surrounded by Navajo land. Government officials have redrawn the reservation boundaries of the Navajo and Hopi many times, never to the satisfaction of all parties. In 1978, congressional and court decisions settled a major land dispute between the two tribes in favor of the Hopi. The victorious Hopi regained part of the territory previously designated for joint use but largely settled by Navajo. To the Hopi this was long-overdue justice, while the Navajo called it The Second Long Walk. The Navajo and Hopi Indian Relocation Commissioners faced the daunting task of resettling hundreds of families in their respective reservations.

INDIAN CULTURES

White people have always had difficulty understanding Arizona's Indians, perhaps because the

THE EXPLORATION OF THE COLORADO RIVER AND ITS CANYONS

Hopi method of dressing the hair

Native American cultures here emphasize very different spiritual values. The Hopi and Navajo exist in accord with nature, not against it, adapting to the climate, plants, and animals of the land. Yet when visiting Native American villages, outsiders often see only the material side of the culture—the houses, livestock, dress, pottery, and other crafts. The visitor has to look deeper to gain even a small insight into Indian ways.

The Hopi and Navajo differ greatly in their backgrounds. The Hopi usually live in compact villages, even if this means a long commute to fields or jobs. The Navajo spread their houses and hogans across the countryside, often far from the nearest neighbor.

Ceremonies

Religion forms a vital part of both Hopi and Navajo cultures. The Hopi have an elaborate, almost year-round schedule of dances in their village plazas and kivas (ceremonial rooms). Some, such as those in the kivas, are closed to outsiders, but others may be open to the public. Nearly all Hopi dances serve as prayers for rain and fertile crops. The elaborate and brilliant masks, the ankle bells, the drums and chanting—all invite the attention of the supernatural spirits (kachinas) who bring rain. Men perform these dances; while they're dancing, they *are* kachinas. At the end of the line of dancers, you might see boys who are learning the ritual; dance steps must be performed precisely. When watching, remember that this is a religious service. Dress respectfully, keep clear of the performers, be quiet, and don't ask questions. Hopi ceremonies generally take place on the weekends; call or ask at the Hopi Cultural Center or the Hopi Tribe Cultural Preservation Office.

Most Navajo ceremonies deal with healing. If someone is sick, the family calls in a healer who uses sand paintings, chants, and dancing to effect a cure. These events, often held late at night, aren't publicized. If you're driving at night and see large bonfires outside a house, it's likely there's a healing ceremony going on. Don't intrude on any ceremony unless invited.

Visiting the Navajo and Hopi

Learning about Native American cultures on the reservation can reward visitors with new insights. It's easy to visit Indian lands; the tribes ask guests to follow only a few simple rules.

INDIAN COUNTRY HIGHLIGHTS

Navajo and Hopi Indian Reservations: Visitors have the opportunity to experience the cultures of these two dynamic, yet very different, Native American peoples.

Navajo National Monument: Two large prehistoric Indian cliff dwellings, which you can hike to, have been amazingly well preserved.

Monument Valley: Towering buttes and pinnacles create an enchanting landscape.

Canyon de Chelly National Monument: Exceptionally beautiful canyons preserve both prehistoric cliff dwellings and traditional Navajo life.

Hopi Country: Centuries-old villages seem to grow out of the mesa tops, where you may be fortunate enough to watch dancers perform religious ceremonies.

Hordes of eager photographers besieged Hopi villages from the late 1800s to the early 1900s, when the Hopi cried "No more!" And that's the way it is now—photography, recording, and sketching by visitors are *strictly* forbidden in all Hopi villages. Even the sight of a camera will upset some tribal members. The Navajo are more easygoing about photos, but you should always ask first; expect to pay a posing fee unless attending a public performance.

Reservation land, though held in trust by the government, is private property; obtain permission before leaving the roadways or designated recreational areas. Don't remove anything—a few feathers tied to a bush may make a tempting souvenir, but they're of great religious importance to the person who put them there. Normal good manners, respect, and observance of posted regulations will make your visit pleasurable for both you and your hosts.

NORTHEASTERN ARIZONA PRACTICALITIES

Accommodations and Food

Because of the distances involved, visitors usually want to stay overnight on or near the reservations. Most towns have a motel or two that can quickly fill up in the summer tourist season, when reservations come in very handy. Motel prices run high due to lack of competition. Most campgrounds offer minimal or no facilities; only a few have water or hookups. Accommodations in towns just outside the reservations—Flagstaff, Winslow, Holbrook, Page, Gallup—are another possibility and generally a much better value.

Indians enjoy American and Mexican dishes as well as the ever-present fast foods. Try the Navajo taco, a giant tortilla smothered with lettuce, ground beef, beans, tomatoes, chilies, and cheese. The Hopi Cultural Center restaurant on Second Mesa has many Indian specialties, but chances are the Hopi family at the next table will be munching on hamburgers and fries. No alcohol is sold or permitted on the Navajo and Hopi reservations; you won't find much nightlife, either.

Information

Not always easy to get! Motels and trading posts can be helpful; tribal police know regulations

SHOPPING FOR INDIAN ARTS AND CRAFTS

The strength of the Navajo and Hopi cultures appears in their excellent arts and crafts. Trading posts and Indian crafts shops on and off the reservations offer large selections. You'll also have the opportunity to buy directly from the person who made the item that you select. Navajo sell from roadside stands, most numerous on the highways to Grand Canyon National Park. Hopi sell directly from their village homes. To learn about Indian art, drop in at the Heard Museum in Phoenix or the Museum of Northern Arizona in Flagstaff. Books—available in trading posts, bookstores, and libraries—describe crafts and what to look for when buying; see the Booklist at the end of the book for more information.

The best work commands high prices but can be a fine memento of a visit to Native American lands. Indians know what their crafts are worth, so bargaining is not normally done. Competition, especially among Navajo at their roadside stands, can make for some very low prices, however. Discounts often mark the end of the tourist season in September and October.

The Navajo have long earned fame for silver jewelry and woven rugs; you'll also see their stone work, pottery, basketry, and sand paintings. Craftsmen learned to work silver from Mexicans in the 19th century, then gradually developed distinctive Navajo styles, such as the squash-blossom necklace with its horseshoe-shaped pendant. Silversmiths also turn out bracelets, rings, concha belts, buckles, and bolo ties. The Navajo are especially fond of turquoise, which appears in much of their work. Navajo once wove fine blankets using sheep obtained from the Spanish and weaving skills learned from pueblo Indians, but factory-made blankets in the late 19th century nearly ended the market for hand-woven ones. At the suggestion of trader Lorenzo Hubbell, weavers switched to a heavier cloth for use as rugs, which became extremely popular. Rugs have evolved into more than a dozen regional styles and may be made from hand-spun and dyed yarn or less expensive commercial yarn. Navajo once used sandpaintings only in ceremonies but now also produce the distinctive designs and colors for the tourist trade.

The Hopi carve exotic kachina dolls from cottonwood and create jewelry, pottery, and basketry. The kachina dolls originally followed simple designs and served to educate children about Hopi religion.

With the rise of interest from outsiders, the Hopi began to carve more elaborate and realistic figures from the diverse Hopi pantheon. The dolls include clowns (painted with black and white stripes and often holding watermelon slices), animal-like forms, solemn masked figures, and fearsome ogres. Much thought and symbolism go into a Hopi carving, so even though its price is high, the doll will be good value. (Some Navajo have cashed in on the kachina-doll trade, but the Hopi may tell you that the Navajo don't really know about the kachina religion; Navajo dolls tend to have more fur, fiercer features, and lower prices.) Hopi silversmiths produce a great variety of inlay work using traditional symbols. The inlay is made from two sheets of silver, one with a design cut out, sandwiched together. This style, now a Hopi trademark, includes earrings, bracelets, rings, bolo ties, and belt buckles. The Hopi also turn out beautiful pottery and baskets, as they have for many generations.

Artists of both tribes create attractive paintings, prints, and sculpture with Indian motifs.

roadside jewelry stall

and road conditions. Try the museums run by the Hopi on Second Mesa and by the Navajo at Window Rock and Tsaile. Local newspapers report on politics, sports, and social events, but not religious ceremonies.

The **Hopi Tribe Cultural Preservation Office** provides information for visitors to the Hopi Indian Reservation at its office in Kykotsmovi, one mile south of AZ 264 in the Tribal Headquarters building; contact Box 123, Kykotsmovi, AZ 86039, tel. (520) 734-2244, Internet: www.nau.edu/~hcpo-p. The **Hopi Cultural Center** on Second Mesa has a museum, motel, campground, and restaurant; write to Box 67, Second Mesa, AZ 86043, tel. (520) 734-2401. People at either place can tell you about upcoming dances open to the public. The Hopi generally don't allow outsiders to hike, fish, or hunt.

The **Navajo Nation Tourism Department** office provides literature and information for visitors to the Navajo Indian Reservation. The desk in the new Navajo Museum, Library & Visitor's Center is open Mon.-Fri. 8 a.m.-5 p.m. and Saturday 10 a.m.-4 p.m. in Window Rock on AZ 264; write to Box 663, Window Rock, AZ 86515, tel. (520) 871-6436, 871-7371, or 871-6659, fax (520) 871-7381, Internet: www.navajoland.com.

For hiking and camping information and permits on Navajo lands, contact the **Navajo Parks & Recreation Department** near the museum and zoo in Window Rock, Box 9000, Window Rock, AZ 86515, tel. (520) 871-6647, 871-6635, or 871-6631, fax (520) 871-6637 or 871-7040. Or, in the western Navajo Nation, which contains most of the open backcountry areas, contact the Visitor Center/Ranger Station at the US 89-AZ 64 junction; it's open Mon.-Fri. 8 a.m.-5 p.m. and maybe extended to daily 7 a.m.-6 p.m. from Memorial Day to Labor Day weekends. You can also write Box 459, Cameron, AZ 86020, tel. (520) 679-2303, fax 679-2330. Backcountry permits cost only $5 per person per entry (less for groups) and $2 per person per night for camping; allow six weeks for processing.

Fishing and hunting on the Navajo Reservation require tribal permits from **Navajo Fish and Wildlife,** Box 1480, Window Rock, AZ 86515, tel. (520) 871-6451 or 871-6452. Of the 12 lakes stocked with fish on the reservation, the most popular are the trout lakes Wheatfields and Tsaile in eastern Arizona and Whiskey nearby in New Mexico. Arizona Game and Fish has no jurisdiction; you need only tribal permits. All photography with commercial intent must be cleared with the **Office of Broadcast Services** at Box 2310, Window Rock, AZ 86515, tel. (520) 871-6655 or 871-6656.

What Time is It?

This must be the question most frequently asked by reservation visitors! While the Navajo Reservation and most of the United States go on daylight saving time from early April to late October, the rest of Arizona stays on mountain standard time. Keep in mind the time difference on Navajo land during daylight saving time or you'll always be one hour late; an easy way to remember is that the reservation follows the same time as its New Mexico and Utah sections. The Hopi, who rarely agree with the Navajo on anything, choose to stay on standard time.

Getting Around

Your own transportation is by far the most convenient, but tours of Indian country do leave from major centers (see "Tours" descriptions in the Grand Canyon and Flagstaff sections).

Navajo Transit System, offers bus service across the Navajo and Hopi reservations Mon.-Fri. and to Gallup on Saturday; no buses run on Sunday and holidays; tel. 520-729-4002. One route connects Fort Defiance and Window Rock in the east with Tuba City in the west, once daily in each direction, $13.05 one way. Stops on this route (east to west on AZ 264) are: Window Rock (Bashas' parking lot), St. Michaels, Ganado Post Office, Burnside Thriftway Store (near junction of US 191), Standing Rock, Steamboat Trading Post, Toyei School, Keams Canyon Trading Post, Polacca Circle-M store, Second Mesa Trading Post, Hopi Cultural Center, Kykotsmovi turnoff, Hotevilla turnoff, Dennebito junction, and Tuba City (Truck Stop Restaurant, Community Center, and PHS Hospital).

Navajo Transit System also heads north from Window Rock and Fort Defiance to Kayenta, $11.85 one way, with stops at Fort Defiance 7 Eleven Store, Navajo (in New Mexico), Diné College at Tsaile, Chinle (Shopping Center and other stops), Many Farms, Rough Rock junction, Chilchinbito junction, and Kayenta (7-Eleven store and police station). Other routes connect

Fort Defiance and Window Rock with the New Mexico towns of Gallup, Crownpoint, Shiprock, and Farmington.

You'll often see Indian people hitchhiking, and you can, too. Be prepared for long waits—traffic is light—and rides in the backs of pickups.

WESTERN NAVAJO COUNTRY

CAMERON

The **Cameron Trading Post,** built in 1916 overlooking the Little Colorado River, commemorates Ralph Cameron, Arizona's last territorial delegate before statehood. The trading post's strategic location near the Grand Canyon makes it a popular stopping point. Facilities include a motel ($69 s, $79 d, less in winter), RV park across the highway ($15 with hookups, no tents, no showers), restaurant, grocery store, Indian crafts shop, post office, and service station. The excellent restaurant, featuring American with some Mexican and Indian food, is open daily for breakfast, lunch, and dinner—try the Navajo taco in meat or vegetarian versions. The separate gallery in a stone building in front contains museum-quality Indian crafts and art for sale, well worth a look by aficionados. The trading post is on the west side of US 89, one mile north of the junction with AZ 64 and 54 miles north of Flagstaff; tel. (520) 679-2231 or (800) 338-7385.

Drop in at the **Visitor Center/Ranger Station,** at the US 89-AZ 64 junction, for information about the Navajo Reservation; you can buy trib-al hiking and camping permits here, too. The center is open Mon.-Fri. 8 a.m.-5 p.m. (may be extended to 7 a.m.-6 p.m. from Memorial Day to Labor Day weekends); write to Box 459, Cameron, AZ 86020, tel. (520) 679-2303, fax (520) 679-2330. **Navajo Arts & Craft Enterprise** next door offers a good selection of Indian crafts. An **RV park** across US 89 is open all year with sites for tents ($8.50) and RVs ($14.50 with hookups) as well as showers ($2) and laundry; check in at the Chevron station; tel. (520) 679-2281. Nearby, the **Trading Post** sells Indian crafts, and **Simpson's Market** has a good selection of groceries.

Vicinity of Cameron
To the west, the high, sheer walls of the **Little Colorado River Canyon** make an impressive sight, even with the Grand Canyon so near. Viewpoints are nine and 14 miles west on AZ 64, about halfway to Desert View in Grand Canyon National Park. For a close look at the "river too thin to plow and too thick to drink," follow signs for the overweight truck route that crosses the Little Colorado River on a low bridge just upstream. The colorful hills of the **Painted**

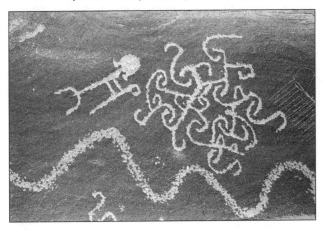

petroglyphs at Inscription Point, north of Wupatki National Monument

Point Hansbrough encircled by the Colorado River—view from Tatahatso Point

Desert lie to the north and east. You'll also have a chance to shop for Navajo jewelry at the many roadside stands in the Cameron area.

Gray Mountain Trading Post, 10 miles south of Cameron on US 89, features the **Anasazi Inn** and a gas station/convenience store on the east side of the highway and a restaurant (lacks a smoke-free area) and an Indian crafts shop on the west side. The inn has a pool and playground; rates run $60-90 d; tel. (520) 679-2214. Moderate-Expensive.

Backcountry Areas

Experienced hikers can explore remote and beautiful areas in the western Navajo lands. The Visitor Center/Ranger Station in Cameron has some information on these, and you'll find descriptions in hiking guidebooks. Navajo permits must be obtained from staff at the Ranger Station in Cameron, Navajo Parks and Recreation in Window Rock near the museum and zoo, or contact Box 9000, Window Rock, AZ 86515, tel. (520) 871-6647, 871-6635, or 871-6631, fax (520) 871-6637 or 871-7040, or possibly at Antelope Canyon. If you'll be camping in Grand Canyon National Park, permits will also be needed from the Backcountry Office there. Navigating the unsigned jeep roads to many of the trailheads may require as much map reading skill as does hiking the routes. When it's not in flood, you can follow the Little Colorado River all the way from Cameron down to the Colorado River in the Grand Canyon, though deep pools, quick-

sand, and flash floods can make the way difficult. The Little Colorado Canyon can also be entered via the Blue Springs Trail, Hopi Trail Crossing, and Hopi Salt Trail, all very challenging and only for knowledgeable canyon hikers. Marble Canyon has difficult rim-to-river routes at Eminence Break, Shinumo Wash, Salt Water Wash, and Jackass Canyon. Rainbow Bridge rates as one of the best hiking destinations on the Colorado Plateau and is only moderately difficult; see description at the end of **Glen Canyon National Recreation Area.**

Tatahatso Point

Spectacular views of Marble Canyon greet adventurous drivers who negotiate the confusing network of roads out to the rim. The name comes from the Navajo *dida'a hotsa'a,* meaning "the edge or top of it is big." The rare visitor experiences the precipitous edge, the vastness, and the solitude here. From Cedar Ridge on US 89, the route is about 20 miles to the Point Hansbrough overlook or 25 miles all the way to the end of the road on Tatahatso Point. High-clearance vehicles must be used, and you'll need 4WD if you drive all the way to the end of the point. The trip should be done only in dry weather with good visibility (to see the landmarks); topo maps will be useful. Bring water, food, and camping gear in case of a breakdown, and leave your plans with a reliable person. Although you can drive out in an hour or so, staying overnight will allow you to see the changing colors and patterns in Marble Canyon and on the plateaus all around. *Arizona Highways* did an illustrated article on Tatahatso Point in the July 1998 issue, though the directions seem suspect: "HOW far is it to the stock pond, Sam?"

First obtain a Navajo permit, most easily done at the Visitor Center/Ranger Station in Cameron, then you can drive to Cedar Ridge on US 89, 40 miles north of Cameron, and turn west on an un-paved road marked by a cairn 0.2 mile north of Milepost 505. This is Indian Route 6110, a wide and bumpy gravel road. Soon the dark, forested Kaibab Plateau comes into view ahead to the west, then Shinumo Altar to the northwest. It's a good idea to look back occasionally for land-marks to help with navigation on the return drive. The route generally heads west, passing sever-al miles to the south of Shinumo Altar, then at a point southwest of Shinumo, curves northwest toward Tatahatso Point. Don't panic if you lose the way, as there's more than one way across the plateau—rather, be amazed if you don't make a wrong turn! The author counted one (1) sign on the entire drive! Just try not to disturb anyone at the widely scattered ranches out here.

Keep right on 6110 where the road forks after 6.8 miles. After another 0.6 mile, take the left fork (a small earthen dam is on the left here). After 0.8 mile take the right fork, then a left fork after 0.3 mile; there's a little outcrop of white rocks to the south. Take a right fork after 1.6 miles, then a left fork after 0.2 mile, then right at the next two forks just 0.1 mile apart; Shinumo Altar is almost due north and the San Francisco Peaks rise to the south. The route continues west or slightly northwest 2.7 miles past several crossroads, then takes a right fork 0.3 mile down to a watering hole for local cows, horses, sheep, and mules. In another 0.3 mile take the right fork, then keep straight on the left fork 0.7 mile farther. After 1.3 miles, take the right fork, then keep straight on the left fork 0.2 mile farther. In half a mile the road veers to the northwest; there's an earthen ridge to the left in another 0.6 mile. Keep straight on the left fork 0.4 mile past the ridge. Marble Canyon reveals itself to the left after 0.7 mile; the road curves north in an-other 0.8 mile, then comes to a fork 0.3 mile far-ther. Turn left here and at the next fork, and you'll have arrived at a cairn marking the end of the road just 0.2 mile farther! The Colorado

River makes a sharp 180-degree bend around Point Hansbrough below your feet. President Harding Rapid lies directly below, though only the lower part can be seen. The little side canyon here and cliffs off to your right mark the Emi-nence Break Fault. Experienced canyon hikers can descend a rough trail from here to Presi-dent Harding Rapid.

This is the best viewpoint, but you can drive or hike out onto Tatahatso Point for additional views. A rough, steep section of rocky road at the fault requires 4WD—don't descend it unless you're sure that you can make it back up! Although just a short walk below the viewpoint, this rough spot is reached by retracing 0.2 mile back to the main road and continuing around and down to the left in 1.7 miles. Once past the rocks, it's an easy three-mile drive across the point, covered in sage, cholla, and Mormon tea, to an old tramway site at road's end. There's a good view down-stream to Buck Farm Canyon on the right. One could hike cross-country about 1.5 miles to the southwest corner of Point Tatahatso or drive half a mile north along the rim to the northwest corner of the point and a view upriver.

TUBA CITY

This administrative and trade center for the west-ern Navajo has nothing to do with tubas and is hardly a city. The town (pop. 7,612, elev. 4,936 feet) commemorates Chief Tuba of the Hopi tribe. The business district isn't much to look at, but the area north of Tuba Trading Post has some fine stone buildings in an oasis of green lawns and shade trees. The springs nearby attracted Mormons who founded a settlement in 1877. They could not gain clear title to the land, how-ever, and the U.S. Indian Agency took it over in 1903. Besides the U.S. government offices, the town has a hospital, schools, and a bank. Tuba City is near the junction of AZ 264 to the Hopi mesas and US 160 to Monument Valley.

Nearby Sights

Dinosaur tracks left by several different species lie preserved in sandstone, 5.5 miles west of Tuba City off US 160, about midway between the Tuba City junction and US 89. The turnoff is on the north side of the highway between Mileposts 316 and 317, marked by signs for dinosaur tracks and Moenave. Some Navajo jewelry stalls will probably be open here.

Elephant's Feet, a pair of distinctive sandstone pillars, stands near Red Lake, 23 miles northeast of Tuba City on US 160 near Milepost 345.

White Mesa Natural Bridge can be viewed from a distance on a seriously corrugated back road north of Red Lake. Turn north off US 160 between Mileposts 349 and 350 through an oval tunnel under the railroad tracks, continue north 3.7 miles on Indian Route 16, then turn left and go about 5.5 miles on Indian Route 6270; you'll see the huge arch off to the left. There's no access to it because of surrounding private ranches. The AAA "Indian Country" map shows the roads but not the arch.

Tuba City Accommodations

Greyhills Inn provides one of the few inexpensive places to stay on the reservation; students of Greyhills High School operate the motel and youth hostel as part of a training program. Rates are $47.52 s plus $5.40 for each additional person; people with hostel cards can stay in shared rooms for $16.20. The bath is down the hall, a kitchen is available, and credit cards are not accepted. It's open 24 hours. You can make reservations by phone or mail with the Hotel Management Program, Greyhills High School, Box 160, Tuba City, AZ 86045, tel. (520) 283-6271, ext. 141/142. From the junction of US 160 and AZ 264, go northeast a half mile on US 160 to just past the pedestrian overpass, turn left 0.2 mile, turn right, then make the first left into the parking lot. Inexpensive.

The **Quality Inn** sits in the center of town behind Tuba Trading Post, one mile north of the highway junction. Rooms cost $85 s, $90 d (less in winter) plus a tax of 14.05%, tel. (520) 283-4545 or (800) 644-8383. Expensive. The RV park here has some trees, showers, and laundry for $21.21 RV w/hookups and $12.73 for tents including tax.

Food

Hogan Restaurant, next to the Quality Inn, serves Mexican-American food and has a fruit and salad bar; it's open daily for breakfast, lunch, and dinner; tel. (520) 283-5260. **Kate's Cafe,** a half block farther east, serves American and pasta dishes; it's open Sunday for breakfast and lunch and Mon.-Sat. for breakfast, lunch, and dinner; tel. (520) 283-4216.

Kentucky Fried Chicken, Taco Bell, Mc-Donalds, and a **Dairy Queen** line the road into town. **The Truck Stop Cafe** on the highway at the turnoff for Tuba City has American food daily for breakfast, lunch, and dinner; tel. (520) 283-4975. **Szechuan Restaurant** prepares Chinese cuisine in the shopping center. It's open daily for lunch and dinner, and there's often a lunch buffet; tel. (520) 283-5807. **Pizza Edge** fixes pizza, calzone, subs, sandwiches, and ice cream at the shopping center; it's open Mon.-Sat. for lunch and dinner; tel. (520) 283-5938. **Toh Nanees Dizi Shopping Center,** a half mile northeast on US 160, offers two restaurants, a Bashas' supermarket and deli, a movie theater, and other shops.

Services

Van Trading Co., west of town on US 160, sells Indian crafts, groceries, and most everything else. The unusually shaped **Tuba Trading Post** next door to Hogan Restaurant sells Indian crafts. It dates to 1870 and had the two-story octagon added in 1920; you can visit the traditional Navajo hogan behind it. The motel and trading post may have information on Indian dances or events, both Navajo and Hopi. The **Western Navajo Fair,** held in October, features a rodeo, carnival, song and dance performances, Miss Western Navajo Pageant, exhibits, and other entertainment; Internet: www.navajoland.com.

NORTHERN NAVAJO COUNTRY

NAVAJO NATIONAL MONUMENT

Navajo National Monument preserves three spectacular prehistoric Indian cliff dwellings, last occupied about 700 years ago. The ancestral pueblo people who once lived here probably have descendants in present-day Hopi villages. Of the three sites, Betatakin is the most accessible; you can see it from a viewpoint near the visitor center. Rangers lead groups into Betatakin during summer.

Keet Seel, a 16-mile roundtrip hike to the northeast, is the largest cliff dwelling in Arizona. Inscription House, to the west, is the smallest of the three ruins; it's closed to the public. The ruins should not be confused with Inscription House Trading Post, which lies some distance away.

You can reach the monument's headquarters and visitor center by following US 160 northeast 52 miles from Tuba City—or southwest 22 miles from Kayenta—then turning north nine miles on AZ 564 at Black Mesa Junction.

Visitor Center

The ancestral pueblo people left many questions behind when they abandoned this area. You can learn what is known about these people and ponder the mysteries at the visitor center. Exhibits of prehistoric pottery and other artifacts attempt to piece together what life was like for them. An excellent 25-minute movie on the ancestral pueblo people is shown on request. A bulletin board lists campfire programs and ranger-led walks. Navajo often demonstrate their art and crafts in or near the visitor center. You can peek into an old-style Navajo forked-stick hogan and a sweathouse behind the center. Rangers answer questions and sell books and maps. A gift shop offers Navajo crafts and Hopi, Navajo, and Zuni jewelry. The **picnic area** lies across the parking area.

The visitor center is open daily 8 a.m.-5 p.m. except Thanksgiving, Christmas, and New Year's Day. Contact monument personnel at HC 71, Box 3, Tonalea, AZ 86044-9704, tel. (520) 672-2366, Internet: www.nps.gov/nava.

Sandal Trail

This easy trail begins behind the visitor center and winds through a pinyon pine and juniper woodland to Betatakin Point Overlook. The paved trail is one mile roundtrip and drops 160 feet to the overlook. Signs along the way identify native plants and describe how Native Americans used them. Bring binoculars to see details of Betatakin ruins across the canyon.

Aspen Trail branches off 400 feet down Sandal Trail, then drops 300 feet into the head of Be-

Betatakin Ruins

tatakin Canyon, 0.8 mile roundtrip. The trail offers pretty scenery along the way and a view of the quaking aspen, Douglas fir, water birch, and redosier redwood trees on the canyon floor below; there's no ruin view or access from this trail.

Visiting Betatakin

The Betatakin (Navajo for Ledge House) ruins lie tucked in a natural alcove on the far side of a canyon. The alcove measures 452 feet high, 370 feet across, and 135 feet deep. It contains 135 rooms and one kiva. Inhabitants built and abandoned the entire village within two generations, between A.D. 1250 and 1300.

You may visit the ruins only with park rangers, who lead one four-hour tour a day from May to September. Groups are limited to 25 people, first-come, first served, so be early. Starting from the visitor center, the five-mile roundtrip trail is primitive and drops 700 feet, which you have to climb on the way back. After passing through an aspen grove on the canyon floor, the trail climbs a short distance to the ruins. Trailhead elevation is 7,300 feet. Thin air can make the hike very tiring—people with heart, respiratory, or mobility problems shouldn't attempt it.

Visiting Keet Seel

This isolated cliff dwelling is one of the best preserved in the Southwest. Keet Seel (Navajo for Broken Pottery) features 160 rooms and four kivas. The ruins look as though they were abandoned just a few years back, not seven long centuries ago. The site, 8.5 miles by trail from the visitor center, is open from the end of May to early September. A permit is required, and there's a limit of 20 people per day. Visitors should make reservations two months ahead with Navajo National Monument, H.C. 71, Box 3, Tonalea, AZ 86044-9704, tel. (520) 672-2366. To pick up your permit, you must attend a scheduled trail orientation in the morning or the afternoon before (remember it's daylight saving time).

The hike's first 1.5 miles run along the rim on a dirt road to Tsegi Point. There the trail descends 1,000 feet to the canyon bottom, travels downstream a short distance, then heads upstream into Keet Seel Canyon. You may have to do some wading. Carry water, as livestock pollute the streams. Visitors may not enter the site without a ranger, stationed nearby. Backpackers can stay in a primitive campground (free, one-night limit) near Keet Seel. Strong hikers can do the roundtrip in a day, though spending a night here makes for an easier, more relaxing visit.

Accommodations and Food

A free **campground** with restrooms is near the visitor center, open mid-May to mid-October with water and the rest of the year without. **Anasazi Inn** ($80 d, less in winter) and its cafe (open daily for breakfast, lunch, and dinner) lie 18 miles away on the road to Kayenta; tel. (520) 697-3793. Moderate. Kayenta, 11 miles farther, offers two motels, a basic RV park, and several restaurants.

Black Mesa Shopping Center, nine miles south of the Visitor Center at the junction of AZ 564 and US 160, has the closest grocery store and service station. The road south from here goes to the coal mines of the Peabody Coal Company, a major place of employment for the Navajo.

Shonto

This Navajo settlement sits in a small canyon southwest of Navajo National Monument. A trading post offers groceries and Navajo crafts. The shaded park in front is a good spot for a picnic. A chapter house and Bureau of Indian Affairs (BIA) boarding school lie nearby. Shonto is 10 miles from the Visitor Center on a sandy road not recommended for cars (except during the school year, when it is kept graded), or 33 miles via US 160 on paved roads.

KAYENTA

The "Gateway to Monument Valley" has a population of 5,200 in a bleak, windswept valley (elev. 5,660 feet). Its name is loosely derived from the Navajo word *Teehindeeh,* meaning "boghole," as there were once shallow lakes here. Kayenta makes a handy stop for travelers, with two good motels, a basic RV park, several restaurants, and shopping.

Accommodations

Wetherill Inn lies in the center of town on US 163, one mile north of US 160. Its name honors John Wetherill, an early trader and rancher in the region who discovered Betatakin, Mesa

Verde, and other major ancestral pueblo sites. Rooms cost $92 s, $98 d in summer, less off-season. Guests can enjoy an indoor pool and a gift shop; tel. (520) 697-3231 or (800) 528-1234 (Best Western reservations). Expensive.

The **Holiday Inn,** on US 160 at the turnoff for Kayenta, features rooms for $129-139 d in summer, as well as a restaurant, gift shop, tours, and an outdoor pool; tel. (520) 697-3221 or (800) HOLIDAY. Premium.

The **Coin-Op Laundry** in town offers basic RV spaces for $10 with hookups; tent campers are welcome too, though campgrounds at Monument Valley or Navajo Natl. Monument are far more scenic. Showers are also available to non-campers for $2.75; tel. (520) 697-3738.

Food

The Holiday Inn's **Wagon Wheel Restaurant** serves up good Navajo tacos and American fare. It's open daily for breakfast, lunch, and dinner; there's also a breakfast buffet in season and a salad bar. **Amigo Cafe** prepares Mexican and American food; it's open Mon.-Fri. for breakfast, lunch, and dinner. You'll find it 0.2 mile in on US 163 between the Kayenta turnoff and town; tel. (520) 697-8448. **Golden Sands Cafe** near the Wetherill Inn offers American food daily for breakfast, lunch, and dinner; tel. (520) 697-3684.

For pizza, calzones, and subs, try **Pizza Edge,** open Mon.-Sat. for lunch and dinner in the Tee-hindeeh Shopping Center; tel. (520) 697-8427. The **Blue Coffee Pot Cafe,** near the shopping center, prepares Mexican and American food weekdays for breakfast, lunch, and dinner; tel. (520) 697-3396. **McDonalds** and **Burger King** also lie near the shopping center; Burger King has a small WWII Navajo Code Talkers exhibit. Buy groceries at Bashas' supermarket/deli in the shopping center or at the Kayenta Trading Post behind the Wetherill Inn.

Shopping and Services

Kayenta Visitor Center, in front of the shopping center, offers Navajo arts and crafts for sale as well as providing some local information; tel. (520) 697-3572. **Navajo Nation Arts & Crafts Showroom,** just east of the highway junction past Thriftway gas station, has a good selection. **Kayenta Trading Post** behind the Wetherill Inn and both motels have Indian crafts, too.

Tours in 4WD vehicles to Monument Valley and the surrounding country can be arranged at the motels and the Kayenta Visitor Center; charges start at about $30 half day or $60 full day with minimums of four or six people. Or wait until you arrive at Monument Valley, where many Navajos offer a variety of driving, horseback riding, and hiking tours.

MONUMENT VALLEY

Towering buttes, jagged pinnacles, and rippled sand dunes make this an otherworldly landscape. Changing colors and shifting shadows add to the feeling of enchantment. Most of the natural monuments are remnants of sandstone eroded by wind and water. Agathla Peak and some lesser summits, roots of ancient volcanoes, rise in the southern part of the valley; their dark rock contrasts with the pale yellow sandstone of the other formations. The valley lies at an elevation of 5,564 feet in the Upper Sonoran Zone; annual rainfall averages about 8.5 inches.

In 1863-64, when Kit Carson was ravaging Canyon de Chelly and rounding up Navajo, Chief Hoskinini led his people to the safety and freedom of Monument Valley. Merrick Butte and Mitchell Mesa commemorate two miners who discovered rich silver deposits on their first trip to the valley in 1880. On their second trip both were killed, reportedly by Paiute Indians. Hollywood movies made the splendor of Monument Valley known to the outside world. *Stagecoach,* filmed here by John Ford in 1938, began a long series of movies, television shows, and commercials shot in the valley that continues to this day; warriors from John Wayne to Susan Sarandon have ridden across these sands.

The Navajo have preserved the valley as a tribal park with a scenic drive, visitor center, restaurant, and campground. It's open 8 a.m.-7 p.m. in summer (May-Sept.) and 8 a.m.-5 p.m. the rest of the year; closed Thanksgiving Day afternoon and Christmas; tel. (435) 727-3353 or 727-3287. A **visitor center** contains an information desk, exhibits, restaurant, and Indian crafts shop. Navajos also sell crafts from little shops at the beginning of the entrance road. Visitors pay a $2.50 per person fee ($1 ages 60 and over, free ages seven and under) collected on the entrance road. From Kayenta, head 24 miles north on US 163 and turn right 3.5 miles.

Monument Valley Drive

A 17-mile, self-guided scenic drive begins at the visitor center and loops through the heart of the valley. Overlooks provide sweeping vistas from several different vantage points. The dirt road is normally okay if you drive cautiously, but don't attempt it with RVs over 27 feet or extremely low-clearance vehicles. Avoid stopping and becoming stuck in the loose sand that sometimes blows across the road. Allow one and a half hours for the drive. No hiking or driving is permitted off the signed route. Only the visitor center and campground have water, so bring some along on the drive.

Valley Tours

Navajos await at booths in the visitor center parking lot to take you on guided tours year-round. The shortest trips last an hour and a half and cover places on the self-guided route. Longer trips of two and a half or three and a half hours visit hogans, cliff dwellings, and petroglyphs in areas beyond the self-guided drive. Guided

Monument Valley

horseback rides from stables near the visitor center run $20 for one and a half hours; longer day and overnight trips can be arranged too. If you'd like to hike in Monument Valley, you must hire a guide at the visitor center parking lot; hiking tours can last from a few hours to a day or more.

Reservations aren't required on most tours, but you can call ahead for information. **Totem Pole Tours** offers jeep trips, photography tours, trail rides, and hiking including cookouts and overnights; tel. (435) 727-3313 or (800) 345-8687. **Black's Hiking and Jeep Tours** has driving trips of 90 minutes to eight hours, plus day and overnight hikes; tel. (800) 749-4226. **Fred's Adventure Tours** will take you on back-road drives for two hours, a half day, or all day, and on hikes for all day or overnight. Fred offers custom photography tours too; tel. (435) 739-4294 (evenings). **Roland's Navajoland Tours** offers a variety of backcountry drives, photography tours, hiking trips, and overnights; tel. (520) 697-3524 or (800) 368-2785. **Sacred Monument Tours** leads jeep, horseback, hiking, and photography tours; tel. (435) 727-3218 or (520) 691-6199; Internet: www.sacredtoursmv.com. **Monument Valley Horseback Trailrides** will take you out for an hour or more—up to a week; tel. (435) 739-4285 or (800) 551-4039.

Accommodations and Food

Sites at **Mitten View Campground** near the visitor center cost $10, with coin-operated showers; no hookups, but there's a fill and dump station. The season runs early April to mid-October; self-contained RVs (only) can park in winter for $5. Tent campers must often contend with pesky winds in this exposed location. Goulding's Lodge offers the nearest motel and store. You'll also find motels at Kayenta in Arizona and at Mexican Hat and Bluff in Utah.

Country of Many Hogan Bed & Breakfast near Monument Valley offers accommodations in hogans with traditional food at $70 d in winter or $125 d in summer with a continental breakfast. Dinner, camping, sweat lodge, horseback rides, hiking tours, and driving trips can be arranged at extra cost; tel. (520) 283-4125 or (888) 291-4397, p.i.n. 4617; e-mail: nezfoster@prodigy.com. Premium.

Hashké Neiniih Restaurant in the visitor center features stunning views with inexpensive

American, Navajo, and Mexican food. It's open daily for breakfast, lunch, and dinner but may close in winter; tel. (435) 727-3312.

Goulding's Lodge and Trading Post
In 1924, Harry Goulding and his wife, Mike, opened a trading post at this scenic spot, just north of the Arizona-Utah border and 1.5 miles west of the US 163 Monument Valley turnoff. **Goulding's Museum,** in the old trading post building, displays prehistoric and modern Native American artifacts, movie photos, period rooms, and Goulding family memorabilia. It's open daily (on request in winter); donations are appreciated.

Motel rooms go for $128 d from June 1 to Oct. 15, dropping to as low as $62 d mid-winter; a stiff 17% tax is added. Guests have a small indoor pool. Premium. The **Stagecoach Restaurant's** menu offers such American favorites as steak, chicken, pork, fish, sandwiches, and a salad bar. Indian specialties include Navajo tacos, both beef and vegetarian, and there are a few Mexican items. The Stagecoach is open daily for breakfast, lunch, and dinner.

A gift shop sells souvenirs, books, and high-quality Indian crafts. A multi-media show, *Earth Spirit,* portrays the region. The nearby store has groceries and gas pumps. An airstrip lies across the road. Monument Valley tours operate year-round at $25 for two and a half hours, $30 for three and a half hours, and $60 full day with lunch; children under 8 pay less. For accommodation and tour information, write Box 360001, Monument Valley, UT 84536; tel. (435) 727-3231 or (800) 874-0902; Internet: www.gouldings.com.

Goulding's Monument Valley Campground offers a spectacular canyon setting one mile west of the lodge turnoff. Tent ($14) and RV ($22 with full hookups) campers enjoy an indoor pool, showers, laundry, and convenience store/gift shop. It's open March 15 to October 15; tel. (435) 727-3235 or (800) 874-0902. The Seventh-day Adventist Church runs a hospital and mission nearby.

FOUR CORNERS MONUMENT

An inlaid concrete slab marks the place where Utah, Colorado, New Mexico, and Arizona meet. This is the only spot in the United States where you can put your finger on four states at once. It is said that more than 2,000 people a day stop at the marker in the summer. Average stay? Seven to 10 minutes. On the other hand, five national parks and 18 national monuments lie within a 150-mile radius of this point. Navajo, and occasionally Ute and Pueblo, Indians set up dozens of craft and refreshment booths here in summer. Navajo Parks and Recreation collects a small fee during the tourist season.

EASTERN NAVAJO COUNTRY

CANYON DE CHELLY NATIONAL MONUMENT

In Canyon de Chelly, you'll find prehistoric cliff dwellings and traditional Navajo life preserved in spectacular canyons. The main canyons are 26-mile-long Canyon de Chelly (pronounced *d'SHAY*) and adjoining 35-mile-long Canyon del Muerto. Sheer sandstone walls rise up to 1,000 feet, giving the canyons a fortress-like appearance. Rim elevations range from 5,500 feet at the visitor center to 7,000 feet at the end of the scenic drives. Allow at least a full day to see some of the monument's 83,840 acres. April to October is the best time to visit. Winter brings cold weather and a chance of snow. Afternoon thunderstorms arrive almost daily in late summer, bringing thousands of waterfalls that cascade over the rims, stopping when the skies clear.

The First Peoples

Nomadic tribes roamed these canyons more than 2,000 years ago, collecting wild foods and hunting game. Little remains of these early visitors, who found welcome shelter from the elements in the natural rock overhangs of the canyons. The ancestral pueblo people (Anasazi

in the Navajo language) made their first appearance about A.D. 1, living in alcoves during the winter and brush shelters in summer. By A.D. 500 they had begun cultivating permanent fields of corn, squash, and beans and were making pottery. They lived at that time in year-round pithouses, partly underground structures that were roofed with sticks and mud.

Around A.D. 700 the population began to move into cliff houses of stone masonry constructed above ground. These pueblos (Spanish for "villages") also contained underground ceremonial rooms, known as kivas, used for social and religious purposes. Most of the cliff houses now visible in Canyon de Chelly date from A.D. 1100-1300, when an estimated 1,000 people occupied the many small villages. At the end of this period the ancestral pueblo people migrated from these canyons and from other large population centers. Archaeologists speculate that possible causes include floods, drought, overpopulation, and soil erosion.

It's likely that some ancestral pueblo people moved to the Hopi mesas, as Hopi religion, traditions, and farming practices have many similarities with the Canyon de Chelly cliff dwellers. During the next 400 years, Hopi farmers sometimes used the canyons during the growing sea-

Navajo paintings in Canyon del Muerto

son, but they returned to the mesas after each harvest.

The Navajo Arrive

First entering Canyon de Chelly about A.D. 1700, the Navajo found it an ideal base for raiding nearby Indian and Spanish settlements. In 1805 the Spanish launched a punitive expedition; soldiers reported killing 115 Navajo, including 90 warriors. The Navajo identified the dead as mostly women, children, and old men. The site of the killing became known as Massacre Cave. During the Mexican era, raids were common in both directions; the Navajo sought food and livestock, while Mexicans kidnapped women and children to serve as slaves.

Contact with Americans also went badly—settlers encroached on Navajo land and soldiers proved deceitful. Conflict came to an end in the winter of 1863-64, when Colonel Kit Carson led detachments of the U.S. Cavalry into the canyons. The Army destroyed the tribe's livestock, fruit trees, and food stores and captured or killed nearly every Navajo it could find. The starving survivors had no choice but to surrender and be herded onto a desolate reservation in eastern New Mexico. In 1868, after four miserable years there, they were permitted to return to their beloved canyons.

Today, Navajo continue farming and grazing sheep on the canyon floors. You can see their distinctive round hogans next to the fields. More than 50 families live in the canyons, but most find it convenient to spend winters on the canyon rims, returning to their fields after the spring floods have subsided.

Visitor Center

Exhibits reveal Indian history from the Archaic Period (before A.D. 1) to the present, with many fine artifacts. A 22-minute video, *Canyon Voices*, provides additional insights into the peoples who have lived here, as do regional books for sale here. You can step into a Navajo hogan next to the visitor center. A bulletin board lists scheduled talks, campfire programs, and hikes. Rangers are happy to answer your questions. The visitor center is open daily 8 a.m.-6 p.m. from May 1 to September 30, and daily 8 a.m.-5 p.m. the rest of the year; contact Box 588, Chinle, AZ 86503, tel. (520) 674-5500, Internet: www.nps.gov/cach.

Sights

Canyons de Chelly and del Muerto each feature a paved scenic rim drive with viewpoints along the edges, or you can travel inside the canyons by 4WD vehicle, horseback, or foot. With the exception of on the White House Ruin Trail, an authorized Navajo guide or monument ranger must accompany visitors entering the canyons. This rule is strictly enforced. It protects the ruins and the privacy of families living in the canyons. All land belongs to the Navajo people; the National Park Service administers policies only within monument boundaries.

Vehicle break-ins have become a major problem at overlooks, especially at White House where visitors head down the trail. Sneak thieves search out cash, cameras, camcorders, computers, and other valuables.

Hiking

White House Ruin Trail is the only hike possible without a guide. If you have a guide, you can hike almost anywhere. Navajos will usually be waiting near the visitor center to accompany you on canyon trips; they can suggest routes depending on your interests and time available. Rangers at the visitor center can help make arrangements and issue the necessary permit. Comfortable walking shoes, water, insect repellent, and a hat will come in handy. Expect to do some wading. In fact, under the hot summer sun with red rocks all around, you may insist on it—the coolness of the water and shade of the trees are irresistible. Autumn can bring especially good hiking weather, with comfortable temperatures and the sight of cottonwoods turning to gold.

Guides charge $10 per hour for up to 15 people. Overnight trips are possible with additional charges (per group) of $10 per night for the guide and a minimum of $20 per night for the landowner; contact Tsegi Guide Association; tel. (520) 674-5500.

Guides sometimes lead scheduled half-day hikes in the lower canyon from late May to the end of September. Meet the guides at the visitor center, and check departure time the day before—hikes leave promptly. Also, it's a good idea to make reservations the day before, as group size is limited.

Horseback Riding

You'll find **Justin's Horse Rentals** near the entrance to South Rim Drive; look for the stables on the north side of the drive just past the Thunderbird Lodge/Cottonwood Campground turnoff. Rides, available all year, cost $10 per hour for each rider and $10 per hour for the guide (one per group). You can arrange trips of two hours to several days; contact Box 881, Chinle, AZ 86503, tel. (520) 674-5678.

Twin Trail Tours, on the north rim of Canyon del Muerto, features two six-hour rides, each 12 miles roundtrip, into the canyon. One goes upstream to Big Cave and Mummy Cave, the other wanders downstream to Standing Cow Ruin and Antelope House Ruin. Riders have to walk during the 700-foot descent. The starting point is 7.7 miles from the visitor center on North Rim Drive. Tours depart Mon.-Sat. at 9 a.m. May-Oct. and cost $70 per person. Two-hour, three-hour, and overnight trips are available as well. Contact Twin Trail at Box 3068, Chinle, AZ 86503, tel. (520) 674-8425, Internet: www.navajoland.com/twintrailtours/.

Tohtsonii Ranch offers four-hour guided horse rides down the Bat Trail in the Spider Rock area at $10 per hour per person, starting daily at 9 a.m. and 2 p.m. The ranch is 1.6 miles down a dirt road off the South Rim Drive of Canyon de Chelly (keep straight where the drive turns left for Spider Rock Overlook); contact Box 434, Chinle, AZ 86503, tel. (520) 755-6209.

You can also ride your own horse by arranging board and feed at one of the stables near the park and by hiring an authorized Navajo guide, preferably from one of the horse concessions.

Canyon Driving Tours

Jeep tours of both canyons leave Thunderbird Lodge daily at 9 a.m. and 2 p.m. during the busy season. From mid-November to early March, you should call ahead to make sure trips are scheduled; there's a minimum of six passengers. The trips, very popular with visitors, run half day ($36.40 adults, $27.96 children 12 and under) and full day ($58.55 per person—all ages—including lunch). You'll enjoy unobstructed views from the back of an open truck that stops frequently for photography and to view ruins. **De Chelly Tours** offers private jeep and hiking trips, from three hours to all day or overnight

starting at $100-125 per vehicle for three hours; tel. (520) 674-3772.

You can also take your own 4WD vehicles into the canyons with a guide and permit arranged at the visitor center; cost is $10 per hour with a three-hour minimum for up to five vehicles; contact the Tsegi Guide Association at (520) 674-5500.

Accommodations

Thunderbird Lodge, within the monument a half mile south of the visitor center, offers attractive landscaping with lawns and shade trees. It also features a cafeteria and large gift shop. The lodge began as a trading post for the Navajo in 1902; tourists later began arriving in sizable numbers and the post expanded to accommodate them. Rates from April 1 to November 15 start at $89 s, $93 d, less in winter; tel. (520) 674-5841/5842 or (800) 679-2473. Expensive.

The free **Cottonwood Campground,** between the visitor center and Thunderbird Lodge, offers pleasant sites with many large cottonwood trees. It's open all year, with water available only from April to October; no showers or hookups are available, though there is a dump station. Rangers present campfire programs from late May to the end of September. Reservations are accepted only for group sites, though there's usually room at the individual spaces. Cottonwood trees also shade a **picnic area** near the campground; water is available there except in winter.

Spider Rock Campground, a primitive, privately owned place in a pinyon-juniper woodland, is eight miles from the visitor center and half a mile before the Spider Rock turnoff on the South Rim Drive; it costs $10 with extra charges for water, solar showers, and local tours.

Holiday Inn, at the Chinle entrance to the monument, has a restaurant, gift shop, and outdoor pool; rates are $99-109 d in season; tel. (520) 674-5000 or (800) 465-4329 (HOLIDAY). Expensive.

Best Western Canyon de Chelly Inn, 2.5 miles west of the visitor center, has a restaurant, indoor pool, and gift shop; rates May 2 to October 31 run $102 d, less off season; tel. (520) 674-5875 or (800) 327-0354. Expensive.

Many Farms Inn, 17 miles north of Chinle on the way to Monument Valley and Four Corners, recently opened in a school dormitory;

rooms with two beds cost $30 d (shared baths); tel. (520) 781-6226/6227 (school office on weekdays). Guests can use the kitchen, TV lounge, and laundry. From the junction of US 191 and Indian Route 59, go north 0.7 mile on US 191, turn left 0.7 mile at the Many Farms High School sign, then right 0.3 mile. Budget.

Food

Thunderbird Lodge features a good cafeteria with low to moderate prices, open daily 6:30 a.m.-8:30 p.m. (shorter hours in winter). **Holiday Inn's** dining room features the most extensive menu and attractive decor in the area; for dinner you can choose from steaks, ribs, lamb, trout, shrimp, Southwestern, and pasta dishes. In high season, there's a breakfast buffet and a salad bar; the restaurant is open daily for breakfast, lunch, and dinner. **Canyon de Chelly Inn's** Junction Restaurant has American and some Navajo dishes daily for breakfast, lunch, and dinner.

Pizza Edge serves up tasty pizza, calzones, and sandwiches Mon.-Sat. for lunch and din-

the White House, Canyon de Chelly

ner in the **Tseyi Shopping Center,** on US 191 just a little bit north of the junction with Indian Route 7. **Bashas'** supermarket/deli, **Taco Bell,** and **Burger King,** are in the shopping center too; **A&W** is across the highway. **Church's Chicken** is several blocks east of the junction on Route 7.

Shopping and Services

Navajo Nation Arts & Crafts Showroom sits opposite the Canyon de Chelly turnoff from US 191. The three lodges also display Indian work in their gift shops. The **post office** is in Tseyi Shopping Center.

SOUTH RIM DRIVE OF CANYON DE CHELLY

All pullouts and turns are on the left. Distances include mileage between turnoffs and overlooks. Allow at least two hours for the drive. Parked vehicles should be locked and valuables removed.

Mile 0: Visitor Center. The nearby canyon walls stand only about 30 feet high where the Rio de Chelly enters Chinle Wash.

Mile 2.0: Tunnel Canyon Overlook. The canyon is about 275 feet deep here. Guides sometimes lead short hikes down the trail in this side canyon. Don't go hiking without a ranger or Navajo guide.

Mile 2.3: Tsegi Overlook. You'll see a Navajo hogan and farm below. Tsegi is the Navajo word for "rock canyon," which the Spanish pronounced "de chegui." American usage changed it to "de chelly" (d'SHAY).

Mile 3.7: Junction Overlook. Here Canyon del Muerto, across the valley, joins Canyon de Chelly. Canyon depth is about 400 feet. Look for two cliff dwellings of ancestral pueblo people. First Ruin is located in the cliff at the far side of the canyon. The pueblo has 10 rooms and two kivas, and dates from the late 11th to late 13th centuries. Junction Ruin lies straight across, where the two canyons join. It has 15 rooms and one kiva. These dwellings, like most others in the monument, were built facing south to catch the sun's warmth in winter.

Mile 5.9: White House Overlook. Canyon walls rise about 550 feet at this point. White House Ruin, on the far side, is one of the largest in the monument. The name comes from the original white plaster on the walls in the upper section. Parts of 60 rooms and four kivas remain in the upper and lower sections; there may have been 80 rooms before floodwaters carried away some of the lower ruin. As many as 12 ancestral pueblo families may have lived in this village about A.D. 1060 to 1275.

From the overlook, **White House Ruin Trail** begins about 500 feet to the right. Many trails connect the rim with the canyon bottom, but few are as easy as this one. The Navajo often used it to move sheep. Allow two hours for the 2.5-mile roundtrip; bring water but no pets. This is the only hike in the canyon permitted without a guide, but you must stay on the trail. You can buy a pamphlet describing the trail at the visitor center.

Mile 12.0: Sliding House Overlook. These ruins, perched on a narrow ledge across the canyon, are well named. The people who constructed the village on this sloping ledge tried to brace rooms with retaining walls. Natural depressions on the overlook collect water and are still sometimes used by the Navajo.

Mile 19.6: Face Rock Overlook. Small cliff dwellings sit high on the rock face opposite the viewpoint. Though the rooms look impossible to reach, the ancestral pueblo people cleverly chipped handholds and toeholds into the rock.

Mile 20.6: Spider Rock Overlook. South Rim Drive ends here, as rock walls plummet 1,000 feet from the rim to the canyon floor. Spider Rock, the highest of the twin spires, rises 800 feet from the bottom of Canyon de Chelly. Spider Woman, a Navajo deity, makes her home here. A darker side of her character, according to one legend, is her taste for naughty children. When Speaking Rock, the lower pinnacle, reports misbehaving children to Spider Woman, she catches and eats them. Look for the sun-bleached bones on top of her spire.

You can see tiny cliff dwellings in the canyon walls if you look hard enough. Monument Canyon comes in around to the right. Black Rock Butte (7,618 feet high), on the horizon, is either the weathered heart of an extinct volcano or a volcanic intrusion.

NORTH RIM DRIVE OF CANYON DEL MUERTO

All turnoffs are on the right. Distances include mileage between turnoffs and overlooks. Allow at least two hours for the drive. Parked vehicles should be locked and valuables removed.

Mile 0: Visitor Center. Cross the nearby Rio de Chelly bridge and continue northeast on Indian Route 64.

Mile 5.9: Ledge Ruin Overlook. The ruin, set in an opening 100 feet above the canyon floor, dates from A.D. 1050 to 1275 and has 29 rooms, including two kivas in a two-story structure. Walk south a short way to another overlook; a solitary kiva is visible high in the cliff face. A handand toehold trail connects it with other rooms in a separate alcove to the west.

Mile 10.0: Antelope House Overlook. This large site had 91 rooms and a four-story building. The village layout is clear—from the overlook you gaze almost straight down on it. The round outlines are kivas. The square rooms were for living or storage. Floods have damaged some of the rooms, perhaps while the ancestral pueblo people still lived there. The site was abandoned about 1260. Its name comes from paintings of antelope, some believed to be the work of a Navajo artist in the 1830s.

The Tomb of the Weaver sits across from Antelope House in a small alcove 50 feet above the canyon floor. Here, in the 1920s, archaeologists found the elaborate burial site of an old man. The well-preserved body had been wrapped in a blanket made of golden eagle feathers. A cotton blanket was enclosed; these were covered with cotton yarn topped with a spindle whorl.

Look for Navajo Fortress, the sandstone butte across the canyon, from a viewpoint a short walk east from Antelope House Overlook. When danger threatened, the Navajo climbed up the east side using log poles as ladders. They pulled in the uppermost logs and pelted attackers with a hail of rocks. Navajo used this natural fortress from the time of the Spanish until the Kit Carson campaign.

Mile 18.7: Mummy Cave Overlook. Archaeologists in the late 1800s named this large cliff dwelling for two mummies found in the talus slope below. Canyon del Muerto (Spanish for Canyon of the Dead) reportedly also took its name from this find. Mummy Cave Ruin sits within two separate overhangs several hundred feet above the canyon floor. The largest section is on the east (to the left), with 50 rooms and three kivas; the west cave contains 20 rooms. Between these sections is a ledge with seven rooms, including a three-story tower of unknown purpose. The tower dates from about A.D. 1284 and is thought to have been built by ancestral pueblo people from Mesa Verde in Colorado.

Mile 20.6: Massacre Cave Overlook. The North Rim Drive ends here. In 1805, Antonio de Narbona led an expedition of Spanish soldiers and allied Indians to these canyons. A group of fleeing Navajo managed to scale the nearly 1,000 feet to this overhang. Narbona's troops, however, ascended the rim overlooking the cave and fired down. Narbona's account listed 115 Navajo killed and 33 taken captive.

From Yucca Cave Overlook nearby, you can see a cave with at least four rooms and a kiva. A small cave to the left was used for food storage; a hand- and toehold trail connected the two alcoves.

VICINITY OF CANYON DE CHELLY NATIONAL MONUMENT

Chinle

This small, spread-out town lies just west of Canyon de Chelly National Monument. The name Chinle is a Navajo word meaning "Water Outlet"—the Rio de Chelly emerges from its canyon here. A trading post opened in 1882, the first school in 1910, and the nearby monument headquarters in 1931. Chinle features motels, several restaurants, a supermarket, shops, post office, laundromat, and service stations.

Diné College (Tsaile Campus)

Recognizing the need for college education, the Navajo in 1957 established a scholarship fund, financed by royalties from oil. Most students had to leave the reservation to receive a college education, but the cultural gap between the Navajo and the outside world proved too great, and many students dropped out. So in 1969, the tribe created Navajo Community College, recently renamed Diné College. ("Diné" is the name Navajo prefer when speaking of themselves.) Students used temporary facilities at Many Farms, Arizona, until 1973, when campuses were completed at Tsaile and in Shiprock, New Mexico. Students can choose from many Navajo and Indian studies courses—crafts, language, politics, music, dance, herbology, and holistic healing. The colleges offer vocational training and adult education too. The website crystal.ncc.cc.nm.us lists programs, visitor information, museum exhibits, and college-published books.

The unusual campus layout resulted from Navajo elders and healers working together with conventional architects. It was decided that because all important Navajo activities take place within a circle, the campus grounds would be laid out in that shape. If you know your way around a hogan, you'll find it easy getting around campus: the library is tucked in where the medicine bundle is kept during a ceremony, the cooking area (dining hall) lies in the center, sleeping (dormitories) is centered in the west, the teaching area (classrooms) occupies the south, and the recreation area (student union and gym) is in the north. The central campus entrance, marked by the glass-walled Ned A. Hatathli Center, faces east to the rising sun.

The **Hatathli Museum** claims to be the "first *true* Indian museum." Managed entirely by Indians, the collection occupies the third and fourth floors of the hogan-shaped Hatathli Center. Exhibits interpret the cultures of prehistoric peoples as well as Navajo and other modern tribes. The museum and adjacent sales gallery are open Mon.-Fri. 8:30 a.m.-4:30 p.m.; tel. (520) 724-6650. A donation is requested. Ned Hatathli was the first Navajo manager of the tribal Arts and Crafts guild and Tribal Council member.

Diné College Press publishes and sells books on the Navajo and related topics on the first floor of the Hatathli Center; it's open Mon.-Fri. 8 a.m.-5 p.m. The college library and dining hall are also open to visitors. The Tsaile campus lies 23 miles east of the Canyon de Chelly Visitor Center and 54 miles north of Window Rock.

Rainbow Inn Bed & Breakfast offers comfortable non-smoking rooms with private bath and a continental breakfast on the west side of campus; $49 d or $69 for a suite (two bedrooms sharing a bath); tel. (888) HOGAN-4U; e-mail: rainbow @crystal.ncc.cc.nm.us. Inexpensive. **Tsaile Lake,** only one mile southeast of Diné College, has trout fishing and primitive camping ($2 per person for ages 13 and over); not suitable for RVs.

Wheatfields Lake
This large mountain lake lies in a ponderosa forest at an elevation of 7,300 feet east of Canyon de Chelly National Monument. Visitors enjoy camping and trout fishing at this pretty spot. The rugged Chuska Mountains that rise to the east have some trails and back roads; get local advice or a guide before entering the mountains. Campground charges run $2 per person for ages 13 and over. You'll need Navajo fishing and boat permits, as on all tribal waters. A store sells groceries and fishing supplies, but no permits. Construction of a new dam may drain the lake in 1999, but the campground should stay open. Wheatfields Lake is 10 miles south of Tsaile and 44 miles north of Window Rock on Indian Route 12. This scenic, high-country road crosses pastures and forests in the foothills of the Chuska Mountains. In winter, check road conditions; snow and ice can be hazardous here.

Navajo, New Mexico
Trees from the extensive woodlands that surround the town of Navajo supply the town's large sawmill. **Navajo Pine Market** has groceries and tribal fishing permits. Nearby **Red Lake,** named for the color of its aquatic vegetation, has fishing. Navajo is 17 miles north of Window Rock on Route 12, on the way to Wheatfields Lake, Tsaile, and Canyon de Chelly. **Assayi Lake** in Bowl Canyon Recreation Area has fishing (catfish) and camping ($2 per person for ages 13 and over) 11 miles northeast in New Mexico; not suitable for RVs. Whiskey Lake is farther east, also on dirt roads, and offers trout fishing.

WINDOW ROCK

In the early 1930s, "The Rock With a Hole in It" so impressed Commissioner of Indian Affairs

Window Rock

John Collier that he chose the site for a Navajo administration center. An octagonal Navajo Council House, representing a great ceremonial hogan, went up, and Window Rock became the capital of the Navajo Nation. Tribal Council delegates meet here to decide on reservation policies and regulations.

Window Rock is a small (area pop. about 8,000) but growing town at an elevation of 6,750 feet. Besides the Council Chambers and offices, the town contains a museum, small zoo, two parks, a motel, and a shopping center. Window Rock's downtown is the shopping center at the junction of AZ 264 and Indian Route 12.

Window Rock hosts the "The World's Largest American Indian Fair," held on the first weekend after Labor Day in September. The five-day festival offers a mixture of traditional and modern attractions, including singing and dancing, a parade, agricultural shows, food, crafts, concerts, rodeo, and the crowning of Miss Navajo. Write for a free brochure from the Navajo Nation Fair office, Box 2370, Window Rock, AZ 86515, tel.

(520) 871-6478 or 871-6702, Internet: www. navajoland.com.

Navajo Museum, Library & Visitor's Center

The entrance of this impressive new building opens to the east, like the traditional log hogan in front. Massive wood pillars soar to the central skylight high above. Staff at the information desk in the lobby will answer questions and provide Navajo and some Arizona travel literature, and you can pick up a map of Window Rock here. The office is open Mon.-Fri. 8 a.m.-5 p.m. and Sat. 10 a.m.-4 p.m.; tel. (520) 871-6436, 871-7371, or 871-6659, Internet: www.navajoland.com.

Museum galleries off to the left exhibit items from the permanent collection and visiting shows; it's open about the same hours as the information desk; tel. (520) 871-6673. The library, to the right of the lobby, has many books on Indian subjects, as well as general reading; it's open Mon.-Fri. 8 a.m.-7 p.m. and Sat. 9 a.m.-5 p.m.; tel. (520) 871-6376 or 871-6526. A gift shop off the lobby is open the same hours as the information desk. The building also has an indoor theater and large outdoor amphitheater. A snack bar and children's museum are in the works. It's on the north side of AZ 264 in Tse Bonito Tribal Park, a half mile east of Window Rock Shopping Center.

Navajo Nation Zoological and Botanical Park

Set beneath towering sandstone pinnacles known as The Haystacks, the zoo offers a close look at animals of the Southwest. Once past the rattlesnakes near the entrance, you'll wander by golden eagles, hawks, elk, wolves, bobcats, mountain lions, coyotes, black bears, and other creatures. Domestic breeds include the Navajo Churro sheep, which has double fleece and often four horns. Prairie dogs, free of restricting cages, run almost everywhere. Native crops grow near the forked-stick and crib-log hogans in summer. Visit daily 8 a.m.-5 p.m.; free admission; tel. (520) 871-6573. You'll find it just northeast of the museum and library building.

Tse Bonito Tribal Park

This open area beside the museum and library building includes some shaded picnic tables, but no water. A spring, now dry, gave the place its Navajo name, meaning Water Between the Rocks. The Navajo camped here in 1864 on the Long Walk to eastern New Mexico.

Window Rock Tribal Park

This beautiful spot shaded by juniper trees lies at the foot of Window Rock. The "window" is a great hole, averaging 47 feet across, in a sandstone ridge. Loose stones just below the hole mark the site of a prehistoric Indian pueblo. You're not allowed to climb up to the hole, though a trail around to the left passes through wonderfully sculptured hills. The park has picnic tables, water, and restrooms; day-use only. The Navajo Nation Veterans Memorial here honors warriors of all eras of war and peace. Turn east at the sign off Indian Route 12 about a half mile north of AZ 264, then head a half mile in, passing the Council Chambers on your left just before the park.

Navajo Nation Council Chambers

The Council meets at least four times a year within the circular walls here. At other times twelve standing committees of the Council carry out legislative work. Colorful murals depict Navajo history. Visitors can arrange tours by calling the Speaker's Office at (520) 871-7160.

Accommodations

Navajo Nation Inn feaures Navajo-style rooms at $62 s, $67 d, and has a restaurant; tel. (520) 871-4108 or (800) 662-6189. The inn is on AZ 264, just east of the shopping center. Moderate.

A new **Days Inn** offers an indoor pool and spa 3.4 miles west in St. Michaels at 392 W. Hwy. 264, tel. (520) 871-5690 or (800) 325-2525. Rates are $65 s, $75 d. Moderate. Window Rock lacks campgrounds; Wheatfields Lake, 44 miles north, and Assayi in New Mexico (17 miles north to Navajo, then 11 miles northeast) are the closest options.

Food

The **Navajo Nation Inn** dining room serves a varied menu of American, Navajo, and Mexican food daily for breakfast, lunch, and dinner. **Hong Kong Restaurant** has Chinese favorites Mon.-Fri. for lunch and dinner in the Window Rock Shopping Center; tel. (520) 871-5622. The shopping center also has **Taco Bell Express, Pizza Hut Express,** and a supermarket. **Bashas'** supermarket/deli lies just west on AZ 264; **Mc-Donald's** and **Church's Chicken** are also nearby. A quartet of fast-food places, **Part Time Pizza, Kentucky Fried Chicken, Blakes Lotaburger,** and **Dunkin' Donuts,** are in New Mexico one mile to the east.

Shopping and Services
Navajo Arts & Crafts Enterprise sells Navajo paintings, rugs, jewelry, jewelry-making supplies, and crafts by other Southwest tribes at the junction of AZ 264 and Indian Route 12; tel. (520) 871-4095 The **post office** is on a hill behind the Navajo Nation Inn.

Information
The **Navajo Nation Tourism Department** has literature and information for visitors in the lobby of the Navajo Museum, Library & Visitor's Center; it's open Mon.-Fri. 8 a.m.-5 p.m. and Sat. 10 a.m.-4 p.m.; tel. (520) 871-6436, 871-7371, or 871-6659; fax 871-7381; Internet: www.navajoland.com. Fishing and hunting on the Navajo Indian Reservation require tribal permits from **Navajo Fish and Wildlife,** located behind the Motor Pool; Box 1480, Window Rock, AZ 86515, tel. (520) 871-6451 or 871-6452. Arizona Game and Fish has no jurisdiction over the reservation; you need only tribal permits. For hiking and camping information and permits on Navajo lands, contact the **Navajo Parks and Recreation Department,** next door to the Zoological and Botanical Park, Box 9000, Window Rock, AZ 86515, tel. (520) 871-6647, 871-6635, or 871-6636.

Transportation
Navajo Transit System connects Window Rock with many communities on the Navajo and Hopi reservations; see "Getting Around" at the beginning of this chapter.

VICINITY OF WINDOW ROCK

Fort Defiance
Permanent springs in a nearby canyon attracted the Navajo, who named the area Tsehotsoi, "Meadow between the Rocks." Colonel Edwin Vose Sumner had another name in mind in September 1851, when, in defiance of the Navajo, he established a fort on an overlooking hillside.

Though the Navajo nearly overran Fort Defiance in 1860, the Army successfully repelled a series of attacks. The fort was abandoned during the Civil War. In 1863-64, Colonel Kit Carson headquartered at the fort while killing, rounding up, and moving the Navajo. After the Navajo returned, destitute, in 1868, the first Navajo Agency offices issued them sheep and supplies here. The first school on the reservation opened in 1869, and the first regular medical service arrived in 1880. The old fort is gone now, but the town remains an administrative center with a hospital, schools, and Bureau of Indian Affairs offices.

St. Michael's Mission
In 1898, Franciscan friars opened a mission to serve the Navajo. St. Michael's School, opened by the Sisters of the Blessed Sacrament in 1902, lies a short distance away. The mission's large stone church dates from 1937, when it replaced an earlier adobe structure; it's usually open, though you may have to use the side entrance. The chapel behind the parking area has a circular shape, earthen floor, and a 16-foot woodcarving. The German artist who did the carving called it "The Redemption of Humanity" or "American Pieta"; it shows a dead Indian being lowered from a tepee tarp to a woman in mourning with two attendants, like the body of Jesus being lowered from the cross.

The original mission building has been restored as a **historical museum** with a chapel, missionary room, displays of Indian culture, and information on the life of the early missionaries. A gift shop sells regional books, cards, and posters; admission is free. It's open daily 9 a.m.-5 p.m. from Memorial Day to Labor Day and at other times by appointment; tel. (520) 871-4171. St. Michael's Mission is 2.9 miles west of Window Rock Shopping Center on AZ 264, then 0.2 mile south at the sign.

GANADO

The Spanish called this place Pueblo Colorado ("Colored House") after a nearby ruin left by ancestral pueblo people. The name was later changed to Ganado, honoring one of the great Navajo chiefs, Ganado Mucho, or Big Water Clansman, a signer of the treaty of June 1868 that returned the Navajo lands. A Presbyterian mission founded here in 1901 provided the Navajo with a school and hospital. The school, now converted into a hospital, grew into the two-year College of Ganado, where students learned forestry, business administration, and general subjects.

Visit the nearby Hubbell Trading Post, Arizona's most famous such post, to experience a genuine part of the Old West. Ganado is on AZ 264, 30 miles west of Window Rock, 44 miles east of Keams Canyon, and 36 miles south of Chinle. There are no accommodations in the area, but you can find bargain-priced cafeteria meals at the **Sage Cafe** on the old college campus. It's open Mon.-Fri. for breakfast, lunch, and dinner. Turn north into the hospital and follow the signs to a two-story building at the north end of an open park; a playground and some picnic tables lie next to the cafe. A small **museum** off the Sage's food line displays many old photos of the Navajo and has historic exhibits of the school and hospital; ask one of the cafe attendants for the key. **Ramon's Restaurant** nearby has American and Mexican food but lacks a smoke-free area; turn north one block on the street opposite the junction of AZ 264 and US 191.

The Conoco station at the highway junction has a little cafe open Mon.-Fri. for breakfast, lunch, and dinner; a grocery store nearby is open daily.

HUBBELL TRADING POST NATIONAL HISTORIC SITE

John Lorenzo Hubbell began trading in 1876, a difficult time for the Navajo, who were still recovering from their traumatic internment at Fort Sumner. Born in New Mexico, Hubbell had already learned some Navajo culture and language by the time he set up shop. Money rarely exchanged hands during transactions; Indians brought in blankets or jewelry and received credit. They would then point out desired items:

coffee, flour, sugar, cloth, harnesses. If after buying the desired items the Indians still had unspent credit, they usually preferred silver or turquoise to money. Tribespeople bringing wool or sheep to the trading post usually received cash, however.

Hubbell distinguished himself by his honesty and appreciation of the Navajo. His insistence on excellence in weaving and silverwork led to better prices for Indian craftspeople. The trading post helped bridge the Anglo and Indian cultures, as Navajo often called on Hubbell to explain government programs and to write letters to officials explaining Indian concerns.

Visitor Center, Hubbell's House, and Trading Post

National Park Service exhibits and programs explain not only Hubbell's work, but how trading posts once linked the Navajo with the outside world. Weavers (usually women) and silversmiths (usually men) often demonstrate their skills in the visitor center. Books about Indian art and culture are available. You can take a scheduled guided tour of Hubbell's house or a self-guided tour of the grounds; both are free. The house contains superb rugs, paintings, baskets, and other crafts collected by Hubbell before his death in 1930 and by the Hubbell family thereafter.

The trading post still operates much as it always has. You can buy high-quality crafts or most anything else. Canned and yard goods jam the shelves, glass cases display pocket knives and other small items, horse collars and harnesses still hang from the ceiling, and Navajo still drop in with items for trade. Check out the Indian baskets and other old artifacts on the ceilings of the jewelry and rug rooms. A tree-shaded picnic area is next to the visitor center. The National Historic Site, tel. (520) 755-3475, Internet: www.nps.gov/hutr, is open daily 8 a.m.-6 p.m. from June to September, 8 a.m.-5 p.m. the rest of the year, and closed Thanksgiving, Christmas, and New Year's Day. It's one mile west of Ganado.

HOPI COUNTRY

For centuries the Hopi people have made their homes in villages atop three narrow mesas, fingerlike extensions running south from Black Mesa. Early European visitors dubbed these extensions First Mesa, Second Mesa, and Third Mesa. Arizona 264 skirts First Mesa and crosses over Second and Third Mesas on the way from Window Rock to Tuba City.

The mesas have provided the Hopi with water from reliable springs as well as protection from enemies, as the 600-foot cliffs discourage assailants. Hardworking farmers, the Hopi are usually peaceable and independent. They keep in close touch with nature and have developed a rich ceremonial life, seeking to maintain balance and harmony with their surroundings and one another. Villages remain largely autonomous even today. The Hopi Tribal Council, which the federal government forced upon the Hopi, serves mainly as a liaison between villages and agencies of the federal and state governments.

Visiting Hopi Villages

The Hopi tend to be very private people, though they do welcome visitors to their lands. Policies vary from village to village and are often posted. All villages *strictly* prohibit such disturbing activities as photography, sketching, and recording. To give residents their privacy, try to visit only between 8 a.m. and 5 p.m. and keep to the main streets and plazas. Walpi asks that visitors enter only with an authorized Hopi guide.

The best time to visit a village is during a ceremony open to the public. Some ceremonies have been placed off limits because of visitors' lack of respect. Please remember that these are important religious rituals and you are a guest. Check with the village having a dance to make sure that visitors are welcome. If so, residents will expect visitors and you'll be allowed to experience Hopi culture. Dances take place in plazas many weekends. For information, try calling the Second Mesa Cultural Center, tel. (520) 734-2401, or the Hopi Tribe's Cultural Preservation Office, tel. (520) 734-2244; Internet: www.nau.edu/~hcpo-p. The village names given below have their old spellings, seen on most maps and signs, along with Hopi spellings in parentheses.

KEAMS CANYON

This, the easternmost community on the Hopi Reservation, is not a Hopi village, but an administrative town with a hospital and various U.S. government agencies. The settlement lies at the mouth of a scenic wooded canyon named

petroglyphs at Hopi Clan Rocks, northwest of Moenave

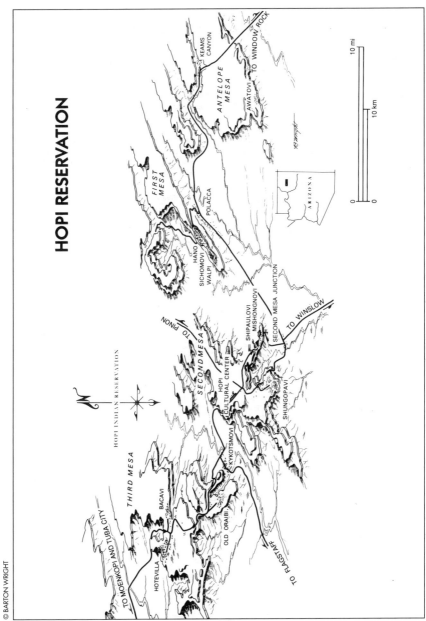

HOPI RESERVATION

© BARTON WRIGHT

HOPI KACHINAS AND CALENDAR

Kachinas appear to the Hopi from the winter solstice on December 21 until mid-July. They dance and sing in unison, symbolizing the harmony of good thought and deed, harmony required for rain to fall and for a balanced life. The rest of the year the kachinas remain in their home in the San Francisco Peaks.

A kachina can take three forms: a powerful unseen spirit, a dancer filled with the spirit, or a wooden figure representing the spirit. Dancers are always male, even when the kachina spirit is female. The men may present gifts of kachina figures to women and children during the dances. Each village sponsors its own ceremonies.

HOPI CALENDAR

Wuwuchim and Soyala
(November to December)

These months symbolize the time of creation of the world. The villages tend to be quiet, as Hopi spend time in silence, prayer, and meditation.

Wuwuchim, a tribal initiation ceremony, marks the start of the ceremonial calendar year. Young men are initiated into adulthood, joining one of four ceremonial societies. The society a man joins depends on his sponsor. Upon acceptance, the initiate receives instruction in Hopi creation beliefs. He's

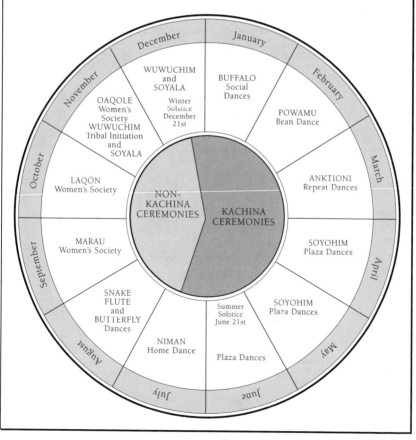

presented with a new name, and his childhood name is never used again.

Only the Shungopavi village performs the entire Wuwuchim ceremony and then not every year. Other villages engage in parts of the Wuwuchim.

The Soyala Kachina appears from the west in the winter solstice ceremony, marking the beginning of the kachina season. As the days get longer, the Hopi begin planning the upcoming planting season; fertility is a major concern in the ceremony.

Buffalo Dances (January)
Men, women, and children perform these social dances in the plazas. They deal with fertility, especially the need for moisture in the form of snow.

Powamuya, the Bean Dance (February)
Bean sprouts are grown in a kiva as part of a 16-day ceremony. On the final day, kachina dancers form a long parade through the village. Children of 13 and 14 years are initiated into kachina societies during the Powamuya. Ogre kachinas appear on First and Second mesas.

Kiva Dances (March)
A second set of nighttime kiva dances consists of Anktioni or "repeat dances."

Plaza Dances (April, May, and June)
The kachina dancers perform in all-day ceremonies lasting from sunrise to sunset, with breaks between dances. The group, and the people watching, concentrate in a community prayer calling on the spirits to bring rain for the growing crops.

Niman, the "Home Dance" (July)
At the summer solstice on June 21, the plaza dances end and preparations begin for the Going Home Ceremony. In this 16-day rite, the last of the season, kachina dancers present the first green corn ears, then dance for rain to hasten the growth of the remaining crops. With their spiritual task completed, the kachinas can now return to their mountain home.

Snake, Flute, and Butterfly Dances (August)
The Snake and Flute ceremonies, held in alternate years, represent the clan groups who perform them in the interests of a good harvest and prosperity. The Snake Dance, usually closed to non-Hopi, takes place in even-numbered years at Shungopavi and in odd-numbered years at Mishongnovi. The snakes, often poisonous rattlers, act as messengers to the spirits.

The Flute Ceremony takes place in odd-numbered years at Shungopavi and Walpi.

The Butterfly Dance, a social dance performed mainly by children, takes place in all villages. It also celebrates the harvest.

Women's Society Dances (September, October, and Early November)
Held in the plazas, these ceremonies celebrate the harvest with wishes for health and prosperity. Chaos reigns during the Basket Dances; female dancers throw out baskets and other valuables to the audience, who engage in a mad free-for-all to grab the prizes. The Society Dances mark the end of the ceremonial year.

---

after Thomas Keam, who built a trading post here in 1875. From the town, the canyon winds northeast for about eight miles; the first three-mile stretch is a road. Kit Carson engraved his name on Inscription Rock, on the left about two miles in from AZ 264. You'll pass the hospital, a picturesque Catholic church, then some pleasant picnic spots on the way in.

Practicalities
The motel and campground once here have closed. **Keams Canyon Shopping Center,** on AZ 264 just west of the Keams Canyon turnoff, features McGee's Indian Art Gallery, a grocery store, an ice cream parlor, and a cafe serving American, Mexican, and Indian food. It's open

daily for breakfast and lunch; dinner is served on weekdays but the restaurant closes at 6 p.m. on Saturday and 3 p.m. on Sunday. A service station is next door. The gallery has an informative website at www.hopiart.com.

Turn north into Keams Canyon for the **post office** (to the right) and the hospital (emergencies only, straight ahead; tel. 520-738-2211).

Awatovi
Beginning as a small village in the 12th century, Awatovi (ah-WAHT-o-vee) had become an important Hopi town by 1540, when Spanish explorers from Coronado's expedition arrived.

Franciscan friars in 1629 built a large church and friary using Indian labor. Their mission lasted 51 years until 1680, when, fearing that their culture would be destroyed by Christianity, Hopi villagers joined their New Mexico Pueblo neighbors in successfully overthrowing Spanish rule, wrecking the Awatovi church and killing most of the priests.

Spaniards re-established the mission in 1700, but other Hopi villages became so angered by this continued alien influence that they banded together and promptly destroyed Awatovi. Of the 800 inhabitants, almost all the men were massacred and the women and children removed to other Hopi villages. Spanish troops retaliated a year later with little effect. Further missionary efforts among the Hopi proved futile. Only ghosts live at Awatovi today—it was never resettled. The ruin sprawls across 23 acres on the southwest tip of Antelope Mesa, with piles of rubble as high as 30 feet. To visit you'll need a permit and a Hopi guide; ask in advance at the Hopi Cultural Center.

FIRST MESA

Polacca

With an increasing population, some Hopi have built houses in settlements below the mesas, as at Polacca (po-LAH-kah). Still, if you ask residents of Polacca where they're from, they'll likely name one of the three villages on the mesa above. Polacca stretches for about a mile along the highway, but offers little of interest. Thrilling views, however, lie atop First Mesa, reached by a paved road that climbs steeply for 1.3 miles to Sichomovi on the crest. If you have a trailer or large vehicle, you must park it in Polacca or at parking areas 0.6 mile or one mile up. A shuttle may be started in the future, in which case all visitors will park below.

Hano (Hanoki)

The first village you reach *looks* Hopi but is really a settlement of the Tewa, a Pueblo tribe from the Rio Grande region to the east. Fleeing from the Spanish after an unsuccessful revolt in 1696, a number of Tewa sought refuge with the Hopi. Hopi leaders agreed, on the condition that the Tewa act as guardians of the access path to the mesa. Despite living close to the Hopi for so long, the Tewa have retained their own language and ceremonies. Hano's fascinating history is detailed in *A Tewa Indian Community in Arizona* by Edward P. Dozier (see the "Booklist" at the end of the book).

Sichomovi (Sitsomovi)

To the visitor, Hano and the Hopi village of Sichomovi (see-CHO-mo-vee) appear as one, but residents know exactly where the line is. Sichomovi is considered a branch of Walpi, the village at the tip of the mesa.

Walpi, "Sky Village"

Walpi (Waalpi)

One of the most inspiring places in Arizona, Walpi (WAHL-pee) stands surrounded by sky and distant horizons. Ancient houses of yellow stone appear to grow from the mesa itself. Coming from Sichomovi, you'll watch the mesa narrow to just 15 feet before widening again at Walpi.

Visitors may enter this traditional village only with an authorized Hopi guide; Walpi is small and its occupants sensitive. Walking tours of 45-60 minutes leave daily from Ponsi Hall in Sichomovi 9 a.m.-5 p.m. in summer and 9:30 a.m.-4 p.m. the rest of the year. The tour cost is $5 adults, $4 children 11-17, and $3 age 5-10 and seniors 65+; tel. (520) 737-2262 (Ponsi Hall) or 737-2670 (Community Development office). Tours may not run on weekends, so it's best to call ahead before making a special trip out.

Unlike other Hopi villages, Walpi lacks electricity and running water. Residents have to walk back toward Sichomovi to get water or to wash. Look for bowl-shaped depressions once used to collect rainwater. Precipitous foot trails and ruins of old defenses and buildings cling to the mesa slopes far below. Inhabited since the 13th century, Walpi is well known for its ceremonial dances and crafts, although most First Mesa dances were closed to the public at press time. Kachina dolls carved by the men and pottery created by the women are sold in the village; signs indicate which houses sell crafts. With sweeping panoramas at every turn and a determined hold on traditions, Walpi is probably the most rewarding of all the Hopi villages.

SECOND MESA

Second Mesa (Junction)

Highways AZ 264 and AZ 87 meet at the foot of Second Mesa, seven miles west of Polacca and 60 miles north of Winslow. Here you'll find a grocery store and a post office. **Honani Crafts Gallery** and a service station lie a half mile west at the turnoff for Shipaulovi and Mishongnovi villages.

Shipaulovi (Supawlavi) and Mishongnovi (Musangnuvi)

These villages are close neighbors on an eastern projection of Second Mesa. Dances often take place; ask at the Cultural Center for dates. You reach Shipaulovi (shih-PAW-lo-vee) and Mishongnovi (mih-SHONG-no-vee) by a short paved road that climbs steeply from AZ 264, a half mile west of the intersection with AZ 87, or by a mesa-top road (also paved, but not to be confused with the Pinon-Hard Rock Road) 0.2 mile east of the Cultural Center. Mishongnovi is the easternmost village, at the end of the mesa.

Shungopavi (Songoopavi)

Shungopavi (shong-O-po-vee or shih-MO-pah-vee) is the largest (pop. 742) of the three Second Mesa villages. Dances performed include the Butterfly Dance (a social dance) and the Snake Dance (late August in even-numbered years), though most have been closed to the public. **Dawa's Art and Crafts** on the road into the village sells locally made work. More galleries lie between the village turnoff and the Cultural Center. Shungopavi is 0.8 mile south off AZ 264, midway between the junction with AZ 87 and the Cultural Center.

HOPI CULTURAL CENTER

Proclaiming itself "At the Center of the Universe," this excellent pueblo-style museum/motel/restaurant/gift shop complex is popular with both visitors and local Hopi. The Hopi Cultural Center is situated on the west side of Second Mesa just before the road plunges down on the way to Third Mesa. For a shortcut to Chinle and Canyon de Chelly, turn north off AZ 264 beside the Cultural Center to Pinon Trading Post, proceed 26 miles (mostly rough and only partly paved), then east 42 miles on paved roads.

The museum displays good exhibits of Hopi culture and crafts with many historic photos. It's open all year Mon.-Fri. 8 a.m.-5 p.m.; from late March to late Oct. it's also open Sat.-Sun. 9 a.m.-3 p.m. There's a small gift shop just inside the entrance. Admission runs $3 adults, $1 children 13 and under; tel. (520) 734-6650. (To learn more of Hopi mythology and customs, dig into off-reservation sources such as the NAU Special Collections or Museum of Northern Arizona libraries, both in Flagstaff.)

The modern motel's nonsmoking rooms run $80 s, ($85 s Fri.-Sat.) and $5 each additional person; rates drop $20 in winter. Reservations are recommended; contact Box 67, Second Mesa, AZ 86043, tel. (520) 734-2401. Moderate. You'll find free camping and picnic grounds next door, between the Cultural Center and the Hopi Arts and Crafts shop. No water or hookups are offered, but you can use the restrooms in the Cultural Center.

The restaurant serves good American and Hopi dishes. This is your big chance to try *paatupsuki* (pinto bean and hominy soup), or maybe some *noqkwivi* (traditional stew of Hopi corn and lamb), or a breakfast of blue pancakes made of Hopi corn. Not to be outdone by Navajo neighbors, the restaurant serves a Hopi taco (with beef) and a Hopi tostada (vegetarian). It's open daily for breakfast, lunch, and dinner.

Hopi Arts & Crafts (Silvercrafts Cooperative Guild), a short walk across the camping area, houses a big selection of traditional works. You can often see Hopi silversmiths at work here.

THIRD MESA

Kykotsmovi (Kiqötsmovi)
The name means Mound of Ruined Houses. Hopi from Old Oraibi (o-RYE-bee) founded this settlement near a spring at the base of Third Mesa. Peach trees add greenery to the town. Kykotsmovi (kee-KEUTS-mo-vee), also known as New Oraibi, is headquarters for the Hopi Tribal Council.

The **Office of the Chairman** provides information for visitors and is near the Tribal Council building one mile south of AZ 264; Box 123, Kykotsmovi, AZ 86039, tel. (520) 734-2441, ext. 102. The **Kykotsmovi Village Store** in town sells groceries and fixes pizza, subs, and snacks in the back. **Sockyma's** is a good source of souvenirs. You can stop for a picnic at Oraibi Wash, 0.8 mile east of the Kykotsmovi turnoff, or the Pumpkin Seed Hill overlook 1.2 miles west on the climb to Old Oraibi. Indian Route 2, leading south to Leupp (pronounced loop), is paved and is the shortest way to Flagstaff.

Old Oraibi (Orayvi)
This dusty pueblo perched on the edge of Third Mesa dates from A.D. 1150 and is probably the oldest continuously inhabited community in the United States.

The 20th century has been difficult for this ancient village. In 1900 it ranked as one of the largest Hopi settlements, with a population of more than 800, but dissension caused many to leave. The first major dispute occurred in 1906 between two chiefs, You-ke-oma and Tawaquap-tewa. Instead of letting fly with bullets and arrows, the leaders staged a strange "push-of-war" contest. A line was cut into the mesa and the two groups stood on either side. They pushed against each other as hard as they could until one group crossed the line and won. You-ke-oma, the loser, left with his faction to establish Hotevilla four miles away. This event was recorded a quarter mile north of Oraibi with the line and inscription: "Well, it have to be done this way now, that when you pass this LINE it will be DONE, Sept. 8, 1906." A bear paw cut in the rock is the symbol of Tawa-quap-tewa and his Bear Clan, while a skull represents You-ke-oma and his Skeleton Clan. Other residents split off to join New Oraibi at the foot of the mesa.

A ruin near Old Oraibi on the south end of the mesa is all that remains of a church built in 1901 by the Mennonite minister, H.R. Voth. Most villagers disliked having this "thing" so close to their homes and were no doubt relieved when lightning destroyed the church in 1942.

Old Oraibi lies two miles west of Kykotsmovi. Avoid driving through the village and stirring up dust; park outside—or next to the Old Oraibi Crafts shop—and walk. Hopi arts and crafts are available at the **Calnimptewa Gallery** east of the turnoff for Old Oraibi, **Monongya Gallery** west of the Old Oraibi turnoff, and **Old Oraibi Crafts** in the village.

Hotevilla (Hot'vela)
Hotevilla (HOAT-vih-lah) is known for its dances, basketry, and other crafts.

Founded in 1906 after the split from Old Oraibi, Hotevilla got off to a shaky start. Federal officials demanded that the group move back to Old Oraibi so their children could attend school there. Twenty-five men agreed to return with their families, despite continued bad feelings; about 53 others refused to leave Hotevilla. The recalcitrant men were jailed for 90 days while their children were forcibly removed to a Keams Canyon boarding school. That winter the women and infants fended for themselves, with little food and inadequate shelter. The next year the men returned, building better houses and planting crops. Exasperated authorities continued to haul You-ke-oma off to jail for lack of cooperation and refusal to send village children to school. In 1912, government officials invited the chief to Washington for a meeting with President Taft, but the meeting didn't soften You-ke-oma's stance.

The turnoff for Hotevilla is 3.7 miles northwest of Old Oraibi and 46 miles southeast of Tuba City.

Bacavi (Paaqavi)

The You-ke-oma loyalists who returned to Old Oraibi under federal pressure continued to clash with the people of Tawa-quap-tewa. When two of the returning women died in quick succession, cries of witchcraft went up. In November 1909, tensions became unbearable. Members of the unwelcome group packed their bags and moved to a new site called Bacavi (BAH-kah-vee) Spring. The name means Jointed Reed, taken from a plant found at the spring. Bacavi lies on the opposite side of the highway from Hotevilla.

Coal Mine Canyon

This is a scenic little canyon 31 miles northwest of Bacavi (15 miles southeast of Tuba City) on AZ 264. Look for a windmill and the Coal Mine Mesa Rodeo Ground on the north side of the highway (no signs), and turn in across the cattle guard. Hopi have long obtained coal from the seam just below the rim.

Moenkopi (Munqapi)

This Hopi village lies two miles southeast of Tuba City. Prehistoric Pueblo Indians built villages in the area but abandoned them by A.D. 1300. Chief Tuba of Oraibi, 48 miles southeast, founded Moenkopi ("The Place of Running Water") in the 1870s. Mormons constructed a woolen mill in 1879 with plans to use Indian labor, but the Hopi disliked working with machinery and the project failed. Moenkopi has two sections—only the upper village participates in the Hopi Tribal Council; the more conservative lower village does not. Water from springs irrigates fields, an advantage not enjoyed by other Hopi villages.

THE EXPLORATION OF THE COLORADO RIVER AND ITS CANYONS

Hopi method of spinning

FLAGSTAFF AND VICINITY

The high country surrounding Flagstaff offers dramatic and remarkably diverse landscapes. Cool forests, which cover much of the region, provide a delightful respite from the desert. Highways wind through many scenic and historic areas, yet backcountry travelers can explore on trails or forest roads all day without ever crossing a paved road. Anglers can choose among many lakes on the Colorado Plateau and the streams below it. In winter, skiers come to enjoy the downhill runs on the San Francisco Peaks near Flagstaff and the shorter runs on Bill Williams Mountain near Williams. Cross-country skiers can strike out on their own or glide along groomed trails near the San Francisco Peaks, at Mormon Lake, or near Williams.

THE LAND

Flagstaff lies atop the Colorado Plateau, a giant uplifted landmass extending into adjacent Utah, Colorado, and New Mexico. As the land rose, vigorous rivers cut deeply through the rock lay-ers, revealing beautiful forms and colors in countless canyons. Sheer cliffs of the Mogollon Rim mark the southern edge of the Colorado Plateau.

While rivers cut down, volcanoes shot up. For millions of years, large and small volcanoes sprouted in the San Francisco Volcanic Field around Flagstaff. The most striking include the San Francisco Peaks, of which Humphrey's Peak at 12,633 feet is Arizona's tallest mountain. Sunset Crater, the state's most beautiful volcano, is the youngster of the bunch, last erupting about 700 years ago—just yesterday, geologically speaking.

Climate

Expect a cool, invigorating mountain climate in most of the Flagstaff area. Spring, summer, and autumn bring pleasant weather to the higher country, where temperatures peak in the 70s and 80s F. Lower valleys may bake in the summer heat, but you can always reach the mountains in less than an hour. From early July into September, thunderstorm clouds billow into the air, letting loose scattered downpours.

Snow and sun battle it out in winter, when temperatures vary greatly—from the bitter cold of storms to the warmth of bright Arizona sunshine. In Flagstaff (elev. 7,000 feet), average winter lows reach the teens, warming to highs in the lower 40s. The winter visitor should be prepared for anything from sub-zero weather to warm, spring-like temperatures. Skiers enjoy the snow, though not many people brave the higher elevations for camping or backpacking. The lower country experiences milder winters, with only occasional snowfalls. Annual precipitation, arriving mostly in summer and winter, varies between 10 and 30 inches, depending on elevation and rain shadows.

Flora and Fauna

The great range in elevation, together with a varied topography, provide many different habitats. Tiny alpine plants hug the ground against strong winds and extreme cold on the highest slopes of the San Francisco Peaks, where no trees can survive. At lower elevations, dense groves of aspen, fir, and pine thrive on the mountainsides and in protected canyons. Squirrels busy themselves storing away food for the long winters here, while larger animals just visit for the summer.

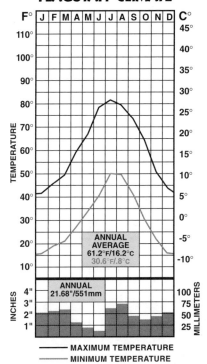

FLAGSTAFF CLIMATE

ANNUAL AVERAGE 61.2°F/16.2°C / 30.6°F/.8°C

ANNUAL 21.68"/551mm

—— MAXIMUM TEMPERATURE
—— MINIMUM TEMPERATURE

FLAGSTAFF HIGHLIGHTS

Flagstaff: This lively university town offers history, science, entertainment, and many traveler's facilities.

San Francisco Volcanic Field: Arizona's highest summit and hundreds of other volcanoes rise in scenic splendor.

Walnut Canyon National Monument: Prehistoric Indian cliff dwellings lie tucked in alcoves of this pretty canyon.

Sunset Crater Volcano National Monument: A beautifully formed and colored volcano stands amidst a lunar-like area of lava flows and cinder craters.

Wupatki National Monument: Large and finely constructed pueblos offer a look into the world of the prehistoric Indians who once lived here.

Vast forests of ponderosa pine and Gambel oak cover much of the Colorado Plateau. Elk, mule deer, a few black bears, coyotes, and smaller animals make these forests their home. Some of the many birds you'll likely see include the ubiquitous common raven, noisy Steller's jay, and feisty hummingbird. Drier parts of the Flagstaff area support woodlands of juniper, pinyon pine, oak, and Arizona cypress. In other semiarid zones, dense shrubs and stunted trees of the chaparral separate the ponderosa forests above from the desert below. Common plants of the chaparral include manzanita, silk-tassel bush, shrub live oak, catclaw acacia, and buckbrush. Streams flowing from the Mogollon Rim often support beavers and attract animals from both the plateau and the desert. The Arizona Game and Fish Department stocks nonnative rainbow trout in lakes and permanent streams.

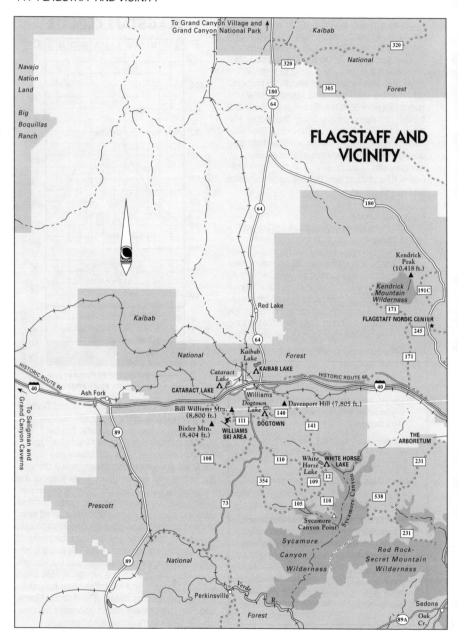

To Grand Canyon Village and
Grand Canyon National Park

Kaibab

National

Forest

Navajo
Nation
Land

Big
Boquillas
Ranch

FLAGSTAFF AND
VICINITY

Red Lake

Kendrick
Peak
(10,418 ft.)

Kendrick
Mountain
Wilderness

191C

Kaibab

FLAGSTAFF NORDIC CENTER

171

National   Forest

Kaibab
Lake

245

HISTORIC ROUTE 66

171

Cataract
Lake

KAIBAB LAKE

HISTORIC ROUTE 66

Ash Fork

CATARACT LAKE

Williams

To Seligman and
Grand Canyon Caverns

Bill Williams Mtn.
(8,800 ft.)

Dogtown
Lake

Davenport Hill (7,805 ft.)

140

THE
ARBORETUM

Bixler Mtn.
(8,404 ft.)

111

WILLIAMS
SKI AREA

DOGTOWN

141

108

110

White
Horse
Lake

WHITE HORSE
LAKE

231

Prescott

354

109

12

105

110

538

231

73

Sycamore
Canyon Point

Sycamore Canyon

Red Rock-
Secret Mountain
Wilderness

Sycamore

Canyon

Wilderness

National

Verde

R.

Forest

Perkinsville

Sedona

Oak
Cr.

89A

89

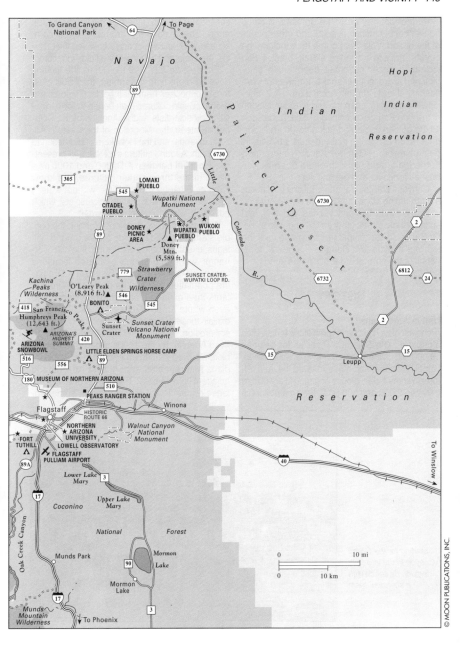

To Grand Canyon National Park
To Page
64

N a v a j o

H o p i

89

I n d i a n

P a i n t e d

I n d i a n

6730

R e s e r v a t i o n

305

LOMAKI PUEBLO
545
Wupatki National Monument
CITADEL PUEBLO
6730
2
89
DONEY PICNIC AREA
WUPATKI PUEBLO
WUKOKI PUEBLO
Doney Mtn. (5,589 ft.)
D e s e r t

Little
Colorado
R.

SUNSET CRATER-WUPATKI LOOP RD.
6732
6812
24
Kachina Peaks Wilderness
779
Strawberry Crater Wilderness
O'Leary Peak (8,916 ft.)
546
545
418
BONITO
San Francisco Peaks
Humphreys Peak (12,643 ft.)
Sunset Crater
Sunset Crater Volcano National Monument
2
ARIZONA'S HIGHEST SUMMIT
420
ARIZONA SNOWBOWL
516
556
89
LITTLE ELDEN SPRINGS HORSE CAMP
15
Leupp
15
180
MUSEUM OF NORTHERN ARIZONA
510
PEAKS RANGER STATION
Winona
R e s e r v a t i o n
Flagstaff
HISTORIC ROUTE 66
Walnut Canyon National Monument
NORTHERN ARIZONA UNIVERSITY
LOWELL OBSERVATORY
FORT TUTHILL
FLAGSTAFF PULLIAM AIRPORT
89A
40
17
To Winslow
3
Lower Lake Mary
Coconino
Upper Lake Mary
National
Forest
Munds Park
Mormon Lake
90
0   10 mi
0   10 km
Oak Creek Canyon
17
Mormon Lake
3
Munds Mountain Wilderness
To Phoenix

© MOON PUBLICATIONS, INC.

In drier country grow the grasses, yuccas, agave, cacti, catclaw acacia, and other plants of the desert. Wildlife at home here include the coyote, gray fox, spotted skunk, black-tailed jackrabbit, desert cottontail, deer mouse, side-blotched lizard, gopher snake, and western rattlesnake. Herds of pronghorn, a graceful, antelope-like creature, roam the arid grasslands north of the San Francisco Volcanic Field. Birds such as the golden eagle, red-tailed hawk, and common raven scavenge in the desert, but usually nest elsewhere. Gambel's quail, roadrunner, horned lark, and black-throated sparrow use bushes for cover and nesting sites.

Canyons create strange variations in climate: a north-facing slope may feature dense growths of fir and pine while only yuccas, grasses, and sparse stunted trees grow on the opposite slope. Or you could see juniper trees growing near the top of a canyon and Douglas firs below, a reversal of the normal order of climate zones.

HISTORY

Native Americans

Archaeologists have dated prehistoric Indian sites along the Little Colorado River as far back as 15,000 B.C., when now-extinct species of bison, camel, antelope, and horse roamed the land. Although some Indian groups engaged in agriculture between 2,000 and 500 B.C., they maintained a seasonal migration pattern of hunting and gathering. These nomadic groups planted corn, squash, and beans in spring, continued their travels, then returned to harvest the fields in autumn.

From about A.D. 200 to 500, as the Indians devoted more time to farming, they built clusters of pithouses near their fields. Regional ancestral pueblo cultures then began to form, classified by scientists as the Anasazi of the Colorado Plateau, the Mogollon of the eastern Arizona uplands, and the Hohokam of the desert to the south. A fourth culture evolved near present-day Flagstaff between A.D. 900 and 1000 as a blend of the three earlier cultures. We know them as Sinagua (Spanish for "without water") because of the area's porous volcanic soil, which quickly absorbs rains and snowmelt.

As these societies developed further, the people started to build pueblos above ground. Villages, usually situated on hilltops or in cliff overhangs, went up in widely scattered locations over north-central Arizona. By about A.D. 1100 the population reached its peak. Most inhabitants then migrated, abandoning villages and even whole areas. Archaeologists attempt to explain these departures with theories of drought, soil erosion, disease, and raids by the newly arrived Apache. By the 1500s, when Spanish explorers arrived in northern Arizona, the Pueblo Indians had retreated to northeast Arizona and adjacent New Mexico. Thousands of empty villages remain in the Flagstaff area, some pro-

starting for the Grand Canyon in the late 19th century, by coach with a six-horse team

COURTESY: AISLINN RACE

tected in the four national monuments of Wupatki, Walnut Canyon, Tuzigoot, and Montezuma Castle-Montezuma Well. You might also discover ruins while hiking in the backcountry.

Americans Settle In

Development in the Flagstaff area started later than in southern and central Arizona. Captain Lorenzo Sitgreaves brought a surveying expedition across northern Arizona in 1851, prompting Lieutenant Edward Beale and others to build rough wagon roads, but hostile Indians and poor farming land discouraged settlement. The coming of the railroad in 1882, thriving lumber mills, and success in sheep and cattle ranching opened up the region and led to the growth of railroad towns such as Flagstaff and Williams.

TRANSPORTATION

You really need your own vehicle to visit the national monuments and most of the scenic and recreation areas. Tours make brief stops at highlights of the region but tend to be rushed; see "Transportation" in the Flagstaff section. Greyhound provides frequent bus service across northern Arizona via Flagstaff and between Flagstaff and Phoenix. Nava-Hopi buses connect Flagstaff and Williams with the Grand Canyon to the north and Phoenix to the south. Amtrak runs daily trains across northern Arizona in each direction between Los Angeles and Albuquerque and beyond. A regional airline serves Flagstaff.

FLAGSTAFF

Surrounded by pine forest in the center of northern Arizona, Flagstaff (pop. 54,280) has long served as an important stop for ranchers, Indians, and travelers. The older, downtown part of Flagstaff still offers a bit of that frontier feeling, expressed by its many historic buildings. Other parts of this small city may seem like endless lines of motels, restaurants, bars, and service stations, but even here one can find reminders of old Route 66 that once linked Flagstaff with the rest of America.

Downtown is an enjoyable place to stroll, admire the architecture, and perhaps sample some of the unique restaurants and shops. Many of the old structures have plaques describing their history. To visit the distant past, when the land rose up, volcanoes erupted, and the early Indians arrived, drop by the Museum of Northern Arizona. To learn about the pioneers of 100 years ago, head over to the Pioneer Historical Museum and the Riordan Mansion State Historic Park. To see the current art scene, swing by the Art Barn and University Art Galleries. For a trip out of this world, visit Lowell Observatory, where astronomers discovered Pluto, or the U.S. Geological Survey, where astrogeologists map celestial bodies.

For the great outdoors, head for the hills— Arizona's highest mountains begin at the northern outskirts of town. In summer, the mountains, hills, and meadows offer pleasant forest walks and challenging climbs. Winter snows transform the countryside into some of the state's best downhill and cross-country skiing areas. As a local guidebook, *Coconino County, the Wonderland of America,* put it in 1916, Flagstaff "offers you the advantages of any city of twice its size; it has, free for the taking, the healthiest and most invigorating of climates; its surrounding scenic beauties will fill one season, from May to November, full to overflowing with enjoyment the life of any tourist, vacationist, camper or out doors man or woman who will but come to commune with nature."

History

Indian groups had settled near the site of present-day Flagstaff, but they had long abandoned their villages when the first white people arrived. Many ruins of old pueblos lie near town. Walnut Canyon National Monument, just east of Flagstaff, contains well-preserved cliff dwellings of the Sinagua people.

Spanish explorers and missionaries knew of the Flagstaff area, but they had little interest in a place with no valuable minerals to mine or souls to save. Beginning in the 1820s, mountain men such as Antoine Leroux became expert trappers and guides in this little-known region between Santa Fe and California. Early travelers sent out glowing reports of the climate, water, and scenery of the region, but hostile Apache, Navajo, Yavapai, and Paiute discouraged settlement.

Samuel Cozzens, a former Tucson judge, traveled east to stir up prospective settlers with a large, well-illustrated book titled *The Marvellous Country; or, Three Years in Arizona and New Mexico, the Apache's Home.* The subtitle expanded upon this theme: *Comprising a Description of this Wonderful Country, Its Immense*

FLAGSTAFF'S FLAGPOLES

It's obvious that Flagstaff was named for a flagpole. The question is, which one?

The first group of settlers to arrive from Boston claimed to have erected a flagpole in April or May of 1876, before the July 4th celebration held by the second Boston group later that year. Either party may have sunk the pole that served as the town's namesake.

Some early settlers regarded a tall tree, trimmed of all branches, at the foot of McMillan Mesa as *the* flagstaff. Others disputed this, stating that Lieutenant Edward Beale delimbed the tree in the 1850s or that it was the work of a later railroad-surveying party. No record actually exists of a flag ever flying from the tree. Another flagpole, standing near Antelope Spring, *did* fly a flag.

At any rate, citizens gathered in the spring of 1881 and chose the name "Flagstaff" for the settlement.

Mineral Wealth, Its Magnificent Mountain Scenery, the Ruins of Ancient Towns and Cities Found Therein, With a Complete History of the Apache Tribe, and a Description of the Author's Guide Cochise, the Great Apache War Chief, the Whole Interspersed with Strange Events and Adventures. Cozzens's book sold well in New England and he stayed busy giving talks to eager audiences. With each retelling, his descriptions of Arizona's climate, forests, water, and mineral wealth grew and improved. By 1875, the Arizona Colonization Company, with Cozzens as president, was established in Boston. In February 1876, a group of about 50 men, each with 300 pounds of tools and clothing, set off for Arizona under the auspices of the company. In May a second group embarked for the "marvellous country."

After 90 days of arduous travel, the first group arrived at their destination on the Little Colorado River only to find the land already claimed by Mormons. The group continued west to the San Francisco Peaks and started to build a settlement, dubbed Agassiz. But finding no land suitable for farming or mining, they gave up and left for Prescott and California even before the second group arrived. The second group gave up, too, but not before erecting a flagpole to celebrate July 4th.

Thomas Forsythe McMillan, who arrived from California with a herd of sheep in 1876, became Flagstaff's first permanent settler. Other ranchers soon moved into the area, bringing the total population to 67 in 1880. On August 1, 1882, the rails reached Flagstaff. Construction of the railroad brought new opportunities, new stores, restaurants, saloons, banks, and Flagstaff's first physician.

SIGHTS

Flagstaff has many free parking spaces along the streets, by the Visitor Center, and in a few lots; these spaces generally have a two-hour limit. A free all-day lot lies off Beaver St.; turn south from Route 66, then right just after the railroad tracks. RVs can park in an adjacent lot by crossing the railroad tracks on Beaver St., turning right on Phoenix Ave., then right into the parking area.

Museum of Northern Arizona

This active museum features excellent displays of the geology, archaeology, anthropology, cultures, and fine art of the Colorado Plateau. Contemporary Native American exhibits illustrate the traditions of northern Arizona tribes and their basketry, pottery, weaving, kachina dolls, and ceremonies; this area of the museum contains a full-size replica of a Hopi kiva. Art galleries display changing exhibits of Indian and Southwestern works.

Enduring Creations, a changing sales exhibition of the finest Hopi, Navajo, and Zuni artwork, runs through the summer. Popular museum-sponsored Hopi, Navajo, Pai, and Zuni shows also take place during this time, exhibiting the best arts and crafts of each tribe: The Hopi Marketplace runs on the weekend nearest July Fourth; Navajo Marketplace is on the first weekend in August; Festival of Pai Arts is on Labor Day weekend; and Zuni Marketplace is held in mid-September. The museum shop sells Native American crafts, including Navajo blankets; Navajo, Hopi, and Zuni jewelry; Hopi kachina dolls; and pottery by various tribes. A bookstore stocks a large selection of books and posters related to the region. Rio de Flag Nature Trail makes a half-mile loop; borrow the trail booklet from the ticket desk. You can use the museum's library—one of the most extensive for Southwest topics—across the highway in the Research Center; it's open Mon.-Fri. 9 a.m.-5 p.m.

A visit to the Museum of Northern Arizona is highly recommended for anyone planning to buy Indian crafts or visit the reservations of northern Arizona, or who wishes to better understand the natural history of the area surrounding the Grand Canyon.

Set beside a little canyon in a pine forest, the museum is open daily 9 a.m.-5 p.m.; admission is $5 adults, $2 ages 7-17, $3 students with I.D., $4 seniors; tel. (520) 774-5213; Internet: www.musnaz.org. From downtown Flagstaff, head three miles northwest on US 180; the museum is on the left.

Scenic Sky Ride

Arizona Snowbowl's chairlift will take you up to 11,500 feet on the San Francisco Peaks for great panoramas. It's open daily 10 a.m.-4 p.m. in summer (June 21-Labor Day weekend) and

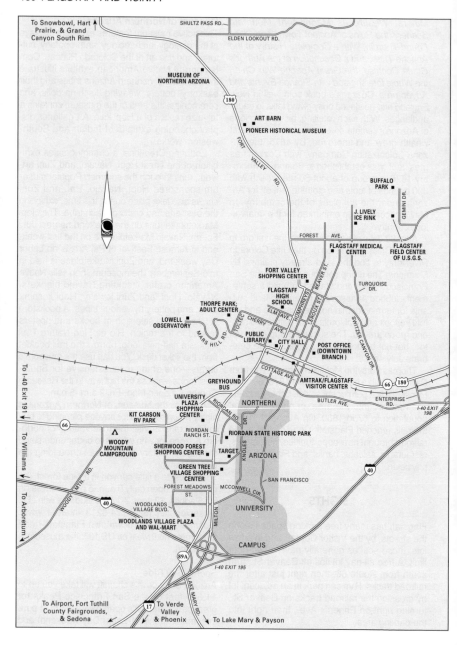

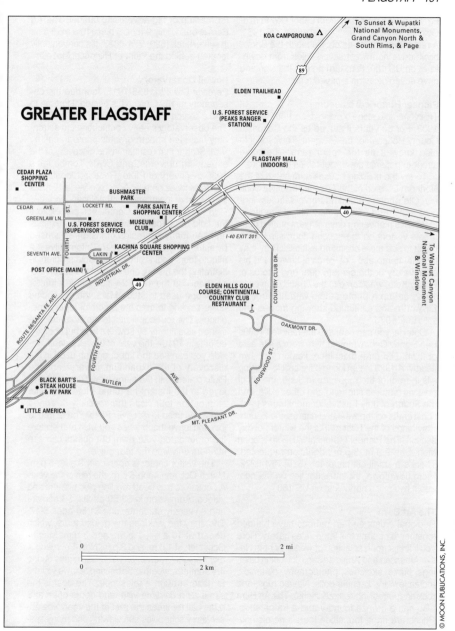

Fri.-Sun. 10 a.m.-4 p.m. from Labor Day to mid-October, weather permitting; tel. (520) 779-1951. A restaurant serves lunch. To reach the Snowbowl, drive northwest seven miles from downtown on US 180, then turn right at the sign and drive seven miles on a paved road.

Pioneer Historical Museum

This venerable stone building dates from 1907 or 1908. For 30 years it served as the Coconino County Hospital for the Indigent. Townspeople also knew it as the "poor farm"—because stronger patients grew vegetables in the yard.

Today the building houses a museum of the Northern Division of the Arizona Historical Society. Old photos, branding irons, saddles, logging tools, and other artifacts illustrate life in Flagstaff's pioneering days. A giant stuffed bear greets visitors on the second floor; slip by the beast to see more changing exhibits. They may include memorabilia of Percival Lowell and his observatory or the camera gear and photos of Emery Kolb, who came to the Grand Canyon in 1902, set up a photo studio with his brother Ellsworth, and continued showing movies and stills until 1976.

Outside, you can peer into the restored 1880s Ben Doney Cabin, moved here from a site east of town. Old farm machinery lies on the lawn nearby. A 1929 steam locomotive built for logging sits in front of the museum. In June, the Wool Festival features shearing and other skills, and the Fourth of July Festival demonstrates traditional crafts on the weekend nearest the Fourth. Playthings of the Past marks the winter holiday season. The Pioneer Historical Museum is open Mon.-Sat. 9 a.m.-5 p.m.; donation requested. There's a small gift shop; tel. (520) 774-6272. From downtown, the museum lies on the right about two miles northwest on US 180.

The Art Barn

Regional artists and art patrons have banded together to operate this large sales gallery. Here you'll find a good selection of works by both Native American and Anglo artisans, including paintings, prints, sketches, photography, ceramics, Indian jewelry, kachina dolls, Navajo rugs, and rock art (petroglyph reproductions). The Art Barn also has a bronze foundry and a frame shop. Prices are right, too, since there's no distribu-

tor markup or big advertising budget. The Art Barn is open daily 9 a.m.-5 p.m. (10 a.m.-5 p.m. in winter); tel. (520) 774-0822. It's conveniently located behind the Pioneer Historical Museum.

Lowell Observatory

Percival Lowell (1855-1916) founded the observatory in 1894, using his personal fortune to fund a search for signs of intelligent life on Mars. The observatory's early contributions to astronomy included spectrographic photographs by V.M. Slipher that resulted in the discovery of the expanding universe, and Clyde Tombaugh's 1930 discovery of Pluto. Research continues with telescopes here, at Anderson Mesa 12 miles southeast of town, and at other locations.

In the Steele Visitor Center, you can explore the field of astronomy with interactive exhibits and see many examples of instruments used by astronomers over the years. Informative 90-minute tours begin with a multimedia program illustrating the history and work of the observatory, then visit the 1896 24-inch Clark refractor telescope used to study Mars, the expanding universe, and to map the Moon for lunar expeditions. The tour continues to the Rotunda, designed as a library by Lowell's wife but completed only in 1916—the year of Lowell's death. Inside you can see the spectrograph used in the discovery of the expanding universe and the Pluto plates, with the same view Tombaugh enjoyed at the instant he found Pluto. The final stop on the tour visits the specially designed telescope used to discover Pluto. You're free to join and leave the tours as you wish and explore the grounds on your own, but guests can see interiors only with the tour guide.

The visitor center is open daily 9 a.m.-5 p.m. March-Oct. and noon-5 p.m. the rest of the year. A bookstore has good reading plus posters and videos. Admission is $3.50 adults, $3 seniors and university students, and $1.50 ages 5-17. The entry fee includes the guided tours, which depart at 10 a.m., 1 p.m., and 3 p.m. March-Oct., then at 1 p.m. and 3 p.m. Nov.-February. A Sky Tonight Program on Mon.-Sat. nights during the summer, weather permitting, allows visitors to gaze through a telescope. The cost is the same as a daytime visit, and doors open at 8 p.m.; call for times the rest of the year. The observatory schedules sun viewing and many special events through the year, so it's worth calling or looking at the website to check times and see what's coming up; tel. (520) 774-2096 (recording); Internet: www.lowell.edu. The observatory sits atop Mars Hill, one mile from downtown; drive or walk west on Santa Fe Ave. to the signed road up. In winter this steep road requires caution and often snow chains.

PLANET X

The ancients recorded five bright star-like wandering bodies. Later generations figured out that Earth was also a planet. In 1781, William Herschel, who was conducting star surveys, discovered a seventh planet. The planet, now known as Uranus, had been plotted on sky charts at least two dozen times as a star. Astronomers used these positions to plot the planet's orbit, but Uranus was not moving according to Newton's mechanics. In the early 1820s it was moving too slowly, but by the end of that decade it was moving too fast.

British astronomer John Couch Adams and French astronomer Urbain Leverrier, working independently, performed laborious calculations based on the assumption that the gravitational pull of an undiscovered eighth planet was affecting Uranus' movement. Both men's predicted positions for the new planet were very close and a short telescopic search soon revealed the "new" planet, which was named Neptune.

Neptune had also been plotted as a star on several charts before its 1846 discovery. Again, the planet did not seem to be following a perfect orbit. Several astronomers started calculations to find a ninth planet, which they dubbed "Planet X." Percival Lowell spent years figuring a position for Planet X but did not have suitable telescopes to search the sky for it. Since his main interest lay in finding signs of life on Mars, his instruments were powerful, did not show wide-angle views, and were so slow photographically that some exposures required guidance hour after hour—night after night in some cases—for a single photograph.

Lowell died before a suitable telescope could be built, and the sky search for Planet X did not begin again for more than a decade. Harvard president A. Lawrence Lowell (Percival's brother) donated money to build a small but wide-angled and photographically fast telescope. This instrument exposed plates 14 inches by 17 inches covering a field 12 by 14 degrees and required less than an hour of exposure.

Each plate showed between 40,000 and one million stars. Since the distant planet was too far away to be recognizable as one by any telescope, only its motion against the background of stars as it circled the Sun would reveal it as a planet. Thus, each plate would be duplicated several days later and then each star image would be compared from plate to plate until one of the "stars" was found to have moved a distance appropriate for a planet that far from the Sun.

Twenty-two-year-old Kansas farm boy and astronomy student Clyde Tombaugh set to work exposing the plates by night and using a blink comparator by day to conduct the search. The blink comparator would flash a view of part of one plate through a microscope eyepiece, then flash a view of the corresponding section of a second plate. If an object had moved it would appear in the eyepiece as if it were jumping back and forth. That sounds easy, but Tombaugh examined hundreds of thousands of star images during a search of about nine months before finding one that moved an appropriate distance. He also discovered some asteroids and variable stars in the process.

Although Tombaugh discovered Pluto on February 18, 1930, using plates made January 23 and January 29, Lowell Observatory cautiously waited several weeks to announce the new planet, studying its motion in the meantime to verify that it was truly the long-sought Planet X. The announcement was made on March 13, 1930—the 75th anniversary of Lowell's birth.

Many people wanted to name the new planet for Percival Lowell; others favored Clyde Tombaugh. An English schoolgirl sent in the winning suggestion "Pluto" in honor of the Greek god of the underworld, brother of Jupiter and Neptune. The planet's astronomical symbol became "P" with an "L" bottom stem. This abbreviation for Pluto also represented Percival Lowell's initials and honored his contribution.

Earth and Planetary Geologic Studies

Many of the scientists at the Flagstaff Field Center of the U.S. Geological Survey study and map Earth's moon, the planets, and other bodies of our solar system using data collected from space missions. They also investigate Earth's landforms such as volcanoes and sand dunes, thought to be formed by the same processes as those on extraterrestrial bodies. The Apollo astronauts received geologic training and tested their equipment here, and were later guided while on the Moon by geologists from this center. Other scientists at the center research and monitor many of Earth's geologic processes. Hydrologists monitor stream flows and geologists study rock layers, faults, and volcanoes. Geologic mapping helps define our landscape, while remote sensing is used to detect environmental change.

You're welcome to visit the Field Center and browse among exhibits throughout the buildings' hallways. Begin by picking up a self-guided tour brochure in the lobby of Buildings 1, 3, or 4. Giant maps and spectacular color images from spacecraft cover the walls. Images include shots of Jupiter and Saturn and their moons, remote-sensing products showing the Earth's features, and views sent back by spacecraft landing on Mars and Venus. The geology of the Moon and most solid-surfaced planets and their satellites have been mapped in surprising detail. Even cloud-covered Venus has been mapped using radar images with computer-generated color. Building 1 features "A Walk Through the Solar System," as well as a specialized library open to the public for reference use. Building 4 displays additional planetary exhibits, while the hallways of Building 3 show maps and photos of geologic and hydrologic studies here on Earth.

You may visit Mon.-Fri. 8 a.m.-4:30 p.m. Remember that the people working here are normally too busy to show visitors around. Also, don't enter offices or labs unless invited. To arrange tours for scientific or educational groups, call or write in advance to the U.S. Geological Survey, 2255 N. Gemini Dr., Flagstaff, AZ 86001, tel. (520) 556-7000. The Flagstaff Field Center's website, wwwflag.wr.usgs.gov, features some of the work done and products available. The Center lies atop McMillan Mesa off Cedar Ave., 1.5 miles northeast of downtown.

Riordan Mansion State Historic Park

The Riordan brothers, Timothy and Michael, arrived in Flagstaff during the mid-1880s and eventually took over the Arizona Lumber & Timber Company. Both became involved with the social, business, and political life of early Flagstaff. In 1904, they built a grand mansion just south of downtown. A "Rendezvous Room" connected the wings occupied by each brother's family. The architect Charles Whittlesey, who also designed El Tovar Hotel on the rim of the Grand Canyon, used a similar rustic style of logs and stonework for the mansion exterior. The brothers christened their joint home *Kinlichi,* Navajo for "Red House."

Tours of the house reveal how the wealthy lived in Flagstaff during the early 1900s. Guides offer history and comment on the furnishings and architectural features. Only the Riordans have lived here, and all the rooms still display their original furniture, most done in an American craftsman style. The park is open daily 8 a.m.-5 p.m. from May to September and daily 11 a.m.-5 p.m. the rest of the year; there's no charge to see the exhibits in the visitor center or to take the self-guided tour of the grounds. Tours inside the mansion last 50-60 minutes and depart on the hour 9 a.m.-4 p.m. May-Sept. and noon-4 p.m. the rest of the year; tour fees are $4 adults, $2.50 ages 7-13; tel. (520) 779-4395. It's best to phone in advance for reservations, as you may enter only in a group and tour times may change. A video shown on request has interior views. Standard wheelchairs can access the lower floor. Picnic tables are near the parking area. You'll find this piece of historic Flagstaff between S. Milton Rd. and Northern Arizona University, about a half mile south of downtown; turn east on Riordan Road toward NAU from S. Milton, then turn right at the sign, opposite Ardrey Auditorium.

Northern Arizona University (NAU)

Flagstaff's character and population owe much to this school, just south of downtown. The university began in 1899 as Northern Arizona Normal School, housed in a vacant reformatory building. Four young women received their diplomas and teaching certificates two years later.

In 1925 the school began offering a four-year Bachelor of Education degree and took the name Northern Arizona State Teachers College. The program broadened over the years to include other degrees, a program in forestry, and graduate studies. In 1966 the institution became a university. NAU's sprawling campus now covers 686 acres, supplemented by the School of Forestry's 4,000-acre laboratory forest. The High Altitude Training Center's programs attract athletic teams from around the world to improve their performance in the thin mountain air.

Be ready for almost anything in the **Marguerite Hettel Weiss Museum and Gallery,** in the historic 1893 Old Main/Ashurst Building (first and second floors) and the **Richard E. Beasley Art Museum** in the Creative Arts Building; call (520) 523-3471 to find what's showing.

Northern Arizona University (NAU) Observatory, built by the U.S. Air Force as an atmospheric research observatory in the early 1950s, is still used today for research, but it primarily serves as an educational tool for university students and the general public. Volunteers, mostly astronomy club members, hold an open house most Friday nights at 7:30 p.m. with special open nights for astronomical events such as eclipses and occultations. It's off S. San Francisco St. just north of a high-rise dormitory and practice field; tel. (520) 523-7170.

Visitors are welcome in the university's art galleries, foodservice facilities, libraries, and indoor swimming pool and at theater and sporting events. To learn about NAU services and events, call or visit the University Union Information Desk, tel. (520) 523-4636, or call the switchboard, tel. (520) 523-9011; Internet: www.nau.edu. A free shuttle bus makes a loop around the northern and southern parts of the main campus. Ask someone for the location of the stop nearest you. The service runs about every 15 minutes Mon.-Thurs. 7:35 a.m.-11 p.m. and Friday 7:35 a.m.-5 p.m. during the main school terms. To park on campus, pick up a free visitor's permit from the **Parking Services/Visitor Information** office at the corner of Dupont Ave. and S. Beaver St.; a small fee applies for permits exceeding seven days. After hours you can obtain a parking permit from the police office at Lumberjack Stadium.

The Arboretum

Plant enthusiasts here do research on native and nonnative flora that thrives in the cool climate of the Flagstaff area. More than 700 species of plants and trees grow on the 200-acre grounds, despite the short 75-day average growing season. At 7,150 feet elevation, the arboretum is the highest botanical garden in the U.S. doing horticultural research.

Tours of 45-60 minutes introduce ongoing projects and take you through the solar greenhouse and outdoor gardens. You'll see endangered species that the staff works to propagate. Exhibits, which you can also see on your own, include gardens of native and adapted plants, wildflowers, herbs, and vegetables. The constructed wetlands area uses native plants to treat wastewater, which gets recycled for watering other plants. A nature trail through the ponderosa pine forest has a 0.6-mile inner loop and a one-mile outer loop. Anyone landscaping or gardening in northern Arizona can gain a wealth of practical information here. The visitor center has exhibits, including mounted specimens of many local species. A gift shop offers books, cards, a bird list, Extension Bulletins (gardening and tree advice), seeds, and gardening supplies. You can purchase plants at the Summer Plant Sale and Garden Fair on the third weekend of June and through the season, then again at the Holiday Plant Sale on the first Saturday in December.

Annual events include the two plant sales and an Open House on the second Saturday in July. The Arboretum is open daily 9 a.m.-4 p.m. May-Oct., open Mon.-Fri. 9 a.m.-4 p.m. Nov.-Dec. 24 and March 14-April, and closed Dec. 24-March 14. No pets permitted. Guided tours begin at 11 a.m. and 1 p.m.; admission is $3 adults, $1 age 6-18; tel. (520) 774-1441; Internet: www.flag-guide.com/arboretum. Summer (June-Sept.) is the best time to visit. Picnic tables offer a place to have your lunch. From S. Milton Rd. in Flagstaff, head west 1.9 miles on Route 66, then turn south four miles on Woody Mountain Road.

Elden Pueblo

Resourceful prehistoric Indians, known by archaeologists as Sinagua, lived at this site below Mt. Elden about A.D. 1150. Some of the pueblo, including a large community room, has been excavated. A leaflet explains and illustrates features of the ruin, open during daylight hours; there's no admission charge. It's on the northeast edge of town; head north on US 89 past the

Flagstaff Mall and the Peaks Ranger Station to the signed turn on the left, just before the Camp Townsend-Winona Road.

RECREATION

Flagstaff Urban Trail System
You don't have to go far for a hike, as this trail network goes right through town. It connects the Mt. Elden trails with the Arizona Trail, Walnut Canyon National Monument, and other areas surrounding Flagstaff. Mountain bikers, joggers, and hikers use them. The City Planning Office in the Flagstaff City Hall at 211 W. Aspen has maps.

Horseback Riding
The Flagstaff area has some great horse country. If you don't have your own steed, local riding stables can provide one; reservations are advised. In winter, stables usually close; horses often head south to join the snowbirds on the desert.

The Flying Heart Barn offers hour-long, half-day, and full-day rides year-round on and near the San Francisco Peaks; head 3.5 miles north on US 89 from I-40 Exit 201; tel. (520) 526-2788. **Hitchin' Post Stables** leads trail rides (one or two hours, half-day, full-day, and overnight), hayrides, sleigh rides, cowboy breakfasts, and steak dinner rides 4.5 miles southeast of town on S. Lake Mary Rd., tel. (520) 774-1719 or 774-7131. **Mormon Lake Riding Stables,** near Mormon Lake Lodge, has trail, wagon, and stagecoach rides May-Sept.; tel. (520) 354-2600; head 20 miles southeast on Lake Mary Rd., then turn right eight miles on Mormon Lake Loop Road.

Downhill Skiing
Arizona Snowbowl, on the San Francisco Peaks, has some of Arizona's best downhill action. Four chair lifts and a tow rope service 30 runs/trails ranging from novice to expert. From the top of Agassiz Chairlift, it's two miles and 2,300 feet down. With sufficient snow, the Snowbowl is open for skiing daily 9 a.m.-4 p.m. from mid-December to Easter. Lift tickets cost $33 ($27 afternoons on weekends and holidays; $20 afternoons on weekdays) for adults; $18 ($13 afternoon) for ages 8-12; $13 seniors 65-69; and free for kids seven and younger and for se-

niors over 70. Call (520) 779-1951 for recorded information about lifts, rentals, and instruction and for weather and road conditions; Internet: www.arizonasnowbowl.com. **Hart Prairie Lodge** (elev. 9,200 feet) offers a ski school, rentals, repairs and a restaurant. **Ski Lift Lodge,** across Hwy. 180 from Snow Bowl Road, has rooms and a restaurant; tel. (520) 774-0729. To reach the Snowbowl, drive northwest seven miles from downtown on US 180 to the sign, then turn right seven miles on a paved road, which sometimes requires chains and/or 4WD.

Cross-Country Skiing
Flagstaff Nordic Center offers more than 40 km of groomed trails ranging from beginner to advanced near Hart Prairie and the San Francisco Peaks. A five-km marked trail leads to the Hochderrfer Hills (maximum elevation 9,200 feet). The center provides ski lessons, a beginner package, a snowshoe-only trail, equipment rentals and sales, and a snack bar. Races, clinics, and moonlight tours highlight the calendar. It's open daily from about mid-November until mid-April, as weather permits. Trail passes run $10, free for kids seven and under and seniors 70 and over; snowshoers pay $5; tel. (520) 779-1951; Internet: www.arizonasnowbowl.com. Take US 180 northwest 16 miles from downtown to near Milepost 232.

Cross-country skiers also head to Hart Prairie and Wing Mountain, two undeveloped skiing areas near the San Francisco Peaks. The rolling meadow and forest country is ideal for ski touring. Reach Hart Prairie by driving 9.5 miles northwest of town on US 180, then turning right on the south end of Forest Road 151 and continuing as far as the road is clear. Parking on US 180 is prohibited, but there are some signed parking areas just off it. For Wing Mountain, continue on US 180 just past Hart Prairie Rd., then turn left onto Forest Road 222B. For road and skiing conditions near the Peaks, call the Forest Service (Peaks Ranger Station) at (520) 526-0866.

The groomed trails of Mormon Lake also attract cross-country skiers. **Mormon Lake Ski Center,** in the village of Mormon Lake, has 20 km of groomed diagonal and skating trails ranging from easy to challenging. It's open daily, snow permitting, with a trail fee of $5 per adult or $15 per family, rental ski sets for $11, and instruction at $15 for 90 minutes in a small group; tel. (520) 354-2240 (toll call from Flagstaff). Drive 20 miles southeast on Lake Mary Rd., then turn right eight miles on Mormon Lake Loop Road. **Mormon Lake Lodge** has rooms, cabins, and a cafe/steakhouse; tel. (520) 774-0462 (Flagstaff) or 354-2227 (local). For Mormon Lake road and ski conditions, call the Forest Service (Mormon Lake Ranger Station) at (520) 556-7474.

ACCOMMODATIONS

Accommodation costs fluctuate greatly with the number of visitors, the season, and the day of the week; summer weekends are the most expensive. Rates listed below apply in summer but go higher on holiday or special-event periods. Off-season, prices can drop substantially, especially at the more expensive establishments. Winter rates may rise a bit during the ski season and weekends, depending on demand. Some motels offer a ski package that can save money.

Bed and Breakfasts

Birch Tree Inn Bed & Breakfast offers comfortable rooms and a hot tub in a 1917 house for $59-99 s and $69-109 d at 824 W. Birch Ave.; tel. (520) 774-1042 or (800) 645-5805; Internet: www.birchtreeinn.com. Moderate-Expensive.

Dierker House Bed & Breakfast offers rooms with antique decor in a 1914 house at 423 W. Cherry Ave.; rates start at $60 d; tel. (520) 774-3249. Moderate.

The Tree House features suites on the second floor of a 1915 house surrounded by large cottonwoods at 615 W. Cherry Ave.; rates are $95 d; tel. (520) 779-6306 or (888) 251-9390. Expensive.

Lynn's Inn (ca. 1905) has beautifully restored early 20th-century furnishings at 614 W. Santa Fe Ave.; rooms and suite run $85 d ($95 d rooms and $105 d suite Fri.-Sat.); tel. (520) 226-1488 or (800) 530-9947. Expensive.

The Inn at 410 offers distinctive guest suites in a stately 1907 residence at 410 N. Leroux St.; rates run $125-175 d; tel. (520) 774-0088 or (800) 774-2008; Internet: www.bbonline.com/az/at410/. Premium-Luxury.

Pinecrest Haven is up the hill on the east side of downtown at 415 E. David Dr., rates run $75-125 d; tel. (520) 774-3939 or (888) 674-3939. Expensive-Premium.

Lake Mary Bed & Breakfast lies out in the country, three miles southeast of town on Lake Mary Rd., with many hiking, biking, and horse riding opportunities. The house was built in Jerome in the 1930s, then moved here and added on; the four guest rooms all have private bath and go for $80 d, $110 four people; tel. (520) 779-7054 or (888) 241-9550. Moderate.

The Sled Dog Inn is in the woods six miles south of town at 10155 Mountainaire Rd. (I-17 Exit 333). Ponderosa Outdoor Adventures is based here and offers guided tours at the beginner's level of hiking, mountain biking, and rock climbing in summer and cross-country skiing and dog sledding in winter. Rooms have private bath and range from $99 d for a regular room to $169 d for a two-bed suite; tel. (520) 525-6212 or (800) 754-0664; www.sleddoginn.com. Expensive.

Hostels

The historic **Weatherford Hotel** and **Monte Vista Hotel** in downtown Flagstaff offer bunk beds in shared rooms; see "Historic Downtown Hotels" below. Neither hotel has a kitchen or common room, though you may meet other travelers in the restaurant or pub downstairs at each establishment. For a lively backpacker scene with an international crowd, head south across the tracks to the Grand Canyon or Du Beau hostels. These two also offer tours to the Grand Canyon, to Sedona (hike/swim), and occasionally to Monument Valley. There's no need for a hostel card or passport at any of the places. Reservations can come in handy on summer weekends, especially if you're in a group, but with four hostels in town you're likely to find a bed.

Grand Canyon International Hostel offers dorm beds at $12-16 and double rooms at $25-35 including tax and breakfast. Guests can use the kitchen and common room, rent bicycles, and receive discounts for car rentals. It's downtown at 19 S. San Francisco and Phoenix Ave., tel. (520) 779-9421 or (888) 442-2696. Budget.

The **Du Beau International Hostel** has dorm spaces at $13 and motel rooms for $27 d including tax, breakfast, kitchen, common room, and e-mail service. It's downtown at 19 W. Phoenix Ave., tel. (520) 774-6731 or (800) 398-7112, Internet: www.dubeau.net. Budget.

Historic Downtown Hotels

Both of Flagstaff's hotels here are registered historic landmarks. The **Weatherford Hotel** at 23 N. Leroux St. is named for J.W. Weatherford, who came to Flagstaff in 1887 from Texas and stayed 47 years. He built the hotel, quite elegant in its day, in 1897. Zane Grey wrote *Call of the Canyon* while staying here, describing the hotel as it was in 1918. Weatherford's other projects included an opera house (now the Orpheum Theatre) and Weatherford Road (now a hiking trail in the San Francisco Peaks). Rooms in this historic hotel cost $35 d ($45 d Fri.-Sat.); hostel beds run $15; tel. (520) 774-2731. Budget-Inexpensive. **Charly's,** the hotel's restaurant and pub, serves food and brew downstairs. Musicians often perform foot-tapping bluegrass, jazz, blues, folk, or rock 'n' roll in the evenings.

Monte Vista Hotel dates only to 1927 but has seen a lot of history. This was Flagstaff's grand hotel where movie stars stayed to film in nearby locations. You can stay in rooms named for those guests, such as the John Wayne, Jane Russell, and Gary Cooper suites. The Monte Vista still has many businesses under its roof, including a restaurant, lounge, hair salon, and gift boutique. Rooms with shared bath cost $40 d, rooms with private bath run $55-90 d, suites are $90-120 d; beds in the hostel go for $12; tel. (520) 779-6971 or (800) 545-3068. It's conveniently located at 100 N. San Francisco Street. Inexpensive-Premium.

Motels and Hotels

Although hostels offer the cheapest places for solo travelers, a party of two or more can do better in a motel. Drive along East Route 66 to look for the bargain places; the "strip" extends three miles. Most motels post prices except on summer weekends, when no bargains exist. The low-priced places usually have satisfactory rooms, but always check them first to make sure they're clean. Light sleepers should be aware that most accommodations lie near the railroad tracks. For quieter nights, try the motels on S. Milton Rd. and adjacent Beulah Blvd. and Woodlands Village Blvd.—all well away from trains.

For a complete listing of Flagstaff motels and hotels, see the **More Accommodations in the Gateway Cities** Appendix.

Campgrounds

You really need your own vehicle to camp. The following places nestle in ponderosa pines; all have showers except as noted. **Fort Tuthill County Campground** is open May 1-Sept. 30 with $9 dry sites for tents or RVs and $13 sites with water and sewer (no electricity); there's a quarter-mile nature trail. The campground is five miles south of downtown off I-17 Exit 337; tel. (520) 774-3464.

Black Bart's RV Park is open all year, $15 tent (three-night limit) and $20 RV with hookups; there's a steak house on the premises. It's two miles east of downtown near I-40 Butler Ave. Exit 198; tel. (520) 774-1912.

Flagstaff KOA is open all year, $23 tent or RV with water and electricity, $25 with full hookups, plus five $19 dry spaces for tents and four $32 "kamping kabins"; it's five miles northeast of downtown on Route 66/US 89, one mile north from I-40 Exit 201; tel. (520) 526-9926 or (800) KOA-FLAG.

Greer's Pine Shadows is an adult RV park for self-contained rigs (no restrooms or showers) open mid-April to October. Sites cost $17 with hookups; it's at 7101 N. Hwy. 89 about two miles north of I-40; tel. (520) 526-4977.

J&H RV Park has sites for RVs only from mid-April to mid-October in an adult-oriented atmosphere at 7901 N. Hwy. 89, three miles north of I-40 Exit 201. Rates are $22.25-27.25 with hookups including tax; there's also a spa; tel. (520) 526-1829.

Kit Carson RV Park is open year-round, $20 RV with hookups; you'll find it two miles west of downtown on W. Route 66 (I-40 Exits 191 or 195); tel. (520) 774-6993.

Woody Mountain Campground is a half mile farther west and open mid-March to October; rates are $16 tents or $21 RVs with hookups; tel. (520) 774-7727.

Munds Park RV Campground offers sites 17 miles south of Flagstaff, near I-17 Exit 322; it's open April 1-Oct. 31. Rates are $19 tent, $19-21 RV with hookups; tel. (520) 286-1309.

Ponderosa Forest RV Park & Campground has year-round sites in the woods for tents ($13) and RVs ($19 with hookups) with showers and a nearby store; tel. (520) 635-0456 or (888) 635-0456. It's north of I-40 Parks Exit 178, 17 miles west of Flagstaff and about halfway to Williams.

Most established campgrounds on U.S. Forest Service land lie 14 or more miles outside Flagstaff: southeast off Lake Mary Road, south in Oak Creek Canyon, and north near Sunset Crater National Monument. The closest National Forest campground to Flagstaff is Little Elden Springs Horse Camp, about seven miles north of town. It offers pull-through campsites, picnic tables, restrooms, water, dumpsters, hitching posts, and ample room for horse trailers from late May to mid October. Sites are $8. Anyone may stay here, but users should be prepared to camp among horses. Head north about five miles on US 89 from the east side of town, turn west two miles on Forest Road 556, then north on Forest Road 556A a short distance to the campground. For more information on this and other campgrounds in the Coconino National Forest near town, contact the Peaks Ranger Station, 5075 N. Hwy. 89, Flagstaff, AZ 86004, tel. (520) 526-0866.

Dispersed camping on Forest Service lands surrounding town provides another option. The ponderosa pine forests offer lots of room but no facilities—just be sure you're not on private or state land. The Coconino National Forest map outlines Forest Service land and shows the back roads. Carry water and be *very* careful with fire; in dry weather the Forest Service often prohibits fires in the woods and may even close some areas.

FOOD

Flagstaff, for its size, offers an amazing number of places to eat. But then, it has a lot of hungry tourists and students to feed. Most restaurants cater to the eat-and-run crowd. You'll find the well-known chains and fast-food places on the main highways, but with a little effort you can discover some unique restaurants and cafes. Come downtown for local atmosphere—old-fashioned homestyle eateries abound.

You'll enjoy Flagstaff's clean mountain air inside restaurants because of the city's non-smoking ordinance. A few places, such as Granny's Closet and Fiddlers on S. Milton, have separate smoking and nonsmoking sections; bars that serve food may be all smoking.

Downtown (north of the tracks)
Chez Marc Bistro offers fine French cuisine with indoor and outdoor seating at a historic 1911 residence; it's open daily for lunch and dinner (dinner only in winter) at 503 N. Humphreys Street. Most dinner entrees run about $30 and reservations are recommended; tel. (520) 774-1343. **Down Under** serves up New Zealand food with a few other styles Mon.-Fri. for lunch and Tues.-Sat. for dinner in a 1910 carriage house at 413 N. San Francisco St.; tel. (520) 774-6677. Reservations are recommended.

Charly's Pub and Restaurant, in the old Weatherford Hotel, serves good American food; it's open weekends for breakfast and daily for lunch and dinner at 23 N. Leroux St.; tel. (520) 779-1919. **Downtown Diner** dishes out bargain-priced breakfasts and lunches daily except Sunday, but don't expect much in the way of decor at 7 E. Aspen Ave.; tel. (520) 774-3492. **Mountain Oasis** has a tasty mix of Mediterranean, Southwestern, and international flavors with many vegetarian options at 11 E. Aspen Ave.; open daily for breakfast and lunch and Tues.-Sat. for dinner; tel. (520) 214-9270. **Pasto** serves Italian food, including vegetarian and wheat-free options, in a casual fine-dining atmosphere with seating indoors or in a courtyard; open nightly for dinner at 19 E. Aspen Ave.; tel. (520) 779-1937. **Alpine Pizza** is open daily at 7 N. Leroux St.; tel. (520) 779-4109.

Café Espress serves homemade natural foods, including many vegetarian items, plus coffees from the espresso bar and baked goodies from the oven; it's open daily for breakfast, lunch, and dinner at 16 N. San Francisco St.; tel. (520) 774-0541. **Kathy's** is a cozy little cafe with American standbys and a few exotic items such as Aussie burgers and Navajo tacos; it's open daily for breakfast and lunch at 7 N. San Francisco St.; tel. (520) 774-1951. The historic Monte Vista Hotel offers a **coffee shop** open daily for breakfast, lunch, and dinner at 100 N. San Francisco St.; tel. (520) 556-3077. **The Quaff & Nosh Restaurant** in a courtyard off 16 E. Route 66 does "World Fusion Cuisine" of ribs, tacos, and sandwiches; tel. (520) 556-1512. Nearby are the **Black Bean Burrito Bar & Salsa Co.,** mainly a take-out place, and **Flagstaff Brewing Company** with brews and snacks, and music some nights.

If you're looking for inexpensive Chinese-American food and don't care about the decor, try the **Grand Canyon Cafe** at 110 E. Route 66, tel. (520) 774-2252 or the **Hong Kong Cafe** at 6 E. Route 66, tel. (520) 774-9801; both are open Mon.-Sat. for breakfast, lunch, and dinner. You'll find good Mexican food at bargain prices at **Martan's Burrito Palace,** open Mon.-Sat. for breakfast and lunch at 10 N. San Francisco St.; tel. (520) 773-4701. **El Metate** offers Mexican dining daily for lunch and dinner at 103 W. Birch and Beaver St.; tel. (520) 774-5527. **Kachina Downtown** also does Mexican food in a pleasant setting Mon.-Sat. for breakfast and lunch and Sunday for dinner at 522 E. Route 66; tel. (520) 779-1944.

Downtown (south of the tracks)
Macy's European Coffee House and Bakery offers a big selection of fresh-roasted coffee and a menu of pasta dishes, sandwiches, soups, salads, quiches, and home-baked goodies; open daily for breakfast, lunch, and dinner at 14 S. Beaver St.; tel. (520) 774-2243. **La Bellavia Sandwich Shoppe** is a cozy little cafe for breakfast and lunch; open daily at 18 S. Beaver St.; tel. (520) 774-8301. **NiMarco's Pizza** is open daily at 101 S. Beaver St.; tel. (520) 779-2691. **Beaver Street Brewery/Whistle Stop Cafe** serves pizza, sandwiches, salads, and fondues along with a selection of local brews daily for lunch and dinner at 11 S. Beaver St.; a beer garden lies outside; tel. (520) 779-0079. **Cottage Place** serves American and continental specialties in an elegant setting; open Tues.-Sun. for dinner at 126 Cottage Avenue. Reservations are recommended; tel. (520) 774-8431.

Thai food devotees can try the **Dara Thai Restaurant,** open Mon.-Sat. for lunch and dinner at 14 S. San Francisco St.; tel. (520) 774-0047. **Morning Glory Cafe** features blue corn tamales, hemp (high protein), chicken pozolé, and a variety of salads and soups for lunch, mostly vegetarian. It's open Mon.-Fri. for lunch and Sat. for breakfast at 115 S. San Francisco St.; tel. (520) 774-3705.

Sundance Bakery & Coffees serves sandwiches, soups, salads, baked goods, and coffees; it's open Mon.-Sat. for breakfast and lunch at 116 S. San Francisco St.; tel. (520) 774-8433. **Cafe Olé** at 119 S. San Francisco St. specializes in homemade Mexican dishes; it's open Mon.-Fri. for lunch and dinner; tel. (520) 774-8272. **Hassib's** serves tasty Middle Eastern, Greek, and Indian specialties (deli and takeout too); it's open

Mon.-Sat. for lunch and dinner at 211 S. San Francisco St.; tel. (520) 774-1037. **El Charro** is a popular Mexican cafe; open Mon.-Sat. for lunch and dinner at 409 S. San Francisco St.; tel. (520) 779-0552.

Northern Arizona University
The Garden Terrace Dining Room at The Inn at NAU serves fine lunches Mon.-Fri. and dinners Tues.-Friday. Friday dinners often feature a seven-course set menu, and reservations are recommended; tel. (520) 523-1625. The Inn is off S. San Francisco Street. University Union, also in the north-central campus, offers a variety of fast-food eateries plus a full-service restaurant, the **Atrium,** which serves lunch Mon.-Fri. and dinner Mon.-Thurs. in a garden atmosphere. **University Dining** features a large cafeteria in the central campus. **North Union** has fast-food establishments on the north edge of campus. **South Campus Dining** offers cafeteria fare and the **South Campus Student Union** contains **The Peaks,** serving food ready to go.

Other Areas
American Cuisine: Galaxy Diner features '50s decor and music with American classics such as sandwiches, platters, milkshakes, and sodas; breakfasts are especially good and are served all day. Open daily for breakfast, lunch, and dinner at 931 W. Route 66; tel. (520) 774-2466. **Woodlands Cafe** serves American food daily for breakfast, lunch, and dinner in a Southwestern atmosphere at Radisson Woodlands Hotel, 1175 W. Route 66; tel. (520) 773-9118. **Granny's Closet** does steak and other meat dishes, seafood, and Italian cuisine at 218 S. Milton Rd. (just south of the railroad underpass); open daily for lunch and dinner; tel. (520) 774-8331. **Mike and Ronda's** pulls in the crowds with generous servings of low-priced American cafe fare at 21 S. Milton Rd., tel. (520) 774-7008, open daily for breakfast and lunch. A second location at Park Santa Fe Shopping Center, 3518 E. Route 66, tel. (520) 526-8138, is open daily for breakfast and lunch and Tues.-Sat. for dinner. Breakfasts are especially popular.

Fiddlers Restaurant serves up ranch-style steaks, chicken, shrimp, and sandwiches at 702 S. Milton Rd.; open daily for breakfast, lunch, and dinner; tel. (520) 774-6689. **Marc's Cafe**

Americain prepares American food—fish, meat, pasta, and crepe dishes—in a French atmosphere at 801 S. Milton Rd.; open daily for lunch and dinner; tel. (520) 556-0093. **Furr's Cafeteria** offers many choices at 1200 S. Milton Rd.; open daily for lunch and dinner; tel. (520) 779-4104. **Souper!Salad!** has a buffet for soups and salads plus sandwiches made to order at 1300 S. Milton Rd., tel. (520) 774-8030. **Buster's** features seafood and an oyster bar along with steak, ribs, chicken, veal, and sandwiches at 1800 S. Milton Rd. in Green Tree Village; open daily for lunch and dinner; tel. (520) 774-5155. The two **Sizzlers** offer good deals on meat and fish entrees plus a big salad bar at 2105 S. Milton Rd., tel. (520) 779-3267, and at 3540 E. Route 66, tel. (520) 526-3391. **Red Lobster's** nautical decor will take you to a Maine lobster house for fish, shrimp, crab, and of course lobster, along with steak and chicken; it's open daily for lunch and dinner at 2500 S. Beulah Blvd. in the Woodlands Village area, tel. (520) 556-9604. Model trains circle the dining areas of **The Crown Railroad Cafe,** which does popular American standbys at 2700 S. Woodlands Village Blvd. near Wal-Mart, tel. (520) 774-6775, and at 3300 E. Route 66, tel. (520) 522-9237.

Little America's Western Gold Dining Room at 2515 E. Butler Ave. serves a buffet lunch Mon.-Fri. and a big brunch on Sunday; the coffee shop is open daily for breakfast, lunch, and dinner; tel. (520) 779-7900. Also in the Butler Ave. area and just off I-40 Exit 198 are the **Country Host Restaurant** and **Kettle Restaurant,** both open daily for breakfast, lunch, and dinner.

Black Bart's Steak House serves up steak, seafood, and other American fare; it's open daily for dinner with singing waiters and waitresses to entertain you at 2760 E. Butler Ave., near I-40 Exit 198, tel. (520) 779-3142. Many locals say you'll find the best steaks in town at **Bob Lupo's Horsemen Lodge,** which serves ribs, chicken, trout, and seafood as well; it's open for dinner nightly except Sunday on US 89, just over three miles north from I-40 Exit 201, tel. (520) 526-2655. **Kelly's Christmas Tree Restaurant** is another American-food favorite, open Mon.-Fri. for lunch and daily for dinner at 5200 E. Cortland Blvd., off Country Club Dr., tel. (520) 526-0776.

Italian Cuisine: The Olive Garden Italian Restaurant serves pasta, seafood, meats from the grill, and breadstick-style pizzas; there's a children's menu too. It's open daily for lunch and dinner at 2550 Beulah Blvd. in the Woodlands Village area; tel. (520) 779-3000. The nearby **Fazoli's** offers "Italian food . . . fast" in an informal setting for pastas, pizza, and salads at 2675 S. Beulah Blvd.; open daily for lunch and dinner; tel. (520) 214-8220. **Mama Luisa's** has excellent Italian cuisine nightly for dinner at Kachina Square, corner of E. Route 66 and Steves Blvd., tel. (520) 526-6809. Reservations are advised at Mama Luisa's. **Dan's Italian Kitchen** is open Mon.-Sat. for lunch and dinner at 1850 N. Fort Valley Rd. (US 180), on the route to the Grand Canyon, tel. (520) 779-9349.

Mexican Cuisine: The large Mexican-American population of Flagstaff provides the town with some tasty food. In addition to the Mexican eateries listed under downtown, try **Jalapeño Lou's** at 3050 E. Route 66, tel. (520) 526-1533; **Ramona's Cantina** at the corner of Woodlands Village Blvd. and Beulah, tel. (520) 774-3397; **Chili's Grill & Bar,** 1500 S. Milton Rd., tel. (520) 774-4546; or **El Chilito,** 1551 S. Milton Rd., tel. (520) 774-4666. All are open daily for lunch and dinner.

Asian Cuisines: Delhi Palace offers fine north Indian food daily for lunch (buffet available) and dinner at 2700 S. Woodland Village Blvd., near Wal-Mart, tel. (520) 556-0019. It's the restaurant where you're most likely to spot the author!

Sakura Restaurant, in the Radisson Woodlands Hotel at 1175 W. Route 66, prepares Japanese teppanyaki and sushi Mon.-Sat. for lunch and nightly for dinner; tel. (520) 773-9118. **Papa-San** serves Japanese fast food at 1312 S. Plaza Way (west of S. Milton Rd.) daily for lunch and dinner; tel. (520) 214-9390.

Dine at Chinese restaurants, all open daily for lunch and dinner except as noted, south of downtown at **August Moon,** 1300 S. Milton Rd., tel. (520) 774-5280; **Szechuan,** 1451 S. Milton Rd., tel. (520) 774-8039; and **Hunan West** (closed Monday) in University Plaza off S. Milton Rd., tel. (520) 779-2229. In east Flagstaff, there's a choice of **Asian Gourmet,** 1580 E. Route 66, tel. (520) 773-7771; **Hunan East,** 2028 N. Fourth St., tel. (520) 526-1009; **Golden Dragon Bowl,** 2730 Lakin Dr. across from Kachina Square, tel. (520) 527-3238; and **Mandarin Gardens,** Park

Santa Fe Shopping Center at 3518 E. Route 66, tel. (520) 526-5033.

Groceries
Nearly every shopping center has a supermarket, and you can find **Smiths** and **Albertsons** at the corner of E. Route 66 and Switzer Canyon Drive. The **Farmer's Market** specializes in fresh produce, often at bargain prices; it's at 1901 N. Fourth St., just off E. Route 66; tel. (520) 774-

4500. **New Frontiers** sells natural foods and offers deli dining and take-out at 1000 S. Milton Rd.; tel. (520) 774-5747.

ENTERTAINMENT AND EVENTS

The free weekly paper *Flagstaff Live!* details the local music scene, movies, arts, restaurants, events, sports, and a hike; look for them on the

THE MUSEUM CLUB

This Route 66 landmark, named one of the top 10 roadhouses in the nation by *Car and Driver* magazine, has a history as unusual as its interior! It began in 1931 as a museum and trading post with such taxidermy oddities as a two-headed calf and a one-eyed lamb along with more conventional animals, Indian artifacts, and a rifle collection. Curious motorists sputtering down early Route 66 dropped in to see the thousands of exhibits inside this huge log structure.

Five years later another entrepreneur converted it into a nightclub to attract the growing crowds of motorists as well as local folk looking for some good music and dancing. Aspiring recording artists traveling cross-country stopped by to perform for appreciative audiences. The Museum Club continues the tradition of fine country music while introducing additional music styles popular with the younger crowd. It's also known as the "The Zoo" because stuffed animals still gaze down from the walls and branches. Branches? Yes, the building incorporates five standing ponderosa pines that tower above the dance floor.

Current owner Martin Zanzucchi has enthusiastically researched the building's history and promoted the Route 66 theme, even successfully petitioning to have the road in front renamed "Route 66." On the way in, you'll pass under an inverted ponderosa tree fork that spans the doorway. Photos and news clippings on the walls to your left inside the entrance tell the story of the Museum Club. Here, too, you can read about the eyewitness accounts of encounters with the ghosts that haunt the place. Wandering on through the rustic interior, you'll cross the dance floor and reach a magnificent late-19th century bar.

Something's happening nightly in the Museum Club; call (520) 526-9434 or check the Internet at

www.museumclub.com. The weekly schedule at press time had country music Thurs.-Sat., swing on Sunday, karaoke on Monday, and a dance mix from the '70s, '80s, and '90s on Tues.-Wed. nights; doors open at noon. Staff offer free dance lessons some evenings; call for times. A gift shop sells Route 66 memorabilia. The Museum Club is east of downtown at 3404 E. Route 66.

the Museum Club and owners Martin and Stacie Zanzucchi

*at the Pine Country
Rodeo, Flagstaff*

Internet at www.mountainliving.com. *Flare,* published weekly by the *Arizona Daily Sun,* also reviews the lifestyle and entertainment scene.

Sports and NAU Culture
Northern Arizona University presents theater, opera, dance, concerts, and a variety of sports events. For information and tickets, contact NAU Central Ticket Office in the University Union at (520) 523-5661. In late July and early August the **Arizona Cardinals** professional football team shows up for summer training camp; call (520) 523-2273 for the times to watch them in action.

Events
People in Flagstaff put on a variety of festivals, fairs, shows, and concerts during the year. The Flagstaff Visitor Center will tell you what's happening; tel. (520) 774-9541 or (800) 842-7293. Major annual events include the Flagstaff **Winter Festival** in February, featuring skiing, sled-dog races, clinics, workshops, games, and entertainment. In May, residents celebrate **Cinco de Mayo** with a parade, coronation, dance, and barbecue. June brings the **Route 66 Festival, Horse Show, Gem and Mineral Show, Pine Country Rodeo and Parade,** and the **Festival of Native American Arts,** featuring Indian art and craft exhibitions, demonstrations, and dance performances. In July comes the **Festival of the Arts,** with concerts, musicals, and plays, July 4th fireworks, and horse racing. The Festival of the Arts continues in August, as does the

Festival of Native American Arts. August also sees **Festival in the Pines**—arts and crafts with musical performances—and the **Coconino County Fair. Luminarios** at Northern Arizona University in early to mid-December brighten the winter season.

SHOPPING AND SERVICES

Art Galleries and Indian Crafts
Shops in downtown Flagstaff display a wealth of regional arts and crafts. Native American artists produce especially distinctive work; you'll see paintings, jewelry, Navajo rugs, Hopi kachina dolls, pottery, and baskets. **Four Winds Traders** at 118 W. Route 66, is one of the largest and best Indian galleries in the state—Indians themselves shop here for stones and jewelry-making supplies; it's closed Sunday and Monday. Look for other shops and galleries nearby on Route 66, N. Leroux St., N. San Francisco St., and Aspen Avenue. The gift shops at the **Museum of Northern Arizona** and the **Art Barn,** both northwest of town on US 180, feature excellent selections of Indian arts and crafts.

Bookstores
McGaugh's Newsstand downtown features a good selection of newspapers, magazines, Arizona books, and general reading at 24 N. San Francisco St.; tel. (520) 774-2131. The **NAU Bookstore** also offers many regional and gen-

eral publications; tel. (520) 523-4041. The **Museum of Northern Arizona** sells excellent books on Southwestern Native American cultures, archaeology, and natural history; it's three miles northwest on US 180; tel. (520) 774-5213. **Northland Publishing** produces outstanding regional and children's books plus some cookbooks and posters; the sales room is open Mon.-Fri. 8 a.m.-5 p.m. at 2900 N. Fort Valley Rd. (US 180); tel. (520) 774-5251; Internet: www. northlandpub.com. **Waldenbooks** in the Flagstaff Mall stocks good regional and general reading selections; tel. (520) 526-5196. **Crystal Magic** features spiritual and New Age titles downtown at 5 N. San Francisco St.; tel. (520) 779-2528.

For new and used books, including many regional titles, drop by **Bookman's Used Books** at 1520 S. Riordan Ranch St.; it offers 250,000 new and used books as well as music, videos, and games; tel. (520) 774-0005. A few doors south, **Hastings** sells discounted books, music, and videos; tel. (520) 779-1880. **Dragon's Plunder** has about 80,000 used books at the corner of S. San Francisco and Butler Ave.; tel. (520) 774-1780. **Starlight Books** at 15 N. Leroux St. has a smaller selection of mostly used books and specializes in out-of-print orders; tel. (520) 774-6813.

Photo Equipment and Supplies

Discount and grocery stores carry print and a bit of slide film. For the best selection of slide, professional, and large format film, try **Photo Outfitters** one block off Route 66 at 25 N. San Francisco St. downtown; tel. (520) 779-5181. **P.R. Camera Repair** offers service at 111 E. Aspen; tel. (520) 779-5263.

Postal Services

The main **post office** is at 2400 N. Postal Blvd., off E. Route 66; tel. (520) 527-2440; General Delivery mail can be sent to you with a zip code of 86004-9998. There's a downtown branch at 104 N. Agassiz St.; General Delivery mail can be sent here with a zip code of 86001-9998. Another post office is in the University Bookstore basement. Bookman's Used Books at 1520 Riordan Ranch St. also provides some postal services.

Medical Services

If you need medical attention, it's cheaper to go directly to a doctor's office or clinic than to the

hospital. You'll find many offices along N. Beaver Street. **Concentra Medical Centers** welcomes walk-in patients daily at 120 W. Fine (west of Beaver); tel. (520) 773-9695. **Walk-in Clinic** provides similar services near the Flagstaff Mall at 4215 N. Hwy. 89; tel. (520) 527-1920. **Flagstaff Medical Center,** the local hospital, is at 1200 N. Beaver St.; tel. (520) 779-3366. In **emergencies**—police, fire, and medical—dial 911.

INFORMATION

Visitor Center

The very helpful **Flagstaff Chamber of Commerce's Visitor Center** staff can answer your questions and tell you what's happening. The office, downtown in the Amtrak depot (1 E. Route 66, Flagstaff, AZ 86001), is open daily 7 a.m.-6 p.m. (until 5 p.m. on Sunday and holidays); tel. (520) 774-9541 or (800) 842-7293; e-mail: visitor@ flagstaff.az.us.; Internet: www.flagstaff.az.us.

Other useful websites include www.flagguide.com and www. mountainliving.com.

Coconino National Forest

The **U.S. Forest Service** provides information and maps about camping, hiking, and road conditions in the Coconino National Forest surrounding Flagstaff. The **Supervisor's Office** is at 2323 E. Greenlaw Lane (Flagstaff, AZ 86004) behind Knoles Village Shopping Center; it's open Mon.-Fri. 7:30 a.m.-4:30 p.m.; tel. (520) 527-3600. You can buy any of the National Forest maps for Arizona here; the Coconino Forest map is also available at the chamber of commerce and sporting goods stores.

For more detailed information on the Mt. Elden, Humphrey's Peak, and O'Leary Peak areas, contact the **Peaks Ranger Station** at 5075 N. Hwy. 89 (Flagstaff, AZ 86004); it's open Mon.-Fri. 7:30 a.m.-4:30 p.m.; tel. (520) 526-0866. For the lake and forest country south of Flagstaff, check with the Peaks Ranger Station or the **Mormon Lake Ranger District** office, 4373 S. Lake Mary Rd. (Flagstaff, AZ 86001); it's open Mon.-Fri. 7:30 a.m.-4:30 p.m. and Saturday during summer; tel. (520) 774-1182.

Arizona Game and Fish Department

This office provides fishing and hunting licenses and dispenses information at 3500 S. Lake Mary

Rd. (Flagstaff, AZ 86001); it's open Mon.-Fri. 8 a.m.-5 p.m.; tel. (520) 774-5045; Internet: www. gf. state.az.us.

Libraries

Looking for a good place to read up on Arizona, keep dry on a rainy day, or just pass the time during a long train or bus wait? The **Flagstaff City Library's** attractive ski-lodge architecture makes it an especially enjoyable spot downtown at the corner of 300 W. Aspen Ave. and Sitgreaves Street. Hours are Mon.-Thurs. 10 a.m.-9 p.m., Friday 10 a.m.-7 p.m., Saturday 10 a.m.-6 p.m., and Sunday 11 a.m.-6 p.m.; tel. (520) 774-4000 (recorded information) or 779-7670 (reference desk). Many good regional books enrich the Arizona Collection. Art exhibits by local artists and photographers change monthly.

NAU's **Cline Library** carries many books and periodicals. Hikers can plan trips and copy maps in the Government Documents section, past the reference area. You can use library computers to access the Internet and local resources, but not for e-mail. The library is open daily during regular school sessions and Mon.-Fri. between terms; tel. (520) 523-2171. Upstairs, the **Special Collections and Archives Department** contains an outstanding array of Arizona-related publications and photos; changing exhibits appear in the entranceway. It's open Mon.-Fri. 8 a.m.-6 p.m.; tel. (520) 523-5551. The library website, www.nau.edu/library, has the entire card catalog online, encyclopedias, plus a searchable database of 3,000 images from Special Collections.

The **Museum of Northern Arizona** has an excellent regional library in the Research Center across the highway from the museum; it's normally open Mon.-Fri. 9 a.m.-5 p.m.; tel. (520) 774-5211.

TRANSPORTATION

Tours

Nava-Hopi Tours (The Gray Line) operates half-day trolley tours in the Flagstaff area with stops at the Museum of Northern Arizona, Riordan Mansion, and Pioneer Museum for $19.50. Bus tours include the Grand Canyon ($38), Oak Creek Canyon-Sedona-Jerome-Montezuma Castle ($36), Petrified Forest-Painted Desert-

Meteor Crater ($58), Lake Powell/Glen Canyon float trip ($89), Grand Canyon Railway ($64), and Monument Valley ($74). Nava-Hopi requires at least 24 hours' advance notice; children 5-15 ride at half price on most trips. Some tours don't operate in winter. Buses leave from the 114 W. Route 66 station; tel. (520) 774-5003 or (800) 892-8687; Internet: www.navahopitours.com.

Sun Tours (Sun Taxi) offers both Flagstaff and northern Arizona tours; tel. (520) 774-7400. Other local tour operators have brochures at the Visitor Center.

Car Rental and Taxi

A rental car allows more extensive sightseeing than public transportation and costs less if several people get together. Rates fluctuate with supply and demand, competition, and the mood of the operators; call around for the best deals. See the Yellow Pages for agencies; you'll find offices in town and at the airport. For a taxi, call **Sun Taxi,** tel. (520) 774-7400; **Arizona Taxi,** tel. (520) 779-1111; or **A Friendly Cab,** tel. (520) 774-4444.

Local Bus

Pine Country Transit serves most of the city with three routes Mon.-Fri. and one route on Saturday; tel. (520) 779-6624 or 779-6635 (TDD). Pick up a schedule at the Flagstaff Visitor Center, public library, or at one of the three Safeway stores in town.

Long-Distance Bus

Greyhound offers daily departures to Phoenix and Sky Harbor Airport (four times daily, $19), Holbrook (five times daily, $19), Gallup (four times daily, $35-37), Kingman (six times daily, $26-28), Los Angeles (nine times daily, $49-52), Las Vegas (three times daily, $47-52), and San Francisco (five times daily, $105-111). Fares listed are one way with the lowest price for weekdays; roundtrips are usually double except for a casino special to Las Vegas at $49-52 roundtrip. The station lies a half mile south of central downtown at 399 S. Malpais Lane; it's open 24 hours; tel. (520) 774-4573 or (800) 231-2222; Internet: www.greyhound.com.

Nava-Hopi buses head north to the Grand Canyon at least once daily ($12.50 each way), with some trips via Williams ($7 each way), and

Flagstaff train station in the late 19th century

south to Glendale and Sky Harbor Airport a few times daily ($22 each way) via Camp Verde; 114 W. Route 66.; tel. (520) 774-5003 or (800) 892-8687; Internet: navahopitours.com.

Train

Amtrak Southwest Chief trains leave every evening for Los Angeles ($52.94 one way), and every morning for Albuquerque ($49-89 one way) and on to Chicago or Orlando. The price depends on availability—book ahead or travel off-season for the lowest rates; roundtrip tickets are double but there are also special All Aboard America and fly/train fares. The station is downtown at 1 E. Route 66; tel. (520) 774-8679 for the station or (800) 872-7245 for reservations; Internet: www.amtrak.com.

Air

America West flies about seven times daily to Phoenix; the regular fare is a stiff $143 each way, but a 21-day advance purchase on a roundtrip costs little more; tel. (800) 235-9292. Pulliam Field, Flagstaff's airport, lies five miles south of town; take I-17 Exit 337.

Airport Shuttles

Many travelers have found it far more economical to reach connections at Sky Harbor Airport in Phoenix by ground shuttle than by flying. **Nava-Hopi Tours** offers a ride two or three times daily for $22 each way; tel. (520) 774-5003 or (800) 892-8687. **Greyhound** offers four daily departures to Sky Harbor Airport for $19 each way; tel. (520) 774-4573 or (800) 231-2222.

NORTH OF FLAGSTAFF: THE SAN FRANCISCO VOLCANIC FIELD

Volcanic peaks, cinder cones, and lava flows cover about 3,000 square miles around Flagstaff. The majestic San Francisco Peaks, highest of all Arizona mountains, soar 5,000 feet above the surrounding plateau. Eruptions beginning about 10 million years ago formed this giant volcano whose center later collapsed, forming a caldera. During Pleistocene ice ages, glaciers then carved deep valleys on its slopes. Hundreds of small cinder cones, of which Sunset Crater is the youngest, surround the Peaks. There's no reason to assume the San Francisco Volcanic Field is finished, either. The area has experienced volcanic activity, with periods of calm, all during its long history. Peaceful today, the volcanic field presents some impressive landscapes and geology.

Indians of northern Arizona regard the San Francisco Peaks as a sacred place. The Hopi believe the Peaks are the winter home of their kachina spirits and the source of clouds that bring rain for crops. The Peaks also occupy a prominent place in Navajo legends and ceremonies, representing one of the cardinal directions.

In 1984 the federal government set aside 18,963 acres of this venerable volcano for the Kachina Peaks Wilderness, selecting the name because of the importance of the site to the Hopi Indians. The Forest Service maintains a network of trails in the wilderness, and any of the peaks and hills makes a good day-hike destination. Cyclists may not ride here, even on the former roads, because of the wilderness designation. Foresters at the **Peaks Ranger Station** offer maps and hiking information for this region; contact 5075 N. Hwy. 89, Flagstaff, AZ 86004, tel. (520) 526-0866. The book *Flagstaff Hikes* by Richard and Sherry Mangum lists 146 hikes around town, many in the San Francisco Peaks area.

SUNSET CRATER VOLCANO NATIONAL MONUMENT

Sunset Crater, a beautiful black cinder cone tinged with yellows and oranges, rises 1,000 feet above jagged lava flows about 15 miles northeast of Flagstaff. Although more than 700 years have passed since the last eruptions, the landscape still presents a lunar-like appearance, with trees and plants struggling to grow.

Eruptions in A.D. 1064 or 1065 sent indigenous people running for safety. By 1110 activity had subsided enough to allow them to settle in the Wupatki Basin, 20 miles northeast of Sunset Crater. You can visit the remains of their community and see a museum in Wupatki National Monument, reached via the Sunset Crater-Wupatki Loop Road, one of the prettiest scenic drives in Arizona. Lava flows and smaller ash eruptions continued from Sunset Crater until about A.D. 1280.

In the late 1920s some Hollywood filmmakers thought Sunset Crater would make a great movie set. They planned to use dynamite to simulate an avalanche, but local citizens put a stop to their plans. Sunset Crater became a national monument in 1930.

Visitor center exhibits illustrate the forces deep within the Earth and their fury during volcanic eruptions. A seismograph tracks the earth's movements. Film clips of Hawaiian volcanic eruptions show how Sunset Crater may have looked during its periods of activity. Rangers give varied programs, mainly during the summer, on geology, seismology, birds, and other topics. Check the bulletin board at the visitor center or call for times and places.

Lenox Crater (elev. 7,240 feet), one mile east of the visitor center at the first pullout on the left, provides a close look at a cinder cone with a crater. It's a short, steep climb, requiring 30-45 minutes to the rim and back; elevation change is 280 feet.

The self-guided **Lava Flow Trail,** which begins 1.5 miles east of the visitor center, loops across the Bonito Lava Flow at the base of Sunset Crater; allow 30-60 minutes for the one-mile walk, less for the one-third-mile loop cutoff. A trail leaflet, available at the start of the trail and at the visitor center, explains geologic features and

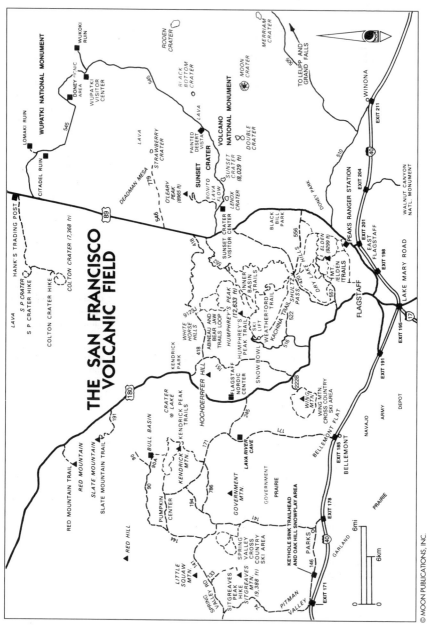

© MOON PUBLICATIONS, INC.

ecology. You'll see fumaroles (gas vents), lava bubbles, squeeze-ups, and lava tubes that seem to have cooled only yesterday. Rangers now forbid hiking on Sunset Crater itself, because earlier climbers wore a deep gash in the soft cinder slopes. Wheelchair users can go out to an observation point from a parking area off the main road.

Bonito Campground, across the road from the visitor center, is open from mid-May to mid-September; it costs $10 a site and offers drinking water and restrooms but no showers; tel. (520) 527-1474 (campground) or 526-0866 (Peaks Ranger Station). Campfire programs run on summer evenings. Dispersed camping is allowed in other areas of the national forest, such as Forest Roads 420, 552, and 418 west of US 89; Forest Road 776 (can be dusty from ATVs) south of Sunset Crater; and Forest Road 150 (hot in summer) south of the road through Wupatki. Visitor center staff can make suggestions and sell you the Coconino Forest map.

You'll find **picnic areas** near the visitor center, at the Lava Flow Trail, and at Painted Desert Vista between Sunset Crater and Wupatki National Monuments. The visitor center is open daily 9 a.m.-5 p.m. (except Christmas) with extended hours in summer; the road and trails stay open all day; tel. (520) 526-0502; Internet: www.nps.gov/sucr. The admission fee of $3 per person age 17 and up includes entry to Wupatki National Monument. You can reach the visitor center by driving north 12 miles from the Flagstaff Mall on US 89, then turning east two miles on a signed road.

O'Leary Peak

Weather permitting, the summit of this 8,965-foot lava-dome volcano provides outstanding views into Sunset Crater. Forest Road 545A begins about a quarter mile west of Sunset Crater visitor center and climbs 5.5 miles to the fire lookout tower at the top. The road is unpaved, with some steep grades. Stay on the roadway to avoid getting stuck in loose cinders. A gate four miles up blocks cars; you can park here and walk the last mile and a half. Mountain bikers can get a good workout on this scenic road. The summit provides the best late-afternoon view of the colors of Sunset Crater and the Painted Desert beyond; the San Francisco Peaks are best viewed in the morning.

WUPATKI NATIONAL MONUMENT

Prehistoric Indian farmers, identified as the Sinagua Culture by archaeologists, settled in small groups near the San Francisco Peaks in about A.D. 600. They lived in partly underground pithouses and tilled the soil in those few areas with sufficient moisture to support corn and other crops. The eruption of Sunset Crater in A.D. 1064 or 1065 forced many to flee, but it improved the farming potential: volcanic ash, blown by winds over a large area, acted as a water-conserving mulch.

Wupatki Pueblo

After about 1110, people returned and were joined by ancestral pueblo people from northeastern Arizona. They settled 20 miles northeast of Sunset Crater in Wupatki Basin, which became the center of a group of cosmopolitan villages. A mix of cultural traits can be seen at Wupatki, including Kayenta Anasazi, Sinagua, Cohonina, and Hohokam. Large, multistoried pueblos replaced the brush shelters and pithouses of former times. Some villages seem defensively built; competition for scarce resources may have created friction or fostered cooperation.

During the 1200s, people began to leave the area. Archaeologists think the inhabitants migrated southward to the Verde Valley and northeastward to the Hopi mesas. Hopi oral histories trace at least eight clans to the Wupatki area. Seven of the best-preserved pueblos have road and trail access; all other sites and the monument's backcountry remain closed to visitors. Please stay on designated trails.

Wupatki Visitor Center

You'll see pottery, tools, jewelry, and other artifacts of early cultures on exhibit here. A Wupatki room reconstruction shows how the interior of a typical living chamber might have looked. You'll also learn a little about the present-day Navajo and Hopi tribes who live near the monument. Insect and flowering plant collections illustrate the flora and fauna of this high-desert country. You can buy books, posters, maps, and videos related to the region. Rangers may offer 15-minute orientation talks and provide demonstrations of prehistoric and modern crafts and activities at Wupatki Pueblo.

Wupatki visitor center is open daily 9 a.m.-5 p.m. with extended hours in summer; closed Christmas; tel. (520) 679-2365; Internet: www.nps.gov/wupa. From Flagstaff, you can drive 12 miles north on US 89, then turn right 21 miles via Sunset Crater National Monument on a very scenic loop road. Or take the northern turnoff from US 89 for the loop road, 26 miles north of Flagstaff, and head east 14 miles. The nearest motels and restaurants are in Flagstaff and Gray Mountain. Hank's Trading Post offers groceries and snacks 1.2 miles north of the US 89-Wupatki junction. See Bonito Campground in the Sunset Crater section above for area camping possibilities.

Doney Picnic Area sits between cinder cones about four miles northwest of the visitor center on the loop road. **Doney Mountain Trail** climbs gradually to a saddle in the Little Doney Craters, from which you can turn left to a lower overlook or right to a higher one, about 0.4 mile one way from the picnic area. Both forks pass small dwellings, probably used by the Indians as field houses while tending nearby gardens. You'll enjoy a panorama of the Wupatki Basin, Painted Desert, and San Francisco Peaks. Interpretive signs explain area ecology and the exploits of prospector Ben Doney.

Wupatki Pueblo

At its peak, Wupatki contained nearly 100 rooms and towered multiple stories. The Hopi name refers to "something long that has been cut or divided." A self-guided trail, beginning behind the visitor center, explains many of the features of Wupatki; pick up a trail brochure at the start.

A community room, where village meetings and ceremonies may have taken place, lies to one side of Wupatki. The ball court at the far end of the village may have been used for games or religious functions. It's one of several found in northern Arizona, probably introduced by the Hohokam Culture of the southern deserts. Archaeologists reconstructed the ball court from wall remnants; the rest of Wupatki Pueblo is stabilized. A blowhole, 100 feet east of the ball court, may have had religious importance. A system of underground cracks connects to this natural surface opening; air blows out, rushes in, or does nothing at all, depending on weather conditions. Researchers once tried to enter the system but couldn't get through the narrow passageways.

Wukoki Pueblo

Indians lived in this small pueblo, the best-preserved structure in the park, for perhaps three generations. You can step inside the rooms for a closer look. From the Wupatki visitor center, drive a quarter mile toward Sunset Crater, then turn left 2.6 miles on a paved road.

Citadel Pueblo

This fortress-like pueblo, perched atop a small volcanic butte nine miles northwest of the Wupatki visitor center, stood one or two stories high and contained about 50 rooms. From the top, look for some of the more than 10 other residences nearby (these are not open to visitation). On the path to the Citadel, you'll pass the pueblo of **Nalakihu,** Hopi for "House Standing Outside the Village." Nalakihu consisted of two stories with 13 or 14 rooms. You can visit both sites on a short, self-guided trail.

Lomaki Pueblo

Lomaki, Hopi for "Beautiful House," sits along a small box canyon. Tree-ring dating of roof timbers indicates the occupants lived here from about A.D. 1190 to 1240. The small, two-story pueblo contained at least nine rooms. A quarter-mile trail from the parking area also passes small dwellings beside Box Canyon. The turnoff for Lomaki lies

northwest of Wupatki visitor center, 0.3 mile beyond Citadel on the opposite side of the road.

Crack-in-Rock Pueblo

Rangers lead overnight backpack trips to this area during April and October. Crack-in-Rock sits atop an easily defended mesa with sweeping views of the Little Colorado River and distant hills. You will see petroglyphs carved around the base of the mesa and on two nearby mesas, as well as many other pueblo sites. The 14-mile roundtrip ranger-guided hike is moderately difficult and costs $25. Call or write for information at least two months in advance; Wupatki National Monument, HC 33, Box 444A, Flagstaff, AZ 86004, tel. (520) 679-2365.

EAST AND WEST OF FLAGSTAFF

TO THE EAST: WALNUT CANYON NATIONAL MONUMENT

Ancestral pueblo people made this pretty canyon their home more than 800 years ago. Ledges eroded out of the limestone cliffs provided shelter from rain and snow—the inhabitants merely had to build walls under the ready-made roofs. Good farmland, wild plant foods, and forests filled with game lay close by. The clear waters of Walnut Creek flowed in the canyon bottom.

Archaeologists call this culture "Sinagua," Spanish for "without water," because the people made such clever use of the small amounts of precipitation and surface water here. People occupied Walnut Canyon from A.D. 1120 to 1250, then moved on. Some Hopi Indian clans trace their ancestors back to this site. More than 300 Sinagua cliff dwellings remain; you can see and enter some along a loop trail constructed by the National Park Service.

Visitor Center

A small museum displays pottery and other artifacts of the Sinagua Culture. Exhibits show how the Indians farmed and how they used wild plants for baskets, sandals, mats, soap, food, and medicine. A map illustrates trading routes to other indigenous cultures. Rangers will answer questions about the archaeology and natural

history of Walnut Canyon. During the summer, they give occasional talks and lead walks; it's best to call ahead for times. A bookstore sells a wide selection of books, maps, and videos related to the monument and region.

The self-guided 0.9-mile **Island Trail** begins behind the visitor center and winds past 25 cliff dwellings. You can get a feeling of what it was like to live here. The paved path descends 185 feet with 240 steps, which you'll have to climb on the way out; allow 45-60 minutes. Because of the high elevation (6,690 feet), the trail isn't recommended for people with mobility, respiratory, or cardiovascular problems. The easy **Rim Trail** visits two scenic viewpoints, a pithouse site, and a small pueblo, and signs describe the varied plants and wildlife found here. Allow 20-30 minutes for the three-quarter-mile loop. Pets cannot go on trails.

Vegetation changes dramatically from the pinyon and juniper forests near the rim to the tall Douglas firs clinging to the canyon ledges. Black walnut and several other kinds of deciduous trees grow at the bottom. Rock layers will be familiar to Grand Canyon visitors. The lower 100 feet of Walnut Canyon belongs to the Coconino Formation, some 265-million-year-old sand dunes that have turned to stone. The 300-foot layer of rock above is Kaibab Limestone, formed in a sea 255 million years ago.

Walnut Canyon National Monument remains open all year (except Christmas), though snows can close the trails for short periods. The visitor center is open daily 9 a.m.-5 p.m.; hours may be extended in summer. Island Trail closes one hour before the visitor center does. The entrance fee is $3 per person age 17 and over. Vehicles pulling cars and large trailers may have trouble negotiating the turnaround loop at the visitor center. You'll find picnic areas near the visitor center and on the drive in. From Flagstaff, head east seven miles on I-40 to Walnut Canyon Exit 204, then turn south three miles on a paved road; tel. (520) 526-3367; Internet: www.nps.gov/waca.

Arizona Trail near Walnut Canyon

Hikers and mountain bikers enjoy forests, canyon scenery, and views of the San Francisco Peaks along this section of trail. A sign 2.5 miles in on the Walnut Canyon National Monument road points the way to a trailhead 1.7 miles to the west along a graded dirt road. From here the path heads southwest, crossing a side canyon of Walnut and paralleling the rim before dropping down into upper Walnut Canyon just west of Fisher Point in about six miles. A branch of Flagstaff's Urban Trail System joins here. In another mile you'll reach the junction for Sandy's Canyon Trail, which climbs the canyon to a trailhead near Lake Mary Road in three-quarters of a mile. The Arizona Trail curves to the southeast and continues four miles to Marshall Lake. Mountain bikers may need to walk the steep sections at the side canyon and at the descent into Walnut Canyon. The monument visitor center may have a map.

TO THE WEST: WILLIAMS

Small and friendly, Williams (pop. 2,700) proudly proclaims itself "Gateway to the Grand Canyon." Arizona 64, on the east edge of town, is the shortest route—58 miles—between I-40 and the famous park. Williams, nestled among pine-forested hills and expansive meadows at an elevation of 6,780 feet, offers a better choice of accommodations and restaurants at lower prices than those at the Grand Canyon. Travelers also enjoy the old architecture downtown, Route 66 nostalgia, and staged gunfights. The popular Grand Canyon Railway puffs its way north to the Grand Canyon daily from the old station downtown. Even if you're not riding the rails, it's worth taking a look at the historic train, the museum, and morning Wild West show. Most travelers, in a hurry to get someplace else, miss the pretty country surrounding Williams—splendid Sycamore Canyon, small fishing lakes, high volcanoes, forest drives, and hiking trails.

History

Charles Rodgers, the first white settler here, started a cattle operation in 1878. The railroad and lumber town founded several years later took its name from Bill Williams Mountain just to the south. The mountain in turn honored mountain man Bill Williams, who roamed the West from 1825 until his death at the hands of Ute Indians in 1849. He earned reputations as a skilled marksman, trapper, trader, and guide—

Grand Canyon Railway train steaming north of Williams

GRAND CANYON RAILWAY

and, some say, as an accomplished horse thief, preacher of profane sermons, and prodigious drinker. An 8.5-foot statue of "Old Bill" stands in Monument Park at the west end of downtown.

Today the Bill Williams Mountain Men perpetuate his adventurous spirit. The group dresses in buckskin clothing and fur hats, stages a 180-mile horseback ride from Williams to Phoenix most years, and works to keep the history of the mountain men alive. The Buckskinners, a family-oriented group, puts on frontier-era garb for black-powder shoots.

A more recent period of Western history came to an end at Williams in October 1984, when I-40 bypassed the last section of old US Route 66. A sentimental ceremony, complete with songwriter Bobby Troup of "Route 66" fame, marked the transition. The famous highway from Chicago to Los Angeles carried many families to a new life in Arizona and California. Its replacement, I-40, now travels an unbroken 2,400-mile path from Durham, North Carolina, to Barstow, California. Local businesses suffered when traffic bypassed town, but I-40 signs attempt to lure Grand Canyon visitors at the west and downtown Williams exits even though the real exit for the park is just east of town!

Grand Canyon Railway

Passenger trains first steamed out of Williams to the Grand Canyon's scenic splendor in 1901, replacing an expensive and arduous stage ride. Railroad service ended with the last passenger train carrying just three customers in 1968, but it started anew after a 21-year hiatus. Once again, Canyon visitors can enjoy a relaxing ride through the forests and ranching country of northern Arizona to the historic log depot in Grand Canyon Village, just steps away from the rim. Grand Canyon Railway runs steam locomotives from Memorial Day weekend through September, then vintage diesels the rest of the year. (If the train is too long for the steam engine to pull by itself, a diesel will be slipped in, too.) Trains run roundtrip daily except December 24 and 25 from the 1908 Williams Depot downtown; the depot is half a mile south from I-40 Exit 163 on Grand Canyon Blvd., or it can be reached via either of the other two I-40 Williams exits to downtown. Wheelchair users can access the depot and some of the train.

Before the ride starts, you can take in the museum (open daily 7:30 a.m.-5 p.m.), outdoor train exhibits, and a Wild West show; all these are free and open to the public. The depot serves a continental breakfast and has a gift shop. Passengers encounter a staged horseback chase and train robbery before "the law" catches up with the outlaws. Strolling musicians and Wild West characters on board also entertain.

The restored 1923 Harriman coaches have reversible seats; roundtrip fare is $54.35 adults and $21.22 children ages 3-16. Travelers can upgrade to Club Class (same as coach but with a bar and coffee, juice and pastries provided in the morning) for $21.76 extra, First Class (reclining chairs and continental breakfast plus appetizers and champagne or sparkling cider on the afternoon journey) for $54.40 extra, Deluxe Observation Class (First Class with dome views; ages 11 and up only) for $76.16 extra, and the Luxury Parlor Car (First Class with seating in overstuffed divans and an open-air rear platform) for $76.16 extra. One-way fares are available. If you have a national park pass, let reservations staff know so that you won't be charged for park admission. The Grand Canyon Railway also offers packages with train tickets, a room at the Fray Marcos Hotel, and some meals, with options for Grand Canyon tours and accommodations; tel. (800) 843-8724 (800-THE-TRAIN); Internet: www.thetrain.com.

Recommended check-in is 8 a.m. or earlier, in time to have breakfast at the station, see the museum and Wild West show, and board the train for its 9:30 a.m. departure. The train arrives at Grand Canyon, across the street from El Tovar Hotel and canyon rim, about 11:45 a.m. Boarding time for the return trip is 3 p.m. for a 3:15 departure and 5:30 p.m. return to Williams. South Rim tours within this time period are available at extra cost when you make reservations or on the train. The three hours at the Grand Canyon is enough for only a quick look, so you may wish to arrange to stay and ride back another day.

Recreation

Mountain Ranch Stables offers a variety of trail rides from half an hour ($11) to overnight during the April-Oct. season; it's behind the Quality Inn, just south of I-40 Pittman Valley Exit 171, six miles east of Williams; tel. (520) 635-0706. **Stable in the Pines** beside the Circle Pines KOA has summer horseback riding ($12 half hour, $18 one hour, and up to full day); it's three miles east at I-40 Exit 167, then east 0.4 mile on the north frontage road; tel. (520) 635-2626. Play golf in the pines at the nine-hole (soon to be expanded to 18 holes) **Elephant Rocks Golf Course;** the golf season runs mid-March to mid-November. Go west on Railroad Ave. across I-40 (or take I-40 Exit 161 and head north) and drive one mile; tel. (520) 635-4936.

Downhill-ski in winter at the small **Williams Ski Area,** four miles south of town on Bill Williams Mountain. It offers a 2,000-foot poma lift (600 vertical feet), 700-foot rope tow for the beginners' slope, lessons, snack bar, rental shop, and ski shop. Full-day weekend lift tickets cost $21 for adults and $13 for children and seniors; rates are lower for weekdays and half days. Cross-country skiers can rent gear and ski on marked trails. The ski season lasts from about mid-December to the end of March; turn south 2.2 miles on Fourth St., then right at the sign; tel. (520) 635-9330.

Spring Valley Cross-Country Ski Trail has three loop possibilities of six and a half to eight miles each, rated easy to moderate; the season at the 7,480-foot-plus elevations runs winter to early spring. Spring Valley is 14 miles east on I-40 to Parks Exit 178, then north six miles on Forest Road 141; Forest Service offices have a ski trail map. Undeveloped cross-country ski areas include Sevier Flat and Barney Flat on the way to Williams Ski Area and other sites at the White Horse Lake area.

Oak Hill Snowplay Area is eight miles east of town on I-40 to the Pittman Valley Rd./Deer Farm Exit 171, then east 2.4 miles on Route 66 on the north side of I-40. Only inner tubes and flexible materials may be used. Separate runs accommodate tubers and skiers.

Motels and Hotels

Business Route I-40 connects Exits 161 and 165; it divides downtown, becoming Route 66 (eastbound) and Railroad Avenue (westbound). Grand Canyon Boulevard meets these streets in the center of downtown from I-40 Exit 163. Most of the town's motels and restaurants lie along Route 66, formerly known as Bill Williams Ave-nue. Downtown offers the most atmosphere and the convenience of being able to walk to many places. The older places can be bargains, with prices getting down into the $20-30 range in summer and in the teens in winter, though it's a good idea to check the rooms first. Don't believe the old sign that still advertises rooms "from $3.50" on the 1892 Grand Canyon Hotel on Route 66—the hotel has been closed awhile! For a complete listing of Williams motels, see the **More Accommodations in the Gateway Cities** Appendix at the back of the book.

The modern **Fray Marcos Hotel** features the same architectural style as the adjacent 1908 Williams Depot. All rooms have two beds and a southwestern motif; they run $119 d March 16-Oct. 14, then $69 d Oct. 15-March 15. Both the lobby and **Spenser's,** a pub with an impressive 1887 bar, are worth a visit for the decor and artwork. Spenser's serves snacks, but it lacks a smoke-free area. The hotel plans to build a full-service restaurant; tel. (520) 635-4010 or (800) 843-8724.

Bed and Breakfasts

For a real sense of history, it would be hard to beat the **Red Garter Bed and Bakery,** a restored 1897 Victorian Romanesque building at 137 W. Railroad Avenue. The upstairs rooms of the former brothel now include the Parlor ($65 d), Madam's Room ($85 d), and Honeymoon Suite ($105 d), all with private bath; Red Garter is closed mid-December to mid-February. Guests awaken to fresh-baked pastries for breakfast in the downstairs bakery, once a rowdy saloon. The establishment had a Chinese chop house and opium den out back at one time. Innkeeper John Holst has photos of the building, saloon-keeper, madam, and customers of the old days; tel. (520) 635-1484 or (800) 328-1484; Internet: www.redgarter.com. Moderate.

The Johnstonian is a 1900 Victorian home at 321 W. Sheridan, three blocks south of Route 66; tel. (520) 635-2178. Rates are $55-70 d. Inexpensive-Moderate.

Canyon Country Inn offers rooms with private bath downtown at 442 W. Route 66, tel. (520) 635-2349 or (800) 643-1020. Rooms cost $55-75 d. Inexpensive-Moderate.

Sheridan House Inn features suites with private bath at 460 E. Sheridan, tel. (520) 635-9441 or

(888) 635-9345, e-mail: egardner@primenet.com. Suites go for $85-195 d; it's closed mid-winter. Expensive-Luxury.

Terry Ranch Bed & Breakfast has a veranda with rocking chairs at 701 Quarterhorse, off Rodeo Drive, tel. (520) 635-4171 or (800) 210-5908, e-mail: terryranch@workmail.com. Rooms are $90-120 d. Expensive-Premium.

Campgrounds
Railside RV Ranch is the closest campground to downtown at 877 Rodeo Rd.; it has showers and a store, but lacks shade trees. Rates run $14 tents (just a few sites available) and $19 RVs with hookups; tel. (520) 635-4077 or (888) 635-4077. From I-40 Exit 165, take the business route west toward town, then turn right on Rodeo Rd.; or from downtown, go north on Grand Canyon Blvd., right on Edison Ave., left on Airport Rd., then right on Rodeo Road.

Red Lake, AZ Campground and Grand Canyon-Red Lake Hostel, 10 miles north on AZ 64 from I-40 Exit 165, is open all year with coin-operated showers, limited cooking facilities, a store, movies, and tour and shuttle booking. A cafe is planned. Rates are $10 tents and $16 RVs with hookups; the hostel facilities cost $11 per person in four-bed rooms or $33 d for a private room; tel. (520) 635-9122 or (800) 581-4753 (reservations); Internet: www.amdest.com/az/williams/redlake. html. Budget.

Two KOA campgrounds lie a short distance from Williams: **Circle Pines KOA** is open year-round in the ponderosa pines three miles east of I-40 Exit 167, then go east 0.4 mile on the north frontage road. Rates are $18 tents, $22-24 RVs with hookups, $30 kamping kabins; amenities include volleyball, badminton, basketball, game room, and indoor pool. In summer, you can take in evening movies, van tours to the Grand Canyon, and horseback riding ($12 half hour, $18 one hour); tel. (520) 635-2626 or (800) 562-9379.

Grand Canyon KOA lies five miles north of Williams on AZ 64 (I-40 Exit 165) on the way to the Grand Canyon; it offers tent ($17.50) and RV sites ($22-25 with hookups) with indoor pool, spa, and showers from March to October; tel. (520) 635-2307 or (800) 562-5771.

Ponderosa Forest RV Park & Campground has year-round sites in the woods for tents ($13) and RVs ($19 with hookups) with showers and a

nearby store; tel. (520) 635-0456 or (888) 635-0456. It's north of I-40 Parks Exit 178, 14 miles east of Williams and about halfway to Flagstaff.

The Forest Service maintains four campgrounds, all on small fishing lakes (trout and catfish) with drinking water but no showers. They're open from early May to about mid-October at elevations of 6,600-7,100 feet. Dispersed camping is allowed throughout most of the forest except within half a mile of developed campgrounds, one-quarter mile of surface water, or where signed "No Camping." Boaters can use motors up to eight hp on Cataract and Kaibab lakes, but only electric motors are allowed on the other lakes.

Cataract Campground lies two miles northwest of town; head west on Railroad Ave. across I-40 to Country Club Dr. (or take I-40 Exit 161 and go north), then turn right one mile immediately after going under railroad tracks and look for the entrance on the left. Sites cost $8.

Kaibab Campground is four miles northeast of town; drive east on Route 66 across I-40 (or turn north from I-40 Exit 165), go north two miles on AZ 64, then left one mile at the sign. Sites are $10.

Dogtown Campground and several trails lie 7.5 miles southeast of town; drive 3.5 miles south on Fourth St. (South Rd./Perkinsville Rd.), turn left three miles on Forest Road 140, then left 1.2 miles at the sign. Campsites go for $8.

White Horse Lake Campground lies 19 miles southeast near Sycamore Canyon; go eight miles south on Fourth St., turn left on Forest Road 110, and follow signs. Sites are $10. Winter visitors to the White Horse Lake area enjoy ice fishing, cross-country skiing, and snowmobiling.

Food
Rod's Steak House is a Western-style restaurant serving good steak, seafood, and sandwiches; it's open daily for lunch and dinner at 301 E. Route 66, tel. (520) 635-2671. **Miss Kitty's Steakhouse and Saloon** serves up cowboy steak, ribs, seafood, and sandwiches in a spacious hall; musicians perform daily on summer evenings. Miss Kitty's is open daily for breakfast, lunch, and dinner (buffets are usually available for breakfast and lunch) at 642 E. Route 66, tel. (520) 635-9161.

The **Red Garter Bakery** is open mornings and evenings for baked goodies at 137 W. Railroad Ave., tel. (520) 635-1484. **Grand Canyon Coffee & Cafe** fixes coffees, sandwiches, and cakes daily for breakfast and lunch and Mon.-Fri. for dinner at 125 W. Route 66, tel. (520) 635-1255. For American cafe food served daily for breakfast, lunch, and dinner, try **Parker House Restaurant,** 525 W. Route 66, tel. (520) 635-4590; **Pine Country Restaurant,** 107 N. Grand Canyon Blvd., tel. (520) 635-9718; and **Hoffman House,** 425 E. Route 66, tel. (520) 635-9955.

Pizza Factory turns out pizza, pasta, calzones, and sandwiches and has a small salad bar. It's open Mon.-Sat. for lunch and daily for dinner at 214 W. Route 66, tel. (520) 635-1090. **Pronto Pizza** fixes take-out pizza and sandwiches (free delivery) daily at 106 S. Third St., tel. (520) 635-4157.

Pancho McGillicuddy's Mexican Cantina serves Mexican cuisine and a few American items daily for lunch and dinner in summer (dinner only the rest of the year) at 141 W. Railroad Ave.; musicians perform daily on summer evenings and some weekends off season; tel. (520) 635-4150. **Rosa's Cantina** offers traditional Mexican food; open daily for lunch and dinner at 106 S. Ninth St. and Route 66; tel. (520) 635-0708.

Safeway supermarket is at 637 W. Route 66.

Events

Downtown rings to the sound of gunfire as cowboys stage shootouts every morning year-round at the train depot; gunfights also break out on the streets every evening during summer. **Bill Williams Rendezvous** on Memorial Day weekend attracts the Buckskinners and Mountain Men to town for a black powder shoot, Saturday parade, street dance, and arts and crafts exhibitions. **Festival in the Pines** on the last weekend of June is a juried arts and crafts show with food and entertainment. Townsfolk celebrate **July 4th** with a parade and fireworks. Working cowboys show what they've learned in the **Cowpuncher's Reunion Rodeo** on the first weekend in August. Top rodeo cowboys compete in the **PRCA Rodeo** on Labor Day weekend. **Old Route 66 "Cruisin' the Loop"**

Day brings back the classic cars and memories of the '50s on the second weekend of October. **Mountain Village Holiday** runs from Thanksgiving to New Year's Day with arts and crafts and, on the second Saturday in December, a parade of lights.

Information

The **Visitor Information Center** has staff from both the Williams-Grand Canyon Chamber of Commerce and the Kaibab National Forest to help you explore and enjoy the region. The office serves so many travelers headed for the Grand Canyon that it stocks brochures and sells maps and books for that area too, as well as the rest of Arizona. It's open all year daily 8 a.m.-5 p.m., in the heart of downtown in a 1901 passenger train depot at 200 W. Railroad Ave. (Williams, AZ 86046); tel. (520) 635-4061 or (800) 863-0546; Internet: www.thegrandcanyon.com. The *Williams Guidebook* by Richard and Sherry Mangum covers local history, walks, hikes, mountain bike trips, and scenic drives.

Kaibab National Forest staff can tell you about backcountry drives, hiking, camping, fishing, and road conditions in the Williams area. Stop by the Visitor Information Center downtown at 200 W. Railroad Ave. or visit the **Williams Ranger District** office, open Mon.-Fri. 7:30 a.m.-4 p.m. The Ranger District office is west 1.5 miles from downtown via Railroad Ave. and the I-40 frontage road; turn left at the sign before I-40; the address is 742 S. Clover Rd., Williams, AZ 86046; tel. (520) 635-2633; www.fs.fed.us/r3/kai.

The **public library** is at 113 S. First St., just south of Route 66; tel. (520) 635-2263.

Tours and Transportation

For backcountry tours, contact **Bronco Charlie's Backwoods Tours;** tel. (520) 635-9033 or (800) 417-8101. To tour the Grand Canyon, try **Grand Canyon Van Tours** at Circle Pines KOA, tel. (520) 635-2626 in summer only; or **Marvelous Marv's Tours,** tel. (520) 635-4948 or (800) 655-4948, Internet: marvelousmarv.com.

Greyhound offers several east- and westbound departures daily from the stop at the Chevron Station, just north of I-40 Exit 163 at 1050 Grand Canyon Blvd., tel. (520) 635-0870 or (800) 231-2222. Tickets must be paid with cash.

Nava-Hopi buses head north to the Grand Canyon once daily in the morning from the Grand Canyon Railway station and return in the evening, $9 each way; buses also make a daily roundtrip to Flagstaff for $7 each way; tel. (800) 892-8687.

VICINITY OF WILLIAMS

Grand Canyon Deer Farm

Visitors enjoy walking among tame deer and hand feeding them at this well-run petting zoo. Llamas, miniature donkeys, pronghorn, wallabies, and talking birds like the attention, too. The farm also has a buffalo, reindeer, exotic goats, a potbellied pig, and other familiar creatures. Peacocks strut across the grounds. The Deer Farm is open daily year-round except Thanksgiving and Christmas; the hours are June-Aug. 8 a.m.-7 p.m., March-May and Sept.-Oct. 9 a.m.-6 p.m., and Nov.-Feb. (weather permitting) 10 a.m.-5 p.m. Admission is $5.50 adults, $4.50 seniors 62 and over, $3 children 3-13; tel. (520) 635-4073 or (800) 926-3337. It's on Deer Farm Rd., eight miles east of Williams off I-40 Pittman Valley/Deer Farm Exit 171. Or from Flagstaff, head west 24 miles on I-40 to Exit 171.

Bill Williams Mountain

You can reach the summit of this 9,255-foot peak by any of three hiking trails or by road. Pine, oak, and juniper trees cover the lower

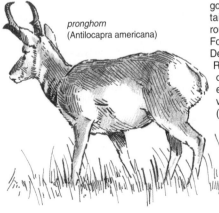

pronghorn
(Antilocapra americana)

mountain slopes, and dense forests of aspen, fir, and spruce grow in protected valleys and at higher elevations. On a clear day, you'll enjoy views of the Grand Canyon to the north, San Francisco Peaks and many smaller volcanoes to the east, Sycamore Canyon and parts of the Verde Valley to the south, and vast rangelands to the west. If it's open, climb up the Forest Service lookout tower at the top for the best views. Hiking season lasts from about June to September; you should always carry water. With a car shuttle, you can go up one trail and down another, or hike a trail just in one direction.

The seven-mile roundtrip **Bill Williams Mountain Trail** climbs the north face of the mountain. You'll reach the road about a half mile from the summit; either continue on the trail across the road or turn up the road itself. The trailhead (elev. 6,900 feet) is near the Williams Ranger District office, 1.5 miles west of town; from I-40, take Exit 161 toward Williams, then turn right (west) 0.7 mile on the frontage road.

The nine-mile roundtrip **Benham Trail** climbs the south and east slopes, crossing the road to the lookout tower several times. To reach the Benham Trailhead (elev. 7,265 feet) from Williams, go south 3.5 miles on Fourth St., then turn right about 0.3 mile on Benham Ranch Road. The gentler grade of this trail makes it good for horseback riders as well as hikers; the trailhead has a corral.

The **Bixler Saddle Trail** starts at Bixler Saddle on the west side of Bill Williams Mountain and climbs past majestic rock formations and good viewpoints. It joins the Bill Williams Mountain Trail fairly close to the top, five miles roundtrip; the summit is another half mile or so. For the trailhead, take I-40 west from Williams to Devil Dog Road Exit 157, head south on Forest Road 108 about a mile, then turn left 3.6 miles on Forest Rd. 45/Bixler Saddle Road to its end. The last bit may require a high-clearance vehicle. The Kaibab National Forest map (Williams District) will help to navigate the forest roads.

You can also drive up if you have a high-clearance vehicle; from Williams head 4.7 miles south on Fourth St., then turn right seven miles on Forest Road 111. The road closes in winter.

Keyhole Sink Trail

A pleasant stroll, also marked for cross-country skiers, leads through ponderosa pines to a seasonal pool in a little box canyon. Aspen, wildflowers, and lush grass thrive here; you're likely to see some birds, too. Prehistoric people left petroglyphs, estimated to be 1,000 years old, on the dark basaltic rock. The easy walk is about 1.2 miles roundtrip with little elevation gain. To reach the trailhead, drive east on I-40 from Williams to Pittman Valley Exit 171, exit north, then head east 2.4 miles on Historic Route 66; parking is on the right at Oak Hill Snowplay Area, which features picnic tables, a warming shed, and toilets. The trailhead is north across the road. Coming from Flagstaff, you can take I-40 Parks Road Exit 178, turn north, then west 4.3 miles on Route 66; you'll pass **Garland Prairie Vista Picnic Area** 1.1 miles before reaching Oak Hill Snowplay Area.

Dogtown Trails

Dogtown Lake (elev. 7,100 feet) offers a campground, picnic area, and good hiking. **Dogtown Lake Trail** makes a pleasant 1.8-mile stroll around the lake from the picnic area. **Davenport Hill Trail** begins near the boat ramp on the east side of the lake, follows Dogtown Wash, climbs to a bench, then switchbacks to the 7,805-foot summit. You'll pass through ponderosa pine, Douglas fir, white fir, and aspen forests with some good views. The trail is five miles roundtrip and has an elevation gain of 700 feet. **Ponderosa Nature Trail** is an easy, level, one-mile loop that branches off the Davenport Hill Trail; interpretive stops tell of the forest environment. Dogtown Lake, named for the prairie dogs common in the Williams area, is 7.5 miles southeast of town; drive 3.5 miles south on Fourth St. (South Rd./Perkinsville Rd.), turn left three miles on Forest Road 140, then left 1.2 miles at the sign

Sycamore Canyon Point

Sycamore Canyon remains wild and rugged, without any roads or facilities. Elk, deer, black bears, and other animals find food and shelter on the canyon's rim and within its depths. Hikers and horseback riders can use a network of trails. Sycamore Canyon Point, 23 miles southeast of

Williams, offers a breathtaking panorama. From town, drive eight miles south on Fourth St./South Rd./Perkinsville Rd., then turn left on Forest Road 110 and travel to its end, approximately 15 miles farther. The last five miles are single lane and may be signed "Not For Low-Clearance Vehicles," but careful drivers may make it. Road signs may direct you left on Forest Roads 109 and 12, then back to 110, but you should be able to get through staying on the 110 road. No trails enter the canyon from this side, though you can spot a path going down the opposite side.

Sycamore Rim Trail

This 11-mile loop overlooks parts of upper Sycamore Canyon and travels past seasonal waterfalls, lumber mill and railroad sites, lily ponds (good swimming), and pretty forest country. Stone cairns mark the trail, shown on both the Kaibab and Coconino Forest maps. Trailheads lie southeast of Williams near the junction of Forest Routes 13 and 56, at the end of Forest Road 56, at Pomeroy Tanks off Forest Road 109, and at Sycamore Falls off Forest Road 109; see the Kaibab or Coconino Forest maps. If you're in the mood for only a short hike, walk 0.3 mile south from the end of Forest Road 56 to an overlook of Sycamore Canyon. The Visitor Information Center downtown at 200 W. Railroad Ave. and the Williams Ranger District office have a map and trail description for Sycamore Rim Trail.

Sycamore Falls

You can easily reach two waterfalls near White Horse Lake. The spectacle, however, occurs only during spring runoff and after heavy rains. From White Horse Lake, turn right two miles (north) on Forest Road 109 to the Sycamore Falls Trailhead, about two miles south of the junction with Forest Road 13. A small waterfall is visible in a canyon just to the right, but walk ahead and a bit to the left to see a larger falls, 80-100 feet high.

Perkinsville Road

Beginning as Fourth Street in downtown Williams, Perkinsville Road heads south through the pine forests of the Mogollon Rim, drops down to the high-desert lands of the Verde Valley, crosses the Verde River at historic Perkinsville

Ranch, then climbs rugged hills to the old mining town of Jerome. The first 25 miles are paved, followed by 27 miles of dirt. Though dusty and bumpy in spots, the route is usually okay in dry weather. No vehicle should attempt the unpaved section after winter snowstorms or heavy summer rains. Allow three hours for a one-way drive, more if you'd like to stop to admire the views. Stock up on gas and water before heading down this lonely road. The Prescott National Forest map covers the entire route.

ASH FORK

Declaring itself the "Flagstone Capital of the USA," Ash Fork occupies high-desert grasslands 19 miles west of Williams and 50 miles north of Prescott. Its location at the junction of I-40 and AZ 89 makes this small community a handy stopping place for travelers. The town grew up around a railroad siding built near Ash Creek in 1882, where passengers and freight transferred to stagecoaches or wagons for Prescott and Phoenix. Ash Fork (pop. 650) now serves as a highway stop and center for livestock raising and sandstone quarrying.

Accommodations
As in Williams, most of the motels and other businesses lie along two parallel one-way streets—Lewis Ave. for westbound traffic and Park Ave. for eastbound. Take I-40 Exits 144 or 146. **Ashfork Inn,** west of downtown near I-40 Exit 144, tel. (520) 637-2514, is the best choice. Rates are $22 s, $25 d. Budget. Other motels in the $20 range include **Stagecoach Motel,** 823 Park Ave., tel. (520) 637-2551; **Copper State Motel,** 101 E. Lewis Ave., tel. (520) 637-2335; and the **Hi-Line Motel** next door.

Ash Fork KOA includes a pool, store, and game room at 783 Old Route 66, tel. (520) 637-2521; rates run $16.50 tents, $19.50-20.50 RV with hookups, and $27 d for rustic cabins; turn in beside the Stagecoach Motel. **Cauthen's Hillside RV Park** is on the south frontage road near I-40 Exit 144, tel. (520) 637-2300; rates are $7 tents or RVs without hookups, $14 with hookups. Both campgrounds stay open all year and have showers. They're also close to the noise of I-40.

Food
Lydia's Fine Mexican Food is at 599 Park Ave., tel. (520) 637-0111. **Route 66 Grill** is on Lewis Avenue. **Picadilly Pizza & Subs** is next to the Chevron station, just south of the west I-40 Exit 144. **Ranch House Cafe,** tel. (520) 637-2710, and the **Bull Pen Restaurant** next door, tel. (520) 637-2330, a 24-hour truck stop, lie on the east side of town. A park on Lewis Ave. has picnic tables.

SELIGMAN

Another old railroad town, Seligman (pop. 900) now relies more on ranching and tourists. The first residents arrived in 1886 and called the place Prescott Junction, because a rail line branched south to Prescott. Though the Prescott line was later abandoned, the town survived. The present name honors brothers who owned the Hash Knife Cattle Company. Modern travelers on I-40 can take Exits 121 or 123 for the motels and restaurants in town or head northwest on old Route 66. This former transcontinental highway is a longer route to Kingman than I-40, but it offers a change of pace and a glimpse of America's motoring past. It also provides access to the Havasupai and Hualapai Indian reservations (see "Western Grand Canyon and The Arizona Strip"). You'll find food and lodging at the Grand Canyon Caverns Inn northwest of Seligman, Hualapai Lodge in Peach Springs, and Frontier Motel in Truxton. There's also a 17.5-mile segment of Route 66 east of town that turns southeast just east of downtown; if approaching Seligman from Ash Fork, you can drive it by turning off I-40 at Crookton Rd., Exit 139.

Accommodations
Nearly all businesses lie along Route 66. Budget category places to stay include **Stagecoach 66 Motel,** just east of town, tel. (520) 422-3470, $28 s, $32 d; **Deluxe Inn,** 203 E. Route 66, tel. (520) 422-3244, $28 s, $30 d; **Comfort Lodge,** 114 E. Chino, tel. (520) 422-3255, $32 s, $35 d; and **Romney Motel/Supai Motel,** 122 W. Chino, tel. (520) 422-3700, $35 d. **Historic Route 66 Motel** on the west edge of town, tel. (520) 422-3204, has rooms for $42 s, $52 d. Inexpensive.

Seligman KOA is open year-round just east of town with a swimming pool and showers; rates are $16.25 tent, $19.70-21 RV with hookups; tel. (520) 422-3358. **Historic Route 66 General Store and Campground,** on the west end of town, is open all year with showers; it costs $10.55 for tents or RVs without hookups and $14.77 with hookups; tel. (520) 422-3549.

Food
Stagecoach 66 Cafe, just east of town, serves breakfast, lunch, and dinner daily; tel. (520) 422-3470. **Patty's Home Cookin'** has Thai-American food daily for breakfast and lunch and Mon.-Sat. for dinner at 223 E. Route 66, tel. (520) 422-0014. Patty's also offers a couple of bed & breakfast rooms for rent and a small grocery. The **Copper Cart Restaurant** downtown offers a varied American menu; it's open daily for breakfast, lunch, and dinner; tel. (520) 422-3241. Get your malts, sodas, fast food, and maybe a joke or two at the colorful **Delgadillo's Snow Cap;** tel. (520) 422-3291. The steak house and cafe on the west end of downtown lack smoke-free sections. A small park downtown has picnic tables.

GRAND CANYON CAVERNS

Vast underground chambers and some pretty cave formations attract travelers on old Route 66. The caverns lie 25 miles northwest of Seligman, then one mile off the highway. A giant dinosaur stands guard in front. On 45-minute guided tours, you descend 21 stories by elevator to the caverns and walk about a quarter mile with some steps and inclines. Tours operate daily 8 a.m.-6 p.m. from Memorial Day to October 16, then 9 a.m.-5 p.m. in winter (closed Christmas Day); admission is $8.50 adults, $5.75 children 4-12. A gift shop at the entrance has some cave exhibits and photos from the early days, when visitors were lowered 150 feet at the end of a rope.

Grand Canyon Caverns Inn offers year-round accommodations near the turnoff on Route 66; rates are $38 s, $46 d, lower in winter. Inexpensive. Self contained RVs only may park in a campground with drinking water but no showers or hookups; the fee is $5. The cavern restaurant is open about the same hours as the tours. For information on cave tours or motel reservations, call (520) 422-3223.

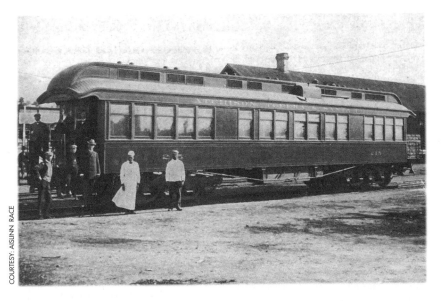

COURTESY: AISLINN RACE

CANYON COUNTRY BASICS

KEEPING THE "WILD" IN WILDERNESS~ KNOW BEFORE YOU GO

As more people seek relief from the confusion and stress of urban life, the use of wilderness areas increases. Fortunately, the Grand Canyon area contains an abundance of this fragile and precious resource. Most of the park's trails and the many designated wilderness areas nearby are closed to mechanized vehicles—including mountain bikes—to protect the environment and enhance the experience of solitude. Hikers need to buy camping permits for the backcountry of Grand Canyon National Park, for any recreation on Indian lands, for camping in the BLM's Paria Canyon, or for day use in the nearby Coyote Buttes area. You're generally free to visit the other designated wilderness areas on Kaibab National Forest and Bureau of Land Management lands anytime without a permit.

Spectacular and memorable hiking and camping await the prepared outdoors enthusiast. But

because Arizona's deserts and canyons are very different from most other parts of the country, even expert hikers can get into trouble. If you're new to these outdoors, read up on hiking conditions and talk to rangers and local hikers. Backpacking stores and the Internet are good sources of information. Start with easy trips, then work up to long hikes gradually.

Suggestions for backcountry travel and camping include these wilderness guidelines:

- Before heading into the backcountry, check with a knowledgeable person about weather, water sources, fire danger, trail conditions, and regulations.

- Tell a reliable person where you're going and when you expect to return.

- Travel in small groups for the best experience; group size may also be regulated.

- Try not to camp on meadows, as the grass is easily trampled and killed.

- Avoid digging tent trenches and don't cut any vegetation.

- Use a campstove to prevent marring the land with fire.

- Camp at least 300 feet away from springs, creeks, and trails. State law prohibits camping within a quarter mile of a sole water source so that wildlife and stock won't be scared away.

- Wash away from streams and lakes.

- Don't drink untreated water in the wilderness, no matter how clean the water appears. It may contain the parasitic protozoan *Giardia lamblia,* which causes the unpleasant disease giardiasis. Boiling your water for several minutes will kill Giardia and most other bacterial or viral pathogens. Filtering and iodine treatments usually work, too, but they're not as reliable as boiling (see the special topic "Giardia").

- Bring a trowel for personal sanitation and dig four to six inches deep. In desert areas it's best to bag and carry out toilet paper because the stuff lasts for years and years in a dry climate; backcountry visitors in the Grand Canyon and Paria Canyon *must* pack it out.

- Carry plenty of feed for horses and mules.

- Leave dogs at home; they foul campsites and disturb wildlife and other hikers. If you do bring one, keep it under physical control at all times. They're not allowed in the Grand Canyon National Park backcountry.

- Take home all your trash, so animals can't dig it up and scatter it.

- Help preserve Indian and historic ruins.

- A survival kit and small flashlight can make the difference if you're caught in a storm or are out longer than expected. A pocket-sized container can hold what you need for the three essentials: **fire building** (matches in a waterproof container and a candle), **shelter** (space blanket, knife, and rope), and **signaling** (mirror and whistle).

- If you get lost, *realize it,* then find shelter and stay in one place. If you're sure of a way to civilization and plan to walk out, leave a note of your departure time and planned route.

STAYING HEALTHY

Hypothermia

Although the Grand Canyon has a well-deserved reputation for intense summer heat below the rims, another danger in the cooler months or at high elevations can sneak up and kill with very little warning. Hypothermia, a drop in the body's temperature below 95° F, causes disorientation, uncontrollable shivering, slurred speech, and drowsiness. The victim may not even realize what's wrong. Unless corrective action is taken immediately, hypothermia can lead to death. That's why hikers should travel with companions and always carry wind and rain protection; close-fitting raingear works better than ponchos.

GIARDIA

It can be tough to resist: Picture yourself hiking in a beautiful area by the banks of a crystal clear stream. The water in your canteen tastes stale, hot, and plastic; the nearby stream looks so inviting that you can't resist a cautious sip. It tastes delicious, clean, and cold, and for the rest of your hike you refresh yourself with water straight from the stream.

Days pass and you forget about drinking untreated water. Suddenly one evening after your meal you become terribly sick to your stomach. You develop an awful case of cramps and feel diarrhea beginning to set in. Food poisoning?

Well, it could be the effects of Giardia, a protozoan that has become common in even the remotest of mountain streams. Giardia is carried in animal or human waste that is deposited or washed into natural waters. When ingested, it begins reproducing, causing a sickness that can become very serious and may not be cured without medical attention.

You can take precautions against Giardia with a variety of chemical purifying and filtering methods or by boiling water before drinking it. Directions for chemical and filtering methods need to be followed carefully to be effective against the protozoan in its cyst stage of life, when it encases itself in a hard shell. The most efficient way to eliminate such threats is to boil all suspect water for a few minutes.

Remember that temperatures can plummet rapidly in Arizona's dry climate—a drop of 40° F between day and night is common. Be especially careful at high elevations, where summer sunshine can quickly change into freezing rain or a blizzard.

If you get cold and tired, don't waste time. Seek shelter and build a fire; change into dry clothes and drink warm liquids. A victim not fully conscious should be warmed by skin-to-skin contact with another person in a sleeping bag. Try to keep the victim awake and drinking warm liquids.

Coping with the Heat

We can take cues from desert wildlife on how best to live in a potentially hostile landscape such as the Grand Canyon. In summer, the early morning and late afternoon have the most pleasant temperatures to be out and about. Photographers also have the incentive of these times having the best light for photography. When captivated by the grand scenery, it's easy to forget to drink enough water, but you'll be glad you did drink enough at the end of the day! For maximum efficiency, the body also needs food when hiking—snacks will increase endurance and prevent water intoxication, caused by sufficient water but too few carbohydrates to go with it.

Medical Services

In emergencies, dial 911. Hospital emergency rooms offer the quickest help, but cost more than a visit to a doctor's office or clinic. Hospital care is very expensive—having medical insurance is recommended. In Grand Canyon National Park, a clinic on the South Rim provides 24-hour medical care.

ACCOMMODATIONS

This book has been written to assist travelers of all budgets! You'll rarely need to spend more than $35 for a room except right at the Grand Canyon, on the Indian reservations, and during peak travel times elsewhere, when camping will be a good option. If you have the funds and the desire to be pampered, top-notch hotels and resorts will do just that. And you'll have plenty of midrange accommodations choices

most everywhere. Expect a sales tax of about 10% to be added to quoted rates at most places. You're sure to find seasonal and long-term price changes, however, so *please* don't use what's listed in this book to argue with staff at businesses. For comparison with other books by Moon Publications, you may find these categories useful; all are based on high-season, double-occupancy rates.

Budget: under $35
Inexpensive: $35-60
Moderate: $60-85
Expensive: $85-110
Premium: $110-150
Luxury: $150 and up

Motels and Hotels

Summer is the Grand Canyon area's busiest season, when reservations come in handy. Off-season prices can be great value, especially in the "gateway towns" of Flagstaff and Williams. You'll find the major hotel and motel chains well represented in northern Arizona. Some of the region's restored historic hotels offer the elegance and romance of the old days.

Bed and Breakfasts

These private homes or small inns offer a personal touch not found in the usual accommodations. Rates range $45-275 d, with most around $75-125. Always call or write for reservations. Although the author didn't find any B&Bs at the Grand Canyon, surrounding towns often have a good selection. Local visitor centers provide listings. **Mi Casa Su Casa** can book many B&Bs at Box 950, Tempe, AZ 85280, tel. (602) 990-0682 or (800) 456-0682; Internet: www.mi-casa.org.

Hostels

The towns of Flagstaff, Tuba City, Williams, Page, and Kanab have independent hostels (no hostel card needed) at a cost of about $15 per night for a bed in shared rooms. Some hostels will accept phone reservations made with a credit card. Check out the website www.hostels.com for news and listings.

Hostel directories can come in handy if you'll be traveling this way. The *Hostel Handbook* lists both Hostelling International places and independents annually for $3; contact Jim Williams at 722 St. Nicholas Ave., New York, NY 10031; tel.

212-926-7030; Internet: www.hostels.com/handbook. *Hostels U.S.A.* provides a comprehensive 395-page guide to Hostelling International members and the independents with descriptions of atmosphere and features. The 1998 first edition book is published by The Globe Pequot Press (Box 833, Old Saybrook, CT 06475, Internet: www.globe-pequot.com) and is sold in bookstores. Both publications cover the U.S. and Canada.

Guest Ranch

Bar 10 Ranch lies in a remote area of the Arizona Strip just north of the Grand Canyon, where you can really "get away from it all." It offers miles of open country, cowboy-style meals, and an informal Western atmosphere. Activities include horseback riding, pack trips, cattle drives, hiking, scenic flights, river trips, cookouts, and entertainment. Many visitors spend a day here when shuttling in or out from a river trip by helicopter and flying by small plane to Las Vegas or other destinations. You can also drive here, though high-clearance vehicles are recommended. Make the required reservations with Bar 10 at Box 910088, St. George, UT 84791-0088, tel. (435) 628-4010 or (800) 582-4139, Internet: www.infowest.com/bar10.

MOTEL AND HOTEL CHAINS

By Stephen Metzger

If you've been on the road at all in the United States in the last few years, you've noticed the amazing proliferation of chain lodging—from Motel 6s to Super 8s to all the Inns (Holiday, Ramada, Comfort, Days . . .). Even many of the ol' Best Westerns have been upgraded and remarketed in recent years; the familiar yellow-crown signs that once rose comfortably into the low skylines of twilight have been replaced by modern deep-blue signs with stylized red crowns and electronic marquees advertising sports bars and exercise rooms. Most of these lodges offer competitive rates; clean, quiet rooms; and a known quantity in terms of price, amenities, and general quality. Unfortunately, they've also helped further the depersonalization of small-town America; the colorful little mom-and-pop places can't compete.

Following is a list of some of the common hotel and motel chains, and what you can expect them to provide. In general, you can count on a swimming pool, laundry, television with a movie channel, free local phone calls, free morning coffee, and a choice of smoking or no-smoking rooms. Many offer discounts to members of various groups and clubs: the American Automobile Association, American Association of Retired Persons, military employees, and others. Always ask.

Refer to this information when you come across a listing for one of the chains described below.

Best Western, tel. (800) 528-1234; Internet: www.bestwestern.com. Best Westerns are individually owned and vary in size and appearance—from roadside motels to downtown high-rises. They all must meet strict standards, however, and you are generally assured of quality and comfort. I stay at them frequently, as I know they'll be clean and quiet and the service dependable and friendly. Most have pools; many have restaurants on the premises.

Days Inn, tel. (800) DAYS INN (329-7466); Internet: www.daysinn.com. Consistently comfortable and clean, though without much personality. Most have pools; no restaurants.

Holiday Inn, tel. (800) HOLIDAY (465-4329); Internet: www.holiday-inn.com. Generally the most upscale of the lodges listed here. Each has a restaurant, lounge, pool, and meeting rooms.
Holiday Inn Express, tel. (800) HOLIDAY (465-4329). Scaled-down versions of Holiday Inns, these lodges offer continental breakfasts, and most have pools.

Motel 6, tel. (800) 4-MOTEL-6 (466-8356); Internet: www.motel6.com. Cookie cutter, but comfortable and inexpensive. Small pool; bathrooms with shower stall but no tub. This chain is extremely popular, and rooms fill up quickly. Often times the No Vacancy sign goes up well before nightfall.

Ramada Inn, tel. (800) 2-RAMADA (272-6232); Internet: www.ramada.com. Ranging from urban highrises to smaller-town motels, Ramadas all offer restaurants, lounges, and meeting rooms and are reliably comfortable and clean.

Super 8, tel. (800) 800-8000; Internet: www.super8.com. Consistently clean, quiet, and inexpensive.

Campgrounds

The best parts of northern Arizona lie outdoors, where you can choose among hundreds of campgrounds—federal, state, Indian, or private. Federal government sites, the most common, are offered by the Forest Service, National Park Service, and Bureau of Land Management; sites commonly feature tables, toilets, and drinking water, with fees ranging from free to $15 per night. The Havasupai, Hualapai, Paiute, Navajo, and Hopi tribes offer campgrounds, too. Commercial campgrounds provide the most frills—showers, laundromats, hookups, stores, game rooms—some even have swimming pools. Rates at these average $15-20 per night; most accept both tents and RVs.

Dispersed Camping

You're welcome to camp almost anywhere in the national forests, Bureau of Land Management (BLM) areas, and the backcountry of the Lake Mead National Recreation Area. This dispersed style of camping costs nothing and, for seasoned campers, provides the best outdoor experience. Because there are no facilities, it's up to you to leave the forest in its natural state. Be very careful with fire—try to use a campstove rather than leave a fire scar. Sometimes high

---

A Word about Hotel Rates

The more I travel the more I realize how capricious hotel rates are, how the rate you get depends on so many variables—whether you phone in your reservation or walk in off the street, whether it's two in the afternoon or 10 at night, whether you asked for a "discount" or not. Keep in mind hotels, and to some degree motels, have widely fluctuating rates, that above all they don't want empty rooms.

True story: I pulled into Fort Collins, Colorado, one afternoon and walked into the lobby of a major hotel chain. Since it was packed with tour groupers, and waiting 10 minutes at the counter got me no closer to a clerk, I walked outside to a pay phone and called the front desk. "Rates are $79 a night," I was told, "but sorry, no rooms available tonight." So I walked next door, where I was told there was one room available, a smoking room. Nope, wouldn't do. So I walked back to the lobby of the first hotel, worked my way to the counter, and asked for a room. "Yes, we do have a room, Sir. For $69."

"Do you offer any corporate discounts?" I asked.

"Why . . . yes, we can give you a room for $59."

Now, this is backward from how it usually works (though it does go to show how arbitrary it can all be). Often you can get a better rate by phone, even if you're calling from just outside the door, as they figure you're not committed yet, and they *want* you. Once you're in the door they figure you're less likely to go somewhere else.

Another true story: One night in Raton, New Mexico, I stopped for the night at dusk at a small independent motel. A man in front of me was talking with the desk clerk.

"How much for a room?"

"Do you qualify for any discounts?" the woman asked.

Shrugging and giving her a blank look, he said, "What do you mean?"

"Triple A, corporate, AARP, you know . . . "

"Uh, I guess not . . . "

"Sixty-four dollars for a single."

He said he'd take it, filled out the registration form, and left with his key.

My turn: "Do you have a nonsmoking single available for this evening?"

"Do you qualify for any discounts?"

"Yes, I do."

"Fifty-four dollars for a single."

"I'll take it."

Is there a lesson here? If there is it's that, like I said, rates are not as fixed as you might think. Some things to keep in mind: The later in the day the better your chance of getting a cut rate. The owners want their rooms full, and, if it looks as if they might not be, they'll offer incentives, in the form of a few bucks off the "standard" rate. (Of course, you also risk not finding a vacancy, and that risk might not be worth it to you.) Also, *ask* about discounts. Most hotels offer at least American Automobile Association, American Association of Retired Persons, and corporate discounts, and you might qualify. Finally, in the case of chain and franchise lodging, I've had better luck phoning the hotel directly than calling the 800 number and talking to an operator who might be booking a room in a town 3,000 miles away from the switchboard.

Bottom line: Phone around, and talk like you do it all the time. You might be pleasantly surprised at the results.

Stephen Metzger is the author of Moon Travel Handbooks' Colorado Handbook, New Mexico Handbook, *and* Santa Fe-Taos Handbook.

Hance's Camp in the late 19th century

COURTESY: AISLINN RACE

fire danger closes the forests in early summer. The Kaibab National Forest covers much of both the South and North Rims of the Grand Canyon on vast expanses of forested plateaus. BLM lands and Lake Mead National Recreation Area extend across much of the Arizona Strip north of the Grand Canyon and west of the Kaibab Plateau. Stop at a national forest office or BLM office for maps and information on camping, hiking, fishing, and back-road travel.

FOOD AND DRINK

People debate whether Arizona actually has a native cuisine. Whether it does or not, you'll find a wide selection of appetizing dishes here. South-of-the-border food is quite popular and every town has a Mexican restaurant. Western-style restaurants dish out cowboy food—beef, beans, and biscuits. You can sample Indian fry bread and the Navajo taco—beans, lettuce, tomatoes, and cheese on fry bread—on or off the reservations. The larger towns offer a cosmopolitan array of ethnic and fine-dining restaurants.

Only the sales tax is added to your bill; you're expected to leave a tip of at least 15% for table service.

Flagstaff and Mesa have laws prohibiting smoking in most restaurants. Nonsmoking sections elsewhere are voluntary, although it's likely that more cities will adopt clean-air policies.

Alcohol
The legal drinking age in Arizona is 21. No alcohol is permitted on the Navajo or Hopi Reservations.

If you choose to drink, don't get behind the wheel of a car. Arizona has strict laws forbidding driving under the influence of alcohol or drugs. A first offense can bring a mandatory jail term, fine, license suspension, and education or treatment.

TRANSPORTATION

The parking facilities at Grand Canyon National Park have been overwhelmed by the sheer numbers of visitors with cars. Shuttle buses have already replaced private vehicles on the West Rim Drive and Yaki Point/S. Kaibab Trailhead areas during the warmer months. In coming years, visitors to the Grand Canyon Village area will park south in Tusayan and use light rail and low-emission shuttle buses to get around. You can reach the South Rim by scheduled bus service from Flagstaff and Williams, by train from Williams, and by plane from Las Vegas, Phoenix, and Page. A shuttle vehicle connects the South and North Rims during the summer season.

By Car
Most people choose their own cars as the most convenient and economical way to get around. High-clearance 4WD vehicles will come in handy

if you plan extensive travel on back roads. Phoenix and Las Vegas have the largest selection of car and RV rentals in the region, as well as the best air connections if you're flying in. See the Driving Tips special topic for advice on travel in the Grand Canyon area.

Driveaways

These are autos scheduled for delivery to another city. If the auto's destination is a place you intend to visit, a driveaway can be like getting a free car rental. You have to be at least 21 years old and pay a refundable deposit of $75-150.

DRIVING TIPS

Summer heat puts an extra strain on both car and driver. Make sure the cooling system, engine oil, transmission fluid, fan belts, and tires are in top condition. Carry several gallons of water in case of breakdown or radiator trouble. Never leave children or pets in a parked car during warm weather—temperatures inside can cause fatal heatstroke in just minutes. Radiator caps must not be opened when the engine is hot because the escaping steam can cause severe burns.

At times the desert has *too much water*—late-summer storms frequently flood low spots in the road. Wait for the water to go down, until you can see bottom, before crossing. If the car begins to hydroplane after a rainstorm, it's best to remove your foot from the accelerator, avoid braking, and keep the steering straight until the tires grip the road again. Drive in the "footsteps" of the car ahead, if you can.

Dust storms also tend to be short-lived but can completely block visibility. Treat them like dense fog: pull completely off the road and stop, turning off your lights so as not to confuse other drivers.

Radio stations carry frequent updates when weather hazards exist. With a VHF radio (between 162.4 and 162.55 MHz), you can pick up continuous weather forecasts in the Flagstaff, Sedona, Lake Powell, St. George, and Las Vegas areas.

If stranded in the backcountry, whether on the desert or in the mountains, stay with the vehicle unless you're *positive* of the way out; then leave a note detailing your route and departure time. Airplanes can easily spot a car—leave your hood and trunk up and tie a piece of cloth to the antenna—but a person trying to walk out is difficult to see. If you're stranded, emergency supplies can definitely help: blankets or sleeping bags, raingear, gloves, first-aid kit, tools and jumper cables, motor oil, shovel, rope, traction mats or chains, flashlight, flares, fire extinguisher, maps, water, food, and a can opener.

School crossings and buses require extra care. You must stop if someone is using a crosswalk.

Crossings in use by school children have a 15 mph posted speed; police have ticketed drivers going 20 mph in them! When you see a school bus stopped with red lights flashing and a stop sign arm extended, you must stop in *both* directions until the lights and arm turn off, unless there is a *physical* barrier dividing the roadway and you're traveling in the opposite direction.

Unless posted otherwise, speed limits are 15 mph when approaching a school crossing, 25 mph in business and residential districts, and 55 mph on open highways and city freeways. Although it's tempting to let loose on long, empty highways, they haven't all been designed for extreme speeds—a speeding car could top a small rise and suddenly find itself bearing down on a flock of sheep crossing the road. Deer, elk, and other stray animals can pose a danger too, especially at night.

You can make right turns from the right lane on a red light, unless prohibited by a sign, after coming to a complete stop and yielding to other traffic. Left turns on a red light can similarly be made only if you're in the far left lane of a one-way street and turning onto another one-way street and there's no sign prohibiting the turn.

Reversible lanes in Phoenix and some other cities have signs designating the lane for certain hours for "Through Traffic," "Do Not Use," and "Other times 2 way left."

Seat belts must be worn by all front-seat passengers. Child safety seats are required for those younger than five years or less than 40 pounds.

Arizona has strict laws against driving under the influence of drugs or drink. Penalties for the first - time offender include mandatory jail term, fine, license suspension, and screening, education, and/or treatment.

The *Arizona Driver License Manual* contains a good review of driving knowledge and road rules. It's available free in most large towns at the state Motor Vehicle Division office or online at www.dot.state. az.us.mvd.dlmanual.

There will be time and mileage limits. Ask for an economy car if you want the lowest driving costs. In a large city—Phoenix or Tucson in Arizona—look in the Yellow Pages under "Automobile Transporters and Driveaways."

By Bus

Greyhound offers frequent service on its transcontinental bus routes across northern Arizona and between Flagstaff and Phoenix; you can connect with other services to the Grand Canyon from Flagstaff or Williams. Greyhound often has special deals on bus passes and "one-way anywhere" tickets; tel. (800) 231-2222; Internet: www.greyhound.com. Overseas residents may buy a Greyhound Ameripass at a discount outside North America.

Nava-Hopi Tours offers a Flagstaff-Phoenix-Sky Harbor Airport (Phoenix) run and connects Grand Canyon National Park (South Rim) with Flagstaff and Williams. **Navajo Transit System** traverses the Navajo and Hopi Indian reservations, but it provides no connections with other bus lines in Arizona.

Local bus services are available at Grand Canyon National Park (South Rim) and Flagstaff; shuttles within the park are free, but there's a charge for ones to Tusayan or the North Rim. Have exact change ready when taking local buses.

By Train

Amtrak runs the luxury Southwest Chief daily in each direction across northern Arizona with stops at Kingman, Flagstaff, and Winslow. It connects Los Angeles with New Orleans, Orlando, Chicago, and other destinations to the east. Amtrak usually charges more than buses but has far roomier seating, as well as parlor cars and sleepers. The cost depends on availability, so advance planning, off-season travel, and luck will get you the lowest fare. Ask about "All Aboard" roundtrips, flight and train packages, and other deals.

For information and reservations, call Amtrak toll-free at (800) 872-7245 or check the excellent website at www.amtrak.com. Travel agents outside North America sell USA Railpasses.

By Air

Nearly all scheduled flights to the Grand Canyon originate in Las Vegas. A few also come from Page and Phoenix. They arrive at the Tusayan Airport, just a short drive south of Grand Canyon Village on the South Rim. No flights land on the North Rim. Passengers have the bonus of a grand overview and may also receive a narrated tour.

More than a dozen major airlines fly to Phoenix and Las Vegas. Fares and schedules tend to change frequently—a travel agent can help you find the best flights. You can also "do it yourself" on the Internet. Big-city newspapers usually run advertisements of discount fares and tours in their Sunday travel sections. You'll have the best chance of getting low fares by planning a week or more ahead and staying over a Saturday night (or any night with Southwest); roundtrip fares will almost always be a better value than one-ways, though changes may be costly.

TOURS

See your travel agent for the latest on package tours to Arizona. Within the state, local operators offer everything from quick bus jaunts to rafting trips through the Grand Canyon. Gray Line offers the largest selection of bus excursions, ranging from half a day to three days; tours leave from Phoenix, Tucson, and Flagstaff. Smaller companies offer jeep trips to scenic spots inaccessible to passenger vehicles; you'll find jeep tours available in Tusayan, Flagstaff, Monument Valley, Page, and Canyon de Chelly. You can also take "flightseeing" trips from many airports, especially at the Grand Canyon. The "Tours" sections in each chapter list tour operators; local chambers of commerce will help you, too.

Grand Canyon Field Institute

Small groups explore the Grand Canyon with day-hikes, backpacking, river-running trips, van tours, and classroom instruction. You can pick up a schedule at Grand Canyon Association bookstores in the park or write the institute at Box 399, Grand Canyon, AZ 86023, tel. (520) 638-2485, Internet: www.grandcanyon.org/fieldinstitute.

Elderhostel

This nonprofit organization offers educational adventures for people 55 and over (spouses can be younger). Many of the programs take place in Arizona, exploring archaeology, history, cultures, crafts, nature, and other topics. Participants join small groups for short-term studies and stay in simple accommodations, which helps keep costs low. For a catalog, write Elderhostel, 75 Federal Street, Boston, MA 02110-1941, tel. (617) 426-7788 or toll-free (877) 426-8056, Internet: www.elderhostel.org.

MONEY MATTERS

National Park Passes
With the Grand Canyon National Park charging a stiff $20 entry fee (good for seven days), you may be best off buying the $50 **Golden Eagle Pass,** which will get you and others in your vehicle into this or any other national park or monument in the U.S. for a 12-month period. Seniors age 62 and older who are U.S. citizens can take advantage of the $10 **Golden Age Pass,** good for a lifetime; it additionally gives a discount at many campgrounds on federal lands. Individuals who receive government benefits because of permanent disabilities should look into the lifetime **Golden Access Pass.** Drop by any national park or regional office to obtain these cards.

Taxes and Tips
The state sales tax in Arizona is five percent, but city and/or county taxes may be tacked onto that amount. Similarly, hotel/motel taxes vary from city to city, but expect roughly 10% to be added to quoted prices for accommodations. Plan to leave a 15% tip for table service at restaurants.

Foreign Currency Exchange
You can change foreign currency in Grand Canyon Village on the South Rim. ATM machines found in almost every town provide cash at good rates. Most businesses gladly cash traveler's checks in U.S. dollars.

ENTERTAINMENT AND EVENTS

Staff at Grand Canyon National Park offer a wide range of programs, such as walks, presentations, campfire talks, and children's activities on both rims. Music concerts are held oc-

VISITING GRAND CANYON NATIONAL PARK ON A SHOESTRING

The steep prices charged for park admission and services can be daunting, yet the Grand Canyon can easily be seen for little more than a song. Getting a small group together will slice costs on the entry, camping, and lodging. A $50 Golden Eagle pass will give unlimited entry to the park and all other National Park Service areas in the country for 12 months, a much better deal than forking out $20 every seven days to visit the Grand Canyon. You can camp free in the Kaibab National Forest that adjoins both the South and North Rims, though you'll need your own wheels to do this. Backpackers and cyclists can stay in cheap walk-in campgrounds at both rims. The cafeterias at Yavapai and Maswik Lodges in Grand Canyon Village offer good deals, or you can fix your own meals. And the best things—the views, sunsets, day-hikes, and interpretive programs—are free.

casionally too. Art exhibits appear in the Kolb Studio on the South Rim and at other venues. The towns of Flagstaff, Williams, and Page offer a full schedule of rodeos, parades, art festivals, historic celebrations, gem and mineral shows, and sporting events; stop by a chamber of commerce to see what's coming up.

Major Holidays
Even though it's not always mentioned in the text, many museums, tourist attractions, and services close on such holidays as Thanksgiving, Christmas, and New Year's Day; call ahead to check. Most places stay open on Easter, as it's observed mainly in churches.

New Year's Day: January 1

Martin Luther King, Jr.'s Birthday: January 15; usually observed on the third Monday in January

Presidents' Day: third Monday in February; honors Washington and Lincoln

Easter Sunday: late March or early April

Cinco de Mayo: May 5; a Mexican festival celebrated in many Southwest communities

Memorial Day: last Monday in May

Independence Day: July 4

Labor Day: first Monday in September

Columbus Day: second Monday in October

Veterans Day: November 11

Thanksgiving Day: fourth Thursday in November

Christmas Day: December 25

COMMUNICATIONS

Telephone

All telephone numbers within Arizona have a **520 area code** except the metro Phoenix area, which uses a **602 area code.** Use the area code when dialing 1+ or 0+ numbers *inside* as well as outside Arizona. To obtain a local number from Information, dial 1-411; for a number within the state, dial 1-520-555-1212 outside the metro Phoenix area and 1-602-555-1212 within the metro Phoenix area; and for a number in another state, dial 1, the area code, then 555-1212. Many airlines, auto rental firms, and motel chains have toll-free 800, 877, or 888 numbers; if you don't have the number, just dial 1-800-555-1212. Pre-paid telephone cards provide much lower costs for long-distance calls than plunking in coins or using a telephone company calling card; discount stores often have the lowest prices for the pre-paid cards.

Postal Services

You'll find **post offices** in most every town; larger cities often support several branches. Normal post office hours are Mon.-Fri. 8:30 a.m.-5 p.m. and sometimes Saturday 8:30 a.m.-noon. You can get a variety of postal information at tel. (800) 275-8777 (ASK-USPS) or Internet: www.usps.gov. A first-class letter sent to a U.S. address requires postage of 33 cents, and a postcard costs 20 cents.

For large parcels, some of the best one-stop shops for packing materials and delivery services are the mail service stores in many towns. Courier services, such as **Federal Express,** tel. (800) 463-3339, and **United Parcel Service,** tel. (800) 742-5877, will pick up packages and also maintain a network of drop-off centers; call for directions to the nearest one.

Photocopying, Faxes, Internet, and E-mail

Photocopying and fax services are available in a variety of places, though they are almost always easier to find in larger urban areas in copy shops and stores specializing in mailing services. Those types of stores are usually the cheapest and most reliable, too. In outlying areas look for signs in the windows of small mom 'n' pop markets, hardware stores, or the local drugstore.

tourist on the rim of the Grand Canyon, late 19th century

COURTESY: AISLINN RACE

Almost all public libraries offer free Internet access, but you'll probably need your own e-mail account to send or receive messages. Computer stores may provide Internet and e-mail service for a charge. Campgrounds sometimes have a telephone jack in the office that can be used by laptop owners to check their e-mail.

INFORMATION

Maps

The *Arizona Travel Map* produced by Arizona Highways magazine has excellent coverage of the state's roads; almost any tourist office will have one. The *Guide to Indian Country* map published by the Automobile Club of Southern California provides superb coverage of the Four Corners region, including the Grand Canyon and the Navajo and Hopi Indian reservations. The map is sold in stores, or AAA members can get it free from AAA offices. The *Arizona Road & Recreation Atlas* by Benchmark Maps covers the state with exceptionally beautiful, accurate, and easy-to-read maps, sold in stores both in atlas and sheet form at a 1:400,000 scale. The National Forest Service maps will be handy when traveling in the Kaibab Forest (separate maps for south and north of the Grand Canyon) and Coconino Forest (Flagstaff area); the scale is 1:126,720; they're cheapest from forest service offices, but stores also have them. For exploring the lonely Arizona Strip, the *Arizona Strip District Visitor Map* will prove essential for navigation; its scale is 1:168,960 and it is published by the Bureau of Land Management and sold at their offices and in stores. Hikers and mountain bikers will appreciate the detailed U.S.G.S. topographic maps of the region, available in a variety of scales and formats from outdoors stores.

Arizona Office of Tourism

Staff offer information on every region of the state. You can find most of their literature at other tourist offices, but this one in Phoenix has the best selection. It's on the fourth floor, set back from the street at 2702 N. Third St., Suite 4015 (Phoenix, AZ 85004); open Mon.-Fri. 8 a.m.-5 p.m.; tel. (602) 230-7733, fax 240-5475. Staff also offer information toll free at tel. (888) 520-3434 and at the Painted Cliffs Welcome Center, I-40 Exit 359 near the New Mexico border, daily 8 a.m.-5 p.m.

The excellent website www.arizonaguide.com hosts many chamber of commerce sites and contains travel tips and event listings.

Grand Canyon

Staff at the South Rim's Visitor Center and at the North Rim Visitor Center can make suggestions for visiting the park and tell you about scheduled events. *The Guide* and other publications list choices for sightseeing, hiking, and programs. The park's mailing address is Box 129, Grand Canyon, AZ 86023.

You can obtain a **weather forecast** and other recordings and reach all park offices through the **automated switchboard,** tel. (520) 638-7888. **Hearing-impaired** people can use the TDD number for park information, tel. (520) 638-7804.

For trail information and backcountry camping permits, drop by the **Backcountry Office** in the Maswik Transportation Center on the South Rim, open daily 8 a.m-noon and 1-5 p.m.; tel. (520) 638-7875. Call between 1 and 5 p.m. to speak with someone in person. The North Rim Backcountry Office near Bright Angel Point is open daily 8 a.m-noon and 1-5 p.m. May 15-Oct. 15, weather permitting; tel. (520) 638-7870.

Kaibab National Forest

The forest extends both south and north from Grand Canyon National Park, offering hiking, mountain biking, developed campgrounds, and primitive camping. The Kaibab National Forest maps show the trails and back roads; the maps are subtitled Williams and Tusayan Districts for the South Rim, North Kaibab District for the North Rim. On the South Rim, stop by the **Tusayan Ranger Station,** open Mon.-Fri. 8 a.m.-5 p.m., in the Tusayan Administrative Site, across from and 0.2 mile south of Moqui Lodge just outside the South Entrance Station; contact Box 3088, Grand Canyon, AZ 86023, tel. (520) 638-2443, Internet: www.fs.fed.us/r3/kai/.

Foresters in the **Kaibab Visitor Center** at Jacob Lake provide information on the many viewpoints, trails, campgrounds, and historic sites in the Kaibab National Forest along the North Rim; they also sell books and maps. Exhibits include a 3-D model of the Grand Canyon and wildlife displays. It's open daily 8 a.m.-5 p.m., though it may close in winter; tel. (520) 643-7298. You can also stop by the **North Kaibab Ranger District** office, open Mon.-Fri. 7 a.m.-5 p.m., for

North Rim information at 430 S. Main St. in Fredonia (Box 248, Fredonia, AZ 86022), tel. (520) 643-7395, Internet: www.fs.fed.us/r3/kai/.

Bureau of Land Management

For hiking and access information to BLM and Lake Mead National Recreation Area land on the Arizona Strip and into Utah, contact the **Interagency Visitor Center**, 345 E. Riverside Dr., St. George, UT 84790, tel. (435) 688-3246, Internet: www.azstrip.az.blm.gov. It's open Mon.-Fri. 7:45 a.m.-5 p.m. (best times for reaching someone with first-hand travel experience) and Saturday and holidays 9 a.m.-5 p.m. Take I-15 Bluff St. Exit 6 and turn southeast one-third mile; the office is on your left.

The BLM **Kanab Resource Area** office takes care of the Paria Canyon-Vermilion Cliffs Wilderness at 318 N. 100 East, Kanab, UT 84741, tel. (435) 644-2672; open Mon.-Fri. 7:45 a.m.-4:30 p.m.

Internet Sites

These offer a great deal of information. The **"Unofficial Grand Canyon National Park Home Page"** is an especially good source at www. kaibab.org. The **National Park Service** site contains visiting information and lists of rules and regulations important for backcountry hikers and river runners at www.thecanyon.com/nps/ or www.nps.gov/grca. The **Grand Canyon Chamber of Commerce** offers a good introduction to the park and links to surrounding towns at www.thecanyon.com. Or look at www.grandcanyon.com, which offers useful information as well as helpful links to the National Park Service and other government organizations, trip planning, books, videos, and maps. Over at **Glen Canyon National Recreation Area,** www.page-lakepowell.com lets you know about visiting Lake Powell and the town of Page. In north-central Arizona, the **Flagstaff Chamber of Commerce** at www.flagstaff.az.us/ and **Flagstaff Guide** at www.flagguide.com will fill you in on the sights and services there with links to nearby towns and recreation areas.

Arizona Highways at www.arizhwys.com offers some of the same beautiful photos, travel infor-

mation, hikes, and entertaining stories found in its magazine pages. You'll find lots of hiking and other outdoor information at **Great Outdoor Recreation Pages** site www.gorp.com/gorp/location/az/az.htm including national forests and wilderness areas. If you're interested in learning about the desert, check **Desert USA's** www.desertusa.com for places to visit and what plants and animals you might meet there. **Adventure in Hiking** at www.swlink.net/~ttidyman/hiking/index.htm features trails, hiking news, links, clubs, and Grand Canyon information.

WEIGHTS AND MEASURES

The Metric System

Except for the nutritional information labels on packaged food and beverages, the metric system is just about nonexistent in the United States. For help converting from the modified English measuring system used in the U.S., consult the conversion table at the back of this book.

Time

Travelers in Arizona should remember that the state is on Mountain Standard Time all year, except for the Navajo Reservation, which goes on daylight saving time by adding one hour from April to October to keep in step with its Utah and New Mexico sections. Note that the Hopi Reservation, completely within Arizona and surrounded by the Navajo Reservation, stays on standard time year-round along with the rest of the state. In summer, Arizona runs on the same time as California and Nevada, and one hour behind Utah, Colorado, and New Mexico. In winter, Arizona is one hour ahead of California and Nevada, on the same time as Utah, Colorado, and New Mexico.

Electricity

Electric current in the U.S. is 110-120 volts, 60-cycle; appliances manufactured for use in Asian and European countries may need an adapter to operate safely outside their typical system of 220-240 volt, 50-cycle current, as well as a plug adapter for the flat two-pin style of the U.S. plug.

APPENDIX

MORE ACCOMMODATIONS IN THE GATEWAY CITIES
FLAGSTAFF MOTELS AND HOTELS

Rates listed below apply in summer but can be higher on holidays or during special events. Lodgings are grouped by weekend rates, often substantially higher than during the week. For other types of accommodations see pages 157-159.

BUDGET TO INEXPENSIVE MOTELS: UNDER $60
SOUTH AND WEST OF DOWNTOWN

Economy Inn is near NAU at 224 S. Mikes Pike, tel. (520) 774-8888, $32 d ($49-59 d Fri.-Sat.).

Crystal Inn features an indoor pool and a spa near NAU at 602 W. Route 66, tel. (520) 774-4581 or (800) 654-4667, $34-49 d ($50 d and up Fri.-Sat.).

Saga Budget Host has a pool at 820 W. Route 66, tel. (520) 779-3631 or (800) BUD-HOST, $38 s, $46 d all week.

Hidden Village has an indoor pool at 822 W. Route 66, tel. (520) 774-1443, $30 d ($45 d Fri.-Sat.).

Arizonan Motel is near NAU at 910 S. Milton Rd., tel. (520) 774-7171, $38 s, $46 d ($42 s, $54 d Fri.-Sat.).

Autolodge is a good value in this part of town at 1313 S. Milton Rd., tel. (520) 774-6621, $28-36 d ($36-69 d Fri.-Sat.).

Motel 6 Woodlands has a pool at 2745 S. Woodlands Village Blvd., tel. (520) 779-3757 or (800) 4MOTEL6, $38 s, $44 d ($44 s, $50 d Fri.-Sat.).

EAST OF DOWNTOWN

"Budget Row" features the best selection in town of bargain places. You can try:

Snowbowl Motel, 618 E. Route 66, tel. (520) 774-4877, $28 s, $34 d ($50 s, $56 d Fri.-Sat.).

Whispering Winds Motel, most with kitchenettes, at 922 E. Route 66, tel. (520) 774-7391, $32-48 d ($38-62 d Fri.-Sat.).

Relax Inn Motel, 1500 E. Route 66, tel. (520) 779-4469, $23 s, $25-36 d ($60 d Fri.-Sat.).

Western Hills Motel, with a pool and Asian Gourmet Restaurant, at 1580 E. Route 66, tel. (520) 774-6633, $30 s, $35 d ($40 s, $45 d Fri.-Sat.).

Chalet Lodge, 1990 E. Route 66, tel. (520) 774-2779, $25-30 d ($35-45 d Fri.-Sat.).

Wonderland Motel, 2000 E. Route 66, tel. (520) 779-6119, $20 s, $22 d ($30 d Fri.-Sat.).

Twilite Motel, 2010 E. Route 66, tel. (520) 774-3364, $25-35 d ($35-55 d Fri.-Sat.).

Timberline Motel with some kitchenettes at 2040 E. Route 66, tel. (520) 774-7481, $20 s, $24 d ($32-42 s, $42-48 d Fri.-Sat.).

66 Motel also has weekly kitchenettes at 2100 E. Route 66, tel. (520) 774-6403, $20 s, $22 d ($28 d Fri.-Sat.).

Royal Inn, 2140 E. Route 66, tel. (520) 774-7308, $25-55 d ($35-75 d Fri.-Sat.).

Flagstaff Motel, 2204 E. Route 66, tel. (520) 774-0280, $20 s, $22 d ($25 s, $27 d Fri.-Sat.).

Alpine Motel, 2226 E. Route 66, tel. (520) 779-3136, $15 s, $19 d ($18 s, $25 d Fri.-Sat.).

Pine Crest Motel with some kitchenettes at 2818 E. Route 66, tel. (520) 526-1950, $25 s, $30 d ($35 s, $39 d Fri.-Sat.).

Carousel Inn Motel, 2918 E. Route 66, tel. (520) 526-3595, $25-28 d ($50-68 d Fri.-Sat.).

Geronimo Motel, 3100 E. Route 66, tel. (520) 527-3377, $30 d ($40 d Fri.-Sat.).

(continues on next page)

BUTLER AVENUE AREA (I-40 EXIT 198)

Motel 6 Butler Avenue has a pool at 2010 E. Butler Ave., tel. (520) 774-1801 or (800) 4MOTEL6, $40 s, $46 d ($44 s, $50 d Fri.-Sat.).

Super 8 has a pool and sauna at 2285 E. Butler Ave., tel. (520) 774-1821 or (800) 962-8695, $49 s, $55 d all week.

Motel 6 has a pool at 2440 E. Lucky Lane, tel. (520) 774-8756 or (800) 4MOTEL6, $38 s, $44 d all week.

Motel 6 nearby also has a pool at 2500 E. Lucky Lane, tel. (520) 779-6184 or (800) 4MOTEL6, $38 s, $44 d all week.

TraveLodge on Lucky Lane includes a pool and spa at 2520 E. Lucky Lane, tel. (520) 779-5121 or (800) 578-7878, $35-45 d ($58-65 d Fri.-Sat.).

MODERATE MOTELS: $60-85

SOUTH AND WEST OF DOWNTOWN

The Inn at NAU puts you in the heart of the campus with large rooms and fine dining; students operate the facilities under the School of Hotel and Restaurant Management; tel. (520) 523-1616; Internet: www.nau.edu/~hrm; $69 d ($79 d Fri.-Sat.) including breakfast.

Townhouse Motel offers a very central (and noisy) location at 122 W. Route 66, tel. (520) 774-5081, $26 d ($65-75 d Fri.-Sat.).

University TraveLodge features two spas, a sauna, and family suites at 801 W. Route 66, tel. (520) 774-3381 or (888) 259-4404, $40-56 s, $50-70 d ($60-66 s, $70-80 d Fri.-Sat.).

Days Inn offers a pool and a cafeteria-style restaurant (breakfast and dinner) at 1000 W. Route 66, tel. (520) 774-5221 or (800) 329-7466, $63 d ($80 d Fri.-Sat.).

Family Inn is at 121 S. Milton Rd., tel. (520) 774-8820, $30-32 d ($60-70 d Fri.-Sat.).

Highland Country Inn sits near NAU at 223 S. Milton, tel. (520) 774-5041, $35-99 d all week.

Rodeway Inn West offers a pool and spa near NAU at 913 S. Milton Rd., tel. (520) 774-5038 or (800) 228-2000, $39-79 d ($69-79 d Fri.-Sat.).

Comfort Inn has a pool near NAU at 914 S. Milton Rd., tel. (520) 774-7326 or (800) 221-2222, $69-79 d ($79-89 d Fri.-Sat.).

Sleep Inn features an indoor pool and spa at 2765 S. Woodlands Village Blvd., tel. (520) 556-3000, $69 s, $74 d, $84 d in a mini-suite.

Econo Lodge West has a pool and two spas at 2355 S. Beulah Blvd., tel. (520) 774-2225 or (800) 553-2666, $69 d ($79 d Fri.-Sat.).

Ramada Ltd. Suites features a pool, sauna, and exercise room and rooms with microwaves and refrigerators at 2755 S. Woodlands Village Blvd., tel. (520) 773-1111 or (800) 2-RAMADA, $59-69 d ($79-89 d Fri.-Sat.).

EAST OF DOWNTOWN

Inn Suites features a pool and rooms with microwave and refrigerator (the most expensive rooms also have a jacuzzi and kitchenette) at 1008 E. Route 66, tel. (520) 774-7356 or (800) 898-9124, $69-109 d ($74-139 d Fri.-Sat.).

King's House Motel (Best Western) offers a pool and some suites at 1560 E. Route 66, tel. (520) 774-7186 or (800) 528-1234, $63-100 d all week.

Pony Soldier Motel (Best Western) includes an indoor pool, spa, and restaurant at 3030 E. Route 66, tel. (520) 526-2388 or (800) 356-4143, $69-89 d all week.

Howard Johnson Inn has the Crown Railroad Restaurant at 3300 E. Route 66, tel. (520) 526-1826 or (800) 437-7137, $69 d all week.

Days Inn East has an indoor pool and a spa at 3601 E. Lockett Rd., tel. (520) 527-1477 or (800) 446-6900, $49-89 d ($79-139 d Fri.-Sat.).

Super 8 is at 3725 Kaspar Ave., tel. (520) 526-0818 or (888) 324-9131, $69 s, $74 d all week.

EXPENSIVE TO LUXURY MOTELS AND HOTELS: $85 AND UP

DOWNTOWN

Comfi Cottages of Flagstaff all have kitchens, 1612 N. Aztec St., tel. (520) 774-0731 or (888) 774-0731; Internet: www.virtualflagstaff.com/comfi; $95 d to $195 for up to six guests.

SOUTH AND WEST OF DOWNTOWN

Radisson Woodlands Hotel offers a pool, indoor and outdoor spas, sauna, and exercise room at 1175 W. Route 66, tel. (520) 773-8888 or (800) 333-3333, $109 d ($119 d Fri.-Sat.).

Starlite Motel has a location near NAU at 500 S. Milton Rd., tel. (520) 774-7301 or (800) 843-5644, $35 s, $37 d ($84-95 s, $89-99 d Fri.-Sat.).

Embassy Suites Hotel has a pool and spa near NAU at 706 S. Milton Rd., tel. (520) 774-4333 or (800) EMBASSY, $121 s, $131 d ($125 s, $135 d Fri.-Sat.).

Quality Inn offers a pool at 2000 S. Milton Rd., tel. (520) 774-8771 or (800) 228-5151, $69-89 d ($75-115 d Fri.-Sat.).

Fairfield Inn by Marriott has a pool at 2005 S. Milton Rd., tel. (520) 773-1300 or (800) 228-2800, $79 d ($85 d Fri.-Sat.).

Hampton Inn & Suites features an indoor pool and spa at 2400 S. Beulah Blvd., tel. (520) 913-0900 or (800) HAMPTON, $89 d ($99 d Fri.-Sat.), jacuzzi rooms cost $10 extra.

AmeriSuites includes an indoor pool, spa and rooms with microwave and refrigerator at 2455 S. Beulah Blvd., tel. (520) 774-8042 or (800) 833-1516, $95-139 d ($105-149 d Fri.-Sat.).

Arizona Mountain Inn nestles in the pines about three miles southeast of downtown at 685 Lake Mary Rd., tel. (520) 774-8959 or (800) 239-5236, $80-110 d rooms (breakfast is $10 per couple extra) and $75 d rustic cabins ($125 d Fri.-Sat.).

EAST OF DOWNTOWN

Hampton Inn offers an indoor pool and spa at 3501 E. Lockett Rd., tel. (520) 526-1885 or (800) HAMPTON, $89 d ($99 d Fri.-Sat.).

Residence Inn by Marriott includes a pool, spa, airport shuttle, and nearby golf at 3440 N. Country Club Dr., tel. (520) 526-5555 or (800) 331-3131, $159 d studio or $199 two-bedroom, all week.

Mountain Country Management & Realty has furnished condos of one to four bedrooms in the Continental Country Club area, 2380 N. Oakmont Dr. (office), tel. (520) 526-4287 or (800) 424-7748, $100-250 per day or you can arrange weekly or monthly stays.

BUTLER AVENUE AREA (I-40 EXIT 198)

Howard Johnson Hotel features an indoor pool and spa in an atrium and a game room at 2200 E. Butler Ave., tel. (520) 779-6944 or (800) 446-4656, $69 d ($89 d Fri.-Sat.), fireplace suites $10 extra.

Little America offers a pool, restaurant, and coffee shop at 2515 E. Butler Ave., tel. (520) 779-2741 or (800) 352-4386, $109-119 d rooms and $135-225 d suites, all week.Holiday Inn features suites, indoor/outdoor pool, and spa at 2320 E. Lucky Lane, tel. (520) 526-1150 or (800) 465-4329, $99 d ($109 d Fri.-Sat.).

Ramada Limited has suites and a pool at 2350 E. Lucky Lane, tel. (520) 779-3614 or (800) 2RAMADA, $69-95 d suites ($150 d suites Fri.-Sat.).

Econo Lodge Lucky Lane includes an indoor pool and spa at 2480 E. Lucky Lane, tel. (520) 774-7701 or (888) 349-2523, $39-89 d ($89-119 d Fri.-Sat.).

WILLIAMS MOTELS AND HOTELS

The following prices were quoted on a somewhat slow summer weekend; they could rise if things get busy.For other types of accommodations see pages 174-175.

BUDGET: UNDER $35

9 Arizona, 315 W. Route 66, tel. (520) 635-4552, $23-35 s, $28-45 d.

Arizona Welcome Inn & Suites, 750 N. Grand Canyon Blvd. off I-40 Exit 163, tel. (520) 635-9127 or (800) 826-4152, $32 d, $75 d suites.

American Inn, 134 E. Route 66, tel. (520) 635-4591 or (888) 635-4591, $25 s, $28 d.

The Downtowner Motel, 201 E. Route 66, tel. (520) 635-4041 or (800) 798-0071, $30 s, $35 d.

Grand Motel/Gateway Motel, 219 E. Route 66, tel. (520) 635-4601, $35 d.

INEXPENSIVE: $35-60

Norris Motel, 1001 W. Route 66, tel. (520) 635-2202 or (800) 341-8000, $50 s, $55 d.

Motel 6, 831 W. Route 66, tel. (520) 635-9000 or (800) 466-8356, $54 s, $60 d.

Countryside Inn, 710 W. Route 66, tel. (520) 635-4464 or (800) 733-4814, $39 s, $49 d.

Budget Host Inn, 620 W. Route 66, tel. (520) 635-4415 or (800) 745-4415, $40-49 d.

Highlander Motel, 533 W. Route 66, tel. (520) 635-2541 or (800) 800-8288, $44 s, $48 d.

Westerner Motel, 530 W. Route 66, tel. (520) 635-4312 or (800) 385-8608, $45 d.

Mountain Country Lodge, 437 W. Route 66, tel. (520) 635-4341, $36 s, $38 d.

Howard Johnson Express Inn, 511 N. Grand Canyon Blvd. off I-40 Exit 163, tel. (520) 635-9561 or (800) 720-6614, $49 s, $59 d.

Route 66 Inn, 128 E. Route 66, tel. (520) 635-4791 or (888) 786-6956, $50 d.

Econo Lodge, 302 E. Route 66, tel. (520) 635-4085, $40 s, $45 d.

Courtesy Inn, 344 E. Route 66, tel. (520) 635-2619, $39 s, $45 d.

TraveLodge, 430 E. Route 66, tel. (520) 635-2651 or (800) 578-7878, $55 d.

El Rancho Motel, 617 E. Route 66, tel. (520) 635-2552 or (800) 228-2370, $52-57 d.

Super 8, 2001 E. Route 66 near I-40 Exit 165, tel. (520) 635-4700 or (800) 800-8000, $54 d.

MODERATE: $60-85

Days Inn, 2488 W. Route 66 near I-40 Exit 161, tel. (520) 635-4051, $62 d.

Comfort Inn, 911 W. Route 66, tel. (520) 635-4045, $68 d.

Fairfield Inn by Marriott, 1029 N. Grand Canyon Blvd. near I-40 Exit 163, tel. (520) 635-9888 or (800) 228-2800, $79 d.

Holiday Inn, 950 N. Grand Canyon Blvd. near I-40 Exit 163, tel. (520) 635-4114, $79 d.

Ramada Inn, 642 E. Route 66, tel. (520) 635-4431 or (800) 462-9381, $75 d.

MODERATE: $60-85

Quality Inn Mountain Ranch has a meadow and forest setting seven miles east, just south of I-40 Exit 171; it offers two restaurants, pool, tennis, and seasonal horseback riding; tel. (520) 635-2693 or (800) 228-5151, $85 d.

EXPENSIVE TO PREMIUM: $85-150

Best Western Inn of Williams, 2600 W. Route 66 near I-40 Exit 161, tel. (520) 635-4400 or (800) 635-4445, $99 d.

Fray Marcos Hotel, downtown at Grand Canyon Railway Depot, tel. (520) 635-4010 or (800) 843-8724, $119 d.

BOOKLIST

DESCRIPTION AND TRAVEL

Annerino, John. *Adventuring in Arizona.* San Francisco: Sierra Club Books, 1996. True to its name, this excellent guide lists back-road driving tours, hiking trails, river trips, and climbing routes through the state's most spectacular country. Includes history and travel tips.

Arizona Highways. 2039 W. Lewis Ave., Phoenix, AZ 85009, tel. (602) 258-1000 or (800) 543-5432, Internet: www.arizhwys.com. Published monthly, this outstanding magazine features superb color photography with articles on the state's history, people, places, wildlife, back roads, hiking, and humor.

Babbitt, Bruce, ed. *Grand Canyon: An Anthology.* Flagstaff: Northland Publishing, 1978. Twenty-three authors from the days of the Spanish to the present relate their experiences of the Grand Canyon.

Casey, Robert L. *Journey to the High Southwest.* Chester, CT: Globe Pequot Press, 1997. The author presents travel experiences and advice for southern Utah and adjacent Arizona, New Mexico, and Colorado.

Fishbein, Seymour L. *Grand Canyon Country: Its Majesty and Its Lore.* (National Geographic Park Profiles) Random House, 1997. Incredible color photography illustrates fine text.

Halper, Evan, and Paul Karr. *Hostels U.S.A.* Old Saybrook, CT: The Globe Pequot Press, 1998. A comprehensive guide to hostelling with an introduction and listings; it also covers some of Canada. Descriptions give a feel for the atmosphere of each place.

Houk, Rose. *The Peaks.* Phoenix: Arizona Highways, 1994. Text and photos capture the beauty and character of the San Francisco Peaks and the land and towns that surround them.

Klinck, Richard E. *Land of Room Enough and Time Enough.* Peregrine Smith Books, 1958, 1984. The geography, legends, and people of Monument Valley.

Kosik, Fran. *Native Roads: The Complete Motoring Guide to the Navajo and Hopi Nations.* Flagstaff: Creative Solutions Publishing, 1996. Many historic photos illustrate this guide to the Navajo and Hopi lands and the surrounding area.

Leydet, Francois. *Time and the River Flowing: Grand Canyon.* New York: Sierra Club-Ballantine Books, 1968. Essays on and color photos of the Grand Canyon.

Rees, Lucy. *The Maze, A Desert Journey.* Tucson: The University of Arizona Press, 1996. A contemporary Welsh woman explores the wilderness of Arizona on horseback from the Verde Valley to the Hopi mesas.

Story Behind the Scenery series: *Grand Canyon; Grand Canyon-North Rim; Glen Canyon-Lake Powell; Rainbow Bridge; Canyon de Chelly; Petrified Forest; Lake Mead & Hoover Dam.* Las Vegas: KC Publications. Beautiful color photos highlight the text in each of these magazine-format titles.

Wallace, Robert. *The Grand Canyon.* The American Wilderness Series. New York: Time-Life Books. A well-illustrated book covering the Canyon with excellent photography by Ernst Haas.

HIKING AND BICYCLING

Adkison, Ron. *Hiking the Grand Canyon National Park.* Helena, MT: Falcon Press, 1997. Detailed descriptions, elevation profiles, and maps cover the most popular trails, along with a good introduction.

Aitchison, Stewart. *A Naturalist's Guide to Hiking the Grand Canyon*. New York: Prentice Hall, 1985. The author introduces you to Canyon climate, geology, "critters," and plants, then guides you on 30 hikes. Good maps.

Annerino, John. *Hiking the Grand Canyon*. A Sierra Club Totebook. San Francisco: Sierra Club Books, 1993. Easily the most comprehensive guide to trails and routes within the canyon. A long introduction provides background on geology, natural history, Indians, and hike planning. The large fold-out topo map clearly shows trails and routes. Riverrunners will be pleased to find a section of trail descriptions beginning at the water's edge.

Butchart, Harvey. *Grand Canyon Treks*. Spotted Dog Press, 1998. This book combines the texts of legendary Grand Canyon hiker and explorer Harvey Butchart's three earlier guides, originally published in the 1970s and 1980s by La Siesta Press. It's a great source of ideas for off-trail hikes and climbs.

Fletcher, Colin. *The Man Who Walked through Time*. New York: Random House, 1989. Well-written adventure tale of Fletcher's two-month solo hike through the Grand Canyon. Fletcher was the first to travel its length within the park on foot.

Kals, W.S. *Land Navigation Handbook*. San Francisco: Sierra Club Books, 1983. After reading this book you'll be able to explore Arizona's vast backcountry with confidence. This handy pocket-guide not only offers details on using map and compass, but tells how to navigate using the sun, the stars, and an altimeter.

Kelsey, Michael R. *Canyon Hiking Guide to the Colorado Plateau*. Treasure Chest Publications, 1995. One of the best guides to hiking in the canyon country, with descriptions and maps for destinations in Arizona, Utah, and Colorado. Geologic cross-sections show the formations you'll walk through. The author uses the metric system, but the book is otherwise easy to follow.

Kelsey, Michael R. *Hiking and Exploring the Paria River*. Treasure Chest Publications, 1997. The classic Paria Canyon hike, with information on nearby Bryce Canyon and other geologically colorful areas. Includes histories of John D. Lee, ghost towns, ranches, and mining.

Mangum, Richard K., and Sherry G. Mangum. *Flagstaff Hikes*. Flagstaff: Hexagon Press, 1998. This comprehensive guide, now in its fourth edition, describes hiking trails surrounding Flagstaff.

Mangum, Richard K., and Sherry G. Mangum. *Williams Guidebook*. Flagstaff: Hexagon Press, 1998. Not many people know about the beautiful country surrounding this town south of the Grand Canyon. Most of the book has been devoted to hikes, but you'll also find local history and visitors' information.

Ray, Cosmic. *Fat Tire Tales and Trails*. Flagstaff: self-published, 1998. "Lots of way cool mountain-bike rides around Arizona . . . both summer and winter fun."

Steck, George. *Grand Canyon Loop Hikes I*. Evergreen, CO: Chockstone Press, 1989. These long trips all involve extensive off-trail hiking with difficult route finding, cliffs, and major changes in elevation. Experienced Grand Canyon hikers who are well-conditioned and mentally prepared can plan adventurous outings with the detailed descriptions.

Steck, George. *Grand Canyon Loop Hikes II*. Evergreen, CO: Chockstone Press, 1997. This newer and larger book offers additional challenging loops.

Thybony, Scott. *Official Guide to Hiking the Grand Canyon*. Grand Canyon Association, 1994. Introduction and guide to the best-known trails of the Grand Canyon.

Tighe, Kelly and Susan Moran. *On the Arizona Trail: A Guide for Hikers, Cyclists, & Equestrians*. Boulder, CO: Pruett Publishing, 1998. The first guidebook to the Arizona Trail takes you all the way from Mexico to Utah with detailed descriptions. New trail sections continue to be constructed, so you'll need to check for the latest conditions, yet this book makes a great place to start planning your trip.

Warren, Scott S. *Exploring Arizona's Wild Areas; A Guide for Hikers, Backpackers, Climbers, X-C Skiers, & Paddlers.* Seattle: The Mountaineers, 1996. Although the author covers only the designated wildernesses, the 87 described will keep you busy for a long time.

Waterman, Laura, and Guy Waterman. *Backwoods Ethics: Environmental Issues for Hikers and Campers.* Stone Wall Press, 1994. Thoughtful commentaries on how hikers can explore the wilderness with minimal impact. Case histories dramatize the need to protect the environment.

RIVER-RUNNING AND BOATING

Abbey, Edward. *Down the River.* New York: E.P. Dutton, 1991. Abbey expresses joy and concern in a series of thoughtful, witty, and wide-ranging essays on the American West.

Belknap, Buzz. *Grand Canyon River Guide.* Westwater Books, 1990. Covers the 288 miles of Colorado River through Marble and Grand Canyons between Lees Ferry and Lake Mead.

Crumbo, Kim. *A River Runner's Guide to the History of the Grand Canyon.* Boulder: Johnson Books, 1981. Highly readable guide with a foreword by Edward Abbey.

Kelsey, Michael R. *Boater's Guide to Lake Powell.* Treasure Chest Publications, 1991. This comprehensive guide will help you explore the lake, whether traveling in a small inflatable raft, as the author did, or a more luxurious craft. Includes many maps, photos, and hiking descriptions.

Ryan, Kathleen Jo (photographer and producer). *Writing Down the River: Into the Heart of the Grand Canyon.* Flagstaff: Northland Publishing, 1998. Fifteen of today's best female

writers tell of their experiences in the Grand Canyon. Impressive color photos illustrate the pages.

Simmons, George C., and David L. Gaskill. *River Runner's Guide to the Canyons of the Green and Colorado Rivers: With Emphasis on Geologic Features, Vol. III.* Flagstaff: Northland Publishing, 1969. This volume covers Marble Canyon and Grand Canyon. It's the only river guidebook to describe the fascinating geology mile by mile through the Grand Canyon National Park.

Stephens, Hal G., and Eugene M. Shoemaker. *In the Footsteps of John Wesley Powell: An Album of Comparative Photographs of the Green and Colorado Rivers, 1871-72 and 1968.* Boulder: Johnson Books and The Powell Society, 1987. Fascinating photo album of identical river views snapped nearly 100 years apart. Photos show how little—and how much—the forces of erosion, plants, and human beings have changed the Green and Colorado River Canyons. The text describes geologic features of each of the 110 pairs of photos. Maps show locations of camera stations.

Stevens, Larry. *The Colorado River in Grand Canyon: A Comprehensive Guide to Its Natural and Human History.* Flagstaff: Red Lake Books, 1998. The introduction and maps guide you from Lees Ferry to Lake Mead with descriptions of geology, Indian history, exploration, flora, and fauna.

HISTORY

Cline, Platt. *They Came to the Mountain: The Story of Flagstaff's Beginnings.* Flagstaff: Northern Arizona University with Northland Publishing, 1976. A highly readable account of Flagstaff's founding and early years. The author has completed his trilogy on the area that began with *Mountain Town: Flagstaff's First Century* (1994) and *Mountain Campus: The Story of Northern Arizona University* (1983).

Coolidge, Dane. *Arizona Cowboys.* Tucson: University of Arizona Press, 1984. Working the range in the early 1900s.

Crampton, C. Gregory. *Land of Living Rock.* New York: Alfred A. Knopf, Inc., 1972, 1985. Story of the geology, Indians, early explorers, and settlers of the high plateaus in Arizona, Utah, and Nevada. Well-illustrated with color and black-and-white photos, maps, and diagrams.

Crampton, C. Gregory. *Standing Up Country.* New York: Alfred A. Knopf, Inc., 1964, 1983. Illustrated historical account of the people who came to the canyon lands of Arizona and Utah—Indians, explorers, outlaws, miners, settlers, and scientists.

Dellenbaugh, Frederick S. *A Canyon Voyage: A Narrative of the Second Powell Expedition Down the Green-Colorado River from Wyoming, and the Expeditions on Land, in the Years 1871 and 1872.* Tucson: University of Arizona Press, reprinted 1984. Dellenbaugh served as artist and assistant topographer on the expedition.

Howard, Kathleen L. and Diana F. Pardu. *Inventing the Southwest: The Fred Harvey Company and Native American Art.* Flagstaff: Northland Publishing, 1996. Illustrated history of how the partnership of the Santa Fe Railroad and Fred Harvey Company brought America and the Southwest Indians together. An optional CD-ROM has additional multimedia material.

Hughes, J. Donald. *In the House of Stone and Light.* Grand Canyon Association, 1978. A well-illustrated history of the Grand Canyon from the early Indians to the modern park.

Lavender, David. *River Runners of the Grand Canyon.* Tucson: University of Arizona Press, 1985. Descriptions of action-packed adventures on the river, beginning with Powell's trip in 1869 through the closing of Glen Canyon Dam in the early 1960s.

Lummis, Charles F. *Some Strange Corners of Our Country.* Tucson: University of Arizona Press, 1891, 1892, reprinted in 1989. Step back a century to visit the Southwest's Indian country, Grand Canyon, Petrified Forest, and Montezuma Castle.

Pattie, James Ohio. *The Personal Narrative of James O. Pattie.* Missoula, MT: Mountain Press Publishing Co., 1988. Reprint of 1831 edition. An early fur trapper, who claimed to be the first white American to see the Grand Canyon, tells of his experiences in the wild lands of the West during the 1820s.

Powell, J.W. *The Exploration of the Colorado River and Its Canyons.* Mineola, NY: Dover Publications, reprinted 1961 and Penguin USA, reprinted 1997. Powell relates the story of his epic 1869 expedition—the first running of the Colorado River through the Grand Canyon—along with a description of the Grand Canyon and travels in the region. His encounters with Indian cultures provide a glimpse of their traditional ways.

Rusho, W.L., and C. Gregory Crampton. *Lees Ferry: Desert River Crossing.* Salt Lake City: Cricket Productions, 1992. A historical study of Lees Ferry, with over 135 rare and unusual photographs.

ARCHAEOLOGY

Ambler, J. Richard. *The Anasazi: Prehistoric Peoples of the Four Corners Region.* Flagstaff: Museum of Northern Arizona, 1977, 1983. One of the best overviews of the ancestral pueblo people's history.

Grant, Campbell. *Canyon de Chelly: Its People and Rock Art.* Tucson: University of Arizona Press, 1978. The author describes the geology, archaeology, and history of the canyons. Nearly half the well-illustrated text is devoted to a discussion of the wealth of petroglyphs and pictographs left by the ancestral pueblo people, Hopi, and Navajo.

Lister, Robert, and Florence Lister. *Those Who Came Before: Southwestern Archaeology in the National Park System.* Tucson: University of Arizona Press, 1983 and Albuquerque: University of New Mexico Press, 1994. A well-illustrated guide to the history, artifacts, and ruins of prehistoric Indian cultures in the Southwest. Includes descriptions of the parks and monuments that contain these sites today.

McGregor, John C. *Southwestern Archaeology.* Champaign: University of Illinois Press, 1982. If you're curious why archaeologists like their work and how they do it, this book presents the motivations and techniques of this special group of scientists. It also describes cultures and artifacts from the earliest known peoples to the present.

Noble, David Grant. *Ancient Ruins of the Southwest.* Flagstaff: Northland Publishing, 1991. A well-illustrated guide to the prehistoric ruins of Arizona, New Mexico, Colorado, and Utah.

Oppelt, Norman T. *Guide to Prehistoric Ruins of the Southwest.* Boulder: Pruett Publishing Co., 1989. An introduction to ancient cultures with descriptions of more than 200 sites in Arizona, New Mexico, Colorado, and Utah.

Patterson, Alex. *A Field Guide to Rock Art Symbols of the Greater Southwest.* Boulder: Johnson Books, 1992. A dictionary-style guide to petroglyphs and pictographs grouped by subject with many illustrations.

Viele, Catherine. *Voices in the Canyon.* Tucson: Southwest Parks and Monuments Assoc., 1980. Highly readable and well-illustrated book about the ancestral pueblo people and their villages of Betatakin, Keet Seel, and Inscription House in northeastern Arizona.

ARIZONA INDIANS OF TODAY

Courlander, Harold. *Hopi Voices: Recollections, Traditions, and Narratives of the Hopi Indians.* Albuquerque: University of New Mexico Press, 1982. A selection of 74 Hopi narratives explaining their mythology, history, exploits, games, and animal stories. One of the best books on Hopi culture.

Courlander, Harold. *The Fourth World of the Hopis: The Epic Story of the Hopi Indians as Preserved in Their Legends & Traditions.* Albuquerque: University of New Mexico Press, 1987.

Dedera, Don. *Navajo Rugs: How to Find, Evaluate, Buy and Care for Them.* Flagstaff: Northland Publishing, 1996. A history of Navajo weaving, including regional styles and practical advice.

Dittert, Alfred, Jr., and Fred Plog. *Generations in Clay: Pueblo Pottery of the American Southwest.* Flagstaff: Northland Publishing, 1980. An introduction to the pottery of the Pueblo Indians, both prehistoric and modern. Well-illustrated with black-and-white and color photos.

Dozier, Edward P. *Hano, A Tewa Indian Community in Arizona.* Orlando: Holt, Rinehart and Winston, 1966. A study of Tewa history, society, religion, and livelihood.

Dyk, Walter (recorded by). *Left Handed Son of Old Man Hat: A Navajo Autobiography.* Lincoln: University of Nebraska Press, 1995, original copyright 1938. This Navajo relates his story of growing up in the late 1800s.

Gillmore, Frances, and Louisa Wetherill. *Traders to the Navajos.* Albuquerque: University of New Mexico Press, 1934, 1983. The Wetherills lived in and explored the Monument Valley region, trading with the Navajo. The authors tell stories about lost mines, early travelers, and the Navajo people.

Gilpin, Laura. *The Enduring Navajo.* Austin: University of Texas Press, 1994. An excellent book of photographs of the Navajo people, their homes, land, ceremonies, crafts, tribal government, and trading posts.

Jacka, Lois Essary and Jerry Jacka. *Art of the Hopi, Contemporary Journeys on Ancient Pathways.* Flagstaff: Northland Publishing, 1998. Beautiful color photos on almost every page of this large-format book show the skills, versatility, and variety of Hopi artists.

James, Harry C. *Pages from Hopi History.* Tucson: University of Arizona Press, 1974. Beginning with the tribe's mythical entrance into this world, the author traces Hopi history through early migrations, encounters with the Spanish, difficulties with Mexicans and Navajo, resistance to U.S. authority, to their lives today.

Locke, Raymond F. *The Book of the Navajo.* Holloway House Publishing, 1992. Navajo legends, art, culture, and history, from early to modern times.

Luckert, Karl W. *Coyoteway: A Navajo Holyway Healing Ceremonial.* Tucson: The University of Arizona Press and Flagstaff: Museum of Northern Arizona Press, 1979. A rare look at an important Navajo ceremony. It requires nine days and involves chanting, fire-making, sand painting, and other rituals. Photos and chant translations provide a peek into intricate Navajo beliefs.

Page, Susanne, and Jake Page. *Hopi.* New York: Harry N. Abrams, Inc., 1982 and Abradale Press, 1994. The authors record Hopi spiritual life in text and large color photos, revealing aspects of everyday living, ceremonies, and sacred places rarely seen by outsiders.

Simmons, Leo, ed. *Sun Chief: The Autobiography of a Hopi Indian.* New Haven: Yale University Press, 1963. A Hopi tells of his experiences growing up in both the Hopi and Anglo worlds, then returning to traditional ways.

Suntracks, Larry Evers. *Hopi Photographers/Hopi Images.* Tucson: University of Arizona Press, 1983. The pages feature photography of the Hopi from 1880 to 1980, including historic photos by Anglos and modern work by Hopi photographers; photos appear in black-and-white and color.

Titiev, Mischa. *Old Oraibi: A Study of the Hopi Indians of Third Mesa.* Albuquerque: University of New Mexico Native American Studies,

1992. Detailed account of Hopi society and ceremonies.

Wright, Barton. *Hopi Kachinas: The Complete Guide to Collecting Kachina Dolls.* Flagstaff: Northland Publishing, 1985. The author explains and illustrates the wide variety of dolls— from clowns to ogres.

Wright, Barton. *Clowns of the Hopi.* Flagstaff: Northland Publishing, 1994. These characters amuse audiences while protecting traditions. The book provides explanations, including the deeper meanings of the clown's antics, with drawings and historic and modern photos.

Wright, Margaret. *Hopi Silver.* Flagstaff: Northland Publishing, 1998. History and examples of Hopi silversmithing.

Yava, Albert. *Big Falling Snow.* Albuquerque: University of New Mexico Press, 1992. A Tewa-Hopi discusses the history and traditions of the Tewa and Hopi, including conflicts with missionaries and government officials who tried to Americanize the tribes.

Zolbrod, Paul G. *Diné bahanè: The Navajo Creation Story.* Albuquerque: University of New Mexico Press, 1988. Deities, people, and animals come to life in this translation of Navajo mythology.

NATURAL SCIENCES

Arnberger, Leslie P., and Jeanne R. Janish. *Flowers of the Southwest Mountains.* Tucson: Southwest Parks and Monuments Association, 1982. Descriptions and illustrations of flowers and common trees found above 7,000 feet.

Barnes, F.A. *Canyon Country Geology for the Layman and Rockhound.* Treasure Chest Publications, 1978. Geologic history and guide to rockhounding with an emphasis on southeastern Utah and adjacent Arizona.

Bowers, Janice Emily. *100 Desert Wildflowers of the Southwest.* Tucson: Southwest Parks and

Monuments Association, 1989. A general introduction with brief descriptions, including a color photo of each flower.

Bowers, Janice Emily. *100 Roadside Wildflowers of Southwest Woodlands.* Tucson: Southwest Parks and Monuments Association, 1989. Brief descriptions and color photos of 100 flowers found above 4,500 feet.

Cunningham, Richard L. *50 Common Birds of the Southwest.* Tucson: Southwest Parks and Monuments Association, 1990. Each bird is represented by a color photo and description of migration, feeding, and nesting habits; the text includes Spanish and Latin names.

Desert Botanical Garden staff, and others. *Desert Wildflowers; A Guide for Identifying, Locating, and Enjoying Arizona Wildflowers and Cactus Blossoms.* Phoenix: Arizona Highways, 1997. Text and color photos take you through the seasons in the different desert regions of the state and provide practical advice for growing your own at home.

Dodge, Natt N., and Jeanne R. Janish. *Flowers of the Southwest Deserts.* Tucson: Southwest Parks and Monuments Assoc., 1985. Desert plant and flower guide for elevations under 4,500 feet.

Doolittle, Jerome. *Canyons and Mesas.* The American Wilderness Series. New York: Time-Life Books, 1974. Text and photos give a feel for the ruggedly beautiful country of northern Arizona and adjacent Utah and Colorado.

Earle, W. Hubert. *Cacti of the Southwest.* Phoenix: Desert Botanical Garden, 1980. Lists the 152 known species of cacti in the Southwest, with black-and-white and color photos.

Elmore, Francis H., and Jeanne R. Janish. *Shrubs and Trees of the Southwest Uplands.* Tucson: Southwest Parks and Monuments Association, 1976. Color-coded pages help locate plants and trees found above 4,500 feet.

Fischer, Pierre C. *70 Common Cacti of the Southwest.* Tucson: Southwest Parks and

Monuments Association, 1989. Each cactus is represented by a color photo and description.

Gray, Mary Taylor. *Watchable Birds of the Southwest.* Missoula: Mountain Press Publishing, 1995. Color pictures of 68 species in wetlands, open-country, and high-country habitats.

Halfpenny, James, and Elizabeth Biesiot. *A Field Guide: Mammal Tracking in Western America.* Boulder: Johnson Books, 1988. No need to guess what animal just passed by. This well-illustrated guide shows how to read the prints of creatures large and small. More determined detectives can peruse the intriguing scatology chapter.

Hare, Trevor. *Poisonous Dwellers of the Desert.* Tucson: Southwest Parks and Monuments Association, 1995. The text describes creatures to watch out for—poisonous insects, snakes, and the Gila monster—with advice on insecticides and bite treatment. Also listed are some nonvenomous animals often mistakenly believed to be poisonous.

McKee, Edwin D. *Ancient Landscapes of the Grand Canyon Region.* Flagstaff: Northland Publishing, 1982. Brief account of the geologic history of the Grand Canyon.

Olin, George, and Dale Thompson. *Mammals of the Southwest Deserts.* Tucson: Southwest Parks and Monuments Association, 1982. Well-illustrated with black-and-white and color drawings.

Peterson, Roger Tory. *A Field Guide to Western Birds.* Chapters Publishing, 1998. Well-illustrated with drawings.

Smith, Robert L. *Venomous Animals of Arizona.* Tucson: University of Arizona Press, 1982. Ever wonder about a scorpion's love life? Good descriptions of poisonous insects and animals, with medical notes.

Whitney, Stephen. *A Field Guide to the Grand Canyon.* Mountaineers Books, 1996. Excellent, well-illustrated guide to the Canyon's geology, early Indians, flowers, trees, birds, and animals. Most of the information also applies to other canyons on the Colorado Plateau. Includes practical advice for visiting and hiking in the Grand Canyon.

ONWARD TRAVEL

Barnes, F.A. *Utah Canyon Country.* Utah Geographic Series, Inc. no. 1; 1994. Stunning color photos illustrate this book about the land, people, and natural history of southern Utah. The text also describes parks, monuments, and practicalities of travel.

Metzger, Stephen. *Colorado Handbook.* Chico, CA: Moon Publications, 1996. Colorado calls you to Mesa Verde National Park, beautiful canyon country, the heart of the magnificent Rocky Mountains, and other fascinating areas.

Metzger, Stephen. *New Mexico Handbook.* Chico, CA: Moon Publications, 1997. Explore the landscapes, ancient pueblos, Spanish sites, wilderness areas, art, and cities of New Mexico with this informative guide.

Weir, Bill, and W.C. McRae. *Utah Handbook.* Chico, CA: Moon Publications, 1997. Explore the magical canyon country north of Arizona with this handy and comprehensive guide. It reveals Utah's unique history, city sights, mountains, and deserts.

REFERENCE

Arizona Atlas & Gazetteer. Freeport, ME: Delorme, 1996. Topographic maps at 1:250,000 scale show great detail along with grids for GPS (Global Positioning System) use, but they are difficult to read.

Arizona Road & Recreation Atlas. Berkeley, CA: Benchmark Maps, 1996. Exceptionally accurate and easy-to-read maps available in either atlas or sheet form at 1:400,000 scale. Both versions include shaded landscape and color-coded land-ownership maps.

Cheek, Lawrence W., and others. *Photographing Arizona; Practical Techniques to Improve Your Pictures.* Phoenix: Arizona Highways, 1992. How do the Arizona Highways photographers get such spectacular results? Find out in this well-illustrated book!

Comeaux, Malcolm L. *Arizona: A Geography.* Geographies of the United States series. Boulder: Westview Press, 1981. A 336-page volume covering Arizona's geography, settlement, population, resources, and agriculture.

Walker, Henry P., and Don Bufkin. *Historical Atlas of Arizona.* Norman, OK: University of Oklahoma Press, 1986. Clear maps and concise text cover the geography, Indian tribes, exploration, and development of Arizona.

HIKING TRAILS INDEX

ACCOMMODATIONS INDEX

RESTAURANT INDEX

INDEX

ARCHAEOLOGICAL SITES

CAMPGROUNDS AND RV PARKS

148; recreation 156-157; services 164; shopping 163-164; sights 149, 152-156; transportation 147, 165-166; *see also* Accommodations in the Gateway Cities Appendix
Flagstaff City Library: 165
Flagstaff Nordic Center: 156
flash floods: 4
Flintstones Bedrock City: 21
flora: 4-6, 34, 38, 59-60, 103-104, 143, 146; The Arboretum 155; *see also specific place*

FESTIVALS AND EVENTS

general discussion: 189-190
Air Affaire: 101
An Evening with the Navajo: 100
Bill Williams Rendezvous: 176
Bullfrog Open Bass Tournament: 100
Bullfrog's Festival of Lights Parade: 101
Cinco de Mayo: 163
Coconino County Fair: 163
Cowboy Days & Indian Nights: 100
Cowpuncher's Reunion Rodeo: 176
Festival in the Pines: 163, 176
Festival of Native American Arts: 163
Festival of the Arts: 163
Fourth of July Festival: 152
Gem and Mineral Show: 163
Grand Canyon Music Festival: 25
Here Comes Santa Parade: 101
High Country Warbirds Air Display: 21
Horse Show: 163
Kanab 10K: 88
Kanab West Fest: 88
Luminarios: 163
Mountain Village Holiday: 176
Mr. Burfel's Softball Tournament: 101
Old Route 66 "Cruisin' the Loop" Day: 176
Pine Country Rodeo and Parade: 163
PRCA Rodeo: 176
Route 66 Festival: 163
Scenic Southwest Art and Photography Competition and Show: 101
Wahweap Festival of Lights Parade: 101
Western Navajo Fair: 118
Winter Festival: 163
Women's Pro Basketball Invitational Tournament: 100
Wool Festival: 152
World's Largest Indian Fair: 130-131

FORESTS AND WILDERNESS AREAS

general discussion: 4-5
Beaver Dam Mountains Wilderness: 80-81
Coconino National Forest: 159, 164
Cottonwood Point Wilderness: 81
Grand Wash Cliffs Wilderness: 81-82
Kaibab National Forest: 20-21, 26-27, 191-192
Kanab Creek Wilderness: 33-34
Mount Logan Wilderness: 84
Mt. Trumbull Wilderness: 83
Paiute Wilderness: 81
Saddle Mountain Wilderness: 36
Vermilion Cliffs Wilderness: 92-95

---

food: 186; *see also* Restaurant Index; *specific place*
football: 163
foreign currency exchange: 189
Forster Rapid: 67
Fort Defiance: 132
Fossil Rapid: 67
4WD touring: general discussion 186-187; Arizona Strip 78-79; Bill Williams Mountain 177; Canyon de Chelly National Monument 125; Cape Solitude 19; Great Thumb Mesa 46-47; Hidden Canyon 82; House Rock Valley 37-38; Mount Logan Wilderness 84; organized tours 28, 101, 122, 126; Point Sublime 36; Tatahatso Point 116-117; Whitmore Wash Road 83
Four Corners Monument: 123
Fredonia: 88-89
Frontier Movie Town: 86

G
Galloway Canyon: 67
Ganado: 132-133
Garcés, Francisco Gomás: 7, 72
Garnet Canyon: 66
Gem and Mineral Show: 163
general stores: 25, 39, 180
geography: *see* land
geology: along the Colorado River 57-71; canyon rocks 59; cross-section 58; Flagstaff Field Center of the U.S. Geological Survey 154; formation of the Grand Canyon 2; Glen Canyon National Recreation Area 103-104;

HOSTELS

MUSEUMS AND EXHIBITS

WHITEWATER RAFTING

ABOUT THE AUTHOR

Bill Weir at Mt. Kangchenjunga, Nepal

Back in school, Bill Weir always figured he'd settle down to a career job and live happily ever after. Then he discovered traveling. After graduating with a B.A. degree in physics from Berea College in 1972, Bill found employment as an electronic technician, but the very short vacation breaks just didn't provide enough time for the trips he dreamed of.

So in 1976 he took off on his trusty bicycle, Bessie, riding across the United States from Virginia to Oregon with Bikecentennial '76. The following year he took off on an even longer bicycle trip—from Alaska to Baja California. Then came the ultimate journey—a bicycle cruise around the world. Bill pedaled the globe from 1980 to 1984, spending most of his time in the South Pacific and Asia. Naturally he used Moon's excellent *South Pacific Handbook* and *Indonesia Handbook*. Correspondence with the authors led to the idea of writing a guidebook of his own. Bill returned to his home base of Flagstaff, Arizona, and set to work researching and writing *Arizona Handbook*.

As soon as the labor on that book came to an end, Bill headed north across the Grand Canyon to the Beehive State to create the *Utah Handbook*. Bill continues to explore Arizona and beyond, always discovering new places and learning more about the old. "Travels in the world and in the mind," he says, "add to life's richness of experiences."

During 1994, for example, he visited the amazing cultures and landscapes of Tibet and Nepal. Then, in the following year, he dusted off ol' Bessie the Bicycle for the final leg of the round-the-world trip started 19 years ago. They flew to Nepal, rode to India, hopped over to Oman and the vast deserts of Arabia, then cycled from Syria to Portugal, the western end of Europe. Poor Bessie, however, was put out to pasture. Bill got his new "Bessie Too the Bicycle" and explored more of the Himalayas—riding from Bangladesh to Nepal via Sikkim—and more of Europe, pedaling north from Greece until the road ran out at Nordkapp in the Norwegian arctic. Then Bill returned to Arizona to write a new edition of *Arizona Handbook* and the first edition of *Grand Canyon Handbook*. You'll find many new places and improved coverage of the old favorites in both books!

Happy Travels!

—Bill

MOON
TRAVEL HANDBOOKS

LOSE YOURSELF
IN THE EXPERIENCE,
NOT THE CROWD

For more than 25 years, Moon Travel Handbooks have been the guidebooks of choice for adventurous travelers. Our award-winning Handbook series provides focused, comprehensive coverage of distinct destinations all over the world. Each Handbook is like an entire bookcase of cultural insight and introductory information in one portable volume. Our goal at Moon is to give travelers all the background and practical information they'll need for an extraordinary travel experience.

The following pages include a complete list of Handbooks, covering North America and Hawaii, Mexico, Latin America and the Caribbean, and Asia and the Pacific.To purchase Moon Travel Handbooks, check your local bookstore or order C/o Publishers Group West, Attn: Order Department, 1700 Fourth St., Berkeley, CA 94710, or fax to (510) 528-3444.

"An in-depth dunk into the land, the people and their history, arts, and politics."
—Student Travels

"I consider these books to be superior to Lonely Planet. When Moon produces a book it is more humorous, incisive, and off-beat."
—Toronto Sun

"Outdoor enthusiasts gravitate to the well-written Moon Travel Handbooks. In addition to politically correct historic and cultural features, the series focuses on flora, fauna and outdoor recreation. Maps and meticulous directions also are a trademark of Moon guides."
—Houston Chronicle

"Moon [Travel Handbooks] . . . bring a healthy respect to the places they investigate. Best of all, they provide a host of odd nuggets that give a place texture and prod the wary traveler from the beaten path. The finest are written with such care and insight they deserve listing as literature."
—American Geographical Society

"Moon Travel Handbooks offer in-depth historical essays and useful maps, enhanced by a sense of humor and a neat, compact format."
—Swing

"Perfect for the more adventurous, these are long on history, sightseeing and nitty-gritty information and very price-specific."
—Columbus Dispatch

"Moon guides manage to be comprehensive and countercultural at the same time . . . Handbooks are packed with maps, photographs, drawings, and sidebars that constitute a college-level introduction to each country's history, culture, people, and crafts."
—National Geographic Traveler

"Few travel guides do a better job helping travelers create their own itineraries than the Moon Travel Handbook series. The authors have a knack for homing in on the essentials."
—Colorado Springs *Gazette Telegraph*

MEXICO

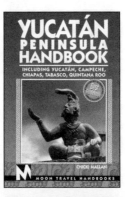

"These books will delight the armchair traveler, aid the undecided person in selecting a destination, and guide the seasoned road warrior looking for lesser-known hideaways."
—*Mexican Meanderings* Newsletter

"From tourist traps to off-the-beaten track hideaways, these guides offer consistent, accurate details without pretension."
—*Foreign Service Journal*

Archaeological Mexico	**$19.95**
Andrew Coe	420 pages, 27 maps
Baja Handbook	**$16.95**
Joe Cummings	540 pages, 46 maps
Cabo Handbook	**$14.95**
Joe Cummings	270 pages, 17 maps
Cancún Handbook	**$14.95**
Chicki Mallan	240 pages, 25 maps
Colonial Mexico	**$18.95**
Chicki Mallan	400 pages, 38 maps
Mexico Handbook	**$21.95**
Joe Cummings and Chicki Mallan	1,200 pages, 201 maps
Northern Mexico Handbook	**$17.95**
Joe Cummings	610 pages, 69 maps
Pacific Mexico Handbook	**$17.95**
Bruce Whipperman	580 pages, 68 maps
Puerto Vallarta Handbook	**$14.95**
Bruce Whipperman	330 pages, 36 maps
Yucatán Handbook	**$16.95**
Chicki Mallan	400 pages, 52 maps

"Beyond question, the most comprehensive Mexican resources available for those who prefer deep travel to shallow tourism. But don't worry, the fiesta-fun stuff's all here too."
—*New York Daily News*

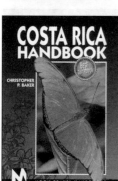

LATIN AMERICA AND THE CARIBBEAN

"Solidly packed with practical information and full of significant cultural asides that will enlighten you on the whys and wherefores of things you might easily see but not easily grasp."

—Boston Globe

Belize Handbook	**$15.95**
Chicki Mallan and Patti Lange	390 pages, 45 maps
Caribbean Vacations	**$18.95**
Karl Luntta	910 pages, 64 maps
Costa Rica Handbook	**$19.95**
Christopher P. Baker	780 pages, 73 maps
Cuba Handbook	**$19.95**
Christopher P. Baker	740 pages, 70 maps
Dominican Republic Handbook	**$15.95**
Gaylord Dold	420 pages, 24 maps
Ecuador Handbook	**$16.95**
Julian Smith	450 pages, 43 maps
Honduras Handbook	**$15.95**
Chris Humphrey	330 pages, 40 maps
Jamaica Handbook	**$15.95**
Karl Luntta	330 pages, 17 maps
Virgin Islands Handbook	**$13.95**
Karl Luntta	220 pages, 19 maps

NORTH AMERICA AND HAWAII

"These domestic guides convey the same sense of exoticism that their foreign counterparts do, making home-country travel seem like far-flung adventure."

—Sierra Magazine

Alaska-Yukon Handbook	**$17.95**
Deke Castleman and Don Pitcher	530 pages, 92 maps
Alberta and the Northwest Territories Handbook	**$18.95**
Andrew Hempstead	520 pages, 79 maps
Arizona Handbook	**$18.95**
Bill Weir	600 pages, 36 maps
Atlantic Canada Handbook	**$18.95**
Mark Morris	490 pages, 60 maps
Big Island of Hawaii Handbook	**$15.95**
J.D. Bisignani	390 pages, 25 maps
Boston Handbook	**$13.95**
Jeff Perk	200 pages, 20 maps
British Columbia Handbook	**$16.95**
Jane King and Andrew Hempstead	430 pages, 69 maps

Canadian Rockies Handbook	**$14.95**
Andrew Hempstead	220 pages, 22 maps
Colorado Handbook	**$17.95**
Stephen Metzger	480 pages, 46 maps
Georgia Handbook	**$17.95**
Kap Stann	380 pages, 44 maps
Grand Canyon Handbook	**$14.95**
Bill Weir	220 pages, 10 maps
Hawaii Handbook	**$19.95**
J.D. Bisignani	1,030 pages, 88 maps
Honolulu-Waikiki Handbook	**$14.95**
J.D. Bisignani	360 pages, 20 maps
Idaho Handbook	**$18.95**
Don Root	610 pages, 42 maps
Kauai Handbook	**$15.95**
J.D. Bisignani	320 pages, 23 maps
Los Angeles Handbook	**$16.95**
Kim Weir	370 pages, 15 maps
Maine Handbook	**$18.95**
Kathleen M. Brandes	660 pages, 27 maps
Massachusetts Handbook	**$18.95**
Jeff Perk	600 pages, 23 maps
Maui Handbook	**$15.95**
J.D. Bisignani	450 pages, 37 maps
Michigan Handbook	**$15.95**
Tina Lassen	360 pages, 32 maps
Montana Handbook	**$17.95**
Judy Jewell and W.C. McRae	490 pages, 52 maps
Nevada Handbook	**$18.95**
Deke Castleman	530 pages, 40 maps
New Hampshire Handbook	**$18.95**
Steve Lantos	500 pages, 18 maps
New Mexico Handbook	**$15.95**
Stephen Metzger	360 pages, 47 maps
New York Handbook	**$19.95**
Christiane Bird	780 pages, 95 maps
New York City Handbook	**$13.95**
Christiane Bird	300 pages, 20 maps
North Carolina Handbook	**$14.95**
Rob Hirtz and Jenny Daughtry Hirtz	320 pages, 27 maps
Northern California Handbook	**$19.95**
Kim Weir	800 pages, 50 maps
Ohio Handbook	**$15.95**
David K. Wright	340 pages, 18 maps
Oregon Handbook	**$17.95**
Stuart Warren and Ted Long Ishikawa	590 pages, 34 maps

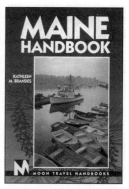

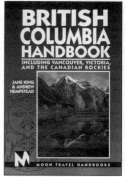

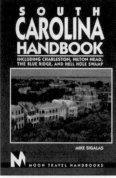

Pennsylvania Handbook	**$18.95**
Joanne Miller	448 pages, 40 maps
Road Trip USA	**$24.00**
Jamie Jensen	940 pages, 175 maps
Road Trip USA Getaways: Chicago	**$9.95**
	60 pages, 1 map
Road Trip USA Getaways: Seattle	**$9.95**
	60 pages, 1 map
Santa Fe-Taos Handbook	**$13.95**
Stephen Metzger	160 pages, 13 maps
South Carolina Handbook	**$16.95**
Mike Sigalas	400 pages, 20 maps
Southern California Handbook	**$19.95**
Kim Weir	720 pages, 26 maps
Tennessee Handbook	**$17.95**
Jeff Bradley	530 pages, 42 maps
Texas Handbook	**$18.95**
Joe Cummings	690 pages, 70 maps
Utah Handbook	**$17.95**
Bill Weir and W.C. McRae	490 pages, 40 maps
Virginia Handbook	**$15.95**
Julian Smith	410 pages, 37 maps
Washington Handbook	**$19.95**
Don Pitcher	840 pages, 111 maps
Wisconsin Handbook	**$18.95**
Thomas Huhti	590 pages, 69 maps
Wyoming Handbook	**$17.95**
Don Pitcher	610 pages, 80 maps

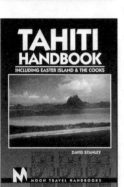

ASIA AND THE PACIFIC

"Scores of maps, detailed practical info down to business hours of small-town libraries. You can't beat the Asian titles for sheer heft. (The) series is sort of an American Lonely Planet, with better writing but fewer titles. (The) individual voice of researchers comes through."

—Travel & Leisure

Australia Handbook	**$21.95**
Marael Johnson, Andrew Hempstead,	
and Nadina Purdon	940 pages, 141 maps
Bali Handbook	**$19.95**
Bill Dalton	750 pages, 54 maps
Fiji Islands Handbook	**$14.95**
David Stanley	350 pages, 42 maps
Hong Kong Handbook	**$16.95**
Kerry Moran	378 pages, 49 maps

Indonesia Handbook	**$25.00**
Bill Dalton	1,380 pages, 249 maps
Micronesia Handbook	**$16.95**
Neil M. Levy	340 pages, 70 maps
Nepal Handbook	**$18.95**
Kerry Moran	490 pages, 51 maps
New Zealand Handbook	**$19.95**
Jane King	620 pages, 81 maps
Outback Australia Handbook	**$18.95**
Marael Johnson	450 pages, 57 maps
Philippines Handbook	**$17.95**
Peter Harper and Laurie Fullerton	670 pages, 116 maps
Singapore Handbook	**$15.95**
Carl Parkes	350 pages, 29 maps
South Korea Handbook	**$19.95**
Robert Nilsen	820 pages, 141 maps
South Pacific Handbook	**$24.00**
David Stanley	920 pages, 147 maps
Southeast Asia Handbook	**$21.95**
Carl Parkes	1,080 pages, 204 maps
Tahiti Handbook	**$15.95**
David Stanley	450 pages, 51 maps
Thailand Handbook	**$19.95**
Carl Parkes	860 pages, 142 maps
Vietnam, Cambodia & Laos Handbook	**$18.95**
Michael Buckley	760 pages, 116 maps

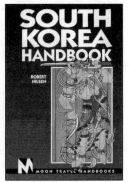

OTHER GREAT TITLES FROM MOON

"For hardy wanderers, few guides come more highly recommended than the Handbooks. They include good maps, steer clear of fluff and flackery, and offer plenty of money-saving tips. They also give you the kind of information that visitors to strange lands—on any budget— need to survive."

—US News & World Report

Moon Handbook	**$10.00**
Carl Koppeschaar	150 pages, 8 maps
The Practical Nomad: How to Travel Around the World	**$17.95**
Edward Hasbrouck	580 pages
Staying Healthy in Asia, Africa, and Latin America	**$11.95**
Dirk Schroeder	230 pages, 4 maps

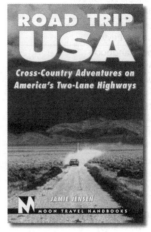

WHERE TO BUY MOON TRAVEL HANDBOOKS

BOOKSTORES AND LIBRARIES: Moon Travel Handbooks are distributed worldwide. Please contact our sales manager at info@moon.com for a list of wholesalers and distributors in your area.

TRAVELERS: We would like to have Moon Travel Handbooks available throughout the world. Please ask your bookstore to contact us for ordering information. If your bookstore will not order our guides for you, please contact us for a free catalog.

Moon Travel Handbooks
C/o Publishers Group West
Attn: Order Department
1700 Fourth Street
Berkeley, CA 94710
fax: (510) 528-3444

IMPORTANT ORDERING INFORMATION

PRICES: All prices are subject to change. We always ship the most current edition. We will let you know if there is a price increase on the book you order.

SHIPPING AND HANDLING OPTIONS: Domestic UPS or USPS priority mail (allow 10 working days for delivery): $6.00 for the first item, $1.00 for each additional item.

UPS 2nd Day Air or Printed Airmail requires a special quote.

International Surface Bookrate 8-12 weeks delivery: $5.00 for the first item, $1.00 for each additional item. Note: We cannot guarantee international surface bookrate shipping. We recommend sending international orders via air mail, which requires a special quote.

FOREIGN ORDERS: Orders that originate outside the U.S.A. must be paid for with an international money order, a check in U.S. currency drawn on a major U.S. bank based in the U.S.A., or Visa, MasterCard, or American Express.

INTERNET ORDERS: Visit our site at: www.moon.com

ORDER FORM

Prices are subject to change without notice. Please check our Web site
at **www.moon.com** for current prices and editions.
(See important ordering information on preceding page.)

Name: _____ Date: _____

Street: _____

City: _____ Daytime Phone: _____

State or Country: _____ Zip Code: _____

QUANTITY	TITLE	PRICE

Taxable Total_____

Sales Tax in CA and NY_____

Shipping & Handling_____

TOTAL_____

Ship: ☐ UPS (no P.O. Boxes) ☐ Priority mail ☐ International surface mail

Ship to: ☐ address above ☐ other _____

_____

Make checks payable to: **PUBLISHERS GROUP WEST**, Attn: Order Department, 1700 Fourth St.,
Berkeley, CA 94710, or fax to (510) 528-3444. We accept Visa, MasterCard, or American Express.
   To Order: Call in your Visa, MasterCard, or American Express number, or send a written order
with your Visa, MasterCard, or American Express number and expiration date clearly written.

Card Number: ☐ **Visa** ☐ **MasterCard** ☐ **American Express**

☐ ☐ ☐ ☐ ☐ ☐ ☐ ☐ ☐ ☐ ☐ ☐ ☐ ☐ ☐ ☐

Exact Name on Card: _____

Expiration date:_____

Signature: _____

Daytime Phone: _____

U.S.~METRIC CONVERSION

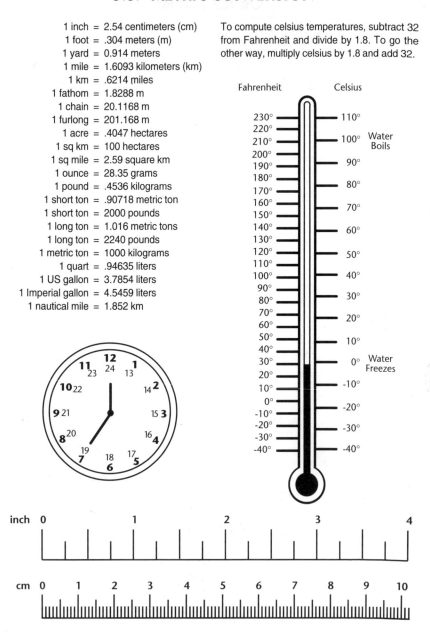

1 inch	= 2.54 centimeters (cm)
1 foot	= .304 meters (m)
1 yard	= 0.914 meters
1 mile	= 1.6093 kilometers (km)
1 km	= .6214 miles
1 fathom	= 1.8288 m
1 chain	= 20.1168 m
1 furlong	= 201.168 m
1 acre	= .4047 hectares
1 sq km	= 100 hectares
1 sq mile	= 2.59 square km
1 ounce	= 28.35 grams
1 pound	= .4536 kilograms
1 short ton	= .90718 metric ton
1 short ton	= 2000 pounds
1 long ton	= 1.016 metric tons
1 long ton	= 2240 pounds
1 metric ton	= 1000 kilograms
1 quart	= .94635 liters
1 US gallon	= 3.7854 liters
1 Imperial gallon	= 4.5459 liters
1 nautical mile	= 1.852 km

To compute celsius temperatures, subtract 32 from Fahrenheit and divide by 1.8. To go the other way, multiply celsius by 1.8 and add 32.